MS ACCESS 2016 SQL
COMPREHENSIVE

Pindaro E. Demertzoglou, Ph.D.

Alpha Press – Albany, New York 2019

About the Author

Pindaro's relationship with databases started with DBase III back in 1991, continuing with all versions of MS Access since early 1993, and working with MS SQL Server, MySQL, Oracle, and IBM DB2 for a number of years. From then on, he is still in love with all of them. After twenty five years, he still works with data, integration, and business analytics.

Pindaro is currently a faculty member in the department of Information Systems at the business school of Rensselaer Polytechnic Institute in Troy, New York where he is teaching databases and business analytics for the last twenty years. Pindaro also completed and collaborated on a myriad of database projects for organizations or in collaborative efforts between the University and various corporations.

Pindaro's interests in information science, transactional systems, and analytics focus on creating more efficient and flexible organizations. The idea is to accomplish more with fewer resources and in less time leaving a small footprint on the environment. Pindaro's education includes a BS from the American College in Thessaloniki Greece, an MS, MBA, and a PhD in the United States.

Nevertheless, the majority of the author's experience came from participating in a multitude of industry projects. There, everything has to work efficiently, reliably and above all be acceptable by the people of the corporation.

Dedication

This book is dedicated to all the teachers in the world and their continuous efforts on education which keep the learning processes going for all of us.

Acknowledgments

I would like to thank the faculty and staff of the American College of Thessaloniki, Greece who made this college a prestigious and internationally recognized institution. Specifically, I would like to express my deepest appreciation to the former president of the college, Dr. William McGrew and the head librarian Mrs. Pat Kastritsis for their decisive and unrelenting guidance and help to their students. Pat is no longer with us today but the difference she made in my life is propagated to the thousands of students I taught over the last fifteen years in New York. She will live through my own students and the students of my students who receive the same values and attention as the ones I received from Dr. McGrew and Mrs. Kastritsis.

Moreover, I would like to express my deepest appreciation to the staff and faculty of Rensselaer Polytechnic Institute, Troy, NY, United States for the collegiate atmosphere and continuous support in my efforts.

Finally, I really want to thank all my students who with their tens of thousands of questions on databases over the last twenty years gave me the spark to think and rethink a multitude of points from different perspectives and learn a lot as a result.

BRIEF TABLE OF CONTENTS

DETAILED TABLE OF CONTENTS

PREFACE: HOW TO USE THIS BOOK

In very few words, the goal of this book is to provide the student of databases with working knowledge of everyday database operations and solutions to actual business tasks. The rationale has been to reduce needless writing and unnecessary pages and concentrate on providing real learning for the professional setting.

1.   How to download the practice database

To download the practice database for the book and stay connected with the latest news and updates please go to http://www.alphapresspublishing.com/Products/default.html, and click on your book link to access its resources.

For faculty members to obtain the companion guides and exercise booklet, please send an email to alphapress@hotmail.com and upon verification of faculty status all resources will be made available to you.

2.   How to start working with the book examples

Start Microsoft Access and open the practice database. Click "CREATE" in the main menu and then from the group "Queries" click on "Query Design".

Click "close" on the "Show Table" dialog box.

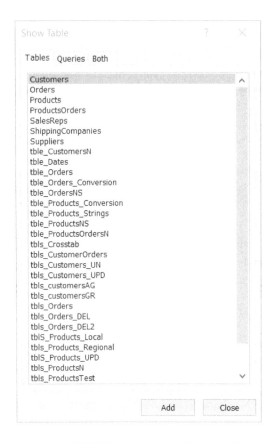

Click the "SQL" button in the "Results" group below:

The following window will come up where you can write your SQL code:

When you want to run your SQL statement and see the result, click the "Run!" button in the "Results" group below:

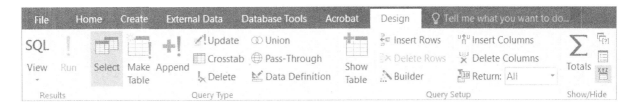

CHAPTER 1
SQL FOUNDATION FOR BUSINESS

3.   The origins of SQL

SQL stands for Structured Query Language and it is the standard language for manipulating relational databases. It was developed by IBM in the mid-seventies and at that point it was named SEQUEL standing for Standard English Query Language.

SQL is based on the Relational Database Model officially defined in June 1970 by E. F. Codd in his amazing paper "A Relational Model of Data for Large Shared Data Banks." In his article Dr. Codd explained the need for a new relational model and language for maximum independence from specific programs and system platforms. To this end the goal set more than 40 years ago has been achieved and SQL is used in a multitude of platforms and database servers.

IBM continued its work on SQL throughout the 1970s and introduced SQL/DS in 1981, and DB2 in 1983. The problem was that Oracle was successful in releasing a relational RDBMS in 1979 beating IBM in its own game by two years. Sybase and Microsoft formed a partnership to produce their own RDBMS and they worked together up until version 4 of their product. After that, Sybase and Microsoft continued to produce their own databases with Sybase working on their SYSTEM products and Microsoft on their SQL Server versions. Today all commercial vendors face severe competition from open source relational databases like PostgreSQL.

> **A tribute to Dr. Codd**
>
> Dr. Codd joined IBM in 1949 and he worked on numerous projects such the logical design of computers and operating systems. He will be remembered for his creation and work on the relational model of databases in 1970 and relational algebra in 1972. Dr. Codd continued his work on SQL and in 1981 received the extremely prestigious Turing Award for his work on database systems. He is considered the father of modern relational databases.

SQL is endorsed by the American National Standards Institute (http://www.ansi.org), and is used by MS SQL Server, dBase for Windows, Paradox, MS Access, INGRES, SYBASE, Oracle, IBM DB2, and other database software. The American National Standards Institute has the role of maintaining SQL, and periodically publishes update versions of the SQL standard. All major database systems comply with the ANSI standards such as SQL-89 and SQL-92 but the constructs and expressions used in a particular environment might be somewhat different because many of the RDBMS were developed prior to standardization and also commercial vendors introduce proprietary features to gain a competitive edge.

4.   What is SQL

SQL is a fourth generation, non-procedural computer programming language. By non-procedural we mean that we are looking at the end result and not the sequence of lines of code. In traditional programming, lines of code execute in sequence, one after the other, to produce the end result. In SQL, a section of code at the end of the SQL statement might execute before a section of code in the beginning of the SQL statement.

The next important characteristic of SQL is that it works to manipulate relational database management systems (RDBMS). These RDBMSs like Access, IBM DB2, Oracle, MS SQL, and PostgreSQL, usually constitute the data layer of the corporation's transaction processing system or at least that should be the case. These transactional databases should be highly normalized which means they consist of a large number of entities with fewer attributes in them or in other words, they consist of many tables with fewer fields in them. It is the job of SQL to manipulate data from multiple tables at the same time. However, in today's working environment transaction processing systems often consist of several relational databases and a host of other heterogeneous data sources (text files, hierarchical files, spreadsheets, etc.) which result in vast amounts of inefficiency for the corporation.

5. SQL in its role as Data Definition Language (DDL)

These SQL statements are further divided into two main categories: In the first category, we have SQL statements we use to create database objects such as tables, indexes, and relationships. In this case we call the SQL code Data Definition Language (DDL). The DDL language supports only three statements which are the CREATE, ALTER, and DROP statements. The ability to use SQL to create database objects does not represent just one additional way to work with a table. By using pure SQL statements, we can understand the inner structure of the objects we are creating. We can also use our knowledge of SQL to enter the realm of other databases like MSSQL Server or MySQL to create objects independent of any design interface, and we can create and delete temporary objects on the fly.

The following is an example of a DDL statement which we use to create a new table with CustomerID as its primary key and two text fields for storing the customer's first and last name.

CREATE TABLE Customer (
[CustomerID] Counter Primary key not null,
[LastName] text(50),
[FirstName] text(50))

The following SQL DDL statement will alter the structure of the existing table "customer" and add one more field called "city". Notice how we can define the data type of the field we are adding as well as its length.

ALTER TABLE Customer
ADD COLUMN City TEXT(25)

Finally, we can delete the table "customer" by using the DROP DDL statement:

DROP TABLE Customer

Now, one might question the practicality of learning how to work with DDL statements since we can do all the above using the design interface. This is correct but the fact is that we use DDL in many more circumstances than for basic database tasks. Specifically, we use DDL within server side pages in web servers like java server pages or active server pages.net or php to add, delete, and modify tables in the back-end database. The same is true for applications developed with hard-coded languages like

C++, Java, or C#. In addition, we use SQL DDL a lot in extraction, transformation, and loading (ETL) packages to move data from one database to another or from a relational database to a data warehouse. Consequently, SQL DDL is a tool that must exist in the belt of any SQL professional and it is part of this book.

6.   SQL as data manipulation language

In the second category, we have SQL statements we use to manipulate table data. In this case we call the SQL code Data Manipulation Language (DML). The DML language supports only four statements which are the SELECT, UPDATE, DELETE, and INSERT statements. We use these statements to retrieve, delete, update, and enter new records in the database. The popularity of these statements corresponds with the way they have been presented above. That is, the SELECT statement is the most popular one followed by the UPDATE, and DELETE statements. We rarely use the INSERT statement in SQL per se. Usually, it is used at the application level to insert a multitude of records at once in the database. The conclusion is that for the whole book we will be practically working with the above seven SQL statements; three DDL and four DML ones.

The following is a sample SELECT statement. The SELECT statement identifies which columns or fields of data we would like to retrieve from a table. In this case, we are retrieving four fields from the customers table. The field names must appear identically in the SQL statement as they do in the database table. Many fields can be selected, simply by separating them with commas in the SELECT statement.

SELECT state, city, lastname, firstname
FROM Customers

We use update statements for two practical reasons: First, we use them to save time by updating multiple records at once. Second, we use them for attaining efficient business operations. The update statement shown below will increase the product price by 10% for all the products coming from a specific supplier. Now, we could go in the table and make the changes manually. That would be ok if we buy only two products from the specific supplier. What if we buy two hundred products? Using an update statement it does not matter if we need to update two, or two hundred, or two thousand records, we can do our job literally in seconds. However, the most important function of update statements is that they let us become more efficient as a business. Specifically, the only constant in business is change. It does not matter if a business expands or contracts, the important thing is to move. A business moves by responding to external or internal stimuli or in other words by responding to initiatives from entities in its external environment like competitors or by initiating actions internally. This means that if a competitor initiates a marketing campaign to obtain market share by reducing their prices, we might respond by reducing prices as well. However, we need to be able to do that quickly at the database level so that the changes in our product catalog are reflected immediately. One way to do that is by using update SQL statements. Then, a couple of days later we might have to change our prices again. We need this agility as a business to be able to stay competitive. The important conclusion is that SQL in general and update statements in particular are not just for the "programming guys" but they can play a central role in any corporation independent of size.

UPDATE Products
SET price = price*1.1,
WHERE supplierID = "15"

A sample delete statement appears below and its function is to delete from the orders table orders that fall between two specific dates. The main purpose of a delete statement is to save us time and effort by allowing us to delete multiple records at once following very specific criteria. Of course delete statements are used at the application level as well whether we talk about a web application or a hard-coded application like VB.NET or C#.

DELETE
FROM Orders
WHERE orderdate BETWEEN #10/15/2014# AND #10/17/2014#

We left the INSERT statement for last and though not often used, it is still a very important statement. For example, the INSERT statement below will take all the customers from New York State in the customers table and place them in an archive table. We can achieve this task in seconds using INSERT instead of trying any other alchemies with multiple queries to achieve the same result.

INSERT INTO CustomersArchive (firstname, lastname, address, city)
SELECT firstname, lastname, address, city
FROM Customers
WHERE State = 'NY'

7.   SQL as an ubiquitous standard

If we understand how to work with SQL we have one additional strong advantage. We will, in essence, be able to work with any relational database, commercial or open source, because all of them use SQL. To make an analogy, let us assume that we want to learn how to create web pages. We can buy or download an HTML editor, as there are plenty to choose from. However, what is our strategic goal? Learn how to work with an editor, or understand how to develop web code? The function of HTML editors is always the same: They convert your clicks to HTML code. The same is true for SQL. There are many design interfaces we can use from multiple different vendors or even download open source ones. However, if we know how to work with SQL we will be able to work with any of those interfaces and many times achieve results that would not have been possible to obtain by using a design interface. Therefore, the knowledge of SQL is a must for the database professional, or actually the basis to become one.

8.   The position and value of SQL within the enterprise data model

As you can see from Figure 1 below, an organization consists of three hierarchical levels. The strategic level is where the top management of the company sets the strategic objectives of the corporation. Strategic objectives are very specific statements and not just general goals. For example, "we would strive to increase sales of product A by 5% in the State of New York in a period of five years" constitutes a strategic objective. Keep in mind that for our purposes the executives at the strategic level of the corporation need information to be able to make decisions for strategic objectives. This information comes from data at the transactional/operational level of the company where all the action takes place.

The tactical level of the corporation is where managers make sure that the company stays on course to achieve the strategic objectives. For example, if for a period of one or two months sales are not materializing as forecasted, tactical management will take action to bring sales back on track and compensate for lost sales. Keep in mind that tactical management needs information to make these tactical adjustments. This information comes again from the transactional level of the corporation.

The third level of the corporation is the transactional/operational level. This is the place where all the business activity takes place daily. For example, taking an order from a customer is a transaction. Processing a quotation for a customer is a transaction. Updating accounts payable is a transaction. Hiring a new employee and creating a new HR record is a transaction. Preparing a shipment for a customer is a transaction. Fulfilling an order is a transaction. Processing payment for an order is a transaction. All these transactions might aggregate to hundreds or thousands or even hundreds of thousands of transactions every day. That is, we have a lot of data generated every day in various parts of the corporation. This is the fragmented data we need to convert to information and direct it to the tactical and strategic levels for decision. This is exactly the place where SQL comes in to help us generate this data. We also, use SQL to aggregate, summarize, group by, add, update, and subtract data to generate information.

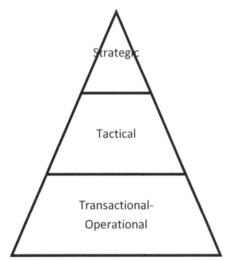

Figure 1: Organizational Hierarchical Levels

In Figure 2, we present a real life corporate transaction system. As you can see, this particular company has a functional design and is divided in four departments: Finance/Accounting, Sales/Marketing, Human Resources, and Production. We also notice that the transactional/operational system has two layers: an application layer and a data layer. The application layer consists of the actual front-end applications corporate employees are using to process transactions. A front-end application is usually made up by a number of forms staff is using to enter, edit, delete, and update data. This front-end is also commonly called the user interface. Notice an additional couple of issues: The various applications do not communicate with each other among departments. Even within the department itself, the departmental units are using different applications. For instance, in the Finance/Accounting department, the accounts receivable, accounts payable, and investment management are all using different applications. This has as a result increased communication times among departments and units which in turn lead to higher cycle times for order processing, fulfillment, accounting debits/credits, and other corporate transactions.

These higher cycle times lead to increased transactional costs which translate to higher operating expenses for the corporation and as a result to a corresponding decrease in our operating margin. Higher operating expenses result in increased risk for the corporation as well which means that in difficult times we will be the ones to have trouble first. To explain it further, the operational cost of a corporation is not directly related to production. This means that we will incur operational cost regardless of the level of business turnover we have. In times of booming business this is not a problem because the added operational cost we experience becomes lower by unit of output. In times of recession however, that operational cost increases by unit of output and its weight shows in full.

It is exactly in these repressed business and economic conditions that managers make their biggest mistakes as well. Instead of trying to make the corporation more efficient, that is, look at cycle times, transactional cost, operating expenses, and risk, they look at the usual culprit: the employee of the corporation. This trend needs to stop at some point and one of the major ways to do it is for management to understand how data processing, analysis, and dissemination affect their businesses. That is why SQL represents an important technology for our business. We will see how this importance is exhibited when we discuss the data layer of the corporate transaction system.

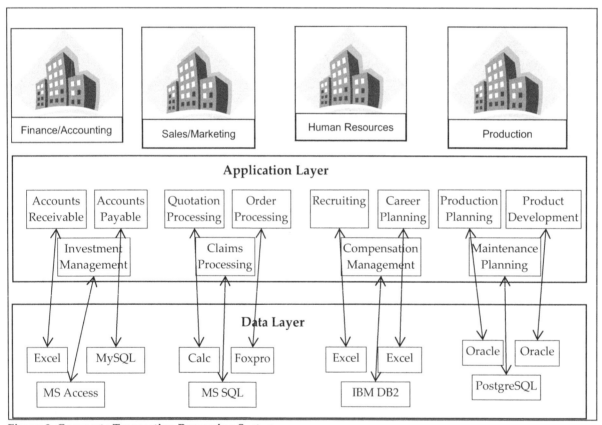

Figure 2: Corporate Transaction Processing System

The second layer we see in Figure 2 is the data layer of the corporation. In the vast majority of cases in the real business world, the corporate data layer consists of many heterogeneous data sources. In theory, in books, and in ERP (Enterprise Resource Planning) package pitches from marketing people an idealized solution is offered where the data layer consists of a single RDBMS (Relational Database Management System). This is very far from the truth and from reality. What actually happens is what you see in Figure 2 where not only departments but also individual units within departments use different data sources. For instance, the Career Planning and Compensation Management units in Human Resources use different and separate data sources. Career Planning is using Excel to store and process its data while Compensation Management is using an IBM DB2 relational database and God help the one who will try to get data from the other or will try to integrate the applications or data sources from multiple departments. It is possible, but get ready for the ensuing political conflict that will lead to a quagmire and finally a compromise to a higher or lesser degree. The real situation for us at this point is that for the data layer of the corporate transaction system we have a suite of multiple and heterogeneous data sources. This of course leads to inefficient data exchange. However, what is inefficient? By inefficient we mean we need more time to exchange data and we are more prone to mistakes when we actually do the exchange. This practically means increased cycle times and increased transactional cost which will again lead to high operating costs for the corporation with direct reductions of the operating margin and net profits as well as an increase of perceived risk.

Now, the question is how can we use SQL in the corporation to help in the above situations? We will list specific situations here from the real world on how SQL is actually used throughout the hierarchical levels of the corporation. In addition, we will explore the possibilities of using SQL to get data from other entities in the external environment of the company like corporate customers, suppliers, partners, distributors, and the government. The following list, though not exhaustive, is still comprehensive enough for a very deep understanding of the role of SQL.

9.   SQL for Inserts, Updates, and Deletes in the Corporate Transaction Processing System

In figure 3 we see how SQL is used for transaction processing at the operational/transactional level of the corporation. A business user can conduct transactions such as updating an order, adding a new order, or deleting an order. Business users use applications, usually forms (Access, Oracle, Visual Basic, Java etc.), to be able to work on these transactions. These forms contain "add", "edit", "delete", and other buttons that initiate the requested transaction. However, in most cases, the end user does not see the SQL statements behind these forms but has the expertise to work with the application.

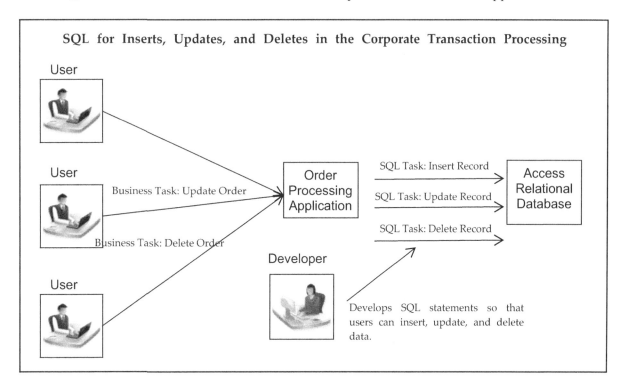

Figure 3: SQL for inserts, updates, and deletes in the transaction processing system

Behind the scenes however, it is the actual database developer who writes the appropriate SQL statements so that business users can do their job. This developer is needed constantly by the corporation because the SQL statements he or she develops will not stay the same but will change as the business conditions change. That is, as the business engages in activities to acquire market share, to reduce cost, to increase revenue, to increase profit, to launch new products, or respond to competitors, the business requirements, or business logic as we call it, for the application will change. This means that the code of the application needs to change to accommodate the new logic and along with the code the SQL statements for processing the corresponding transactions. Consequently, the role of the SQL developer is ongoing to help the corporation achieve its strategic and tactical objectives. The SQL developer in this role is not the technical person who writes code all day long. Actually, most of his or her time will be spent on communication with users at any level of the corporation so that he or she can understand in detail the business expectations behind his or her code. Consequently, the SQL developer becomes a business person and an integral part of the business operations of the company.

10. SQL for information generation – from the TPS to tactical and strategic levels.

In this scenario SQL is used to convert data to information. Specifically, instead of using INSERT, UPDATE, and DELETE statements to process transactions, we now use GROUP BY statements, aggregate functions, conditional statements, pivot queries and a multitude of other techniques to generate information out of data in existing transactions. A lot of data is generated at the data layer of the transaction processing system (see Figure 4) as the various departments interact with customers, suppliers, partners, distributors, and the government. For instance, hundreds or thousands of orders and order quotations might be processed every month. All these orders generate data that stays in the data layer of the transaction processing system.

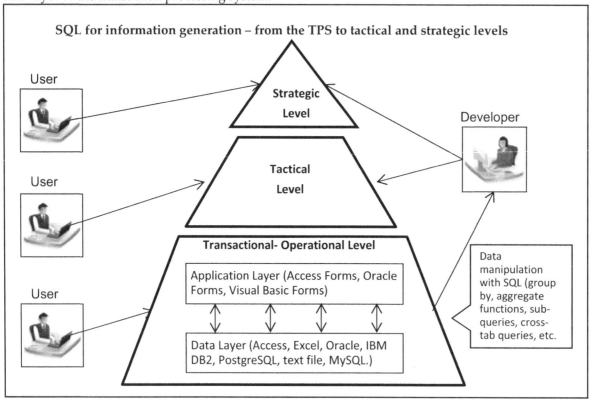

Figure 4: SQL for information generation – from the TPS to tactical and strategic levels

It is the job of the SQL professional to provide intelligence to the tactical and strategic levels of the corporation by using the data stored at the corporate TPS. This process has two tasks. As you can see from Figure 4, not all the data in the data layer of the TPS is in the same format. That is, we have multiple and heterogeneous data sources. Specifically, in this case we need to retrieve data from five different databases, one Excel data source, and one text file. This is because the corporation does not use a single database as the basis for its transaction processing system. Even in the case where corporations engaged in ERP implementations, departmental, unit, and even personal databases emerge like mushrooms. Consequently, we need to accept a degree of heterogeneity of data sources in any corporate environment. The consequence is that the SQL developer needs to do some staging in the first place. That is, he or she needs to import data from various sources such as Excel and text files into the relational database so that he or she can then manipulate this data to extract information. Now, this staging procedure might be something as simple as a simple import or something as intricate as the creation of multiple Extraction Transformation and Loading (ETL) packages. ETL has become an expertise area itself and a whole book can be devoted to it. In any case, a SQL developer who augments his or her portfolio with ETL knowledge positions himself or herself very strongly in the market.

Once the data is in a common relational format (in relational tables) then the SQL developer can work with SQL statements to convert this data into information. This is actually one of the major goals of this book. Specifically, the SQL developer will use calculated fields, concatenated fields, string and date functions, the group by clause, crosstab queries, union operators, aggregate functions, parameter queries, and other techniques to convert pieces of data to information that makes sense and is needed by the strategic and tactical levels of the corporation. This information is usually provided in the form of web based reports for larger corporations, or at least corporations that have the know-how to work with web servers. If not, usually a reporting capability is provided by the database software itself like in the case of the MS Access. No matter what the reporting platform is, the SQL professional has a central role in the provision of intelligence to the corporation and in many occasions this is a full time job with important responsibilities for the medium and long term planning of the company.

11. SQL and its relation to web server side pages technologies

Another area in which you will work as a SQL professional is the web. Specifically, you might be asked to participate in a team for the development of server side web pages like asp.net, java server pages (jsp), and hypertext preprocessor (php) pages. These pages contain code in languages like java script, vb script, vb.net, c#, and others. They also contain HTML code. However, in many cases they also contain SQL code used to communicate with back-end databases. In these cases, you might be called to write the SQL part of the page since web developers might not have the depth required to write complex SQL statements.

In Figure 5, you can see a scenario of a web site that contains multiple php pages. Specifically, there are four php pages: SubmitOrder.php, UpdateOrder.php, ReviewOrder.php, and DeleteOrder.php. These four pages constitute an application to which customers connect through the web to place and manage orders. Notice that each customer uses a dissimilar browser as the client to connect to the web site on the web server. The beauty of server side pages is that they are browser independent. Consequently, we do not need to worry about the browser used by the customer. In addition, as you can see from Figure 5, the php pages connect to a database on the back-end database server. Now, in most occasions, the web server and the database server are in different machines but it might be the case that both the web server software and the relational database software are installed on the same machine. For our purposes, the fundamental point is that php pages use SQL to connect to back-end databases. This in turn means that a SQL professional can find his or her way to the world of web development and this is of the essence for our discussion since it constitutes an additional career path.

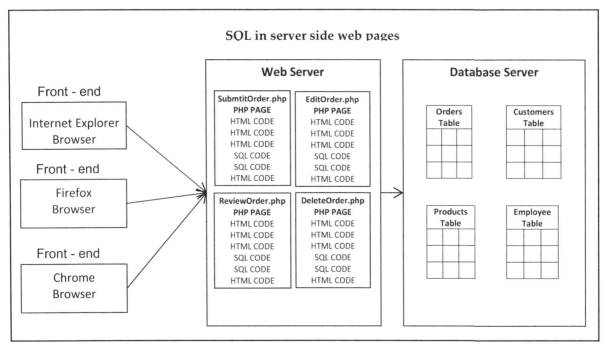

Figure 5: SQL in server side web pages

12.   SQL to obtain data from entities in the external environment of the company

An additional area where you can work, shine, and show your true potential as a SQL developer is when connecting client databases like Access to server databases like MS SQL, Oracle, IBM DB2, and MySQL.   Actually, you can connect Access to any back-end database provided you can find and download the corresponding Open Database Connectivity Drivers (ODBC). Well, this is too technical already. Let us take a step back and first see why do we want to do this from a business point of view and second, what is in it for us, the SQL developers, so that our motivation stays high.

In today's business environment, when we do business with our customers, suppliers, distributors, and other entities, we practically buy or sell products or services. Those products or services have associated "paperwork" which we need to process for every selling, purchasing or other transaction. This paperwork is what leads to the development of the purchasing department, accounts payable, accounts receivable, and other places within the corporation where people go around with pieces of papers in their hands for the most part. Now, there are many ways to process this paperwork with corresponding consequences for the well-being of the company.   For instance, let us consider the scenario in which we would like to re-order parts from our suppliers, a process we call replenishing. When we replenish our inventories we can communicate, i.e. transact with our supplier, in many different ways. First, we can call them and give our order on the phone. Second, we can send them a fax. Third, we can send them an email with an attached spreadsheet of what we need. Fourth, we can go to their online system and order the materials we need online, right away through the web. Fifth, we can have access to their databases through pre-defined queries so that we can look at the latest

10

products, their descriptions, special pricing for us, and any other piece of information we might need. In this last case, we can also create reports for the tactical management of our company to look at before we make our purchase. We do not imply that the fifth method is always the best method to communicate with external entities but is the best from the four mentioned above. There are other methods to integrate corporate information systems well beyond the scope of this SQL book. However, the SQL developer can make a real difference in the efficiency of transaction processing if he or she has the knowledge to connect and manipulate external databases.

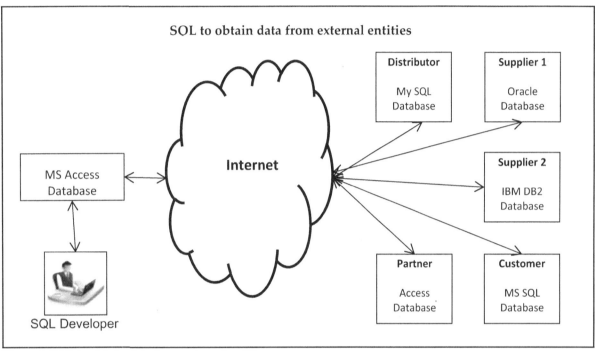

Figure 6: SQL to obtain data from external entities

What is the source of this corporate efficiency? The answer is reducing cycle times and reducing transactional cost. It is one of the primary goals of every corporation to reduce transactional cost and cycle times. That is why banks went from tellers to ATMS and from ATMs to the web. The plain goal was to reduce transaction cost and they got it down to pennies per transaction. However, you need to have the know-how and the technology to do it. That is, you need to have access to database technology and know how to work with it. Going back to our scenario, we would like to do replenishing directly from within the supplier database and without involving any people who would call each other or exchange messages. Some problems might be that the sales person we try to find is out on vacation, the fax machine is not working, the message went to the junk folder, there was a mistake in the order and a multitude of other things that can go wrong. All these situations lead to extended cycle times for replenishing that have multiple consequences all of which lead to increased costs. For example, we might need to keep more inventory which is costly, we lose a customer because we did not have the parts we needed on time, we re-ordered because someone typed in the wrong order amounts or wrong parts, and in general we make our corporation more expensive to operate.

By accessing our supplier databases and doing the work ourselves we avoid all the above and many more tricky situations. As we can see from Figure 6, we can use Access to connect to the databases our customers, partners, and suppliers are using through the Internet. We can literally use the IP address of the database server of the external entity to connect through ODBC drivers or native data providers. ODBC is somewhat slower but nevertheless universal to use with any database and readily available for download through the web. Usually, the supplier or customer will not give us access to their whole database but have some queries available for us to use with the appropriate security setup. From those basic queries then, we can create our own queries and retrieve the data we need exactly the way we would like to retrieve it.

For these purposes a strong SQL developer is needed to work with multiple systems and since in this book we learn how to work with SQL which is the standard for all relational databases, it means that we will be able to write queries against any relational database management system without much difficulty. That is why it is imperative to know how to work with SQL and not just the design interface of Access or any other database.

13.   SQL and its relation to XML

The major business goal in this scenario is to outsource replenishing. That is, we want our suppliers to assume the cost of re-supplying us with inventory. Practically, we want to avoid devoting any human or financial resources to this process so that we can reduce our operational costs and decrease our replenishing cycles as well. At the same time the suppliers will be willing to do this since they will be selling more products. Incurring zero cost for inventory replenishing sounds like an excellent idea but how can we achieve this in technical terms and what would be the role of the SQL developer in the process?

As you can see from Figure 7, the SQL developer is working with an MS Access front-end database to connect to the back-end SQL server and its tables as shown. Now, the SQL developer will write queries that contain all the product related items for inventory purposes. For example, fields included might be the product name, product units per box, unit price, quantity on hand, reorder level, and quantity on order. Then, automation packages will be established in SQL server using integration services so that the result of the SQL statements written by the SQL developer are exported as XML files on the web server. For illustration purposes we named such a file "Inventory.xml" in Figure 7. Today's database servers support the automated importing and exporting of XML data with easily set procedures. Then, the suppliers can access these XML files through the Internet. They check to see what we need from each product and they replenish our inventory without us getting involved in the process. The basic premise of this process is that it is repeatable. That is, every day, or every three days, or every week we replace the XML files on the web server so that the suppliers have access to all the latest data about the status of our inventory. Though the whole process can run manually once or twice a week we should strive to automate it given the flexibility we have by using today's advanced database software.

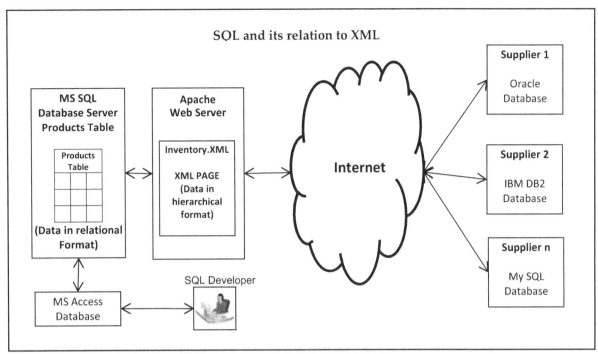

Figure 7: SQL and its relation to XML

On a more technical level, when we export data from a relational database to an XML file there are a couple of items we need to be aware of. First, databases follow the relational data model which means we have a set of related entities (tables) to store data. This for a business task of exchanging data is a problem since the data we need to send to our suppliers might be in four, five or even more related tables and there is no way to send those tables and their relationships across the web. Consequently, what we do is use SQL to get the data we need from those tables in a single query and then we export the result of this query to an XML file which follows the hierarchical model of storing data. But what is an XML file? XML files are practically text documents containing elements. An element can be a book, an employee, a product etc. This single element contains sub-elements and these sub-elements contain additional elements down the hierarchy. Have you noticed the word hierarchy?

In Figure 8, we see a simple XML file. Notice that this file contains information about two employees. In a usual relational database they would represent two records in the employee table. In this XML file we notice that we have a root element called <Employees> which contains two instances of the sub-element <Employee> or in other words information about two employees of ours. We also notice that there are sub-elements like LastName, FirstName, Title, etc. We see that between the element tags we have the actual name, title, and hire date for each employee. Consequently, this single XML file contains both the data and the description of this data by means of its tags. When we receive a file like this, it is very easy to make sense of the data it contains. As a result, when our suppliers connect to a file like this through the Internet, they can read it, they know its meaning, import it into their database for processing, and finally send us the products we need to do our work with no or minimal cost to us.

```
<?xml version="1.0" encoding="UTF-8" ?>
<Employees>
  <Employee>
  <LastName>Smith</LastName>
  <FirstName>George</FirstName>
  <Title>Sales Representative</Title>
  <Address>507 - 20th Ave. E. Apt. 2A</Address>
  <City>Seattle</City>
  <Region>WA</Region>
  <PostalCode>98122</PostalCode>
  <Country>USA</Country>
</Employee>
  <Employee>
  <LastName>Fuller</LastName>
  <FirstName>Andrew</FirstName>
  <Title>Vice President, Sales</Title>
  <Address>908 W. Capital Way</Address>
  <City>Tacoma</City>
  <Region>WA</Region>
  <PostalCode>98401</PostalCode>
  <Country>USA</Country>
  </Employee>
</Employees>
```

Figure 8: Sample XML file

14.   SQL and its relation to ETL

Another area with lots of opportunity and work potential for the SQL developer is the area of extraction, transformation, and loading of data (ETL). This area has a lot of potential for work or consulting since all corporate entities, from the business itself down to the departmental unit, need to move data for transaction processing or for intelligence/analytics. We can define ETL as the general process of extracting data from one or more data sources, transforming this data to appropriate formats and have the ability to load it in one or more data destinations. An ETL process might involve extracting data from a transaction processing system and load this data to a data warehouse (see Figure 9). ETL might also involve the exchange of data between two transaction processing databases, an Excel file to an XML file, or an XML file to a data warehouse. The important point is that ETL is a process that needs to be considered in any data moving scenario.

One of the major differences between ad hoc data moves and rigorous ETL processes is the notion of the timing of data exchanges. A simple import of data from an Excel spreadsheet to an Access database can hardly be described as an ETL process but rather as a data export procedure. However, when we have a process in place that takes data from ten heterogeneous data sources and processes any transformations automatically with workflow and error checking support, and it does this every week, every day, or even every hour, then we can say we have an ETL process in place.

Data sources might be homogeneous or heterogeneous in nature. For example, let us suppose that we have an ETL process in place which takes data from ten data sources. These data sources are two Oracle databases, one Access database, one MySQL database, three XML files, an Excel spreadsheet, two text files, and an ODBC connection to our own DB2 database system. The two Oracle databases are considered to be homogeneous data sources but an XML file and the ODBC connection to IBM DB2 are considered to be heterogeneous data sources. In a data warehouse scenario we will usually have to work with a number of heterogeneous data sources so that we can have all the data needed for advanced business analytics.

Such a scenario is shown in Figure 9, where we get data from multiple heterogeneous data sources from our suppliers, partners, and our own transaction processing system. The goal is to integrate all this data into a data warehouse which will function as the basis of our business intelligence system. A data warehouse is practically a historical data repository, or in other words, a repository of completed transactions. We will use this data to come up with information by using tools such as Data Mining, Online Analytical Processing (OLAP), and Multi-dimensional Expressions (MDX).

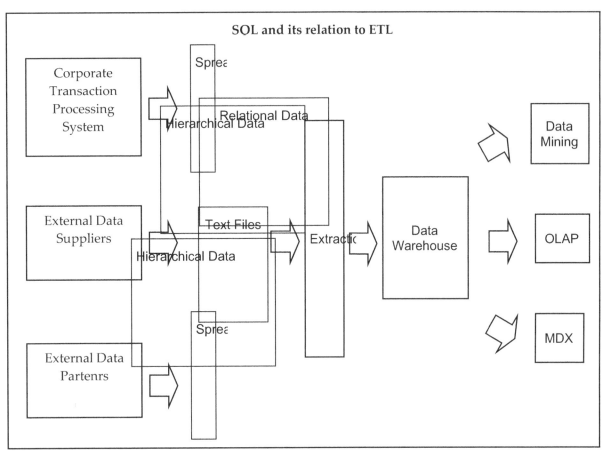

Figure 9: SQL and its relation to ETL

The job of the SQL developer is to provide his or her expertise in designing, developing and implementing the ETL packages. He or she needs to be able to connect to data sources (databases or others), write SQL code, develop queries, concatenate fields, write functions to alter existing data, convert data from text to numeric or other formats, write criteria, and a host of additional tasks that require real command of the SQL language. This is ongoing work as we might have tens or even hundreds of ETL packages setup. Moreover, ETL packages need repetitive editing since business conditions change. For instance, we might need to include a new supplier, delete a partner, include one more data source, delete a field, change scrubbing rules, and a myriad of other tasks. We see at this point how important the role of the SQL developer becomes at any hierarchical level of the company.

15.   SQL and its relation to OLAP

As we get away from business transaction processing and we enter the realm of business analytics, we discover that a knowledgeable SQL developer is very well needed in this field as well. An OLAP cube contains data from the historical transactions of the company. For example, a sales OLAP cube will contain data from past sales of the company.   A customer service cube might contain data from past customer claims records. These cubes are not archival systems that contain all of the data from those past sales or service records. They are developed to contain only relevant information that we need for decision making such as sales and service financial forecasts. Consequently, it is the job of the SQL developer to write the appropriate queries that will feed the OLAP cubes with data from the transactional database of the company. The point here is that SQL is a language needed even at the analytical level to help setup the business intelligence processes of the company.

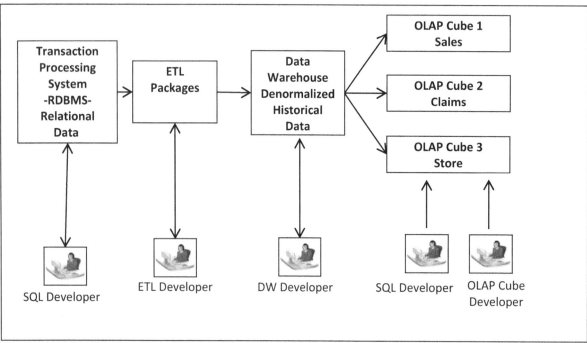

Figure 10: SQL and its relation to OLAP

16.   SQL and its relation to Data Mining

In data mining we use algorithms such as decision trees, neural networks, and clustering so that we can predict the future. Practically, we try to develop a model using an algorithm which will be able to predict the future as accurately as possible. This model is developed and tested using historical data for which we know exactly what happened. Then, we try to apply the same model to predict the future. For instance, let us assume we need to predict the buying behavior of a set of potential customers from a list of fifty thousand leads given to us by a marketing company. The problem is we do not have the financial resources to market to all these customers. Second, we do not want to market to a random set. Third, we do not want to market to a segment that we think it makes sense based on our biased thinking.   Instead we would like to concentrate on the customers with the highest propensity to buy our products. That is why we study the buying behavior of our past customers, we develop a data mining model using an algorithm, and then we test this model with our past customers so that we know it works. Then, we take this model and we apply it on the list of fifty thousand leads to select the best two thousand customers for our company. The SQL developer in this case is indispensable again since he will be the person who will provide the data mining models with data from either the transaction processing system of the company or the data warehouse. In figure 11 we assume there is a data warehouse but even if there is none, the logic of our thought remains the same. The job of the SQL professional is key because he needs to make sure the data provided is the data intended to be provided for the mining model to work effectively.

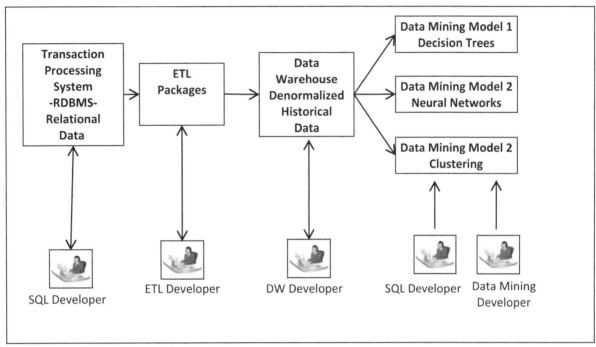

Figure 11: SQL and its relation to Data Mining

17. SQL and its relation to MDX

The power of business analytics comes through the use of multidimensional data stores like data warehouses and OLAP cubes. MDX appeared in commercial products for the first time in 1998 and it was quickly accepted as a fast and efficient way to access multidimensional analytical data. Products that offer MDX capabilities include SAP, SAS, Microsoft, Microstrategy and others.

MDX is a tool designed to unlock the wealth and depth of dimensional data coming from data warehouses, OLAP cubes and dimensional sources in general. If we think about it, MDX is to a dimensional database what SQL is to a relational database. However, this is as close as the two languages come; in terms of syntax MDX is very different from SQL. However, some of the strengths of MDX are SQL's weaknesses and vice versa. In SQL we are working on two dimensions of columns and rows and there is nothing we can do to expand this two dimensional model. In MDX we can practically create and work on multiple dimensions based on the results that we want to have. Moreover, we can define what data goes to each dimension which means that we can manipulate on the fly the content and behavior of each dimension in the multidimensional result.

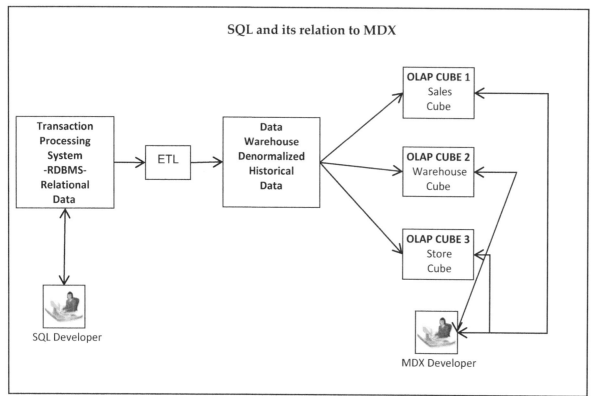

Figure 12: SQL and its relation to MDX

The result of any MDX statement is a virtual cube itself and additional MDX statements can be written against existing MDX statements. It works the same way as SQL queries or views where we can use existing queries as data sources to write more SQL statements and obtain refined results. As you can see from Figure 12, a SQL developer works with relational data in the relational database management system (MySQL, Oracle, DB2) of the company. This RDBMS constitutes the data store of the transaction processing system of the corporation as we examined it in detail in the beginning of this chapter. An MDX developer works with client MDX tools that use OLAP cubes as the data sources. MDX is different in syntax and expressions from SQL. However, a SQL professional who knows how to work with data will be able to make the transition to MDX and add MDX to his or her toolbox. Knowing how to work with MDX statements, opens a whole new stream of career opportunities for the already sought after SQL developer. Below we present some MDX statements for demonstration purposes so that you know how they look like and what kind of information they produce. Our goal in this book is to show you that this road exists. If you decide to follow this path, there are plenty of books focusing on the concepts of OLAP and MDX. Let us have a look at some examples.

The goal in this example is to access a sales cube and provide total cost and sales figures for all stores for the year 2014. Notice that we use two dimensions of the sales cube: time and measures. "Time" is an ordinary dimension and "Measures" is a kind of dimension that contains all the counting and arithmetic (unit sales, store cost, store sales, and sales count) we have previously defined for the cube. Moreover notice that the "on columns" specification means that the time dimension will appear in columns and the "rows" specification means that the "measures" dimension and its members will appear as rows. Practically, this MDX statement contains three specifications: columns, rows, and the cube where the data comes from.

MDX:

```
SELECT
{[Time].[2014]} on columns,
[Measures].members on rows
FROM Sales
```

	2014
Unit Sales	266,773.00
Store Cost	225,627.23
Store Sales	$565,238.13
Sales Count	86837

In this example we are looking for total cost and sales figures for all stores for the year 2014 presented by quarter. Notice that only the quarters for the year 2014 appear and not the individual months. This is the case since quarters are children to years. Months on the other hand, are children to quarters.

MDX:
```
SELECT
{[Time].[2014].children} on columns,
[Measures].members on rows
FROM Sales
```

	Q1	Q2	Q3	Q4
Unit Sales	66,291.00	62,610.00	65,848.00	72,024.00
Store Cost	55,752.24	52,964.22	55,904.87	61,005.90
Store Sales	$139,628.35	$132,666.27	$140,271.89	$152,671.62
Sales Count	21588	20368	21453	23428
Store Sales Net	83,876.11	79,702.05	84,367.02	91,665.72

In this example we are looking for total cost and sales figures for the year 2014 as well as the quarterly figures. Notice that we provide analytics for the whole year and by quarter in the same result pane and those familiar with SQL code will start realizing the power of MDX in that in one short line of code we get such useful results. Also, notice that we can specify exactly the amount of detail that we want by including or excluding parameters in the DESCENDANTS function.

MDX:
```
SELECT
{[Time].[2014], DESCENDANTS ([Time].[2014], [Time].[Quarter])} on columns,
[Measures].members on rows
FROM Sales
```

	2014	Q1	Q2	Q3	Q4
Unit Sales	266,773.00	66,291.00	62,610.00	65,848.00	72,024.00
Store Cost	225,627.23	55,752.24	52,964.22	55,904.87	61,005.90
Store Sales	$565,238.13	$139,628.35	$132,666.27	$140,271.89	$152,671.62

| Sales Count | 86837 | 21588 | 20368 | 21453 | 23428 |
| Store Sales Net | 339,610.90 | 83,876.11 | 79,702.05 | 84,367.02 | 91,665.72 |

As you can see from the MDX statements above, we can obtain information from a multidimensional data store which we cannot acquire using SQL statements. The opposite is true as well: We can get data at a very refined level (highly normalized) from the relational database using SQL which we cannot get from the denormalized data in a data warehouse. In addition, it is imperative to keep in mind that transactional data are current data. That is, the transactional database contains data referring to current orders, quotations, invoices, and other current work. In the data warehouse, we keep only historical data, or in other words, data from completed transactions. Consequently, we use SQL for current, highly normalized data while we use MDX for historical, denormalized data.

18.   SQL and its relation to Reporting Appplications

The role of a SQL developer is essential in reporting applications as well. Today's reporting applications such as SAP Crystal Reports, IBM Cognos, and Microsoft SSRS (SQL Server Reporting Services) are capable of connecting to a multitude of heterogeneous data sources like databases of any kind, spreadsheets, and text files to provide the company with the information it needs to compete. By the way, knowing how to work with any of these reporting applications can lead to a full time job or a consulting position as a simple search on monster.com will confirm. However, no matter how user friendly these applications are, a report developer with knowledge of SQL will always have an advantage both with respect to her colleagues with no knowledge of SQL and with respect to the quality of reports she produces. As you can see from figure 13, the SQL developer will connect the

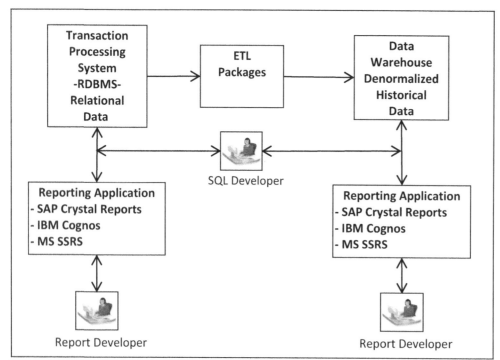

Figure 13: SQL and its relation to reporting

reporting applications to the various data sources, he will make sure that the right data is provided to the report developer, and he might also do some preliminary work in preparing data for analysis. Notice also from figure 13, that we access data both from the transactional database and from the data warehouse database (we make the assumption that the data warehouse is based on relational database) which means that for reporting purposes a SQL developer is needed throughout the organization.

19. CHAPTER 1 DISCUSSION QUESTIONS

1. Is SQL a procedural or non-procedural language?
2. Is SQL working with relational or hierarchical databases?
3. What is the purpose of the SQL Data Definition Language?
4. Can you give some examples of DDL statements?
5. Why do we need to know how to work with DDL statements?
6. What is the purpose of the SQL Data Manipulation Language (DML)?
7. What are the main SQL DML statements?
8. Why SQL is working primarily with highly normalized databases?
9. Is SQL a language associated with a particular database product or vendor?
10. At what corporate level do we use SQL to insert, edit, and delete data?
11. Why do the strategic and tactical corporate levels need information?
12. Why do we need to pay attention to transactional cycle times from a business point of view?
13. What is the role of the SQL professional in web development?
14. What is the difference between relational and hierarchical data?
15. Why do we want to export relational data in hierarchical (XML) format?
16. What is the role of extraction, transformation, and loading (ETL) packages in the corporation?
17. Can the SQL developer help with the development of ETL packages?
18. What is the role of SQL in developing data mining models?
19. Why do we need SQL when we build OLAP cubes?
20. Why do we need SQL with reporting applications such as SAP Crystal Reports?

CHAPTER 2
CREATE, EDIT, AND DELETE TABLES USING SQL

In this chapter, we will work with three DDL statements: CREATE TABLE, ALTER TABLE, and DROP TABLE. We use the CREATE statement to create new tables, the ALTER statement to modify existing ones, and the DROP statement to delete existing tables. The basic structures of the three statements appear below:

CREATE TABLE "tablename" (
fieldname1 datatype (size),
fieldname2 datatype (size),
fieldname3 datatype (size)
)

ALTER TABLE "tablename"
[ADD] [ALTER] [DROP] COLUMN fieldname datatype(size)

DROP TABLE "tablename"

20. Create a simple table using SQL
Create a customer table using pure SQL
Discussion:
This is a simple example of creating a table using SQL in MS Access. The Access help file says that we need to use data definition queries to create objects. Actually, we can enter this code in the SQL view of a select query, and it will work. The table in this example contains only six text fields and is bare without any primary keys defined, NULLs handling, or indexes.

Code:
```
CREATE TABLE Customer1 (
[LastName] text(50),
[MiddleName] text(50),
[FirstName] text(50),
[Address] text(100),
[State] text(2),
[Zip] text(5))
```

Result:
As soon as you run the SQL statement a new Customer1 table is created in the objects pane in Access on the left part of the screen.

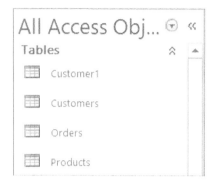

Right click on the name of the "Customer1" table and select "**Design View**". The design of the new table along with its fields appears below.

Field Name	Data Type
LastName	Short Text
MiddleName	Short Text
FirstName	Short Text
Address	Short Text
State	Short Text
Zip	Short Text

21.   Create a table using SQL, and populate it with data on the fly
Create a customer table and populate it with data from an existing table
Discussion:

In most of our work tasks, we do not just need to create a table. We also need to insert some data in it at the same time. Creating a table and populating it on the fly is possible using the SELECT INTO statement in MS Access. In this example, we create the table customer2, and we populate it with data from the customers table.

Code:
```
SELECT * INTO Customer2
FROM customers
```

Result:
Click "Yes" in the dialog box below to create the Customer2 table.

22.   Create a table using SQL, and populate it with specific rows and columns

Create a customer table, and populate it with specific columns and rows from an existing table

Discussion:

In this example, we create the table Customer3 and we populate it with only three fields and 14 records from the Customers table.

Code:

```
SELECT lastname, firstname, address INTO Customer3
FROM Customers
WHERE city = 'Boston'
```

Result:

Double click on the name of the Customer3 table to open it. It will look like the following image.

23.   Create a table defining its primary key

Create a customer table, and assign the CustomerID field as the primary key

Discussion:

In this scenario, we create a table with a primary key of data type "Number" and two simple text fields. Notice the primary key picture on the left of the CustomerID field in the table design view in the picture below:

Code:

```
CREATE TABLE Customer4 (
[CustomerID] number Primary key,
[LastName] text(50),
[FirstName] text(50))
```

Result:
Notice the key icon in front of the CustomerID field.

Customer4	
Field Name	**Data Type**
🔑▶ CustomerID	Number
LastName	Short Text
FirstName	Short Text

24. Create a table defining a field as the primary key and as an autonumber

Create a customer table, and assign the PK CustomerID as an autonumber

Discussion:

In this scenario, we create a table with the primary key of data type "AutoNumber" and two simple text fields.

Code:
```
CREATE TABLE Customer5 (
[CustomerID] Counter Primary key,
[LastName] text(50),
[FirstName] text(50))
```

Result:

Customer5	
Field Name	**Data Type**
🔑 CustomerID	AutoNumber
LastName	Short Text
FirstName	Short Text

25. Create table with a field that does not accept nulls

Create a customer table, and assign the lastname field as required

Discussion:

On some occasions, we might want to create a table with a field that will not accept null or empty values. Null values are different from zero-length strings or zeros. (Check chapter 24 for a full discussion of null values). To avoid nulls for a field, we simply make the field required. In other words, we force users to enter a value, or they will not be able to save the record in the database. We can do this with the following code, which makes the lastname field required.

Code:
```
CREATE TABLE Customer6 (
[CustomerID] Counter PRIMARY KEY,
[LastName] text(50) NOT NULL,
[FirstName] text(50),
[Address] text(50))
```

Result:

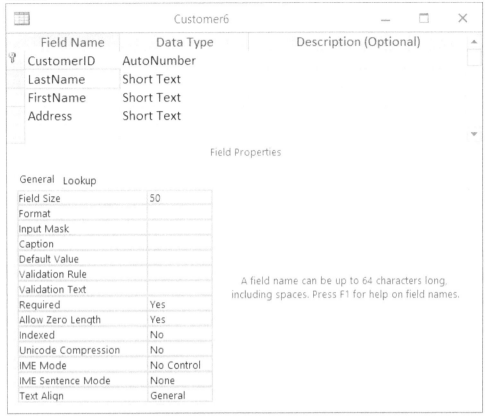

26.   Create a table with the primary key consisting of two fields

Create a tbls_ProductsOrders table and assign the combination of the ProductID and OrderID as the PK

Discussion:

We must know how to setup concatenated keys which means how to setup primary keys consisting of two or more fields. This knowledge is imperative for creating join tables in many to many relationships. In this example, we will create the tbls_ProductsOrders table whose primary key will consist of the combination of the values of the ProductID and OrderID fields.

Code:

```
CREATE TABLE tbls_ProductsOrders (
[ProductID] number,
[OrderID] number,
PRIMARY KEY (ProductID, OrderID))
```

Result:

Notice how the key icon is in front of both fields.

27.   ALTER table: add a column

Add a city field in the customer1 table
Discussion:

On most occasions, we modify the design of existing tables instead of creating new ones. We can alter table designs at will using pure SQL. In this example, we add the city field to the customer1 table.

Code:
```
ALTER TABLE Customer1
ADD COLUMN City TEXT(25)
```

or if you would like to make it a required field:

```
ALTER TABLE Customer1
ADD COLUMN City TEXT(25) NOT NULL
```

Result:

⊞	Customer1	
Field Name	**Data Type**	
LastName	Short Text	
MiddleName	Short Text	
FirstName	Short Text	
Address	Short Text	
State	Short Text	
Zip	Short Text	
City	Short Text	

28.   ALTER table: delete a column

Delete the city field from the customer1 table
Discussion:

We can easily delete a field from a table using the DROP statement. In this case, we delete the "city" field from the customer1 table.

Code:
```
ALTER TABLE Customer1
DROP COLUMN City
```

Result:

Customer1	
Field Name	**Data Type**
LastName	Short Text
MiddleName	Short Text
FirstName	Short Text
Address	Short Text
State	Short Text
Zip	Short Text

29.   ALTER table: change an existing text column to accept more characters

Change the size of the lastname field from 50 to 80 characters

Discussion:

In this example, we will change the size of the lastname field from 50 to 80 characters. Notice the data type of the lastname field is already text. We can also change the data type or the name of the field, if we wish, using the ALTER COLUMN statement.

Code:

```
ALTER TABLE Customer1
ALTER COLUMN LastName TEXT(80)
```

Result:

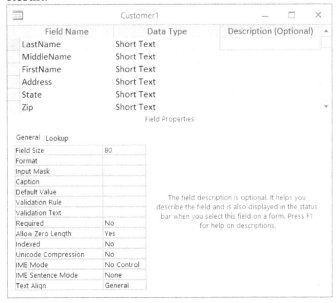

30.   ALTER table: Change the data type of an existing column

Change the data type of the address field from Text to Long Text

Discussion:

In this example, we modify the address field of the Customer2 table from text to long text. This means that the field will be able to store up to a 1 GB of data. Access forms and reports though will be able to display only the first 64000 characters. For the LONGTEXT data type we do not specify the number of characters.

Code:

ALTER TABLE Customer2
ALTER COLUMN Address LONGTEXT

Result:

Customer2	
Field Name	**Data Type**
CustomerID	AutoNumber
FirstName	Short Text
LastName	Short Text
Address	Long Text
City	Short Text
State	Short Text
Zip	Short Text
Country	Short Text

31.   Delete Table

Delete the table customer1 from the database

Discussion:

We can use SQL to delete tables using the DROP statement. In this example, we delete the customer1 table. We must pay attention, however, when we delete tables using the DROP statement because there is no warning or undo action for it. The table will be deleted permanently from the database.

Code:

DROP TABLE Customer1

Result:

The table customer1 has been deleted from the database.

32.   CHAPTER 2 DISCUSSION QUESTIONS

1.   What type of SQL do we use when we create tables? DDL or DML?
2.   What DDL keyword do we use to create a table?
3.   Do we need to enclose field names in brackets in DDL statements?
4.   Can we use DDL to alter the structure of an existing table? What is the keyword used?
5.   Can we create and populate a table using a single DDL statement?
6.   What DDL statement do we use to delete a table?
7.   What keyword do we use to define a field as an autonumber?
8.   What keyword do we use to define a field as the primary key?
9.   What is the SQL keyword we use so that a field does not accept null values?
10. Can we use DDL to change the size of an existing field?

33.   CHAPTER 2 HANDS-ON EXERCISES

Chapter 2 Case 1:

Create a new Access database and name it Chapter2_1.accdb. Copy the table "Products" from the PracticeDatabase.accdb and paste it to Chapter2_1.accdb.

1.   Create a new table with the fields: ProductName (text 50), ProductPrice (currency), UnitsInStock (number), and ReorderLevel (number). Name the table tbl_Products1. Save the query you are using to create the table as Qry1_ Products1.

Your result should look like:

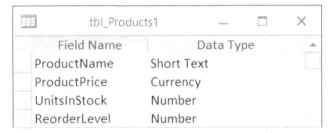

2.   Create a new table with the fields: ProductID (primary key) ProductName (text 50), ProductPrice (currency), UnitsInStock (number), and ReorderLevel (number). Name the table tbl_Products2. Save the query you are using to create the table as Qry2_ Products2.

Your result should look like:

31

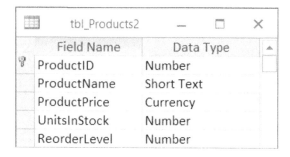

3. Create a new table with the fields: ProductID (primary key and autonumber) ProductName (text 50), ProductPrice (currency), UnitsInStock (number), and ReorderLevel (number). Name the table tbl_Products3. Save the query you are using to create the table as Qry3_ Products3.

Your result should look like:

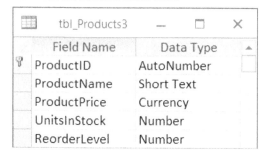

4. Create a new table that matches the structure of the products table. Populate the new table with all the data from the Products table in one step. Name the new table tbl_Products4. Save the query you are using to create the table as Qry4_ Products4.

Your result should look like:

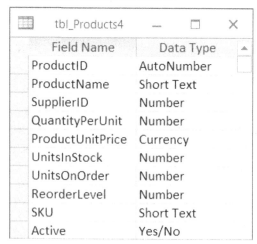

5. Delete the field UnitsOnOrder from the table tbl_Products4. Save the query you are using as Qry5_ Products4_DropColumn.

Your result should look like:

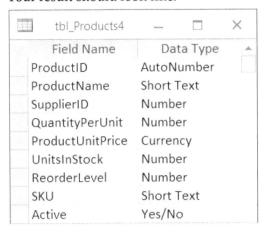

Chapter 2 Case 2:

Create a new Access database and name it Chapter2_2.accdb. Copy the table "Customers" from the PracticeDatabase.accdb and paste it to Chapter2_2.accdb.

1. Create a new table that matches the structure of the customers table. However, it should contain only customers from Florida. Name the table tbl_Customers_FL. Save the query as Qry1_Customers_FL. Assign the CustomerID field as the PK of the table.

   Your result should look like:

   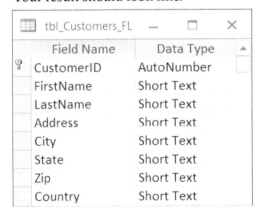

2. Add a new column named Address2 text (100) to the table tbl_Customers_FL. Save the query as Qry2_Add_Address2.

   Your result should look like:

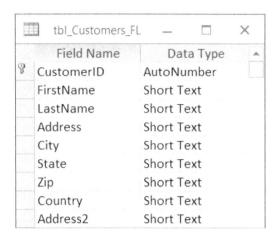

3. Delete from the table tbl_Customers_FL the column Country. Save the query as Qry3_Del_Country.

    Your result should look like:

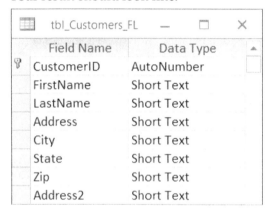

4. In the table tbl_Customers_FL, modify the size of the column named Zip from 255 to 5 characters. Save the query as Qry4_Alter_Zip.

    Your result should look like:

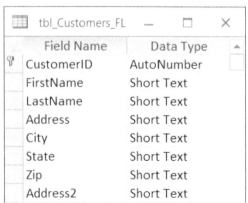

5. Delete the table tbl_Customers_FL from the database. Save the query as Qry5_Del_tbl_Customers_FL.

Your result should look like:

The table tbl_Customers_FL has been deleted from the database.

CHAPTER 3
CREATE, EDIT, AND DELETE INDEXES USING SQL

The use of indexes is another low-lighted topic in the world of databases. It is common knowledge that indexes are useful, but the guidelines to use them are obscure at best. First, indexes will speed up searching operations. They work great with WHERE and ORDER BY clauses. However, they will slow down INSERT and UPDATE statements since every insert or update needs to be saved in both the table and the index. Third, they should be avoided in small tables with few records. They work better in large tables with thousands of records. Fourth, it is a good idea to create indexes for fields used a lot in searching operations. If we have a form in Access or a web form that we use as the front-end in which we provide the users with the option to search customers by first and last name fields, then we need to index those two fields.

In addition, indexes can be set up as unique or non-unique. In this case, the indexes accept unique or non-unique values and they can function as constraints disallowing duplicate values for the indexed field or fields. For example, if we set up a unique index on a last name field, all of the last names in the table will have to have unique values. Primary key fields in Access are automatically indexed when created, and those indexes are set up as unique.

We can also use indexes as constraints to disallow null values for fields in Access tables. If we want to make the last name field a required field, we can use an index to assign a field as required. In this case, we force the users to make an entry for this field.

Finally, we can create multi-field indexes that will index the combination of values of multiple fields instead of just indexing the values of each individual field. That is, we can create a multi-field unique index on both the last and first name fields that will accept duplicate values for the individual last and first name fields but will not accept duplicate values for their combinations. Let us go through some examples to demonstrate the points we mentioned above in practice.

34.   Create a table and set a unique index for one of its fields
Optimize customer searches on the last name field
Discussion:
Since we expect heavy searching activity on the LastName field, we need to create an index to accelerate these searches. In this example, we create a new table and a unique index on the LastName field. That is, we do not allow duplicate values on the lastname field which means two customers cannot have the same last name.

Code:

```
CREATE TABLE tblCustomer21 (
[CustomerID] Counter Primary key,
[LastName] text(50),
[FirstName] text(50),
[Address] text(50),
CONSTRAINT indLastName UNIQUE (LastName))
```

Result:

In the figure below, the LastName field is indexed and, at the same time, does not accept duplicates due to the unique index we created on this field.

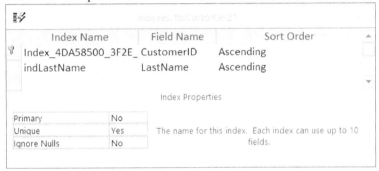

To check the index you just created go to the table design and in the design tab go to the group "Show/Hide" and click on "Indexes".

35.   Create a non-unique index for an existing table

Add a non-unique index for the first name field in the customer table

Discussion:

Let us assume we have a table with data in it. If later on we decide we would like to add an index, we can easily do it using SQL. Notice in the figure below that the indFirstName is non-unique. This means that we allow duplicate values for the FirstName field. In other words, we can have two "Johns" or two "Marys" in the table, but they definitely have to have different last names as defined by the indLastName, which is a unique index in the previous example.

Code:

CREATE INDEX indFirstName ON tblCustomer21 (FirstName)

Result:

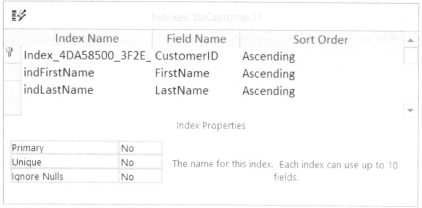

To check the index you just created go to the table design and in the design tab go to the group "Show/Hide" and click on "Indexes".

36.   Create a unique index for an existing table

Add a unique index for the last name field in the existing customer table

Discussion:

As we can see from the figure in the previous example, the indFirstName index is non-unique, and it does not ignore nulls. What is the exact meaning of a unique index? What is the meaning of an index ignoring or not ignoring nulls?

First, by a unique index, we mean that no duplicate values are allowed for that field. We know very well that unique values are not allowed for fields that have been designated as primary keys. However, by defining a unique index, we can disallow duplicate values for a field that is not the primary key of the table. For example, if we are working with the LastName field, and we create a unique index on it, we cannot have two customers in our table with the same last name. If we try to enter two customers with the same last name, the database will not allow their entry. The SQL code below will create a unique index on a field other than the primary key for an existing table. Let us create the table first:

Code:
```
CREATE TABLE tblCustomer22 (
[CustomerID] Counter Primary key,
[LastName] text(50),
[FirstName] text(50),
[Address] text(50))
```

Code:
```
CREATE UNIQUE INDEX indLastName ON tblCustomer22 (LastName)
```

Result:

As we can see from the figure below, the indLastName is a unique index now. However, this is not always a desirable scenario since there might be multiple customers with the same last name. How can we set up index constraints so that we allow multiple customers to have the same last name or the same first name, but disallow multiple customers to have the same last and first names at the same time? Let us see the next example with multiple-field indexes.

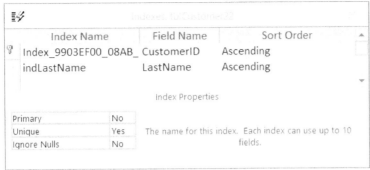

To check the index you just created go to the table design and in the design tab go the the group "Show/Hide" and click on "Indexes".

37.   Create multiple-field indexes to avoid duplicates
Add a unique multi-field index for the last and first name fields
Discussion:

When working with customers, we would like to make sure that no duplicate customer records exist in our database. At the same time, it is logical that many customers might have the same last name, and many of them will have the same first name.

With a multi-field unique index on the last and first name fields, our database will accept values such as Smith John and Smith Tracy. However, if we try to enter another Smith John in the database, we will get a message that such an entry violates existing index rules and it will not be accepted. Multi-field indexes are extremely useful to keep our data in a good state.

Code:

CREATE UNIQUE INDEX indLastFirst ON tblCustomer22 (LastName, FirstName);

Result:

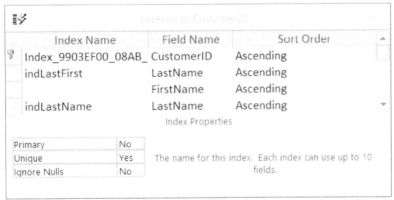

To check the index you just created go to the table design and in the design tab go the the group "Show/Hide" and click on "Indexes".

38. **Create an index on a field that will not accept nulls.**

Add a unique index for the last name field that will not allow null values

Discussion:

In this scenario, we would like the indexed field not to accept duplicate values and null values at the same time. It will not accept duplicate values because we use the "UNIQUE" keyword and it will not accept null values because we use the "DISALLOW NULL" keywords. Practically, the "DISALLOW NULL" keywords will not permit any blank entries in the last name field.

Code:

```
CREATE TABLE tblCustomer23 (
[CustomerID] Counter Primary key,
[LastName] text(50),
[FirstName] text(50),
[Address] text(50))
```

Code:

```
CREATE UNIQUE INDEX indLastName ON tblCustomer23 (LastName) WITH DISALLOW NULL
```

Result:

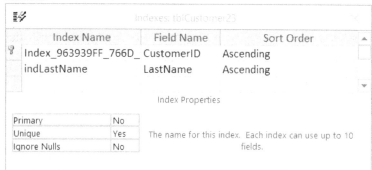

To check the index you just created go to the table design and in the design tab go the the group "Show/Hide" and click on "Indexes".

39. **Create an index that ignores nulls**

Create an index on lastname that ignores null last name values

Discussion:

By default when we create an index for a field, this index will include the field's null values in the indexed entries. We might, however, want nulls to be excluded from our index and only entries with data in the field to be included. This is not the same as setting a field to not accept nulls. In this example, the keywords "WITH IGNORE NULL" will simply exclude null values from the index list. That is, a list of last names will be created and kept in the database as an index and this list will not have any blank entries in it.

Code:
CREATE TABLE tblCustomer24 (
[CustomerID] Counter Primary key,
[LastName] text(50),
[FirstName] text(50),
[Address] text(50))

Code:
CREATE UNIQUE INDEX indLastName ON tblCustomer24 (LastName) WITH IGNORE NULL

Result:
As you can see from the result set, the "Ignore Nulls" property is set to "yes."

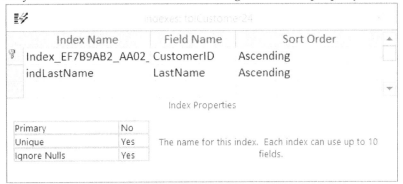

To check the index you just created go to the table design and in the design tab go to the group "Show/Hide" and click on "Indexes".

40.   Delete Index
Delete the "indLastName" index from the customer table using SQL
Discussion:
In our previous example, we have created an index on the LastName field for the tblCustomer24 table and we named it indLastName. In this example, we write a DROP statement to delete that index from our tblCustomer24 table.

Code:
DROP INDEX indLastName ON tblCustomer24

Result:
The index "indLastName" has been deleted from the tblCustomer24 table.

41.   CHAPTER 3 DISCUSSION QUESTIONS

1. Why do we need to use indexes?
2. On what fields does it make sense to use indexes?
3. What does it mean to use indexes as constrains?
4. How can we use an index to disallow nulls in a field?
5. How can we avoid duplicate values in a field by using indexes?
6. What are the consequences of indexes on inserts and updates?
7. How can we avoid duplicate values in multiple fields by using indexes?
8. What are the consequences of indexes on WHERE and ORDER BY clauses?
9. Does it make sense to use indexes on small or large tables?
10. Can we setup indexes to ignore null values in the field?

42.   CHAPTER 3 HANDS-ON EXERCISES

Chapter 3 Case 1:
Create a new Access database and name it Chapter3_1.accdb.

1. Create a new table with the fields: CustomerID (Primary key, autonumber), Lastname (text, 50), FirstName (text 50), Address (text,50), City (text, 50), State (text, 2), and Zip (text, 5). Name the table tbl_Customers31. Save the query you are using to create the table as Qry1_ tblCustomers.

   Your result should look like:

   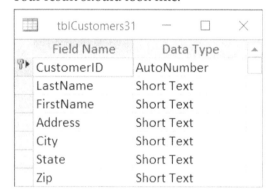

2. Create a non-unique index on the FirstName field. Name the index "IndFirstName". Save the query you used to create the index as Qry2_IndFirstName. Open the indexes for the table tbl_Customers and look at the new index you have just created.

   Your result should look like:

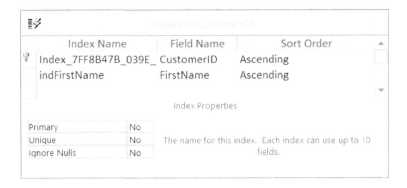

3. Create a non-unique index on the LastName field. Name the index "IndLastName". Save the query you used to create the index as Qry3_IndLastName.

Your result should look like:

4. You have decided that you want to disallow entries of customers with the same first and last names. You consider those entries as very probable duplicates. To achieve this goal create a unique multiple-field index on the first and last name fields. Save the query you used to create the index as Qry4_IndFirstLastName.

Your result should look like:

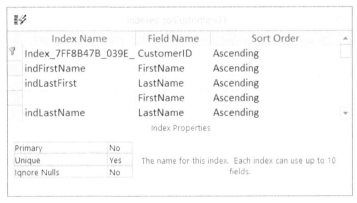

5. You have also decided not to allow null values on the last name field. Create a unique index on the lastname field that will also not allow null values for this field. Save the query you used to create the index as Qry5_IndLastNameNulls. HINT: Delete the index IndLastName first and then

recreate it.

Your result should look like:

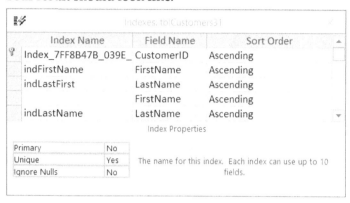

Chapter 3 Case 2:

Create a new Access database and name it Chapter3_2.accdb.

1. Create a new table with the fields: ProductID (Primary key, autonumber) ProductName (text 100), ProductDescription (text, 200), ProductPrice (currency), UnitsInStock (number), and ReorderLevel (number). Name the table tbl_Products32. While creating the table, create a unique index on the field ProductName and name it IndProductName. Save the query you are using to create the table as Qry1_ tblProducts.

   Your result should look like:

   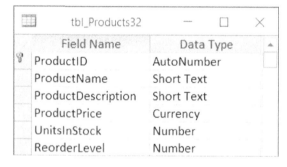

2. Change the unique index on the ProductName field in table tbl_Products32 to a non-unique index. Name the index IndProductName. Save the query you are using to create the index as Qry2_IndProductName_NonUnique. Hint: You need to drop and recreate the index.

   Your result should look like:

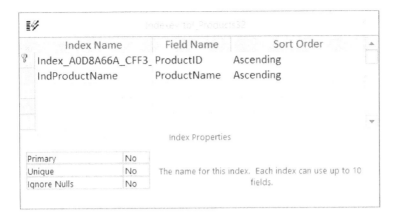

3. Change the IndProductName index to be unique and disallow null values in the field at the same time. Save the query you are using to create the index as Qry3_IndProductName_Nulls. Hint: You need to drop and recreate the index.

Your result should look like:

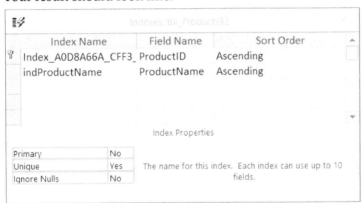

4. Create a unique index on both the ProductName and ProductPrice fields. Name the index IndNamePrice. Save the query you are using to create the index as Qry4_IndNamePrice.

Your result should look like:

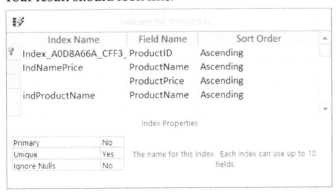

5. Create a non-unique index on the ProductDescription field. This index should ignore null values in this field. That is, null values for the ProductDescription field should not be included in the index. Save the query you are using to create the index as Qry5_IndProductDescription.

Your result should look like:

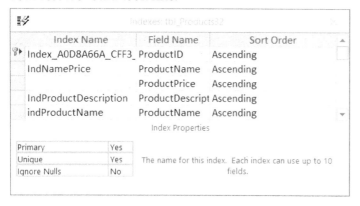

CHAPTER 4
CREATE, EDIT, DELETE
RELATIONSHIPS USING SQL

Our manager asked us to create a customer database to store information about our customers and their orders. One of our tasks will be to create relationships among tables. After almost 20 years of working with databases, I can attest that this process is much more art than science. There are neither rigid rules to follow nor guidelines to cover all of the situational scenarios we might encounter.

However, we have two great tools at our disposal: First, we should have a total and complete understanding of the meaning of relationships and their related topics like primary keys, foreign keys, referential integrity, cascade updates, cascade deletes, and join types. Second, we can use our logic to achieve a well-built relationship resulting in a solid database. The purpose of this chapter is to completely demystify the obscure area of relationships not only with respect to building them but, most importantly, with respect to their interpretation and usage.

43.   Why and how to create a one-to-many relationship
Create a one-to-many relationship between customers and orders

Our first task is to create a relationship between the customers and orders tables. The logic here is that each customer can have multiple orders while one order definitely belongs to one customer only. This is the case for a one-to-many relationship. This one-to-many relationship is depicted graphically in the figure below. I have included data values on purpose to actually show how records from one table relate to records in the other table. This is because when we talk about relationships among tables, we are actually talking about record relations.

CUSTOMERS		ORDERS		
CustomerID	Name	OrderID	CustomerID	OrderDate
1	John	1	2	9/10/2017
2	Mary	2	2	10/10/2017
3	George	3	1	11/10/2017
4	Stacy	4	3	11/11/2017

Primary Key   Primary Key   Foreign Key

The steps for creating a one-to-many relationship between two database tables (customers and orders in this case) are the following:

1. Assign a primary key to both tables if they do not already have one. In this example, the primary key for the Customers table is "CustomerID", and the primary key for the Orders table is "OrderID".

2. Make sure your primary key is not a "natural" key like a social security number, or driver's license number. The data types for the primary keys in both tables should be of the "Auto Number" data type.

3. Create a field in the Orders table, which we will name "CustomerID." The "CustomerID" field in the Orders table is the "Foreign key" of the table. The data type of the "CustomerID" field in the Orders table should be of the number data type so that it can be joined with the CustomerID in the Customers table.

4. Click on the "Database Tools" tab on the ribbon. In the "Relationships" group, click on the relationships button. In the "relationships" group again click on the "Show Table" button." The "Show Table" dialog box opens. Add the tables we would like to join.

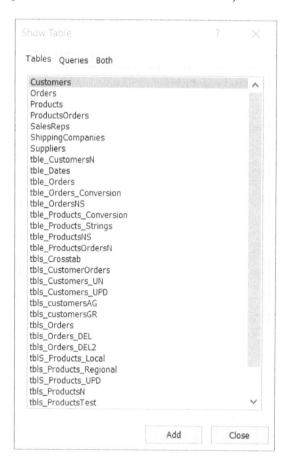

5. The relationships window in Access shows the entity relationship diagram (ERD) of the database. In the ERD, all related tables appear along with the field names and the primary and foreign keys. The ERD allows us to understand the structure and design of the database, and it constitutes the place in which we can create, edit, and delete relationships. In this case, we will create a new relationship between customers and orders.

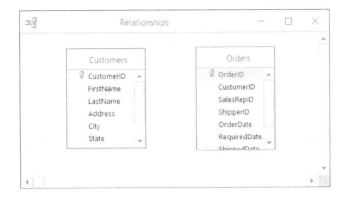

6. Click on the CustomerID field in the Customer table, and drag it on the CustomerID field on the Orders table. The "Edit Relationships" window will come up.

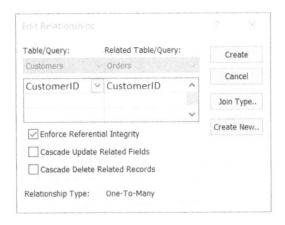

7. We can just click "Create", and our relationship is ready. However, in this case, we will also click on "Enforce Referential Integrity" so that our database remains sound when inserting new records and deleting existing ones. When referential integrity is on, we have two specific consequences: first, we will not be able to add an order in the orders table without a corresponding customer in the customers table. Second, we will not be able to delete a customer from the customers table for whom there are orders in the orders table. We will have to first delete the orders for that customer and then delete the customer. For a full understanding of referential integrity and its important implications, read the corresponding section in this chapter.

8. Finally, our Entity Relationship Diagram (ERD) will look like this:

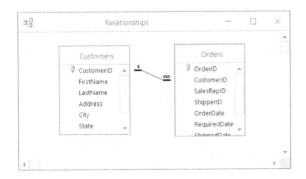

44.   How to create a one-to-many relationship using pure SQL code
Create a one-to-many relationship between the tables Customers41 and Orders41

Discussion:
In this example we simply use pure SQL code to attain the same result as in the previous example. We will create the tables Customers41 and Orders41 first.

Create the Customers41 table:
CREATE TABLE Customers41 (
[CustomerID] Counter Primary key,
[LastName] text(50),
[FirstName] text(50))

Create the Orders41 table:
Pay attention here: we designate the data type of the CustomerID FK below as integer since Access designates the CustomerID PK in the Customers41 table as integer. If you designate the CustomerID FK as simply "number" you will not be able to create the relationship since PK and FK data types need to be the same.

CREATE TABLE Orders41 (
[OrderID] Counter Primary key,
[CustomerID] integer,
[ShippedDate] Date)

Create the one-to-many relationship between Customers41 and Orders41:
ALTER TABLE Orders41
ADD CONSTRAINT FK_CustomerID
FOREIGN KEY (CustomerID)
REFERENCES Customers41 (CustomerID)

Result:

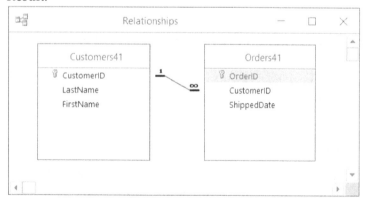

45.   How to read, understand, and use a one-to-many relationship
The meaning of one-to-many relationship between customers and orders

Learning how to create a one-to-many relationship is really a minimal goal in itself. The essential objective is to actually understand its meaning, be able to apply it, and take advantage of its many possibilities. In this respect, let us try to read what is happening in our two related tables of customers and orders.

First, when looking at the foreign key values in the orders table (the values of the CustomerID field in the Orders table), we notice that only John, Mary, and George have orders. Second, we see that John and George have one order each, while Mary has two orders. Third, we see that Stacy does not have any orders at all, so we might want to initiate a marketing effort for her. Fourth, when we look at the orders table and examine order number 3 (with OrderID = 3), we immediately understand that this order belongs to John because the corresponding foreign key value is 1. If we look up this value in the customer table, we find that the corresponding customer name is John. This is the way relational databases work and are able to retrieve related records from two or more tables.

CUSTOMERS		ORDERS		
CustomerID	Name	OrderID	CustomerID	OrderDate
1	John	1	2	9/10/2017
2	Mary	2	2	10/10/2017
3	George	3	1	11/10/2017
4	Stacy	4	3	11/11/2017

Primary Key   Primary Key   Foreign Key

46. Why and how to create a many-to-many-relationship
Create a many-to-many relationship between orders and products

Our task this time is to create a database to keep track of customers, orders, and products. We already know how to create a one-to-many relationship between customers and orders. Now, we need to create a relationship between orders and products. Whenever we design a database, the setup of relationships is the cornerstone of the design process. We do have an ally in this process, which is our logic.

In this respect, we examine and make conclusions on the relation of each table to the other or of relations among entities because this is how we refer to tables in database parlance. From the orders point of view, we conclude that each order in the orders table can contain more than one product. It is only logical that a customer can order multiple products in one order. From the products point of view, we conclude that each product can participate in more than one order. It is logical that we can sell the same product to multiple customers through their orders. When this is the case, we need to establish a many-to-many relationship between Orders and Products.

To create a many-to-many relationship between the Orders and Products tables, we need to create a join table between them like the Products_Orders table in this example. The primary key of the join table is the combination of the primary keys of the tables that we would like to join in a many-to-many relationship. In other words, the primary key of any join table in a many-to-many relationship is a composite key consisting of two fields. As we know already, the values of a primary key in a relational table must always be unique, and this uniqueness is expressed in this case by the combination of the values of OrderID and ProductID. For example, in Figure 17 the value (1,2) of the first record in the Products_Orders table is different from the value (2,2) in the second record. This is how we obtain uniqueness of primary key values of join tables in many-to-many relationships.

Customers	
CustomerID	Name
1	John
2	Mary
3	George
4	Stacy

Orders		
OrderID	CustomerID	OrderDate
1	2	9/10/2017
2	2	10/10/2017
3	1	11/10/2017
4	3	11/11/2017

Products	
ProductID	ProductName
1	A
2	B
3	C
4	D

ProductsOrders		
OrderID	ProductID	Quantity
1	2	2
2	2	5
3	1	3
4	2	4

Figure 17: A many-to-many relationship

To create a many-to-many relationship in Access, we follow these steps:
1. Make sure that the two tables that you are about to join in a many-to-many relationship already have primary keys. These primary keys should be of the autonumber data type.
2. Create a new table whose name is the combination of the names of the two tables that you would like to join—in this case "Products_Orders." You can follow any other naming convention you prefer as long as you can remember in the future that this is a join table between Orders and Products.
3. In the join table "Products_Orders", create two fields whose names are: ProductID and OrderID. The data types of both OrderID and ProductID should be "Number". This is because we need to join these fields with the corresponding keys in the Orders and Products tables, and we cannot join two fields with dissimilar data types. Your table should look like this:

4. We are not finished yet, however. Let us assume that a customer orders two units of product (A) and three units of product (B). This customer is ordering multiple quantities of the same product in

the same order. In addition, we might want to give discounts on particular products in the same order while extending no discounts for other products. How do we accomplish this? The answer is to include additional fields in the Products_Orders table so that we can enter this information. Our final table will look like this:

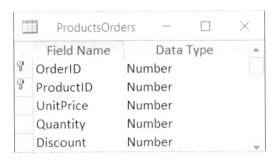

5. The next step is to join the Orders table to the ProductsOrders table by dragging the OrderID field from the Orders table on the OrderID field in the ProductsOrders table. We do the same by dragging the ProductID field from the Products table on the ProductID field in the ProductsOrders table. Our relationships window will now look like the figure below:

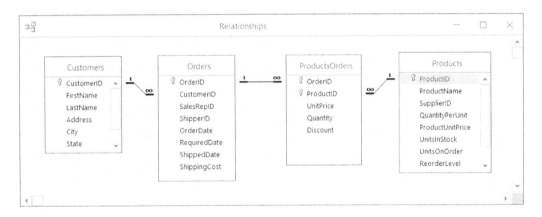

47. How to create a many-to-many relationship using pure SQL code
Create a many-to-many relationship between the tables Orders41 and Products41

Discussion:
In this example, we use SQL code to create a many-to-many relationship between the tables Orders41 and Products41.

Create the Orders41 table:
CREATE TABLE Orders41 (
[OrderID] Counter Primary key,
[CustomerID] integer,
[ShippedDate] Date)

Create the Products41 table:
CREATE TABLE Products41 (

53

[ProductID] Counter Primary key,
[ProductName] text (50))

Create the OrdersProducts41 join table:
This is the join table that we need to have to establish the many-to-many relationship between Customers41 and Orders41. We designate the data type of the OrderID and ProductID fields as integers since Access designates the CustomerID PK in the Customers41 table and the OrderID PK in the Orders41 table as integers. The last line of the code designates the combination of the OrderID and ProductID values as the PK of the Products41 table. That is, the PK of this table is composite consisting of two fields.

```
CREATE TABLE OrdersProducts41 (
[OrderID] integer,
[ProductID] integer,
PRIMARY KEY (OrderID, ProductID))
```

Create a one-to-many relationship between Orders41 and OrdersProducts41:
ALTER TABLE OrdersProducts41
ADD CONSTRAINT FK_OrderID
FOREIGN KEY (OrderID)
REFERENCES Orders41 (OrderID)

Create a one-to-many relationship between Products41 and OrdersProducts41:
ALTER TABLE OrdersProducts41
ADD CONSTRAINT FK_ProductID
FOREIGN KEY (ProductID)
REFERENCES Products41 (ProductID)

Result:

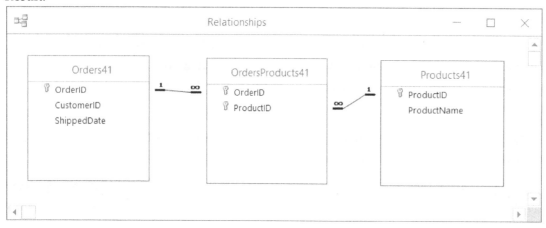

48.   How to "read", understand, and use a many-to-many relationship
The meaning of many-to-many relationship between orders and products

The important goal with relationships is to understand what we are doing and not so much the process of doing it. If we do not remember the series of clicks to achieve the task, we can always resort to a handy reference. However, if we do not understand how many-to-many relationships work, we will not be able to use them or, at the very least, cannot take full advantage of them.

Let us examine the meaning of a many-to-many relationship from A to Z. The figure below depicts a many-to-many relationship between the Orders and Products tables. Let us try to answer a couple of questions:

What specific products were included in John's order?

To answer this question, we should go to John's record in the customer table. There, we see that John's primary key value is 1 (PK=1). Then, we proceed to the Orders table, which is joined with the customer table through a one-to-many relationship. There, we see that John appears in the third record of the table where CustomerID = 1. In database parlance, this translates to foreign key value = 1 or FK=1. Next, we see that the corresponding OrderID value for FK=1 is 3 (OrderID =3). From there, we are looking for OrderID = 3 in the ProductsOrders table. We see that we have one OrderID with the value of 3 in the ProductsOrders table. The corresponding ProductID value is 1. Next, we go to the Products table and see that ProductID = 1 corresponds to product A. Since the quantity for the pair (3,1) in the Products_Orders table is 3, we can finally answer that John ordered three units of product (A). This is exactly how relational databases use associations (relationships) to store and retrieve information.

Customers	
CustomerID	Name
1	John
2	Mary
3	George
4	Stacy

Orders		
OrderID	CustomerID	OrderDate
1	2	9/10/2017
2	2	10/10/2017
3	1	11/10/2017
4	3	11/11/2017

Products	
ProductID	ProductName
1	A
2	B
3	C
4	D

ProductsOrders		
OrderID	ProductID	Quantity
1	2	2
2	2	5
3	1	3
4	2	4

Figure 18: Understanding a many-to-many relationship

What specific products were included in Mary's orders?

Mary's PK is 2. For FK=2 in the orders table, the corresponding PK values are 1 and 2. We now know that Mary placed two orders. For OrderID 1 and 2 in the ProductsOrders table, the corresponding ProductIDs are 2 and 2. The quantities are 2 and 5. Therefore, we know right away that Mary ordered seven product Bs in two separate orders. We also note that Mary has a pattern of ordering only product Bs, which allows us to direct our marketing efforts.

49.   What is referential integrity, how to apply it, and what it means
The meaning and implications of referential integrity in table relationships

Referential Integrity is a concept misunderstood and underused in the database professional world. Some developers will turn this option on in Access because it is a good "thing" to do even though they do not fully understand its implications. Let us take it one step at a time and explain the ins and outs of referential integrity.

Referential integrity in relational databases means that relationships among joined tables remain consistent. Of course, as is the case with all definitions, we do not understand much. Let us try to approach it from a more practical perspective. First, we set referential integrity on table relationships (not tables themselves), and we have the choice to apply it when we create those relationships.

Here is how we do it. Let's say that we would like to create a one-to-many relationship between customers and orders. To achieve this, we drag the CustomerID field (PK in the Customer table) on the CustomerID field in the Orders table (FK in the orders table). The relationships window then opens up as we can see below:

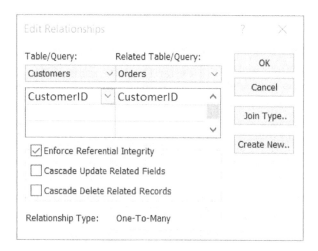

The only thing we need to do is to click on the Referential Integrity check box. In some cases, you might find that the database does not allow you to apply referential integrity. If this is the case, then you should immediately look for orphaned records in the table at the many part of the relationship and it would mean that we have CustomerID (FK) values in the Orders table without corresponding CustomerID values (PKs) in the customers table. In short, we have orders without corresponding customers. Check chapter 23 for a full explanation of orphaned records. I have devoted a whole chapter on orphaned and unrelated records because this topic is crucial in any database work.

Once referential integrity is on, we have several consequences: First, the database will not allow us to enter an order in the orders table without a corresponding customer. If we have an order from a new customer, we have to enter that customer's data in the Customers table first and then, the orders in the Orders table.

Second, if we try to enter an order in the orders table with a CustomerID value (FK value) that does not exist in the Customers table the database will produce an error message that a related record is required in the Customers table.

Third, in Access we need to pay attention since if we try to enter an order in the orders table leaving the CustomerID field blank (FK value null) this will be ok for the database but very bad for the integrity of our data since we will not know who this order belongs to. In this case, referential integrity will not be enforced. The solution is to make the CustomerID field (FK field) in the orders table required as shown in the figure below:

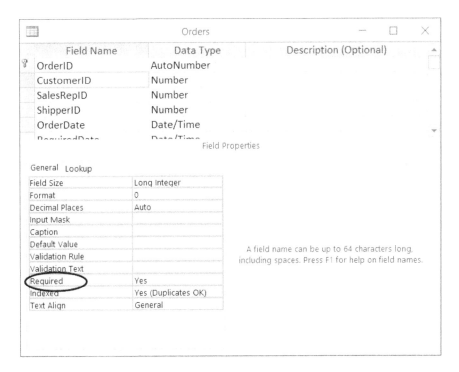

The next major consequence of referential integrity is that the database will not allow us to delete a customer who has orders in the database. To delete such a customer, we first need to delete all the orders associated with him or her and then delete the customer. If we try to delete a customer with existing orders, the following message will appear.

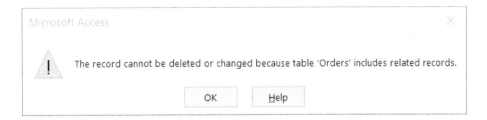

If we want to delete a customer with existing orders in one step, we can click on "Cascade Deletes". This option helps the professional delete all related information about a customer in the database, but it is very dangerous to leave on because users might delete customers and their related information by mistake. Check chapters 28 and 29 on "Cascade Updates" and "Cascade Deletes" for full details on their use since they are an important productivity tool for developers and power users.

50. CHAPTER 4 DISCUSSION QUESTIONS

1. What kind of a scenario are we in if we have customers without orders in our database?
2. What kind of a scenario are we in if we have orders without customers in our database?
3. How do we establish a many-to-many relationship between two tables, for example, orders and products?
4. Why do we have to establish a many-to-many relationship between singers and songs?
5. Why do we have to establish a one-to-many relationship between customers and orders?
6. How do we setup a one-to-many relationship between customers and orders? How many primary keys we need? How many foreign keys?
7. If referential integrity is on, can we enter orders without customers in the database?
8. If referential integrity is on, can we enter customers without orders in the database?
9. What scenario are we in if we try to apply referential integrity for a relationship but the database does not allow us to do so?
10. If referential integrity is on, can we delete a customer with existing orders in the database?

51. CHAPTER 4 HANDS-ON EXERCISES

Chapter 4 Case 1:

Create a new Access database and name it Chapter4_1.accdb.

1. Create a new table and name it "Actors". Setup three fields: ActorID as the primary key and auto number, ActorFirstName text (50) and ActorLastName text (50).   Create the table using pure SQL code. Save the query you are using to create the table as Qry1_Actors.

   Result:

   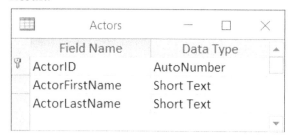

2. Create a new table and name it "Films". Setup three fields: FilmID, FilmTitle, and FilmDate. Assign FilmID as the primary key and auto number, FilmTitle as text (200), and FilmDate as date. Create the table using SQL code. Save the query you are using to create the table as Qry2_Films.

Result:

3. Create a new table and name it FilmsActors. This table will serve as the middle table for the many-to-many relationship between the tables Actors and Films. Setup the primary key and data types of its fields using pure SQL. Save the query you are using to create the table as Qry3_FilmsActors.

Result:

4. Setup a one-to-many relationship between the tables Actors and FilmsActors. Save the query you are using to create the relationship as Qry4_Actors_FilmsActors. Go to "Database Tools" click on "Relationships" and show the Actors and FilmsActors tables in the Entity Relationship Diagram. It should look like the one in the image below:

Result:

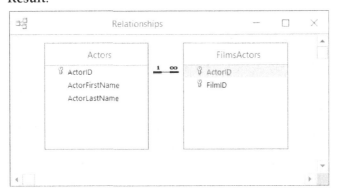

5. Setup a one-to-many relationship between the tables Films and FilmsActors. Save the query you are using to create the relationship as Qry5_Films_FilmsActors. The Entity Relationship diagram of the database should look like the following:

Result:

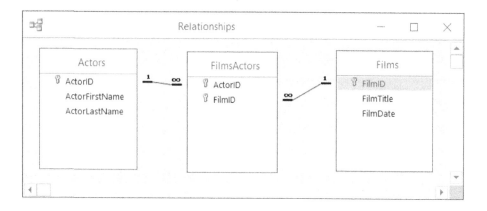

Chapter 4 Case 2:

Create a new Access database and name it Chapter4_2.accdb.

1. Create a new table and name it "Patrons". Setup three fields: PatronID as the primary key and auto number, PatronFirstName text (30), and PatronLastName text (50). Create the table using pure SQL code. Save the query you are using to create the table as Qry1_Patrons.

    Result:

    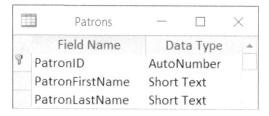

2. Create a new table and name it "Events". Setup three fields: EventID as the primary key and auto number, EventTitle text (200), and EventDate as date. Create the table using pure SQL code. Save the query you are using to create the table as Qry2_Events.

    Result:

    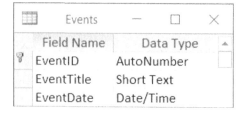

3. Create a new table and name it PatronsEvents. This table will serve as the join table for the many-to-many relationship between the tables Patrons and Events. Setup the primary key and data types of its fields using pure SQL. Save the query you are using to create the table as Qry3_PatronsEvents.

Result:

4. Setup a one-to-many relationship between the tables Patrons and PatronsEvents. Save the query you are using to create the relationship as Qry4_Patrons_PatronsEvents. Go to "Database Tools" click on "Relationships" and show the Patrons and PatronsEvents tables in the Entity Relationship Diagram. It should look like the one in the image below:

Result:

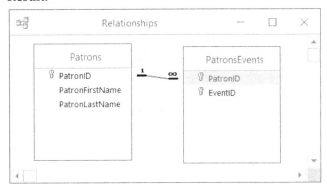

5. Setup a one-to-many relationship between the tables Events and PatronsEvents. Save the query you are using to create the relationship as Qry5_Events_PatronsEvents. The Entity Relationship diagram of the database should look like the following:

Result:

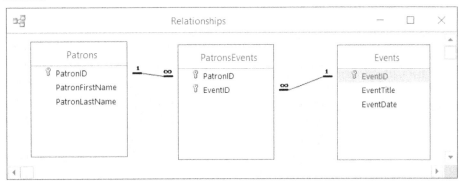

CHAPTER 5
THE SELECT STATEMENT

The SELECT statement is the most widely used keyword in any relational database, and it constitutes the basis for a multitude of Structured Query Language (SQL) code statements. We will go through examples of how to use the SELECT statement alone or in combination with its various clauses like WHERE, GROUP BY, HAVING, and ORDER BY. However, we will devote whole chapters to its clauses since there are many ways and tricks in using them to achieve the intricate results we need in our daily business tasks. In this chapter, we will focus on the SELECT statement in detail, and you will be surprised to see that SELECT can be used in many more ways than simply selecting records. The general structure of the SELECT statement in Access appears below. The keywords in brackets are optional.

SELECT [ALL, TOP, DISTINCT, DISTINCTROW] field1, field2, field3
FROM table
[WHERE]
[GROUP BY]
[HAVING]
[ORDER BY]

The SELECT statement has a set of four predicates (ALL, TOP, DISTINCT, DISTINCTROW) used to manipulate the number of records returned from a SQL statement. All four of them are used right after the SELECT keyword, and all of them are optional. If none of them is used the ALL predicate is used by default.

52.   SELECT with * to retrieve all columns and rows from a table
Create a quick report selecting all columns and rows from the customer table
Discussion:
We can use the * wildcard character to quickly retrieve all of the columns and rows from a table. Note that a SELECT statement used this way will retrieve records in the order they are stored in the table.

Code:
SELECT *
FROM Customers

Result:

53. SELECT to retrieve only field names

Provide documentation for the Orders table by retrieving a list of its fields

Discussion:

There are occasions when we want to retrieve only the field names and not any records. This is usually for documentation purposes or for just having a look at the field names before we write a query. We can easily do this by using the following code, which will result in no records because there is no way for 0 to equal 1.

Code:

```
SELECT *
FROM Orders
WHERE 0=1
```

Result:

54. SELECT to retrieve specific columns from a table

Create a quick customer list for mailing labels

Discussion:

In this example, we define exactly what columns to get using the SELECT statement.

Code:

```
SELECT lastname, firstname, address, city, state, zip
FROM Customers
```

Result:

55.   SELECT to retrieve specific records from a table

Create a report of customers in Boston

Discussion:

SQL statements provide great flexibility for retrieving records. For instance, we can retrieve all columns from a table, all rows, some columns and all rows, some rows and all columns, or some rows and some columns. In this example, we are retrieving all of the columns in the customer table but limiting the rows to customers who reside in Boston. The code would work with double quotes for the criterion "Boston" as well.

Code:

```
SELECT *
FROM Customers
WHERE city = 'Boston'
```

Result:

CustomerID	FirstName	LastName	Address	City	State
163	Arnold	Cormack	31 2nd Street	Boston	MA
164	Carolyn	Currier	58 Holmes CT	Boston	MA
165	Catherine	Davis	87 Coral Street	Boston	MA
166	Cristopher	Geisler	93 Kate Street	Boston	MA

Record: ◄ ◄ 1 of 14 ► ►I ►▣ No Filter Search

56.   SELECT to retrieve specific columns and specific rows

Create a list of suppliers from NY but do not display the state

Discussion:

Sometimes, we need to retrieve specific columns and specific rows from a table. When in this situation, always work with the process of getting the columns first and then, apply the appropriate clauses (WHERE) and criteria ("Houston", "Texas") to get the rows that you need. In this example, we are retrieving only the company name and the contact name of suppliers who operate in New York. In addition, notice that although we use the state as a criterion field, the state itself will not appear in the result set. For the state field to appear in the result set, it needs to be part of the SELECT statement. Fields used for filtering only in the where clause do not appear in the result set.

Code:

```
SELECT companyname, contactname
FROM suppliers
WHERE state = 'NY'
```

Result:

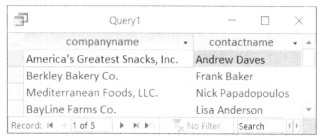

companyname	contactname
America's Greatest Snacks, Inc.	Andrew Daves
Berkley Bakery Co.	Frank Baker
Mediterranean Foods, LLC.	Nick Papadopoulos
BayLine Farms Co.	Lisa Anderson

Record: ◄ ◄ 1 of 5 ► ►I ►▣ No Filter Search

57.   SELECT AS: column aliases

Retrieve data from the suppliers table but change the column titles

Discussion:

In many cases, table fields have names that make sense to the database developer but not to the end user. For example, Cust_LN and Cust_FN might make sense to the database developer because they represent naming conventions for the last name and first name fields. However, if we use them as titles for queries or reports, no one will be able to discern their meaning.

In these cases, we use the SELECT AS statement to assign field aliases or column titles that make sense for all of us. We can do this on the fly in the SELECT statement. In the example below, we change the titles of the fields for two columns in the suppliers table. Notice, we enclose the second alias [Supplier Contact] in brackets because we have a space between the two words. If we forget the brackets, the SQL statement will not run.

Code:

SELECT companyname AS Company, contactname AS [Supplier Contact]
FROM suppliers

Result:

58.   SELECT combined with plain text

Create a quick letter to customers

Discussion:

SQL allows us to mingle field data with plain text, which results in the creation of some interesting results. In this example, we are writing a quick letter to customers. Notice that we enclose plain text in single quotes (" "). In addition, note that the characters (+ ' ' +) add spaces between fields. Finally, the whole statement in the code below is just one concatenated field named "CustomerLetter." For a full understanding of concatenated fields, refer to chapter 16 where you will find many tips and tricks working with them.

Code:

SELECT 'Dear' + ' ' + [firstname] + ',' + ' ' + 'we would like you to know that our full product catalog is on sale in the city of' + ' ' +[city] + ' ' + 'Please visit our website at: http://www.company.com' As CustomerLetter
FROM customers

Result:

59.   SELECT with ORDER BY

Sort a customer list by last name

Discussion:

In this example, we use the * wildcard character to retrieve all of the columns and rows in the customers table and then, sort the data on last name. To sort data in SQL, we use the ORDER BY clause. Specifically, to sort in ascending order, we use ORDER BY ASC, and to sort in descending order, we use ORDER BY DESC. If like in this example, the ORDER BY clause is not followed by the ASC or DESC keyword, then the ASC keyword is used as the default one.

Code:

```
SELECT *
FROM Customers
ORDER BY lastname
```

Result:

60.   SELECT with WHERE and ORDER BY

Retrieve all customers except those in Boston and sort by last name

Discussion:

In this example, we use the * wildcard character to retrieve all columns in the customers table. For rows, we filter the result set by using the WHERE clause with the inequality predicate "<>" to select all customers except those in the city of Boston. Then, we sort ascending on lastname.

Code:
SELECT *
FROM Customers
WHERE city <> 'Boston'
ORDER BY lastname

Result:

CustomerID ▾	FirstName ▾	LastName ▾	Address ▾	City ▾	State ▾	Zip ▾
93	Nicholas	Ackerman	5 Buckingham Dr	Dallas	TX	52347
141	Alfred	Allen	29 Water Street	New York	NY	12189
15	Pindar	Ames	23 Cornell Dr	New York	NY	45357
50	Thomas	Andersen	52 Betwood Street	Orlando	FL	89754

Record: 1 of 187   No Filter   Search

61.   SELECT with WHERE, GROUP BY, HAVING and ORDER BY

Calculate the number of customers in all states except NY and show states with more than ten customers

Discussion:

Our business manager asked us to calculate the number of customers in each state. She asked us to exclude New York State from the results. From the remaining states, she also asked us to exclude states with less than ten customers. Finally, states with bigger numbers of customers should appear first in the result set.

To comply with the above requirements, we need to use SELECT, WHERE, GROUP BY, HAVING, and ORDER BY in combination. Let us examine the purpose of each statement: First, we use the SELECT statement to select two fields from the customers table. Specifically, we select the state field as it is and the CustomerID field on which we apply the Count() function to calculate the number of occurrences of CustomerID in the table. Since the CustomerID is the primary key of the table, we know that Count() will produce reliable results because there is no way to have null values in a primary key field.

Then, we use the WHERE clause with the inequality operator "<>" to exclude customers from New York State. Practically, "<>" means retrieve everything else except 'NY'. Next, we use the GROUP BY clause to aggregate calculations by state. The database will calculate the number of customers and produce results by state since we group on that field.

The next point is a bit tricky if not understood well. The WHERE and HAVING clauses are both filtering statements. We use them both to obtain a subset of records. However, they have different roles in SQL statements, and they can be used individually or in combination. In this specific example, we use the WHERE clause to exclude customers from the state of New York from the result set. The WHERE clause will run before any groupings and calculations by the GROUP BY clause. The WHERE clause will exclude customers from NY, and the GROUP BY clause will produce groups and count customers for the remaining records. After the groups of customers by state are generated from the GROUP BY clause, and the customer numbers are calculated by the count() function, the HAVING clause takes effect. It will exclude from the final result any states with less than ten customers. Therefore, the HAVING clause will wait until all the groupings and calculations are complete before it

67

takes effect. This is logical since the numbers produced by the count() function are not known in advance.

Finally, the ORDER BY clause will take effect, and it will sort results by the highest number of customers. What you need to remember in one sentence is that when using the WHERE and HAVING clauses in combination, the WHERE clause always takes effect first, while the HAVING clause takes effect after the groups by the GROUP BY clause have been established. The ORDER BY clause will take effect last.

Code:
SELECT State, Count(CustomerID) As NumberOfCustomers
FROM Customers
WHERE State <> 'NY'
GROUP BY State
HAVING Count(CustomerID) >10
ORDER BY Count(CustomerID) DESC

Result:

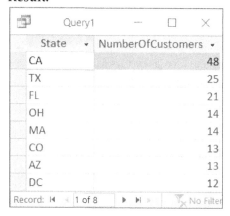

State	NumberOfCustomers
CA	48
TX	25
FL	21
OH	14
MA	14
CO	13
AZ	13
DC	12

Record: ◄ 1 of 8 ► ►► ► No Filter

62. SELECT with INSERT INTO to append records in an existing table
Append records from the customer table to a historical customer table
Discussion:
Our goal in this example is to copy (append) a number of records from our customer table to another table in which we keep historical customer data. This scenario applies in situations where we no longer do business with some customers, but we do not want to delete them from the database. At the same time, we do not want these old customers to clutter our operational customer table, slow it down, or interfere with our calculations. We can easily copy them to a historical table by using the INSERT INTO statement. The general structure of the INSERT INTO statement appears below:

INSERT INTO TargetTable (field1, field2, field3…)
SELECT (field1, field2, field3…)
FROM SourceTable

In this particular example, we copy records from the customers table to the customer51 table. Since customer51 does not exist, we create it with the CREATE statement below. Then, we use the INSERT

INTO statement to append three fields with 201 records (all records in the customer table) in the customer51 table.

Code:
CREATE TABLE Customer51 (
[CustomerID] Counter Primary key,
[LastName] text(50),
[FirstName] text(50),
[Address] text(100),
[City] text(50))

INSERT INTO Customer51 (firstname, lastname, address, city)
SELECT firstname, lastname, address, city
FROM customers

Result:

63.   SELECT with INSERT INTO to append specific records in a table
Append selected customer records to a historical table
Discussion:
In some occasions, we might want to copy only a subset of records into another table. We can easily achieve this by using the INSERT TO statement and the WHERE clause in combination. Here, we append customer records from NY only.

Code:
INSERT INTO Customer51 (firstname, lastname, address, city)
SELECT firstname, lastname, address, city
FROM customers
WHERE State = 'NY'

Result:

64.   SELECT INTO to create a backup or temp table
Create a quick backup copy of the products table
Discussion:

The SELECT INTO statement accomplishes two tasks simultaneously. First, it can create a new table, and second, it can populate this table with records from another table. We do not need to use the CREATE statement to create a new table. In addition, we do not need the INSERT INTO statement to copy records from one table to another. The SELECT INTO statement can accomplish both tasks at once.

We can use the SELECT INTO statement to create quick backup copies of tables, or we can create temporary tables and work on their data leaving the original tables untouched. For instance, we might want to manipulate data in the products table, but we would like to see the results of the edits first before we apply them in the operational products table. In this particular example, we create a backup copy of the products table, and we name it Products_Backup.

Code:
```
SELECT *
INTO Products_Backup
FROM Products
```

Result:

65.   SELECT INTO to create a backup table with a subset of data from the original table
Create a temporary table that contains a subset of data from the products table
Discussion:

We can use the SELECT INTO statement and the WHERE clause in combination to create a new table that will contain a subset of data from the original table. Here, we create a new table named "Products_Subset" which will contain only three fields and product records from suppliers with supplier ID 1, 2, 3, and 4 only.

Code:
```
SELECT ProductName, UnitsInStock, UnitsOnOrder
INTO Products_Subset
FROM Products
WHERE SupplierID IN (1,2,3,4)
```

Result:

66.   SELECT INTO to create a new table with a subset of data from three joined tables

Create a new table that contains data from the three joined tables

Discussion:

The SELECT INTO statement can create a new table with data from multiple joined tables. In this example, we create a new table that contains fields from the customers, orders, and productsorders tables. In addition, we restrict the number of records it will contain by using the WHERE clause for customers in NY only. Why do we need to create a new table since we can easily retrieve the same records using a query? Actually, a move like this serves multiple purposes. First, we might want to give access to this data to other people and not worry if they edit it or change it any way they want. If we provide them with a query, they could affect the data in our own underlying tables. Another scenario might be that we would like to hide the complexities of the joins to the people working with this data. It is much easier to work with one table than with two inner joins from three tables. Finally, we might be in a business scenario in which this table is the data source for XML or PHP or ASP.Net or other server side pages on our website, and we generate this table every week. Those pages will return results much faster working out of a table data source instead of multiple joins and WHERE clauses.

Code:

```
SELECT customers.lastname, customers.firstName, Orders.OrderDate,
ProductsOrders.UnitPrice, ProductsOrders.Quantity
INTO TempCustomersOrders
FROM (customers INNER JOIN Orders ON customers.CustomerID = Orders.CustomerID)
INNER JOIN ProductsOrders ON Orders.OrderID = ProductsOrders.OrderID
WHERE customers.State='NY'
```

Result:

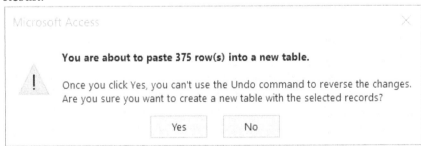

67.   SELECT INTO to create a new table with the structure of an existing table but without the data

Discussion:

Using the code below, we will create a new table named "Products51" which will be identical to the Products table but without any data. Field names and corresponding data types transfer wonderfully but remember to define the primary key and any indexes in your new table.

Code:

```
SELECT * INTO Products51
FROM Products
WHERE 1=2
```

Result:

68.   SELECT INTO to create a new table with part of the structure of an existing table

Discussion:

As a continuation from the previous example, you can transfer part of the structure of an existing table to a new one as in the code below. Remember, no data will move to the new table.

Code:

```
SELECT ProductID, ProductName, QuantityPerUnit, ProductUnitPrice INTO Products52
FROM Products
WHERE 1=2
```

Result:

CHAPTER 5 DISCUSSION QUESTIONS

1. What is the primary purpose of the SELECT statement?
2. What is the purpose of using column aliases in SELECT statements?
3. Can we insert plain text in SELECT statements? How can this help in our business communications?
4. What is the purpose of the WHERE clause in the SELECT statement?
5. What is the purpose of the ORDER BY clause in the SELECT statement?
6. What is the purpose of using the GROUP BY clause with SELECT?
7. Is HAVING a clause we can use with SELECT? What is its purpose?
8. Which clause runs first? WHERE or HAVING?
9. What statement can we use with SELECT to append records to an existing table?
10. What keyword do we use to create and populate a new table using a single SELECT statement?

70. **CHAPTER 5 HANDS-ON EXERCISES**

Chapter 5 Case 1:

Create a new Access database and name it Chapter5_1.accdb. Copy the table Products from the PracticeDatabase.accdb and paste it to Chapter5_1.accdb.

1. Create a query to select all columns and rows from the products table. Save the query as Qry1_All_Products.

   Your result should look like:

   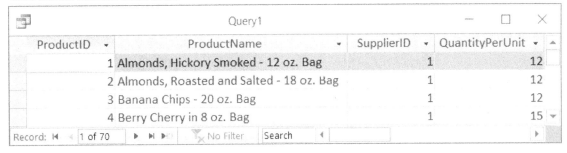

2. Retrieve all records from the products table but only include the following fields: ProductName, ProductUnitPrice, UnitsInStock, and UnitsOnOrder. Name the query Qry2_Products_Columns.

   Your result should look like:

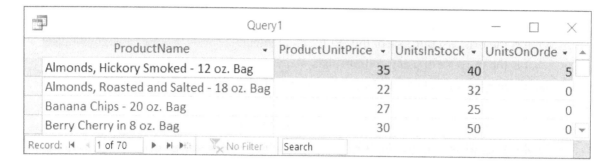

3. Create a query for the fields ProductName, ProductUnitPrice, UnitsInStock, and UnitsOnOrder. However, only retrieve products for which the UnitsOnOrder quantity is zero. Name the query Qry3_UnitsOnOrder.

Your result should look like:

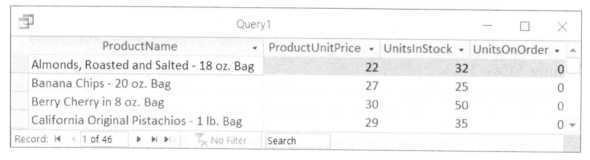

4. Create a query for the fields ProductName, ProductUnitPrice, UnitsInStock, and UnitsOnOrder. The query should include all the records in the table. However, in the result set the field names should appear as: Product Name, Price, Units In Stock, and Units On Order. Name the query Qry4_Alias.

Your result should look like:

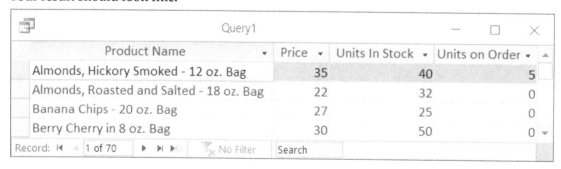

5. Create a query for the fields ProductName, ProductUnitPrice, UnitsInStock, and UnitsOnOrder. The query should retrieve all columns and rows in the products table. Sort the result set ascending by ProductUnitPrice so that cheaper products appear first. Name the query Qry5_ProductsSort.

Your result should look like:

Chapter 5 Case 2:

Create a new Access database and name it Chapter5_2.accdb. Copy the table Products from the PracticeDatabase.accdb and paste it to Chapter5_2.accdb.

1. Create a backup copy of the entire products table. Name the backup products table tbl_Products_Backup. Save the query as Qry1_Products_Backup.

   Your result should look like:

2. Create a backup table of the products table. However, only include the ProductName, QuantityPerUnit, ProductUnitPrice, and UnitsInStock fields. In addition, the backup table should include products from suppliers 5,6,7,8, and 9 only. Name the backup products table tbl_Products_Backup_Subset. Save the query as Qry2_Products_Backup_Subset.

   Your result should look like:

3. Create a new table and name it Products2. This table should have the following fields: ProductID (primary key and auto number), ProductName (ShortText, 50), QuantityPerUnit (number), Price (currency), UnitsInstock (number), and UnitsOnOrder (number). Then, use the INSERT INTO

statement to insert all records from the Products table into the Products2 table. Save the query as Qry3_Products_Insert1.

Your result should look like:

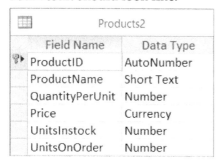

4. Now, insert into the Products2 table only those products from the Products table whose price is more than $25. Save the query as Qry4_Products_Insert2.

Your result should look like:

5. Now, select all fields from the Products2 table for those products whose price is above $30 and sort ascending by productname. Save the query as Qry5_Products_Select.

Your result should look like:

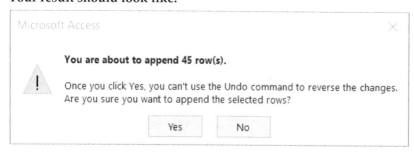

CHAPTER 6
THE OR AND AND OPERATORS

The OR and AND operators are widely used in relational databases. There are four points you need to remember about them: First, their task is to produce a subset of records from the total records in a table or query. Second, they have no effect on the columns we retrieve from that table or query. Third, they are always used with other operators such as LIKE, with equality and inequality predicates, or with wildcard characters. Fourth, the OR and AND operators can be used individually or in combination with varying results as we shall see in the following examples.

The OR operator is inclusive which means that records will be returned for every OR condition satisfied in our query. For example, if we want to retrieve invoice information from suppliers in three different cities ('New York' OR 'Portland' OR 'Houston'), we will use the OR operator twice. If we have misspelled the word "Houston" to "Houston1" the query will still give us results for "New York" or "Portland".

The AND operator on the other hand is exclusive which means it will produce results only when all of the conditions are met. Using the above example if we misspell any of the three cities in the expression such as ('New York' AND 'Portland' AND 'Houston1'), we will not get any result at all from the query.

71.   Using OR on the same column
Create a quick report with customers in New York or Houston
Discussion:
Let us suppose we have a request to generate a list of customers who reside in New York or Houston. In this case, we need to use the OR operator on the city field with two equality predicates. Note that since we use the SELECT statement with *, the database will return all columns from the table. However, when it comes to records, only 39 out of 201 will be returned. This is because we filtered the recordset to include customers in the cities of New York or Houston only.

We can use the OR operator on the same column multiple times as in this example to retrieve customers from multiple cities. However, we cannot use the AND operator multiple times on the same column because we would ask the impossible: that is, having a customer who resides in many cities simultaneously.

Code:
```
SELECT *
FROM customers
WHERE (city = 'New York') OR (city = 'Houston')
```

Result:

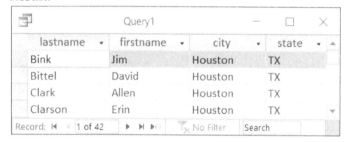

72. Use the IN operator to replace multiple OR operators

Produce a report of customers from four cities

Discussion:

The OR operator works fine with two cities as we have seen in the previous example. What if we need to use OR on the city field multiple times? We have two problems in this case: First, we need to write a long SQL statement using multiple OR operators. Second, if we have a big number of records in the table, the query will be slow to return results. In cases like this one, we can use the IN operator that produces much cleaner code. It is easy to modify and maintain as you can see below:

Code:

```
SELECT lastname, firstname, city, state
FROM customers
WHERE city IN ('Albany', 'Denver', 'Houston', 'Phoenix')
ORDER BY lastname
```

Result:

lastname	firstname	city	state
Bink	Jim	Houston	TX
Bittel	David	Houston	TX
Clark	Allen	Houston	TX
Clarson	Erin	Houston	TX

Record: 1 of 42   No Filter   Search

73. Using OR on multiple columns

Create an inventory report listing product quantities for units in stock and units on order

Discussion:

A very efficient way to use the OR operator is to apply it on multiple columns. For instance, we might have a business request to create an inventory report that lists products for which we have more than 10 units in stock and products for which we have more than 10 units on order. As you can see from the result set, we obtained a total number of 70 products. This means that 70 records satisfied at least one condition. This is because any record that satisfies at least one of the conditions will appear in the result set.

In addition, this is why the second record in the result set with 32 units in stock and 0 on order appears as well. We asked for units in stock >10 or units on order >10. This particular record satisfies only the first condition, and this is enough to appear in the result set. The outcome will be very different when we use the AND operator as we will see presently.

Code:
SELECT productname, unitsinstock, unitsonorder
FROM products
WHERE (UnitsInStock > 10)
OR (UnitsOnOrder > 10)

Result:

productname	unitsinstock	unitsonorder
Almonds, Hickory Smoked - 12 oz. Bag	40	5
Almonds, Roasted and Salted - 18 oz. Bag	32	0
Banana Chips - 20 oz. Bag	25	0
Berry Cherry in 8 oz. Bag	50	0

Query1 — □ ×

Record: 1 of 70   No Filter   Search

74. Use UNION instead of OR to speed up results

Create an inventory report using UNION instead of OR operators
Discussion:
We can use the UNION statement instead of multiple OR operators to speed up the response time of the database engine. This is a trick and the difference in response times is enormous. The SQL statement below with the UNION operation achieves the exact same results as the SQL code in the previous example. However, the response is instant using UNION, while it takes quite a few seconds using the OR operators.

Response times deteriorate as the number of records or the number of OR operators increase. Consequently, if you have statements with multiple OR operators that you use often, you might consider replacing them with UNION statements. The only difference is the order in which the retrieved records appear since in this case, the results of the first SELECT statement in the UNION operation will appear first. The results of the second SELECT will follow and so on. You can easily reorder the recordset using the ORDER BY clause with a UNION statement. For a full understanding of UNION operations, plus related tips and tricks refer to chapter 22.

Code:
SELECT productname, unitsinstock, unitsonorder
FROM products
WHERE (UnitsInStock > 10)
UNION
SELECT productname, unitsinstock, unitsonorder
FROM products
WHERE (UnitsOnOrder > 10)

Result:

productname	unitsinstock	unitsonorder
All-Purpose Marinade I	27	15
All-Purpose Marinade II	26	15
Almonds, Hickory Smoked - 12 oz. Bag	40	5
Almonds, Roasted and Salted - 18 oz. Bag	32	0

Record: 1 of 70   No Filter   Search

75.   Using AND on multiple columns

Produce a report of customers from a specific state and a specific city

Discussion:

This time, we have a business request to produce a report of customers who reside in the state of NY and, in particular, the city of Albany. In this case, we need to use the AND operator to isolate records which satisfy both criteria at the same time. Note that if we use the OR operator, we will get all of the customers in the state of NY irrespective of city and all the customers from all of the cities named "Albany" around the country. This is a problem because there are 28 cities in the U.S. named Albany! If we do business worldwide, there are six additional cities named Albany. An experienced database user will always use AND to isolate the customers for Albany, New York. As you can see from the result set, we have only four customers that satisfy both criteria.

Code:

```
SELECT lastname, firstname, city, state
FROM customers
WHERE (state = 'NY')
AND (city = 'Albany')
```

Result:

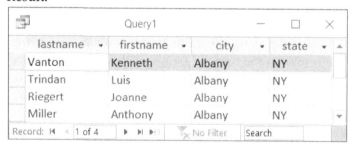

lastname	firstname	city	state
Vanton	Kenneth	Albany	NY
Trindan	Luis	Albany	NY
Riegert	Joanne	Albany	NY
Miller	Anthony	Albany	NY

Record: 1 of 4   No Filter   Search

76.   Using OR and AND in combination

Produce a report of customers from one state and two cities

Discussion:

Our objective in this scenario is to produce a report that will list customers from the cities of Albany and New York in NY State. In this case, we need to use the AND operator twice and the OR operator once as it appears in the code below:

Code:
SELECT lastname, firstname, city, state
FROM customers
WHERE
state = 'NY' AND city = 'Albany'
OR
state = 'NY' AND city = 'New York'
ORDER BY lastname

Result:

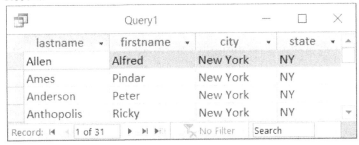

77.   Using multiple OR and multiple AND operators in combination

Produce a report of customers from three states and three cities

Discussion:

This time, we have a request to create a customer report that will list customers in the cities of Houston, Albany, and Phoenix from the states of Texas, New York, and Arizona respectively. In this case, we need to use the AND operator three times and the OR operator twice as it appears in the code below.

Code:
SELECT lastname, firstname, city, state
FROM customers
WHERE
state = 'NY' AND city = 'Albany'
OR
state = 'TX' AND city = 'Houston'
OR
state = 'AZ' AND city = 'Phoenix'
ORDER BY lastname

Result:

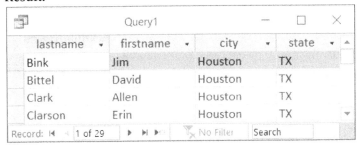

78.   CHAPTER 6 DISCUSSION QUESTIONS

1. What is the primary purpose of the OR and AND operators in a query?
2. Is the OR operator inclusive or exclusive? What is the implication of this?
3. Is the AND operator inclusive or exclusive? What is the implication of this?
4. When using the OR and AND operators, can we control what columns (fields) will appear in the result set?
5. Can we use the OR and AND operators alone or do we need to use them in conjunction with other operators and predicates?
6. Can we use the OR operator multiple times on the same column? What is the meaning of doing this?
7. What will the result be if we use the OR operator on multiple columns? How many conditions need to be true to obtain results?
8. What operator can we use to replace multiple OR operators?
9. Can we use the AND operator multiple times on the same column?
10. When we use the AND operator on multiple columns how many conditions need to be true to obtain results?

79.   CHAPTER 6 HANDS-ON EXERCISES

Chapter 6 Case 1:

Create a new Access database and name it Chapter6_1.accdb. Copy the table Customers from the PracticeDatabase.accdb and paste it to Chapter6_1.accdb.

1. Create a query to select all customers from the states of New York and Massachusetts. Save the query as Qry1_Customers_NY_MA.

    Your result should look like:

2. Create a query to select all customers from the states of New York, Massachusetts, Ohio, Texas, and Colorado. Hint: Use the IN operator. Save the query Qry2_Customers_FiveStates.

    Your result should look like:

3. Create a query to select all customers from the city of Boston and the State of California. Save the query as Qry3_Customers_Boston_California.

Your result should look like:

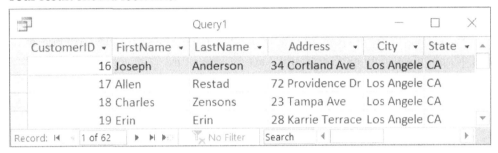

4. Create a query to select all customers from the city of Albany in the state of New York and the city of San Jose in the state of California. Name the query Qry4_Customers_Albany_SanJose.

Your result should look like:

5. Create a query to select all customers form the cities of San Jose, Phoenix, and Boston, for the states of California, Arizona, and Massachusetts respectively. Save the query as Qry5_Customers_MultipleCitiesStates.

Your result should look like:

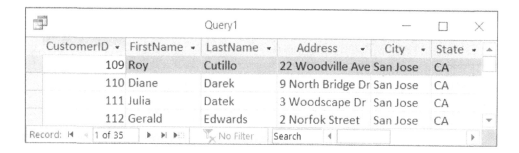

Chapter 6 Case 2:

Create a new Access database and name it Chapter6_2.accdb. Copy the table Customers from the PracticeDatabase.accdb and paste it to Chapter6_2.accdb.

1. Create a query to select all customers from the states of New York, Massachusetts, Arizona, and Texas. Use the OR operator to achieve your result. Save the query as Qry1_Customers_MultipleStates.

   Your result should look like:

2. Create the same query as in step 2 but this time use the IN operator to achieve your result. Name the query Qry2_Customers_MultipleStates_IN.

   Your result should look like:

3. Create the same query as in step 2 but this time use the UNION operator to achieve your result. Name the query Qry3_Customers_MultipleStates_UNION. You will notice that the record number 83 at the bottom of the result set appears instantly while in the queries in steps 2 and 3 it takes a few seconds to appear.

Your result should look like:

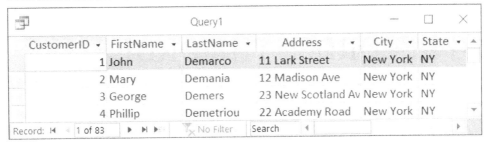

4. Create a query to select all customers except those in the states of California, Arizona, and Massachusetts. Hint: Use the NOT IN operator. Save the query as Qry4_Customers_MultipleStates_NOTIN.

Your result should look like:

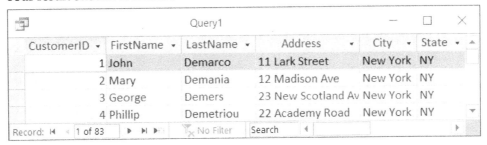

5. Create a query to select all customers except those in the area code 22459. Save the query as Qry5_Customers_AreaCode.

Your result should look like:

CHAPTER 7
SORTING RECORDS: THE ORDER BY CLAUSE

The ORDER BY clause, with the ASC or DESC keywords, allows the sorting of records in ascending or descending order respectively. Sorting ascending means text is sorted from A to Z and numbers from 1 to 9. Sorting descending means Z-A and 9-1. When no ASC or DESC keyword is used after the ORDER BY clause, then ASC is assumed by default. The ORDER BY clause is much stronger than what is generally assumed and it allows for some cool tricks with the data.

80.   Sorting ascending on one column
Create a list of customers sorting by last name in ascending order
Discussion:

In this example, we sort our customers by last name in ascending order. Customers whose last names start with an "A" will appear first. The keyword "ASC" is not required to sort records in ascending order. If we leave the keyword "ASC" out, the ORDER BY clause will sort ascending by default.

Code:
```
SELECT *
FROM Customers
ORDER BY lastname ASC .
```

Result:

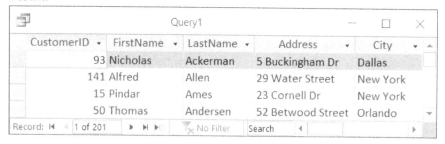

81.   Sorting descending on one column
Create a list of customers sorting by last name in descending order
Discussion:

Sometimes, we want to see names in reverse alphabetical order—names that start with Z, Y, or X first. In this case, we add the DESC keyword to our SQL statement. Note that if we want to sort descending, the DESC keyword is required.

Code:
```
SELECT *
FROM Customers
ORDER BY lastname DESC
```

Result:

CustomerID	FirstName	LastName	Address	City
48	Stephen	Zinter	110 Johnson Ave	Philadelphia
21	Lauren	Zentons	23 Crescent Dr	Los Angeles
18	Charles	Zensons	23 Tampa Ave	Los Angeles
20	Lisa	Zartons	34 Home Ave	Los Angeles

Record: 1 of 201   No Filter   Search

82.   Use the ORDER BY clause to sort on multiple columns

Create a customer list sorting by city and last name simultaneously

Discussion:

We can sort records on the values of multiple columns. For example, we might want to obtain a report which will include a list of customers sorted first by city and then, by last name.

Let us assume we have some customers in Albany and some customers in Boston. Sorting ascending on both city and last name fields will create the following result: The customers from Albany will appear first, followed by the ones in Boston. Now, for the city of Albany, customers will be sorted ascending by last name and then for the city of Boston, customers will again be sorted in ascending order by last name. We should not be surprised to see a customer from Boston whose last name starts with an "A" being listed after a customer in Albany whose last name starts with a "Z".

Code:
```
SELECT city, lastname, firstname
FROM Customers
ORDER BY city, lastname ASC
```

Result:

city	lastname	firstname
Albany	Miller	Anthony
Albany	Riegert	Joanne
Albany	Trindan	Luis
Albany	Vanton	Kenneth

Record: 1 of 201   No Filter   Searc

83.   Use the ORDER BY clause to sort multiple columns with different sorting directions

Create a customer list sorting by city ascending and customer name descending

Discussion:

We also have the ability to sort on multiple columns forcing a different sorting direction for each column. In this example, we sort ascending on the city and then within each city we sort descending on the last name.

Code:

SELECT city, lastname, firstname

FROM Customers

ORDER BY city ASC, lastname DESC

Result:

84. Use ORDER BY clause with null values

Find customers who do not have a first name in the database

Discussion:

Let us suppose that we have a suspicion that some first name values are missing from our records. We can quickly find out which ones they are by creating a query that includes the first name and sorting ascending on the first name. As you can see from the result set, we immediately found one customer without a first name.

Code:

SELECT lastname, firstname

FROM Customers

ORDER BY firstname ASC

Result:

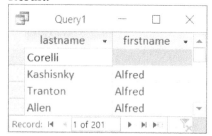

85. Use the ORDER BY clause with numbers

List the products with the biggest quantities on hand first

Discussion:

In this scenario, we would like to list products from our inventory with the highest quantities of units in stock first. We can achieve this task using the DESC keyword with numbers. When sorting numbers, the DESC keyword will cause the biggest ones to show first, while the ASC keyword will cause the smallest numbers to show first.

Code:

```
SELECT productname, unitsinstock
FROM products
ORDER BY unitsinstock DESC
```

Result:

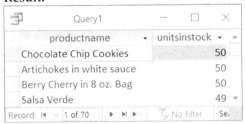

86.   The ORDER BY clause with dates

Create a list of orders with the latest orders on top

Discussion:

The ORDER BY clause works with dates the same way it works with numbers. Therefore, to list the newest order dates first, we use the DESC keyword. If we would like to show the oldest order dates first, we use the ASC keyword.

Code:

```
SELECT orderid, orderdate, shippeddate
FROM ORDERS
ORDER BY orderdate DESC
```

Result:

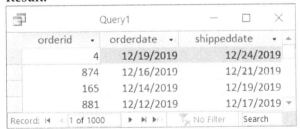

87.   Combine the ORDER BY and TOP clauses with numbers to control the result set

List the top five products in the inventory with the biggest quantities on hand

Discussion:

The ORDER BY clause produces very meaningful results when used in combination with the TOP clause. For instance, let us say we want to list the top five products with the biggest quantities on hand. We can achieve this task by combining the ORDER BY and TOP clauses. Notice the number of records in the result set. Only five products appear, and these five products have the largest unit quantities in stock in our inventory.

Code:

SELECT TOP 5 unitsinstock, productname
FROM products
ORDER BY unitsinstock DESC

Result:

You need to pay attention to the results of the TOP clause however. It will provide consistent results as soon as there are distinct values in the field on which we are using it. If there are identical values, then all of them will appear in the result set if the first one appears. For example, let us say we have four products with quantity per unit at 50 units and ten products with quantity per unit at 49 units. If we use TOP 5 to get the top five quantities per unit, we will actually get fourteen records.

88.   Combine the ORDER BY and TOP clauses with PERCENT to control the result set

List the top five percent of products in the inventory with the biggest quantities on hand

Discussion:

In this example, we use TOP with the PERCENT keyword to retrieve the ten percent of the products with the most units in stock. We will get the ones with the most units in stock because we sort descending on the UnitsInStock field. Since we have seventy products in the products table, we would expect to see seven products in the result but we get nine. This is because product 7 in the result set has 45 units in stock. Since however we have another two products with the same quantity of units in stock they will appear in the result set as well. This is a behavior inherent to the TOP clause.

Code:

SELECT TOP 10 PERCENT unitsinstock, productname
FROM products
ORDER BY unitsinstock DESC

Result:

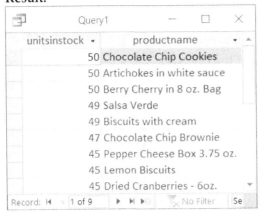

89.   CHAPTER 7 DISCUSSION QUESTIONS

1. What is the difference between sorting ascending and sorting descending?
2. Is the keyword "ASC" ascending optional or required in the ORDER BY clause?
3. Is the keyword "DESC" optional or required in the ORDER BY clause?
4. Can we use the ORDER BY clause to sort multiple fields? In what order are multiple fields sorted?
5. If we sort ascending on a field that contains null values, do those values appear at the top or the bottom of the sorted column?
6. If we sort descending on a number field, do big numbers appear at the top or the bottom of the sorted column?
7. We want to sort a date field so that the most recent dates appear first. Shall we use ASC or DESC?
8. You need to obtain the five most recent orders. Shall you use ORDER BY, TOP, and DESC or ORDER BY, TOP, and ASC on the date field?
9. You need to obtain the top five most expensive products. Shall you use ORDER BY, TOP, and DESC or ORDER BY, TOP, and ASC on the price field?
10. You need to find the five least productive sales people. Shall you use ORDER BY, TOP, and DESC or ORDER BY, TOP, and ASC on the commission field?

90.   CHAPTER 7 HANDS-ON EXERCISES

Chapter 7 Case 1:

Create a new Access database and name it Chapter7_1.accdb. Copy the table "Products" from the PracticeDatabase.accdb" and paste it to Chapter7_1.accdb.

1. Create a query that includes the fields ProductName, ProductUnitPrice, UnitsInStock, and UnitsOnOrder from the Products table. Your supervisor wants the records sorted in a way so that products with less UnitsOnOrder show first in the result set. Save the query as Qry1_UnitsOnOrder.

Your result should look like:

ProductName	ProductUnitPrice	UnitsInStock	UnitsOnOrder
Dark Chocolate Apricots in 20 oz. Bag	46	38	0
Cocoa and Hazelnut Biscuits	35	42	0
Cream and honey biscuits	22	22	0
Fried Jalapeños	15	32	0

Record: 1 of 70   No Filter   Search

2. Create a query that includes the fields ProductName, ProductUnitPrice, UnitsInStock, and UnitsOnOrder from the Products table. Your supervisor wants the records sorted in a way so that products with the most UnitsInStock show first in the result set. Save the query as

Qry2_UnitsInStock.

Your result should look like:

3. Create a query that includes the fields ProductName, ProductUnitPrice, and UnitsInStock from the Products table. Your supervisor needs a list of the ten products with the highest number of units in stock. Save the query as Qry3_Ten_UnitsInStock. Why are there 11 records instead of ten?

Your result should look like:

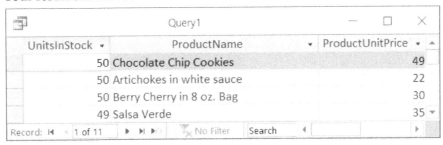

4. Create a query that includes the fields ProductName, ProductUnitPrice, and UnitsOnOrder from the Products table. Your supervisor wants a list of the five products with the highest number of units on order. Save the query as Qry4_Five_UnitsOnOrder.

Your result should look like:

5. Create a query that includes the fields ProductName, ProductUnitPrice, UnitsInStock, and ReorderLevel from the Products table. Your supervisor wants a list of the ten products with the lowest reorder level. Save the query as Qry5_Ten_ReorderLevel. You see that you get 26 records in the result set and not ten. Why is that?

Your result should look like:

ProductName ▾	ProductUnitPrice ▾	UnitsInStock ▾	ReorderLevel ▾
Almonds, Roasted and Salted	22	32	20
Banana Chips - 20 oz. Bag	27	25	20
Cream and honey biscuits	22	22	20
Chocolate Covered Dried Tart	23	37	20

Record: ◄ ◄ 1 of 26 ► ►I ►≡ No Filter   Search

Chapter 7 Case 2:

Create a new Access database and name it Chapter7_2.accdb. Copy the tables Customers and Orders from the PracticeDatabase.accdb and paste them to Chapter7_2.accdb.

1. Create a query that includes the fields State, City, LastName, and FirstName from the Customers table. Your supervisor wants the records sorted simultaneously by State and then City in ascending order. Save the query as Qry1_StateCity_ASC.

   Your result should look like:

   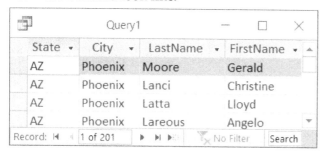

State ▾	City ▾	LastName ▾	FirstName ▾
AZ	Phoenix	Moore	Gerald
AZ	Phoenix	Lanci	Christine
AZ	Phoenix	Latta	Lloyd
AZ	Phoenix	Lareous	Angelo

   Record: ◄ ◄ 1 of 201 ► ►I ►≡ No Filter   Search

2. Create a query that includes the fields State, City, LastName, and FirstName from the Customers table. Your supervisor wants the records sorted simultaneously by State ascending and then City in descending order. Save the query as Qry2_StateCity_Asc_Desc.

   Your result should look like:

   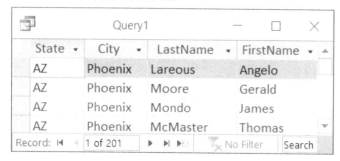

State ▾	City ▾	LastName ▾	FirstName ▾
AZ	Phoenix	Lareous	Angelo
AZ	Phoenix	Moore	Gerald
AZ	Phoenix	Mondo	James
AZ	Phoenix	McMaster	Thomas

   Record: ◄ ◄ 1 of 201 ► ►I ►≡ No Filter   Search

3. Create a query that includes the fields OrderID, CustomerID, ShippedDate, and ShippingCost. Provide a list with the ten most recent shipped orders. Save the query as Qry3_LatestShippedOrders.

Your result should look like:

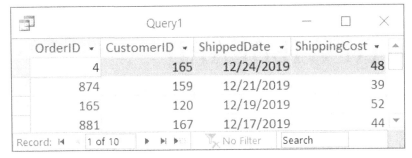

4. Create a query that includes the fields OrderID, CustomerID, ShippedDate, and ShippingCost. Provide a list with the ten orders with the most expensive shipping cost. Save the query as Qry4_MostExpensiveShippingCost. Why the query returns 57 records instead of 10?

Your result should look like:

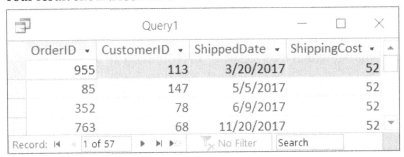

5. Create a query that includes the fields OrderID, CustomerID, ShippedDate, and ShippingCost. Provide a list with 5% of the orders with the most expensive shipping cost. Save the query as Qry5_MostExpensiveShippingCostPercent. Why the query returns 101 records?

Your result should look like:

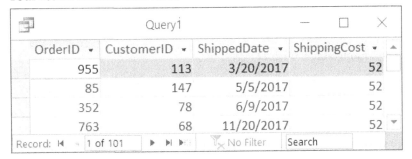

CHAPTER 8
WORKING WITH WILDCARD CHARACTERS

Wildcard characters like (*, ?, !, [], -, #) provide essential functionality and power in databases. They are used in combination with operators such as (LIKE, OR, AND, BETWEEN, IN, etc.) and predicates like (<, >, <>, =, >=). They allow for the formulation of very sophisticated search criteria on text and number data.

Character	Description	Example
*	Matches any number of characters. You can use the asterisk (*) anywhere in a character string.	**wh*** finds what, white, and why, but not awhile or watch.
?	Matches any single alphabetic character.	**B?ll** finds ball, bell, and bill.
[ ]	Matches any single character within the brackets.	**B[ae]ll** finds ball and bell, but not bill.
!	Matches any character not in the brackets.	**b[!ae]ll** finds bill and bull, but not ball or bell.
-	Matches any one of a range of characters. You must specify the range in ascending order (A to Z, not Z to A).	**b[a-c]d** finds bad, bbd, and bcd.
#	Matches any single numeric character.	**1#3** finds 103, 113, and 123.

Figure 19: List of wildcard characters

Source: https://support.office.com/en-us/article/Access-wildcard-character-reference-af00c501-7972-40ee-8889-e18abaad12d1

91.   The * wildcard character
Create a list of customers whose last name starts with D
Discussion:

The * is the wildest of the wildcard characters, and it will match any numeric or alphabetic character whether we put it in the beginning, middle, or end of a search condition. For example, we can search for all the customer last names that start with the letter D. As we can see in this example, every customer whose last name starts with a D will appear in the result set. Notice in the code the * is positioned after the letter D. This means that entries such as Dem, D1a, d123, or Dzo will appear in the result set.

Code:

```
SELECT *
FROM customers
WHERE lastname Like 'D*'
```

Result:

CustomerID ▾	FirstName ▾	LastName ▾	Address ▾	City ▾
1	John	Demarco	11 Lark Street	New York
2	Mary	Demania	12 Madison Ave	New York
3	George	Demers	23 New Scotland Ave	New York
4	Phillip	Demetriou	22 Academy Road	New York

Record: ◄ ◄ 1 of 21 ► ►I ►▪ ⛉ No Filter Search

92. The ? wildcard character in combination with *

Create a customer list using ? and * to create intricate search patterns

Discussion:

The ? character matches any single character. Though not used as much as the *, it can still make the difference and enable us to get exactly the results we want in certain cases. Usually, we use it in combination with other wildcard characters. For instance, let's say we want to find names starting with "Da", have one character after the "Da" pattern, the next letter is "e" followed by any number of characters—"Da?e*". This will give us results such as Darek, Datek, Dale, and Daleney.

Code:

```
SELECT *
FROM customers
WHERE ((lastname) Like 'Da?e*')
```

Result:

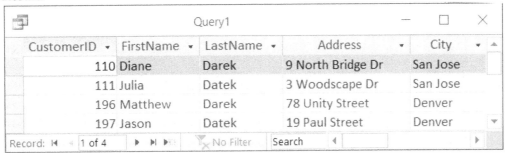

CustomerID ▾	FirstName ▾	LastName ▾	Address ▾	City ▾
110	Diane	Darek	9 North Bridge Dr	San Jose
111	Julia	Datek	3 Woodscape Dr	San Jose
196	Matthew	Darek	78 Unity Street	Denver
197	Jason	Datek	19 Paul Street	Denver

Record: ◄ ◄ 1 of 4 ► ►I ►▪ ⛉ No Filter Search

93. Create multi-character search strings with [ ]

Create a customer list using multi-character search patterns

Discussion:

Using the brackets [ ] wildcard, we can search for any characters included within the brackets. For example, C[ru]* will find Croney, Culey, but not Colonie. Note that we use the * in this example to allow any characters to be included after the brackets.

Code:
```
SELECT *
FROM customers
WHERE ((lastname) Like 'C[ru]*')
```

Result:

CustomerID	FirstName	LastName	Address	City
99	Kenneth	Crondos	158 West Lawrence A	Houston
100	Pindar	Crooney	16 Warren Street	Houston
101	Joseph	Crandil	192 Tampa Ave	Houston
107	Mary	Crawford	21 Aegean Dr	Houston

Record: 1 of 8 — No Filter — Search

94. Use the ! and [ ] wildcard characters to create exclusion patterns

Create a customer list using specific characters as exclusion search patterns

Discussion:

Sometimes, we need to exclude a set of characters to obtain the results we need. For example, we might want to retrieve all customers except those whose names start with an A, B, C, D, or E. We can use the [!] wildcard to get the results we want. Any of the customers whose names start with a letter [abcde] will be excluded from the recordset. Note that the returned recordset is sorted by last name, and the first customer record to appear has a last name value starting with "F".

Code:
```
SELECT *
FROM customers
WHERE ((lastname) Like '[!abcde]*')
ORDER BY lastname
```

Result:

CustomerID	FirstName	LastName	Address	City
115	Sonya	Ford	5 Beach Ave	San Jose
166	Cristopher	Geisler	93 Kate Street	Boston
116	William	Gibson	17 Grove Street	San Jose
117	Kathy	Giordano	21 Garden Ave	San Diego

Record: 1 of 130 — No Filter — Search

95. Use the ! and [ ] and - wildcards to create exclusion ranges

Create a customer list using sets of characters as exclusion ranges

Discussion:

What if we continue from the previous example using ! and [], but instead of typing in all of the characters one by one, we use ranges? For example, we might want to obtain a recordset of customers whose names do not start with a letter in the range A-P. We can do this by using the "[!a-p]*" exclusion pattern. As you can see from the figure below, the customers who appear in the list have names starting with an "R", which is the one immediately following "P" that was included in our exclusion range.

Code:
SELECT *
FROM customers
WHERE ((lastname) Like '[!a-p]*')
ORDER BY lastname

Result:

	CustomerID	FirstName	LastName	Address	City
	61	Richard	Ramirez	48 Mereline Ave	Miami
	184	Lisa	Read	12 Madison Ave	Washington
	17	Allen	Restad	72 Providence Dr	Los Angeles
	139	Joanne	Riegert	31 Arizona Ave	Albany

Record: 1 of 59   No Filter   Search

96. Use the - and [ ] wildcards to create inclusion ranges
Create a customer list using sets of characters as inclusion ranges
Discussion:
We can continue from the previous example and use [] and - to obtain a recordset of customers whose names do start with a letter between A and P. We simply need to take out the exclamation mark.

Code:
SELECT *
FROM customers
WHERE ((lastname) Like '[a-p]*')
ORDER BY lastname

Result:

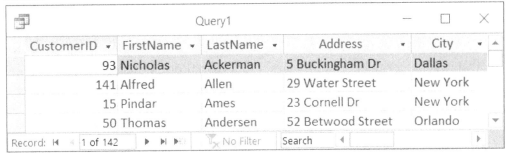

	CustomerID	FirstName	LastName	Address	City
	93	Nicholas	Ackerman	5 Buckingham Dr	Dallas
	141	Alfred	Allen	29 Water Street	New York
	15	Pindar	Ames	23 Cornell Dr	New York
	50	Thomas	Andersen	52 Betwood Street	Orlando

Record: 1 of 142   No Filter   Search

97.   CHAPTER 8 DISCUSSION QUESTIONS

1. What is the role of the * wildcard character?
2. How is the ? wildcard character different from the * one?
3. What is the role of the ! wildcard character?
4. Can the * wildcard character find only letters, only numbers, or both?
5. What is the function of the [] wildcard character?
6. What is the difference between a range and a pattern?
7. What wildcard character can we use if we want to look for ranges?
8. What wildcard character can we use if we want to look for patterns?
9. How can we define exclusion ranges using wildcard characters?
10. How can we define inclusion ranges using wildcard characters?

98.   CHAPTER 8 HANDS-ON EXERCISES

Chapter 8 Case 1:

Create a new Access database and name it Chapter8_1.accdb. Copy the table "Products" from the PracticeDatabase.accdb and paste it to Chapter8_1.accdb.

1. Create a query that includes all fields from the Products table. The query should return all records having a product name that starts with "ch". Save the query as Qry1_ch.

    Your result should look like:

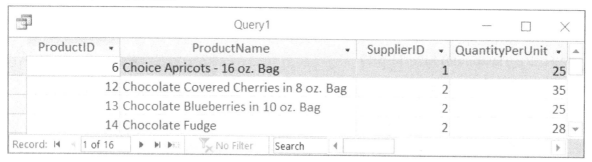

2. Create a query that includes the fields ProductName, ProductUnitPrice, UnitsInStock, and ReorderLevel from the Products table. The inventory department needs a list of all the products whose name starts with a "C", the second character is any character, the third character is a "C", followed by any characters after that. Save the query as Qry2_Inventory_ProductName.

    Your result should look like:

3. Create a query that includes the fields ProductName, ProductUnitPrice, UnitsInStock, and SKU from the Products table. This time, the inventory department needs a list of all the products whose SKU starts with "ASD", followed by any of the characters T,D,L, followed by any character or number. Save the query as Qry3_Inventory_SKU_Pattern.

Your result should look like:

4. Create a query that includes the fields ProductName, ProductUnitPrice, UnitsInStock, and SKU from the Products table. The inventory department needs a list of all the products for which the SKU does not start with "ASD". Save the query as Qry4_Inventory_SKU_Exclusion_Pattern.

Your result should look like:

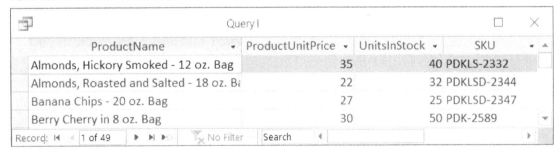

5. Create a query that includes the fields ProductName, ProductUnitPrice, UnitsInStock, and SKU from the Products table. Your manager needs to send to the inventory department a list of all the products whose ProductName does not start with any letter in the range of A to K. Save the query as Qry5_Inventory_Name_Exclusion_Range.

Your result should look like:

ProductName	ProductUnitPrice	UnitsInStock	SKU
Raw Sunflower Seeds in 19 oz. Bag	25	12	PDKLS-2347
Sesame Crackers in 20 oz. Pack	39	43	DKLS-4732
Roasted & Salted Almonds	19	35	PDKL-2389
Roasted & Salted Cashews	30	22	PDKL-2389

Record: ◄ ◄ 1 of 18 ► ►I ► No Filter Search ◄

Chapter 8 Case 2:

Create a new Access database and name it Chapter8_2.accdb. Copy the table "products" from the PracticeDatabase.accdb and paste it to Chapter8_2.accdb.

1. Create a query that includes the fields ProductName, ProductUnitPrice, UnitsInStock, and ReorderLevel from the Products table. The query should return products having a product name starting with the letters a through e. Save the query as Qry1_NameRange.

Your result should look like:

ProductName	ProductUnitPrice	UnitsInStock	ReorderLevel
Almonds, Hickory Smoked - 12 oz. Bag	35	40	45
Almonds, Roasted and Salted - 18 oz. Bag	22	32	20
Banana Chips - 20 oz. Bag	27	25	20
Berry Cherry in 8 oz. Bag	30	50	30

Record: ◄ ◄ 1 of 49 ► ►I ► No Filter Search

2. Create a query that includes the fields ProductName, ProductUnitPrice, UnitsInStock, and ReorderLevel from the Products table. The query should return products having a product name starting with the letters a,d,e,k, and l. Save the query as Qry2_NamePattern.

Your result should look like:

ProductName	ProductUnitPrice	UnitsInStock	ReorderLevel
Almonds, Hickory Smoked - 12 oz. Bag	35	40	45
Almonds, Roasted and Salted - 18 oz. Bag	22	32	20
Dried Blueberries - 1 lb. Bag	28	28	30
Dried Cranberries - 34 oz.	35	15	20

Record: ◄ ◄ 1 of 15 ► ►I ► No Filter Search

3. Create a query that includes the ProductName and SKU fields from the Products table. The query should return all products having an SKU starting with the letters PD, having any characters after PD, followed by a dash and ending with exactly four digits. Save the query as Qry3_SKU_Pattern.

WORKING WITH WILDCARD CHARACTERS

Your result should look like:

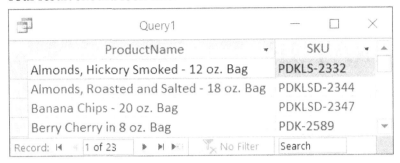

4. Create a query that includes the ProductName and SKU fields from the products table. The query should return all products having an SKU starting with any letters between A and P, any characters after those letters, followed by a dash, and ending with exactly four digits. The first two digits should be any digits and the last two 89. Save the query as Qry4_SKU_Range.

Your result should look like:

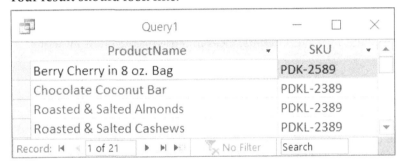

5. Create a query that includes the ProductName and SKU fields from the products table. The query should return all products having an SKU starting with any character, followed by a dash, and ending in 2345. Save the query as Qry5_SKU_ExactEnding.

Your result should look like:

CHAPTER 9
THE LIKE OPERATOR

The major aspect of the LIKE operator is its flexibility in creating search expressions. In other words, it has the flexibility to work on text, number, and date data using intricate expressions to produce results. In addition, its usefulness is greatly enhanced when used in combination with wildcard characters like (*, ?, !, [], -) for the creation of elaborate search expressions.

However, we need to remember two points when using the LIKE operator. First, to supply this flexibility and functionality, it consumes resources, so it should not be the first operator that we resort to for all of our search expressions. Second, we should really know how to use it to get the results we need since it might not always return the expected results.

In this chapter, we approach the usage of the LIKE operator from all perspectives, and we point out tips for using it optimally. To demonstrate the cool functionality of the LIKE operator, all of the examples in this chapter use the table called tbls_CustomerOrders. The records of this table are edited with special values to show how LIKE applies to various circumstances in our working environment.

99.   The LIKE operator with the * wildcard character
Create a list of customers whose last name starts with M
Discussion:
This simple example uses the LIKE operator to find customers whose last names start with an "M". The LIKE operator is used within the WHERE clause, we enclose the search expression in single quotes, and we use the * wildcard to obtain the result we need.

Code:
```
SELECT *
FROM tbls_CustomerOrders
WHERE (lastname like 'M*')
```

Result:

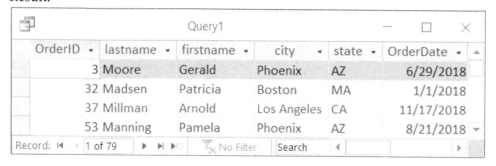

OrderID	lastname	firstname	city	state	OrderDate
3	Moore	Gerald	Phoenix	AZ	6/29/2018
32	Madsen	Patricia	Boston	MA	1/1/2018
37	Millman	Arnold	Los Angeles	CA	11/17/2018
53	Manning	Pamela	Phoenix	AZ	8/21/2018

Record: 1 of 79   No Filter   Search

100.   The LIKE operator with [ ] and * to search for ranges
Find customers whose zip code starts with a number between 1 and 4
Discussion:
This time, we have a request to prepare a customer report showing customers whose zip codes start with numbers between 1 and 4, such as 12189, 26890, 34123, or 41289 (as opposed to 58659, which would not be included). To obtain the report, we use the LIKE operator with the [ ] and * wildcard characters. The [ ] wildcard will retrieve all zip codes starting with 1, 2, 3, and 4. Then, the * will retrieve any number of characters after 1, 2, 3, and 4.

Code:
SELECT lastname, firstname, city, zip
FROM tbls_CustomerOrders
WHERE (zip like '[1-4]*')

Result:

lastname	firstname	city	zip
Riegert	Joanne	New York	12189
Read	Lisa	Washington	11882
Moore	Gerald	Phoenix	44895
Davis	Catherine	Boston	22459

Record: 1 of 492   No Filter   Search

101.   The LIKE operator with date fields
Create a report of orders for the month of April for all years
Discussion:
In this particular example, we look for orders in the month of April irrespective of the day or the year they were placed. To achieve this, we use the LIKE operator with the * wildcard character. Notice how we use the * twice for days and years, while we fix the month at 4 (April). In your own working environment, dates might not be in the format of "Month number/Day number/Year" (1/1/2018), but perhaps like January 12 2018, for example. This is not a problem at all since we can manipulate dates and change their format on the fly any way we need. We have devoted a whole chapter (chapter 27) on date manipulation for your reference. In the same way, using LIKE, we can fix the day, the year, or any combination of month, day, and year and retrieve the corresponding results.

Code:
SELECT lastname, firstname, orderdate
FROM tbls_CustomerOrders
WHERE (OrderDate Like '4/*/*')

Result:

lastname	firstname	orderdate
Cambell	Veronica	4/1/2019
Stoll	Nicholas	4/14/2019
Stoll	Nicholas	4/9/2019
Stoll	Nicholas	4/14/2019

Record: 1 of 83   No Filter   Search

102.   The LIKE operator with number fields

Create a report of customer orders with order totals of exactly $200

Discussion:

We can use the LIKE operator with number fields as well. In this example, we have a request to find all customers with a total of orders equal to $200. When we use LIKE with numbers, we do not enclose the numbers in quotes.

Code:

```
SELECT lastname, firstname, orderdate, OrderTotal
FROM tbls_CustomerOrders
WHERE (OrderTotal Like 200)
```

Result:

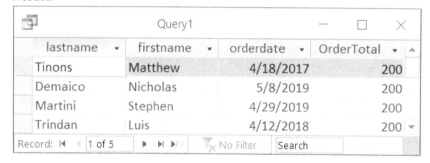

lastname	firstname	orderdate	OrderTotal
Tinons	Matthew	4/18/2017	200
Demaico	Nicholas	5/8/2019	200
Martini	Stephen	4/29/2019	200
Trindan	Luis	4/12/2018	200

Record: 1 of 5   No Filter   Search

Although we can use LIKE to search for numbers, it is a much better practice to use equality and inequality predicates such as (<, >, <>, =, >=). The above example could be written with the equality predicate "=", and it will produce the same results.

Code:

```
SELECT lastname, firstname, orderdate, OrderTotal
FROM tbls_CustomerOrders
WHERE (OrderTotal = 200)
```

103.   Compare LIKE, BETWEEN, and "<=" "=>" for number ranges

Create a report of customer orders with order totals between $200 and $400

Discussion:

In this scenario, we have a request from management to prepare a report showing customer orders with order totals between $200 and $400. To achieve this goal, we have three alternatives: We can use the LIKE operator, the BETWEEN operator, and the "<=" "=>" predicates. Which one is the best solution? Let us explore the three cases before we make a decision. In the first case, we use the LIKE operator with the [ ] wildcard for ranges and the "?" to establish the number of characters to be returned at 3. In other words, we are looking for numbers such as 234, 345, or 385. If we have used * after the [ ], we will also get numbers such as 26, 30, and 35, which is not what we want. The result set includes 230 records starting with order totals at $200 and going all the way up to the order total of $393. Attention, here. The LIKE operator with this expression is not able to include order totals that are exactly $400. It can go as far up as $399. Consequently, if we want to include order totals at exactly $400 we have to write an additional expression. Since the data does not include any order totals at exactly $400 we will not write any additional expressions.

Code:
```
SELECT lastname, firstname, orderdate, OrderTotal
FROM tbls_CustomerOrders
WHERE (OrderTotal LIKE '[2-3]??')
ORDER BY OrderTotal ASC
```

Result:

lastname	firstname	orderdate	OrderTotal
Platt	Colleen	9/26/2019	200
Demaico	Nicholas	5/8/2019	200
Trindan	Luis	4/12/2018	200
Tinons	Matthew	4/18/2017	200

Record: 1 of 230 — No Filter — Search

Discussion:
Now we use the BETWEEN operator to achieve the same task. The BETWEEN operator is inclusive which means that it will include values in the range plus the boundaries of the range. For the range of order totals between $200 and $400, it will also include the order totals of exactly $200 and exactly $400 if they are available.

Code:
```
SELECT lastname, firstname, orderdate, OrderTotal
FROM tbls_CustomerOrders
WHERE (OrderTotal BETWEEN 200 AND 400)
ORDER BY OrderTotal ASC
```

Result:

lastname	firstname	orderdate	OrderTotal
Platt	Colleen	9/26/2019	200
Demaico	Nicholas	5/8/2019	200
Trindan	Luis	4/12/2018	200
Tinons	Matthew	4/18/2017	200

Record: ◄ ◄ 1 of 230 ► ►I ►＊ No Filter Search

Discussion:

Now, we are using the "<=" "=>" predicates to achieve the same goal of finding orders between $200 and $400. When it comes to numbers, the "<=" "=>" predicates are the most flexible and trusted to work with. For example, we can use the "<" ">" to exclude lower and upper limits. In addition, predicates will produce consistent results, while operators have issues with result accuracy and performance.

Code:

```
SELECT lastname, firstname, orderdate, OrderTotal
FROM tbls_CustomerOrders
WHERE (OrderTotal >= 200 AND OrderTotal <=  400)
ORDER BY OrderTotal ASC
```

Result:

lastname	firstname	orderdate	OrderTotal
Platt	Colleen	9/26/2019	200
Demaico	Nicholas	5/8/2019	200
Trindan	Luis	4/12/2018	200
Tinons	Matthew	4/18/2017	200

Record: ◄ ◄ 1 of 230 ► ►I ►＊ No Filter Search

104.   The NOT LIKE operator

Find customer orders with order totals different than $200

Discussion:

We can use the keyword "NOT" to reverse the result set of an operation using LIKE. In this example, we are looking for order totals different from $200. Though we use LIKE to achieve this, we will be better off using the inequality predicate "<>" for which we include the code below as well. Both pieces of code will produce the same result but prefer to use the predicate instead of the operator.

Code1:

```
SELECT lastname, firstname, orderdate, OrderTotal
FROM tbls_CustomerOrders
WHERE (OrderTotal NOT Like 200)
```

Code2:
SELECT lastname, firstname, orderdate, OrderTotal
FROM tbls_CustomerOrders
WHERE (OrderTotal <> 200)

Result:

lastname	firstname	orderdate	OrderTotal
Riegert	Joanne	11/6/2018	30
Read	Lisa	7/25/2018	210
Moore	Gerald	6/29/2018	231
Davis	Catherine	12/14/2019	45

Record: 1 of 914   No Filter   Search

105. TIP: Use LIKE with the trim() function to get the right results

Filter customer names effectively by eliminating blank spaces

Discussion:

In this example, we look for customers with a Mary first name so that we can send them a card for their name day. We know how to use the LIKE operator, so we write a statement like the one below and get 20 records. We provide the report to our manager, and two weeks later, she comes back and says we missed three customers. What happened? Well, for three Marys, there were spaces in front of their first names and the LIKE operator did not pick them up. When it comes to LIKE, the statement (LIKE ' Mary') is different from (LIKE 'Mary'). Consequently, if there are any spaces, the two LIKE statements above will produce different results. We can solve this by using the trim() function as shown below:

Code without trim():
SELECT lastname, firstname, orderdate, OrderTotal
FROM tbls_CustomerOrders
WHERE (firstname LIKE 'Mary')

Result:

lastname	firstname	orderdate	OrderTotal
Stewart	Mary	3/9/2019	196
Simmons	Mary	6/24/2017	253
Simmons	Mary	2/26/2018	105
Simmons	Mary	9/16/2019	115

Record: 1 of 20   No Filter   Search

Discussion:

The trim() function will eliminate any spaces before or after a string in a field, and this will allow the LIKE operator to function properly. Notice that this time, the database returned 23 records instead of 20. For a full understanding of string functions and their cool functionality, please refer to chapter 26 where there are numerous examples.

Code with trim() function:
SELECT lastname, firstname, orderdate, OrderTotal
FROM tbls_CustomerOrders
WHERE (trim(firstname) LIKE 'Mary')

Result:

lastname	firstname	orderdate	OrderTotal
Stewart	Mary	3/9/2019	196
Simmons	Mary	6/24/2017	253
Simmons	Mary	2/26/2018	105
Simmons	Mary	9/16/2019	115

Record: I◄ ◄ 1 of 23 ► ►I ►⁎ No Filter   Search

106.   TIP: Use LIKE to test a field for the presence of spaces

Check for the presence of blank spaces in a city field

Discussion:

The same supervisor comes back and says she needs a report of customers from certain cities. This time, we are wise enough to check for spaces first. Then, however, we reason that some city names do contain spaces. For example, New York contains a space, and Los Angeles contains a space. In addition, we realize that the trim() function is good enough for leading and trailing spaces. What if we have a space right in the middle of the word, however? We can actually look for spaces in any part of the name of the city using the LIKE operator with the * wildcard character. In this example, we are looking for two spaces in any part of the field assuming a maximum of one space in the city name. To achieve this, we use the * three times. We can test for one space using two asterisks ("* *"). The cool thing is that we have found two city names with two blank spaces as you can see in the figure below:

Code:
SELECT lastname, firstname, city, orderdate
FROM tbls_CustomerOrders
WHERE (city LIKE '* * *')

Result:

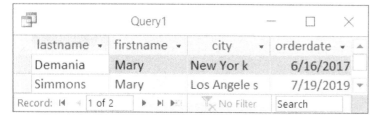

lastname	firstname	city	orderdate
Demania	Mary	New Yor k	6/16/2017
Simmons	Mary	Los Angele s	7/19/2019

Record: I◄ ◄ 1 of 2 ► ►I ►⁎ No Filter   Search

107.   TIP: Use LIKE to test a field for the presence of numbers

Check for the presence of numbers in a city field

Discussion:

Now, what if someone entered some city names and did not pay attention, and as he was typing, he mingled some numbers with the name of the city? For example, he might have entered "New 9York". How can we check a field for the presence of numbers within text strings? The answer is by using the LIKE operator, the [ ] wildcard character for ranges, and the * wildcard character as in the code below. Notice we use the [ ] to check for any number between 0 and 9. In addition, we use the * twice to look for the presence of a number at any part of the field, including the end and the beginning of its value. We actually caught two records with numbers mistyped in them.

Code:

```
SELECT lastname, firstname, city, orderdate
FROM tbls_CustomerOrders
WHERE (city LIKE '*[0-9]*')
```

Result:

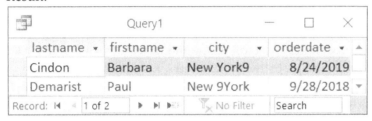

111

108. CHAPTER 9 DISCUSSION QUESTIONS

1. What is the purpose of the LIKE operator?
2. On what kind of data types can we use the LIKE operator?
3. What is the most appropriate data type to use with LIKE?
4. Can we use the LIKE operator by itself or do we need to combine it with special characters?
5. What is the tradeoff for the LIKE operator's flexibility?
6. How can we use the LIKE operator to test for the presence of spaces?
7. How can the LIKE and BETWEEN operators get the same results on numeric data?
8. What wildcard character can we use with LIKE to search for patterns?
9. What wildcard character can we use with LIKE to search for ranges?
10. How can we use the LIKE operator to test field values for the presence of numbers?

109. CHAPTER 9 HANDS-ON EXERCISES

Chapter 9 Case 1:

Create a new Access database and name it Chapter9_1.accdb. Copy the tables tbls_CustomerOrders and Products from the PracticeDatabase.accdb and paste them to Chapter9_1.accdb.

1. Create a query that includes all fields from the tbls_CustomerOrders table. Your manager wants to see all customers whose first name starts with the letter K. Save the query as Qry1_Customers_LetterK.

Your result should look like:

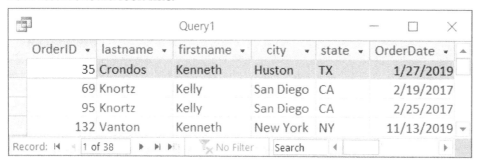

2. Create a query that includes all fields from the tbls_CustomerOrders table. Your supervisor wants to see all customers whose total order amount is between $60 and a $100. Sort results by OrderTotal ascending. Save the query as Qry2_Customers_Orders60-100.

Your result should look like:

3. The finance department ordered a report to include all orders for the month of March 2018. Create a new query that will include all fields from the tbls_CustomerOrders table, satisfy the demand of the finance department, and name it as Qry3_Customers_MarchOrders.

Your result should look like:

4. The inventory department asked for a report of all products whose quantity per unit is 35. This is because they need to plan for the handling of heavy packages. Create a new query that will include all the fields from the Products table, satisfy the request of the inventory people, and name it Qry4_Products_Quantity35.

Your result should look like:

5. The marketing department asked for a report that includes all products with prices between 30 and 40 dollars. Create a new query that includes the fields ProductName, ProductUnitPrice, UnitsInStock, and UnitsOnOrder from the products table and satisfies the request of the marketing department. Sort results by ProductUnitPrice ASC. Name the query as Qry5_Products_Price30-40.

Your result should look like:

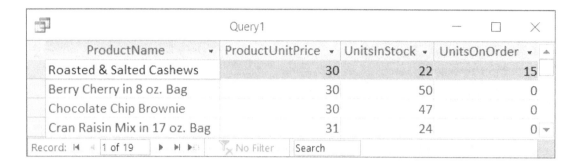

Chapter 9 Case 2:

Create a new Access database and name it Chapter9_2.accdb. Copy the table "Products" from the PracticeDatabase.accdb and paste it to Chapter9_2.accdb.

1. You need to test the ProductName field for the existence of spaces before or after the name of the product. Create a new query that includes the ProductName, ProductUnitPrice, and SKU fields from the Products table and remove from the ProductName field any spaces in the beginning and end of the field. Name the query as Qry1_Spaces.

   Your result should look like:

2. The inventory people made a peculiar request. They want to know the weight quantities of the various products in the inventory. However, you do not have a weight field in your products table. On the other hand, you do have weights in the product name field. Create a new query that will include only the ProductName field from the products table and will retrieve all the products for which there is a weight indication in the product name field. Name the query as Qry2_Weights.

   Your result should look like:

3. It is a business rule that all SKUs start with a three-letter code, followed by a dash, followed by a four digit numeric code. Create a new query that includes the product name and SKU fields. This query should list all products, which have a blank space anywhere in the SKU field. Name the query Qry3_SKUs.

Your result should look like:

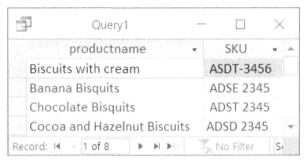

4. The marketing people asked for a report of all products with a ProductName that does not start with the letters a, d, n, r, or s. Create a new query that will include all the fields from the Products table, satisfy the request of the marketing people, and name it Qry4_Pattern.

Your result should look like:

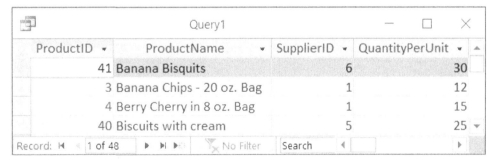

5. Your marketing department is reviewing pricing to initiate a new marketing campaign. They think that pricing is skewed at the extremes. That is, products in the $10 range are priced too low and products in the upper range of $50 are priced too high. They need a report that includes products priced at the $10 dollar range and those at the $50 dollar range to adjust prices. Create a query that will list the ProductName and ProductUnitPrice fields from the Products table and will include products in the 10 and 50 ranges. That is, if a product is priced at 11, 12, 14, 19 or 51, 55, 59 should

appear in the result set. You must use the LIKE operator to achieve your results. Sort results by ProductUnitPrice ascending. Name the query Qry5_Pricing.

Your result should look like:

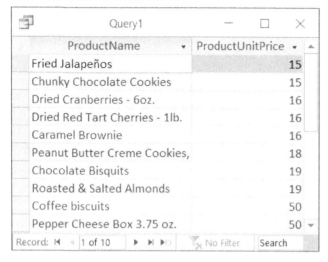

CHAPTER 10
EQUALITY AND INEQUALITY PREDICATES

The primary goal of equality and inequality predicates in search expressions is to find absolute matches. Their results are solid and unquestionable. They are used in the WHERE clause of a SQL statement, and they can be used by themselves to construct a search condition without the need of any wildcard characters. For instance, the statement (WHERE lastname = 'Smith') is valid. They should be given priority over operators such as LIKE, BETWEEN, and TOP.

Meaning	Predicate
Equal to	=
Not equal to	<>
Less than	<
Less than or equal to	<=
Greater than	>
Greater than or equal to	=>

Access 2016 equality and inequality predicates reference

110. The equality predicate "=" for absolute searches in text data
Find a specific customer record searching on last name
Discussion:
In this example, we use the equality predicate to retrieve the record of a particular customer. What we need to know about the equality predicate is that we search for a known value. That is, we know the last name of the customer we are looking for in advance. Then, we use the equality predicate to find that customer. This is very different when we conduct approximate searches using the LIKE operator where we might know the customer last name starts with "Ma", but we are not certain about the rest of it. This is why we use the expression (LIKE 'Ma*') to find all of the customers whose last names start with "Ma" and then, select the one we need to work with. The point to remember is that whenever we can, we should give preference to the equality predicate over the LIKE operator because it will retrieve exactly what we need, faster, with less overhead for the database, and no ambiguity in the results.

Code:
```
SELECT *
FROM Customers
WHERE (lastname = 'Delaney')
```

Result:

CustomerID ▾	FirstName ▾	LastName ▾	Address ▾	City ▾	State ▾	Zip ▲
11	Jason	Delaney	92 Madison Ave	New York	NY	898
45	Dolores	Delaney	25 Marwood Street	Philadelphia	PA	567 ▾

Record: ◄ ◄ 1 of 2 ► ►I ►∷ | ▼x No Filter | Search ◄ | ►

111. The equality predicate "=" for absolute searches in number data

Find a specific customer record searching on CustomerID

Discussion:

The equality predicate is very efficient with numbers. For example, let us assume we need to use an UPDATE statement to change the record of a customer. We should unequivocally identify the customer using the equality predicate on the primary key of the table so that we are certain we are updating the right customer. The same logic is valid with DELETE statements where we should use the equality predicate to identify the correct customer for deletion. Another scenario is for those who work with server side pages like ASP.Net, PHP, ASP, JSP, etc. and who need to connect back to the database server to get customer records. Obviously, they would want to transfer the exact data they need between the database server and web server, so the equality predicate is the one of choice. In this example, we retrieve all of the information on a particular order searching on the OrderID, which is the primary key of the Orders table.

Code:
```
SELECT *
FROM Orders
WHERE OrderID = 972
```

Result:

OrderID ▾	CustomerID ▾	SalesRepID ▾	ShipperID ▾	OrderDate ▾	RequiredDate ▾
972	199	10	3	8/24/2017	9/3/2017
✱ (New)					

Record: ◄ ◄ 1 of 1 ► ►I ►∷ | ▼x No Filter | Search ◄ | ►

112. The ">" inequality predicate with date data

Retrieve orders placed after a certain date

Discussion:

The ">" inequality predicate means "greater than", and we can freely use it with numbers and dates. For instance, we might want to find orders placed after June 2018. The last day of June will not be included in the result set because we are using a "greater than" argument instead of a "greater than or equal to" one. In the next example, we will see how we can include the last day of June as well. In addition, we sort by orderdate ascending so that older orders appear first.

Code:

```
SELECT OrderID, OrderDate, ShippedDate, ShippingCost
FROM Orders
WHERE OrderDate > #6/30/2018#
ORDER BY OrderDate
```

Result:

OrderID	OrderDate	ShippedDate	ShippingCost
479	7/1/2018	7/6/2018	52
99	7/2/2018	7/7/2018	36
3	7/4/2018	7/9/2018	34
790	7/4/2018	7/9/2018	36

Record: 1 of 543   No Filter   Search

113.   The "=>" inequality predicate with date data

Retrieve orders placed after a certain date including the date specified

Discussion:

The ">=" inequality predicate means "greater than or equal to". In this example, we want to fetch orders placed after June 2018 including the last day of June. In addition, we sort by orderdate ascending so that older orders appear first.

Code:

```
SELECT OrderID, OrderDate, ShippedDate, ShippingCost
FROM Orders
WHERE OrderDate >= #6/30/2018#
ORDER BY OrderDate
```

Result:

OrderID	OrderDate	ShippedDate	ShippingCost
661	6/30/2018	7/5/2018	50
479	7/1/2018	7/6/2018	52
99	7/2/2018	7/7/2018	36
3	7/4/2018	7/9/2018	34

Record: 1 of 544   No Filter   Search

114.   The "<" inequality predicate with number data

Find orders for which the shipping cost was less than $35

Discussion:

The "<" inequality predicate means "less than", and, in this example, we use it to retrieve orders with a shipping cost lower than $35. Notice that we do not use quotes or other symbols to enclose numerical data in criteria expressions. We simply type the number. In addition, the first number appearing in the result set is 34 because we specifically asked for numbers "less than 35".

Code:

```
SELECT OrderID, OrderDate, ShippedDate, ShippingCost
FROM Orders
WHERE ShippingCost < 35
ORDER BY ShippingCost DESC
```

Result:

OrderID	OrderDate	ShippedDate	ShippingCost
541	1/26/2017	1/31/2017	34
288	5/5/2019	5/10/2019	34
838	10/3/2018	10/8/2018	34
833	6/7/2019	6/12/2019	34

Record: ◄ ◄ 1 of 180 ► ►I ►= No Filter Search

115.   The "<=" inequality predicate with number data

Find orders for which the shipping cost was less than or equal to $35

Discussion:

The "<=" inequality predicate means "less than or equal to". In this example, we are looking for orders with a shipping cost of less than 35 per order, including those orders with a shipping cost of exactly 35.

Code:

```
SELECT OrderID, OrderDate, ShippedDate, ShippingCost
FROM Orders
WHERE ShippingCost <= 35
ORDER BY ShippingCost DESC
```

Result:

OrderID	OrderDate	ShippedDate	ShippingCost
462	11/9/2018	11/14/2018	35
893	10/12/2017	10/17/2017	35
892	3/24/2019	3/29/2019	35
339	9/17/2018	9/22/2018	35

Record: ◄ ◄ 1 of 219 ► ►I ►= No Filter Search

116.   The "<>" inequality predicate with number data

Find orders for which the shipping cost is not equal to $35

Discussion:

The "<>" inequality predicate means "not equal to" and in this example we retrieve orders with a shipping cost different from $35. Notice that we do not use quotes or other symbols to enclose numerical data as criteria. We can also use the inequality predicate very efficiently with date and text data.

Code:

SELECT OrderID, OrderDate, ShippedDate, ShippingCost
FROM Orders
WHERE ShippingCost <> 35
ORDER BY ShippingCost DESC

Result:

OrderID	OrderDate	ShippedDate	ShippingCost
225	4/4/2017	4/9/2017	52
745	6/13/2018	6/18/2018	52
856	6/4/2019	6/9/2019	52
868	5/27/2017	6/1/2017	52

Record: 1 of 960   No Filter   Search

117.   The ">" predicate with number and date data concurrently

Find orders placed after a certain date and with shipping cost less than $35

Discussion:

In this example, we are looking for orders placed after June 2018, which also have shipping costs of less than $35.

Code:

SELECT OrderID, OrderDate, ShippedDate, ShippingCost
FROM Orders
WHERE OrderDate > #6/30/2018#
AND ShippingCost < 35
ORDER BY ShippingCost DESC

Result:

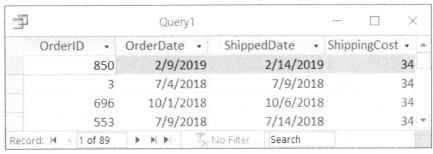

OrderID	OrderDate	ShippedDate	ShippingCost
850	2/9/2019	2/14/2019	34
3	7/4/2018	7/9/2018	34
696	10/1/2018	10/6/2018	34
553	7/9/2018	7/14/2018	34

Record: 1 of 89   No Filter   Search

1.   What is the difference between absolute and approximate data searches?
2.   What operator do we use to conduct approximate data searches?
3.   What is the rationale behind absolute data searches?
4.   Why equality and inequality predicates are the first choice for number searches?
5.   Do we have to use wildcard characters with equality and inequality predicates?
6.   On what data types can we use equality and inequality predicates?
7.   Why is it a very good idea to use the equality predicate "=" in delete and update statements?
8.   What is the difference between the "=>" and ">" inequality predicates?
9.   How does the BETWEEN operator compare with the "=>" and ">" inequality predicates?
10. Why do we prefer equality and inequality predicates over operators such as BETWEEN and LIKE which can achieve the same results?

119.   **CHAPTER 10 HANDS-ON EXERCISES**

Chapter 10 Case 1:

Create a new Access database and name it Chapter10_1.accdb. Copy the tables Customers, Orders, and Products from the PracticeDatabase.accdb and paste them to Chapter10_1.accdb.

1.   The marketing department is about to initiate a new promotion and they are asking for a list of customers in the state of New York. Create a new query that includes the fields FirstName, LastName, Address, City, and State from the Customers table for customers in New York State only. Save the query as Qry1_Customers_NY.

Your result should look like:

2.   The accounting people are calling for help because a customer has complained about the number of invoices she received to pay. In particular, they need to know what is happening with the orders of customer with CustomerID 199. Create a new query that includes the fields OrderID, CustomerID, OrderDate, and ShippedDate from the orders table. This query should list all the orders for the customer with customerID 199. Save the query as Qry2_Customer_199.

Your result should look like:

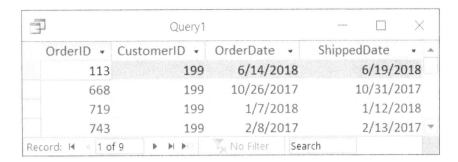

3. The inventory people want to plan stock replenishment and are asking for a list of products with a reorder level higher than 35 units. Create a new query that includes the ProductName, UnitsInStock, UnitsOnOrder, and Reorder Level fields and which query satisfies the inventory department requirements. Save the query as Qry3_Products_ReorderLevel_a.

    Your result should look like:

4. A few weeks later the inventory department complains heavily to your supervisor. Apparently, many products were left out from the report you gave them. Create a new query that includes the ProductName, UnitsInStock, UnitsOnOrder, and Reorder Level fields and which query also includes the products that have a reorder level at exactly 35 units. Save the query as Qry4_Products_ReorderLevel_b.

    Your result should look like:

5. Finally, for replenishing purposes again, the Inventory department asks for a report of products with current UnitsInStock between the levels of 15 and 20. They want to see the products with less units in stock appear first. Create a new query that includes the ProductName, UnitsInStock, UnitsOnOrder, and Reorder Level fields and satisfies the inventory people request. Save the query

as Qry5_Products_UnitsInStock.

Your result should look like:

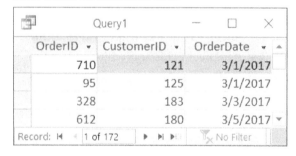

Chapter 10 Case 2:

Create a new Access database and name it Chapter10_2.accdb. Copy the tables Orders and Shipping Companies from the PracticeDatabase.accdb and paste them to Chapter10_2.accdb.

1. The marketing department needs to understand the seasonality effects on sales. For this reason, they asked for a preliminary report on sales for the months of March and April for the whole country and for all years. Create a new query that includes the fields OrderID, CustomerID, and OrderDate from the Orders table and satisfies the above criteria. Sort results so that oldest Order dates show first. Save the query as Qry1_Orders_Seasonality_a.

    Your result should look like:

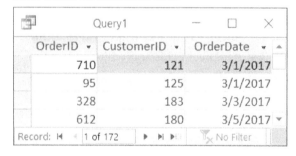

2. Achieve the same result you have achieved in step 1 but using an alternate criterion in your WHERE clause. Save the query as Qry2_Orders_Seasonality_b.

    Your result should look like:

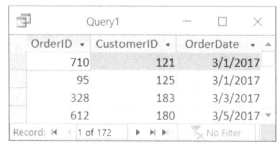

3. Accounting is asking for a report that lists the orders with a shipping cost between $30 and $40, boundaries included. Create a new query that includes the fields OrderID, CustomerID, OrderDate, and ShippingCost from the Orders table and satisfies the above criteria. Sort results by shipping cost so that lower shipping costs appear first. Save the query as Qry3_Orders_ShippingCost.

   Your result should look like:

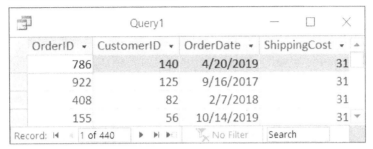

4. Your supervisor is asking for a report of orders that includes the fields OrderID, CustomerID, OrderDate, and ShippingCost from the Orders table. It should list all orders except those in March and April of every year. He needs this as a follow up to a report you created for marketing. Sort results so that the latest orders appear first. Save the query as Qry4_Orders_Seasonality_c.

   Your result should look like:

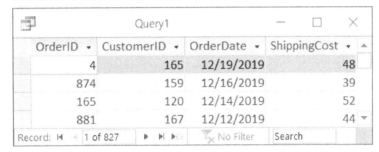

5. The six-sigma team is evaluating new shipment processes. They need a report that will list all the orders from the United Postal Service. Create a new query that includes the fields OrderID, CustomerID, OrderDate, and ShippingCost from the Orders table and satisfies the above criteria. Save the query as Qry5_Orders_PostalService. **Hint:** First, check the ShipperID value for the United Postal Service in the ShiipingCompanies table.

   Your result should look like:

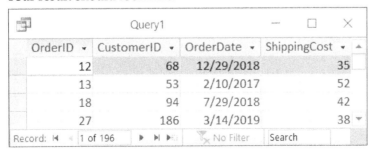

CHAPTER 11
THE BETWEEN OPERATOR

The BETWEEN … AND operator is designed to retrieve subsets from a data set. It works primarily with number and date data. In this sense, it can be used to retrieve records that exist between two values acting as boundaries. Those two boundary values can be numbers or dates. In addition, while we cannot use BETWEEN with wildcard characters or predicates, we can still use functions to augment its range of applicability. It is important to state that BETWEEN is inclusive which means that the values acting as boundaries will be included in the result set.

120. The BETWEEN operator with numbers
Find products with prices between $15 and $18
Discussion:

In this example, we are looking for product prices between the $15 and $18 values. The BETWEEN operator is inclusive, so the products with unit prices of $15 and $18 will be included in the result set.

Code:

SELECT productname, productunitprice
FROM products
WHERE productunitprice BETWEEN 15 AND 18
ORDER BY productunitprice

Result:

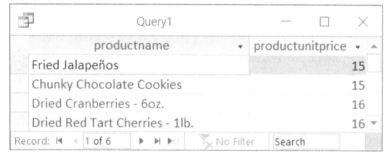

121. The BETWEEN operator with the left function()
Find suppliers with zip codes starting between 12 and 22
Discussion:

In this example, we are looking for a range of zip codes between 12+ any number and 22+ any number. We can use the left() function to extract the two leftmost characters of the zip code and get the result we need.

Of course, one might raise an objection and say: Why do we need to use the left function and not put the lower and upper boundaries in directly as 12189 and 22459? The answer is two-fold: First, the BETWEEN operator does not work with text data and we will get a type mismatch error since the zip code is a text field (and it should be). Second, in working with the supplier table, we deal with only 10 records which makes it easy for us to see the values we have for the zip codes. If we have hundreds of records to work with, we need to run two SQL statements, one with the min() and max() functions to identify the boundaries, and then a second with BETWEEN.

Code:
```
SELECT companyname, address, city, zip
FROM suppliers
WHERE left(zip, 2) BETWEEN 12 AND 22
ORDER BY zip
```

There is a turnaround to the above code by using a type conversion function (see CHAPTER 25 TYPE CONVERSION FUNCTIONS) to convert the text data in the Zip field into numeric data. Now, if you use the CInt() function you will get a stack overflow error since the CInt() function can convert numbers from -32,768 to 32,767 and with no decimals. Notice in the supplier table, that we have two zip code entries of 52347. Consequently, we can use the Clng() function as it shown below to get the same results. Even though we used a couple of tricks to use the BETWEEN operator with text data, it is highly recommended to use this operator with numbers and dates and retrieve your results with the simplest SQL Statement possible.

Code:
```
SELECT companyname, address, city, zip
FROM suppliers
WHERE clng(zip) BETWEEN 12000 AND 23000
ORDER BY zip
```

Result:

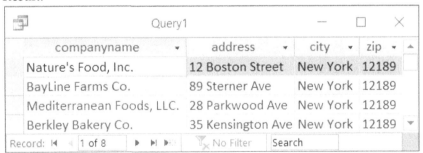

122.   The BETWEEN operator with dates
Find orders placed within a date range
Discussion:
In this example, we retrieve order dates that fall between 6/15/2017 and 8/15/2018. The BETWEEN operator is inclusive, and it will include orders placed on 6/15/2017 and 8/15/2018 as it is shown in the result set.

Code:

```
SELECT OrderID, orderdate, shippeddate
FROM orders
WHERE orderdate BETWEEN #6/15/2017# AND #8/15/2018#
ORDER BY orderdate DESC
```

Result:

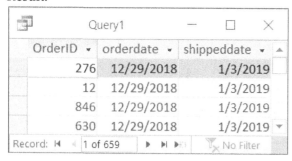

OrderID	orderdate	shippeddate
499	8/15/2018	8/20/2018
278	8/13/2018	8/18/2018
376	8/13/2018	8/18/2018
137	8/12/2018	8/17/2018

Record: 1 of 364   No Filter

123.   The BETWEEN operator with the year() function

Find orders placed within a year range

Discussion:

In this example, we use the year() function to extract the year out of the orderdate field so that we can use year values as the lower and upper boundaries. All orders from 2017 and 2018 will be included in the result set due to the inclusivity characteristic of the BETWEEN operator.

Code:

```
SELECT OrderID, orderdate, shippeddate
FROM orders
WHERE year(orderdate) BETWEEN 2017 AND 2018
ORDER BY orderdate DESC
```

Result:

OrderID	orderdate	shippeddate
276	12/29/2018	1/3/2019
12	12/29/2018	1/3/2019
846	12/29/2018	1/3/2019
630	12/29/2018	1/3/2019

Record: 1 of 659   No Filter

124.   The NOT BETWEEN operator with numbers

Find products with prices outside a price range

Discussion:

In this instance, we are looking for products with prices outside the $10 to $40 range, so we are asking the database to give us all products whose prices do not fall between $10 and $40. In practical terms, when we use the BETWEEN operator with NOT, we are usually looking for extreme values or outliers. The products with prices of exactly $10 or $40 will not be included in the result set.

Code:

SELECT productname, productunitprice
FROM products
WHERE productunitprice NOT BETWEEN 10 AND 40
ORDER BY productunitprice ASC

Result:

125.   Comparison of BETWEEN with "<=" or "=>"

Find products with prices within a price range

Discussion:

In this paradigm, we show that using the BETWEEN operator is the same as using the two inequality predicates "<=" and "=>". Both SQL statements below will produce the same result. However, we should always give preference to equality and inequality predicates since they produce faster results with less overhead for the database engine.

Code:

SELECT productname, productunitprice
FROM products
WHERE productunitprice BETWEEN 15 AND 18
ORDER BY productunitprice ASC

Or

SELECT productname, productunitprice
FROM products
WHERE productunitprice >=15 AND productunitprice <=18
ORDER BY productunitprice ASC

Result:

CHAPTER 11 DISCUSSION QUESTIONS

1. What is the primary goal of the BETWEEN operator?
2. Which equality/inequality predicates can we use to simulate the function of the BETWEEN operator?
3. Are boundary values included in the result set when we use the BETWEEN operator?
4. Can we use the BETWEEN operator with wildcard characters or predicates for more intricate searches?
5. With what data types do we primarily use the BETWEEN operator?
6. How can we use the BETWEEN operator with functions to augment its functionality?
7. Can we use the LIKE operator to simulate the functionality of the BETWEEN operator?
8. Why would someone prefer to use equality and inequality predicates instead of the BETWEEN operator?
9. Why do we need to use conversion functions with BETWEEN to work with text data?
10. The BETWEEN operator allows us to get the range within two numbers or within two dates. What keyword can we use to retrieve the respective outside ranges?

127.   **CHAPTER 11 HANDS-ON EXERCISES**

Chapter 11 Case 1:

Create a new Access database and name it Chapter11_1.accdb. Copy the table tbls_CustomerOrders from the PracticeDatabase.accdb and paste it to Chapter11_1.accdb.

1. The marketing department needs a list of customers with orders between $100 and $200 for customer segmentation purposes. Create a new query that includes the lastname, city, state, and OrderTotal fields from the tbls_CustomerOrders table and satisfies the marketing request. Order results by OrderTotal ascending. Save the query as Qry1_Orders100-200.

    Your result should look like:

    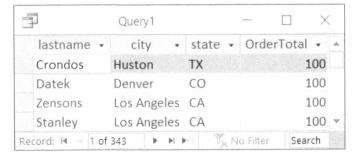

2. The inventory people need a quick list of all orders placed in May and June 2017 to compare it against their shipments for accuracy. Create a new query that includes the lastname, city, state, and OrderDate fields from the tbls_CustomerOrders table satisfying the inventory department's request. Order results by OrderDate ascending. Save the query as Qry2_OrdersMayJune.

Your result should look like:

3. The management of the corporation asked for a report that will include all orders in the years 2017 and 2018. They need this data for a historical assessment of orders. Create a new query that includes the OrderDate, ShippedDate, and OrderTotal fields as well as a field that shows only the year out of the OrderDate date. Order the results by year, ascending. Save the query as Qry3_Orders_2017_2018.

Your result should look like:

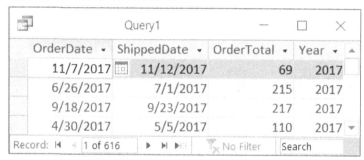

4. Management is asking for a report of orders shipped within 2017 but outside the period between June 2017 and August 2017 for reviewing performance outside the summer months. Create a new query that includes the OrderID, OrderDate, ShippedDate, and OrderTotal fields and satisfies the managerial request. Sort results by ShippedDate ascending. Save the query as Qry4_Orders_NoSummerMonths.

Your result should look like:

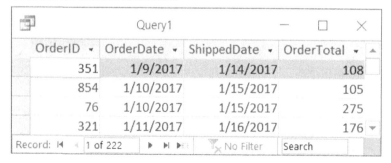

5. The sales people need a list of customers residing in the areas with zip codes ranging from 12000 to 12999. They need this data for follow up with sales to existing customers. Create a new query that includes the OrderID, lastname, city, state and zip fields from the tbls_CustomerOrders table and satisfies the sales people request. Order results by Zip ascending. Save the query as Qry5_Orders_ZipCodes.

    Your result should look like:

Chapter 11 Case 2:

Create a new Access database and name it Chapter11_2.accdb. Copy the table tbls_CustomerOrders from the PracticeDatabase.accdb and paste it to Chapter11_2.accdb.

1. The management of the company needs to review shipped orders within the year 2017 but outside the months of January through March. Create a new query that includes the fields OrderID, State, City, ShippedDate, and OrderTotal from the tbls_CustomerOrders table and satisfies the above criteria. Order the result set by ShippedDate so that older orders appear first. Save the query as Qry1_Orders_OutsideWinter.

    Your result should look like:

2. The marketing people need a list of orders shipped within the period of June 2017 to December 2017, which also have order total amounts between $200 and $300. Create a new query that includes the OrderID, State, City, ShippedDate, and OrderTotal fields from the tbls_CustomerOrders table and satisfies the above criteria. Sort results by OrderTotal so that bigger orders show on top. Save the query as Qry2_Orders_DoubleCriteria.

    Your result should look like:

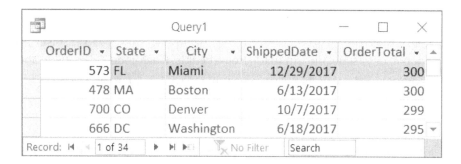

3. The inventory people need a report of all orders shipped within the month of June 2017. They had a breakdown with their trucks and they need to compare their shipment slips with your report data to see if they missed to report a shipment. Create a new query that includes the OrderID, State, City, ShippedDate, and OrderTotal fields from the tbls_CustomerOrders table and satisfies the above criteria. Save the query as Qry3_Orders_Inventory.

Your result should look like:

4. The accounting department asks for a report of customer orders with OrderTotals between $0 and $50. There have been discrepancies in the billing of small orders, which need to be checked. Create a new query that includes the OrderID, State, City, ShippedDate, and OrderTotal fields from the tbls_CustomerOrders table and satisfies the above criteria. Sort results so that smaller order totals appear first. Save the query as Qry4_Orders_50.

Your result should look like:

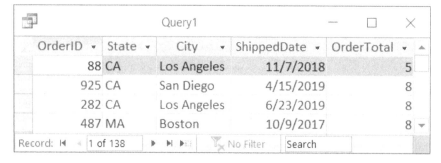

5. The senior management of the company wants a report that lists all the orders placed in the months between September and December 2017. It has been reported to them that orders in that period experience higher processing cycles because of the holiday volume. Consequently, they want to

compare the intervals between the order dates and shipped dates, especially for large orders such as those between $300 and $500. Create a new query that includes the fields OrderID, OrderDate, ShippedDate, and OrderTotal from the tbls_CustomerOrders table and satisfies the above criteria. Sort the results so that bigger orders appear first. Save the query as Qry5_Orders_CheckCycles.

Your result should look like:

OrderID	OrderDate	ShippedDate	OrderTotal
858	10/3/2017	10/8/2017	435
256	9/11/2017	9/16/2017	410
422	11/14/2017	11/19/2017	382
763	11/10/2017	11/15/2017	366

Record: 1 of 11   No Filter   Search

CHAPTER 12
THE IN OPERATOR

The major role of the IN operator is to participate in search conditions for filtering records. It is always used within the WHERE clause of a SQL statement and usually takes the place of multiple OR operators. It is an extremely useful search operator, and it will check the existence of a value against a list of values provided or constructed dynamically. Moreover, the IN operator can be used with text, number, and date data, making it suitable for a wide range of applications. Finally, it is indispensable when used with subqueries, as we will show you in this chapter and in chapter 31. Using IN with subqueries allows the database professional to obtain results that would have been very difficult or impossible to obtain otherwise. The IN operator should be well understood and at the top of the toolbox of a database user or developer.

128.   The IN operator with text data
Create a report of customers from multiple cities
Discussion:
Our supervisor is requesting a report that lists all customers from the cities of New York, Boston, Chicago, Los Angeles, and Dallas. Of course, we could use the OR operator to produce this report:

```
SELECT LastName, FirstName, City
FROM customers
WHERE (city='New York')
OR (city='Boston')
OR (city='Chicago')
OR (city='Los Angeles')
OR (city='Dallas')
```

Using multiple OR operators to obtain a solution is rather tedious in both time and effort. Then, as soon as we provide the report to the supervisor, she comes back and says: "This is excellent; can I please have another report with our customers in the rest of the cities in the country?" To produce the second report, we will need to create an additional multitude of OR statements with the remaining cities. The IN operator solves these problems quickly and efficiently.

Code:
```
SELECT lastname, firstname, city
FROM customers
WHERE city in ('New York', 'Boston', 'Chicago', 'Los Angeles', 'Dallas')
```

Result:

129. The NOT IN operator with text data

Create a report of customers excluding several cities

Discussion:

This time, our supervisor reverses the request and asks for a report of customers from all cities not included in our previous report—every city except New York, Boston, Chicago, Los Angeles, and Dallas. Since we have the code using the IN operator from the previous example, the only thing we need to do is put the keyword "NOT" in front of the IN operator.

Code:

```
SELECT lastname, firstname, city
FROM customers
WHERE city NOT IN ('New York', 'Boston', 'Chicago', 'Los Angeles', 'Dallas')
```

Result:

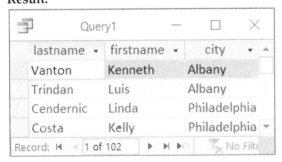

130. The IN operator with numeric data

Create a report of products based on prices

Discussion:

In this scenario, we need to produce a report that lists products from our product catalog with the following prices: 15, 19, 22, 23, and 42. Since the numbers are not sequential, we cannot use the BETWEEN operator to get our results. We can, however, use the IN operator to produce the report almost as fast. When we employ IN with numbers, we do not use quotes.

Code:

```
SELECT productname, quantityperunit, productunitprice
FROM products
WHERE productunitprice in (15, 19, 22, 23, 42)
```

Result:

productname	quantityperunit	productunitprice
Almonds, Roasted and Salted - 18 oz. Bag	12	22
Chunky Pretzels	30	22
Roasted & Salted Almonds	35	19
Cream and honey biscuits	28	22

Record: 1 of 11 — No Filter — Search

131. The IN operator with date data

Create a report of orders for several specific dates

Discussion:

We have a request from the sales department to have a look at the orders in the first day of the three summer months of the year 2017 because they are missing an order. They want to know what happened so that they can communicate it to the customer. We can absolutely use IN with date fields as can be seen in the code below. Notice the special character (#) in which we enclose date criteria in Access. Pay attention that the dates provided are all actual date values and not ranges. We cannot use date ranges with the IN operator.

Code:

```
SELECT OrderID, OrderDate, ShippedDate, ShippingCost
FROM Orders
WHERE
OrderDate IN (#6/1/2017#, #7/1/2017#, #8/1/2017#)
```

Result:

OrderID	OrderDate	ShippedDate	ShippingCost
170	6/1/2017	6/6/2017	40
201	7/1/2017	7/6/2017	41
905	7/1/2017	7/6/2017	51
959	6/1/2017	6/6/2017	32

Record: 1 of 4 — No Filter — Search

132. Create dynamic lists for the IN operator using subqueries

Generate a report of orders in which there is at least one non-discounted product

Discussion

The IN operator shows its real power when used with lists generated dynamically through SQL code. Instead of typing the values within the parenthesis, we can actually use SQL to create value lists automatically. This leads to the concept of subqueries, which we will discuss in detail in chapter 31, but we will go through a few examples here to get introduced to the ultimate use of the IN operator.

In this example, management wants to have a report of orders in which no discount was extended for at least one of the products included in the order. Each order might contain multiple products, and for each product, we might or might not have extended a discount. In other words, the database is set up so that discounts are given on a per product basis and not per order. This way, we have the flexibility to extend discounts on a per product basis, which is a much more flexible way of doing business.

To answer this request, we need information from two different tables: the Orders table and the ProductsOrders table. The subquery in this case will generate a list of OrderIDs from the ProductsOrders table for which the discount = 0. Then, this list of OrderIDs will be used with the IN operator as criteria to retrieve the OrderID, OrderDate, and ShippedDate from the Orders table.

Code:
SELECT orderid, orderdate, shippeddate
FROM orders
WHERE orderid
IN (SELECT orderid FROM ProductsOrders WHERE (Discount) =0)

Result:

orderid	orderdate	shippeddate
2	7/30/2018	8/4/2018
5	11/19/2017	11/24/2017
7	12/1/2018	12/6/2018
24	3/12/2017	3/17/2017

Record: 1 of 136   No Filter

133. The IN operator with GROUP BY and HAVING in subqueries

Generate a report of orders for which the total extended discount was 0

Discussion

Continuing from the previous example, we now have to produce a report that will list orders in which all of the included products have a discount of zero. That is, if four products are included in an order, the discount rate for all four of them should be zero for the order to be included in the report. To reply to this request, we will again use the IN operator to look in the ProductsOrders table for OrderIDs of orders with zero discounts for all their included products. Our next concern is to compute the sum of discount for every order which should be equal to zero. Consequently, we will have to filter orders after we know the results of the sum() function keeping those that equal zero and excluding all others with any amount of discount.

All of the above issues can be solved by using the IN operator, a subquery, the WHERE clause, the GROUP BY and HAVING clauses, and the sum() function as per the example below. In the example, the GROUP BY clause with the sum() function will run first and produce a list of unique orders and their total discounts. From this list, the HAVING clause will keep only the ones with a zero total discount. Then, the SELECT statement in the subquery will generate a list of OrderIDs as filtered out by the HAVING clause. Finally, the WHERE clause from the main query will use the OrderIDs generated from the subquery to filter orders from the Orders table and produce a result set of orders whose orderID matches the OrderID produced by the subquery.

As we can see from the result set, we have only ten orders for which the discount is zero for all the products they contain. We will discuss the GROUP BY clause in detail in chapter 17 and subqueries in chapter 31 but it is imperative to know that the IN operator is not just a replacement for multiple OR operators.

Code:
SELECT orderid, orderdate, shippeddate
FROM orders
WHERE orderid
IN (SELECT orderid FROM ProductsOrders GROUP BY orderid HAVING sum(Discount) =0)

Result:

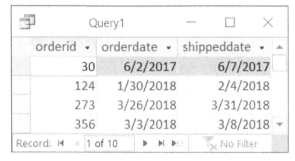

134.   The IN operator with subqueries and dates
Find customers who have not placed any orders in the second half of 2017
Discussion
Our task in this scenario is to find customers who have not placed any orders in the second half of the year 2017. Management needs this information for initiating promotions to inactive customers. To achieve this task, we will use the NOT IN and BETWEEN operators and a subquery. Remember that the purpose of the subquery is always the same—to generate a list of values to be used by the IN operator. Here, the subquery will generate a list of CustomerIDs from the Orders table, which will serve as criteria by the main query to filter records from the Customers table.

Code:
SELECT CustomerID, FirstName, LastName, City, State
FROM Customers
WHERE CustomerID NOT IN
(Select CustomerID FROM Orders WHERE
OrderDate BETWEEN #6/1/2017# AND #12/1/2017#)

Result:

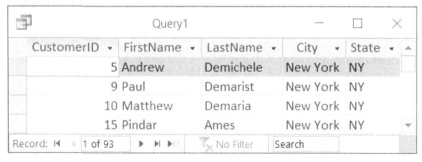

135.   The IN operator with subqueries, dates, and date functions
Find customers who have not placed any orders in the year 2017
Discussion
The request in this case is to find customers who have not placed any orders in the year 2017. Of course, we do not track years separately in the orders table, but we can easily extract the year out of the OrderDate filed using the year() function. Then, we can use it in the subquery as shown below. This type of query is excellent to keep track of customer retention rates in a business.

Code:
SELECT CustomerID, FirstName, LastName, City, State
FROM Customers
WHERE CustomerID NOT IN
(Select CustomerID FROM Orders WHERE
year(orderdate) = 2017)

Result:

CustomerID	FirstName	LastName	City	State
10	Matthew	Demaria	New York	NY
15	Pindar	Ames	New York	NY
19	Erin	Erin	Los Angele	CA
24	Roy	Sars	Los Angele	CA

Record: 1 of 50   No Filter   Search

1. What is the primary role of the IN operator?
2. What is the clause within which we must always use the IN operator?
3. Why is it a good idea to use IN instead of multiple OR operators?
4. What are the data types with which we can use the IN operator?
5. What is the purpose of the NOT IN operator?
6. Can we use the IN operator with dates?
7. Can we use date ranges with the IN operator?
8. How can we provide dynamic lists for the IN operator?
9. Can we use the IN operator to look for data in different tables?
10. How can we create dynamic lists with the IN operator?

137. **CHAPTER 12 HANDS-ON EXERCISES**

Chapter 12 Case 1:

Create a new Access database and name it Chapter12_1.accdb. Copy the tables Customers and Orders from the PracticeDatabase.accdb and paste them to Chapter12_1.accdb.

1. The marketing department is asking for a report of all the customers in the States of New York, California, and Florida. Create a new query that includes the lastname, firstname, city, and state fields from the Customers table satisfying the marketing request. Order results by State ascending. Save the query as Qry1_Customer_States.

    Your result should look like:

2. Your supervisor needs a report of all the customers who do not reside in the States of Ohio and Texas. Create a new query that includes the lastname, firstname, city, and state fields from the Customers table satisfying your supervisor's request. Order results by state ascending. Save the query as Qry2_Customers_OH_TX.

    Your result should look like:

3. The shipping people called in and are asking for a report of all the orders processed by the sales reps with SalesRepIDs 2, 5, and 9. They want to check those orders again. Create a new query that includes the fields OrderID, SalesRepID, OrderDate, and ShippingCost from the Orders table satisfying the request from shipping. Order results by SalesRepID ascending. Save the query as Qry3_SalesReps.

Your result should look like:

4. The sales department is asking for a report of orders placed on the first and third day of March 2017. Create a new query that includes the fields OrderID, SalesRepID, OrderDate, and ShippingCost from the Orders table satisfying the request from sales. Order results by OrderDate ascending. Save the query as Qry4_MarchOrders.

Your result should look like:

OrderID ▾	SalesRepID ▾	OrderDate ▾	ShippingCost ▾
710	7	3/1/2017	34
95	1	3/1/2017	48
328	3	3/3/2017	31

Record: ◄ 1 of 3 ► ►► No Filter Search

5. The sales people need a list of customers who have not placed any orders so that they can market to them. Create a new query that includes the customerid, firstname, lastname, city, and state fields from the Customers table and satisfies the sales people request. Save the query as Qry5_CustomersNoOrders.

Your result should look like:

Chapter 12 Case 2:

Create a new Access database and name it Chapter12_2.accdb. Copy the tables Customers, SalesReps, and Orders, from the PracticeDatabase.accdb and paste them to Chapter12_2.accdb.

1. Your supervisor is asking for a list of sales representatives who reside in the zip codes 22459 and 12189. Create a new query that includes the lastname, title, city, state, and zip fields from the SalesReps table and sort results ascending by lastname. Save the query as Qry1_SalesRepsZip.

    Your result should look like:

2. The marketing department needs a list of orders for three particular customers: Andrew Demichele, Lisa Zartons, and William Teall. Create a new query that includes the fields CustomerID, OrderDate, ShippedDate, and ShippingCost from the Orders table satisfying the marketing request. Order results by customerID. Save the query as Qry2_CustomerOrders.

    Your result should look like:

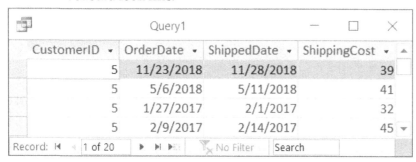

3. The HR department is asking for a report of the sales representatives who do not have any orders yet. If they exist, HR feels these employees should get more help from everyone to be successful in their jobs. Create a new query that includes the fields FirstName, LastName, Title, and DateOfHire from the SalesReps table satisfying the HR request. Order results by lastname ascending. Save the query as Qry3_SalesReps_NoOrders.

Your result should look like:

4. Your supervisor is asking you to look for orphaned records in the orders table. That is, you need to check and see if there are any orders without associated customers. This would be very bad for the integrity of the database and if there are any they need to be deleted. Create a new query that includes the fields OrderID, CustomerID, and OrderDate from the Orders table and save it as Qry4_OrdersWithNoCustomers.

Your result should look like:

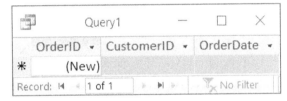

5. The marketing department is asking for a list of customers who placed orders after the holiday season and specifically in February and March 2017. They would like to know who these customers are so they can market to them and compensate for out of season sales drops. Create a new query that includes the fields CutomerID, LastName, and FirstName from the Customers table and order the results by lastname asc. Save the query as Qry5_CustomersFebruaryMarch.

Your result should look like:

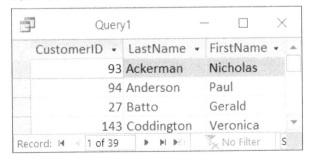

CHAPTER 13
THE DISTINCT PREDICATE

We use the DISTINCT predicate to eliminate duplicate rows from the results of a SELECT statement. It belongs to a set of four predicates (ALL, TOP, DISTINCT, DISTINCTROW) which we use to manipulate the number of records returned from a SQL statement. All four of them are used right after the SELECT keyword, and all of them are optional. If we do not use a predicate with the SELECT statement, [ALL] is assumed by Access.

SELECT [ALL] [TOP] [DISTINCT] [DISTINCTROW] field1, field2, ... fieldn
FROM table

From the four predicates above, we will focus on DISTINCT in this chapter and TOP in the next one, since they are the two most useful ones. [ALL] is assumed as the default when no predicate is used while the DISTINCTROW has very specific applications. Specifically, the difference between DISTINCT and DISTINCTROW is that DISTINCT is looking for unique values for the field or fields included in the SQL statement while DISTINCTROW will retrieve distinct records overall. We also need to know that the results of a query in which we use DISTINCT are not updatable while the results of a query in which we use DISTINCTROW are updatable. Also, keep in mind that DISTINCTROW might not be supported by other database engines like MSSQL, DB2, Oracle, or MySQL. To conclude, we should focus on understanding the DISTINCT and TOP predicates well because they are essential to retrieving the results we need in various business scenarios.

The column on which we use the DISTINCT predicate will return only its unique values and if we apply it on a combination of columns—lastname and firstname, for example—the database will return the unique combinations of those values. Let us see how this works through examples in our familiar customers and orders database.

138.   Run a SELECT statement without the DISTINCT predicate
Find cities in which we have customers
Discussion:
Using a classic SQL statement to retrieve the "city" from the customers table will return multiple instances of the same city since it is logical to have multiple customers in the same city. For example, as we can see from the result set, New York appears as many times as the number of customers we have in this city. There are 201 records returned with multiple instances of various cities.

Code:
SELECT city
FROM customers

Result:

139. Run a SELECT statement with the DISTINCT predicate
Find unique cities in which we have customers
Discussion:
In thiss case, we want to obtain only the unique or distinct names of the cities where we have customers. The business goal is to create a list of cities where we do business. In this scenario, we would like New York to appear only once, Boston only once, and Los Angeles only once. This is a case where we use the DISTINCT predicate. This time, only 15 records returned, and the value for each city is unique. From this recordset, we know that the number of cities where we have customers is 15.

Code:

```
SELECT DISTINCT city
FROM customers
```

Result:

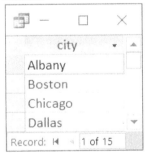

140. Use DISTINCT on one column
Finding unique job titles
Discussion:
Suppose our next business goal is to retrieve the unique job titles of people who replenish our inventory and manage our orders from various corporate suppliers. It is a good thing to know if we deal mostly with managers, directors, or other positions. Maybe we can get better discounts if we talk to people in higher positions with more decision-making flexibility. We can easily achieve this goal using the DISTINCT keyword. The unique corporate titles of people with whom we do business are seven.

Code:
SELECT DISTINCT ContactTitle
FROM suppliers

Result:

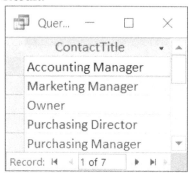

141.   Use DISTINCT on multiple columns

Finding unique customer names in various states
Discussion:
Experience indicates that DISTINCT works at its best when applied on a single column. However, if we want to apply DISTINCT on multiple columns, we need to know exactly what to expect. Let us work with our customers table and go through some examples to fully understand this concept.

Code Case 1:
If we run a simple SELECT statement such as:

SELECT firstname, state
FROM customers
WHERE (firstname='John')

We will get four customers with a first name John. Actually, these are all the Johns we have in our customers table.

Result:

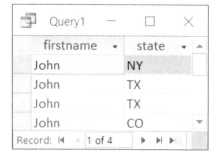

If we include the DISTINCT clause such as:

Code Case 2:
SELECT DISTINCT firstname, state
FROM customers
WHERE (firstname='John')

We will get only three customers with a first name John. This is because we told the database to return unique combinations of first names and states. In the previous result set, we have two Johns in Texas. When we use DISTINCT on both firstname and state, only one of the two will appear. The problem with DISTINCT on multiple columns is that we cannot exactly control which ones will appear in the result set, and we might get results that we haven't intended. So, be very careful when using DISTINCT on multiple columns.

Result:

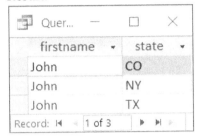

142.   Getting more information beyond DISTINCT
Find unique job titles and their Corresponding Numbers
Discussion:
Although it does not thematically belong here, your next logical thought is probably: I know how to retrieve unique values for names, states, job titles, and other fields. However, what is the total number I have from each? To answer this question, we need to use the GROUP BY clause, which we explore in detail in chapter 17. Here, we will use the job titles as an example to find the number of people holding each title.

To obtain this result set, we simply use one aggregate function count() and the GROUP BY clause to get the result we need. The "CountNumber" is the title we give ourselves to the counting column.

Code:
SELECT ContactTitle, Count(ContactTitle) AS CountNumber
FROM suppliers
GROUP BY ContactTitle

Result:

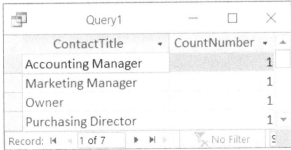

143. The DISTINCTROW predicate

Find customers with at least one order

Discussion:

In this scenario, we are looking for customers who have at least one order in the Orders table. That is, the result set will leave out customers without orders. There are three ways to achieve this goal. We can use a subquery (see chapter 31), a join (chapter 30), or DISTINCTROW. I would suggest using a subquery to obtain this result because it is the cleanest way and will provide guaranteed results. We can do it by using joins, but we will create a lot of code, while DISTINCTROW has its own peculiarities, as you shall see in a second. From the result set below using DISTINCTROW, we see that we have 190 unique customers with at least one order. However, we used fields only from the customers table. If we include at least one field from the Orders table, the DISTINCTROW will not work. DISTINCTROW will work with any number of joined tables as soon as we select fields from some of the joined tables but not all of them. Finally, I have included the code using a subquery, which will produce the exact same result. Always use subqueries to find related, orphaned, and unrelated records. See chapter 23 for multiple examples.

Code:

SELECT DISTINCTROW lastname, firstname, city, zip

FROM Customers

INNER JOIN Orders ON Customers.CustomerID = Orders.CustomerID

Code:

SELECT lastname, firstname, city, zip

FROM Customers

WHERE CustomerID

IN (SELECT CustomerID from tbls_Orders)

Result:

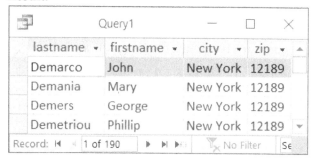

144.   CHAPTER 13 DISCUSSION QUESTIONS

1.   What is the primary role of the DISTINCT predicate?
2.   What other predicates similar to DISTINCT can be used to manipulate the number of rows retrieved?
3.   Is DISTINCT a required predicate or an optional one?
4.   Can we use the DISTINCT predicate on multiple columns?
5.   What is the default predicate used if we do not use DISTINCT in the SQL statement?
6.   If we use DISTINCT on one column what kind of values do we retrieve from that column?
7.   If we use DISTINCT on multiple columns what kind of values do we retrieve from those columns?
8.   Where in the SELECT statement do we place the DISTINCT predicate?
9.   From the four possible predicates of the SELECT statement which are the two most useful?
10.   What is the difference between DISTINCT and DISTINCTROW?

145.   CHAPTER 13 HANDS-ON EXERCISES

Chapter 13 Case 1:

Create a new Access database and name it Chapter13_1.accdb. Copy the tables Customers and Products from the PracticeDatabase.accdb and paste them to Chapter13_1.accdb.

1.   Your supervisor is asking for a list of unique states in which we have customers. Create a new query that satisfies your supervisor's request. Order results by State ascending. Save the query as Qry1_States.

Your result should look like:

2.   The marketing department wants to prepare a nameday list so that they can send greeting cards to customers. They are asking you to give them a list of unique first names of customers.   Create a new query that satisfies the marketing request. Order results by firstname ascending. Save the query as Qry2_CustomersFirst.

Your result should look like:

Notice, the first blank row in the result set. This means we are missing the first name for a customer.

3. The inventory people need a list of the different SKUs in the Products table. Create a new query that satisfies the inventory department request. Order results by SKU ascending. Save the query as Qry3_SKU.

Your result should look like:

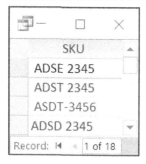

4. The inventory people came back and they are now asking for a list that will display the unique SKUs as well as the number of products associated with each SKU. Create a query that satisfies this request and order results by SKU ascending. Save the query as Qry4_SKU_Numbers.

Your result should look like:

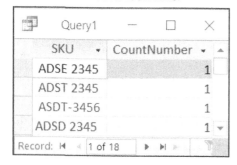

5. The marketing people are asking for a list of unique first names of customers and their respective numbers so that they know how many customers they have for each nameday occasion. Create a query that satisfies this request and order results by firstname ascending. Save the query as Qry5_FirstName_Numbers.

Your result should look like:

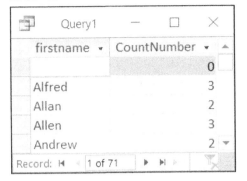

Chapter 13 Case 2:

Create a new Access database and name it Chapter13_2.accdb. Copy the tables Products, SalesReps, and Suppliers from the PracticeDatabase.accdb and paste them to Chapter13_2.accdb.

1. The inventory people need a list of unique states in which we have suppliers. Use the suppliers table and create a new query that satisfies the inventory department request. Order results by state ascending. Save the query as Qry1_States_Suppliers.

    Your result should look like:

2. The sales people are asking for a list of unique cities in which we have sales representatives. Use the SalesRep table to create a new query that satisfies the sales department request. Order results by city ascending. Save the query as Qry2_Cities_SalesReps.

    Your result should look like:

3. The sales people are now asking for a list that will display the unique cities in which we have sales representatives as well as the number of sales reps in each city. Create a query that satisfies this request and order results by city ascending. Save the query as Qry3_SalesReps_Numbers.

Your result should look like:

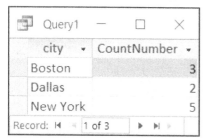

4. The inventory people are asking for a list of unique reorder level amounts for our products in the products table. They feel that some of the reorder levels are set too high resulting in higher inventory cost. Create a new query that satisfies the inventory department request. Order results by reorder level descending. Save the query as Qry4_ReorderLevels.

Your result should look like:

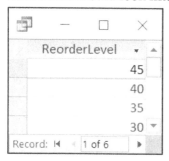

5. The inventory people are also asking for a list that will display the unique reorder levels for products as well as the number of products for each reorder level. Create a query that satisfies this request and order results by reorder level ascending. Save the query as Qry5_ReorderLevels_Numbers.

Your result should look like:

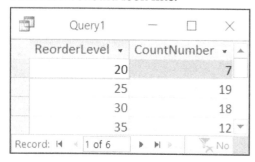

CHAPTER 14
THE TOP PREDICATE

The TOP predicate is useful for retrieving a specified number or a specified percentage of records from a table. It belongs to a set of four predicates (ALL, TOP, DISTINCT, DISTINCTROW) used to manipulate the number of records returned from a SQL statement. All four of them are used right after the SELECT keyword, and all of them are optional. If we do not use a predicate with the SELECT statement, [ALL] is assumed by Access.

SELECT [ALL] [TOP] [DISTINCT] [DISTINCTROW] field1, field2, … fieldn
FROM table

The TOP predicate used alone is not useful since it does not return records in any special order; it simply returns the first n or n% of the records as they are stored in the table. However, when the TOP predicate is used with the ORDER BY, GROUP BY, and WHERE clauses, it shows its real potential and practicality.

146.   The TOP predicate alone with numbers
Retrieve 5 records from the products table
Discussion:
The TOP predicate in this example will return the first five records from the products table in the order these records are stored in the table. This process is practically useless for our business needs since it does not provide any special information at all. It might be useful for technical reasons if we want to retrieve the first five records from the table or if we want to see a sample of records in the table without retrieving all of them.

Code:
SELECT TOP 5 productname, unitsinstock, unitsonorder
FROM Products

Result:

productname	unitsinstock	unitsonorder
Almonds, Hickory Smoked - 12 oz. Bag	40	5
Almonds, Roasted and Salted - 18 oz. Bag	32	0
Banana Chips - 20 oz. Bag	25	0
Berry Cherry in 8 oz. Bag	50	0
California Original Pistachios - 1 lb. Bag	35	0

Record: 1 of 5   No Filter   Search

147.   The TOP predicate with ORDER BY and numbers

Find the five products with the most units in stock

Discussion:

In this example, the business goal is to retrieve the five products with the highest levels of inventory. The use of the TOP predicate in combination with the ORDER BY clause can show its usefulness and practical application. As you can see from the result set, the five products with the highest inventory levels appear first. We use the DESC keyword with the ORDER BY clause so that highest quantities appear first (see chapter 7 for the ORDER BY clause).

We need to be very careful when using TOP. In this example, we get five records because we have three products with 50 units in stock and two with 49 units in stock. If we had three products with 50 units in stock and five with 49 units in stock, then the query would display eight records though we asked for five. This is how the query will work. First, it will retrieve the three products with 50 units in stock. Then, it will go to the third record with 49 units in stock and display this record as well. Then, it will go the fifth record with the value of 49 and display this as well. However, the query will not stop at the above five records. Since, the value of 49 units in stock is already included in the query, any number of records with 49 units in stock will be displayed as well.

Code:

SELECT TOP 5 productname, unitsinstock, unitsonorder
FROM Products
ORDER BY unitsinstock DESC

Result:

productname	unitsinstock	unitsonorder
Chocolate Chip Cookies	50	0
Artichokes in white sauce	50	0
Berry Cherry in 8 oz. Bag	50	0
Salsa Verde	49	0
Biscuits with cream	49	0

Record: 1 of 5   No Filter   Search

148.   The TOP predicate with ORDER BY and percentages

Retrieve 10% of the products with the highest prices

Discussion:

This time, management asked for the top 10% of the most expensive products in the inventory. We can reply to this request by using the TOP predicate with the ORDER BY clause as shown below. In Access, we use the word "10 PERCENT" and not "10%" with the TOP predicate. In addition, notice that the order of the fields in the SELECT statement is insignificant. What really matters is the field included in the ORDER BY clause. This is the field with which the TOP predicate will work.

Code:

```
SELECT TOP 10 PERCENT productname, productunitprice
FROM Products
ORDER BY productunitprice DESC
```

Result:

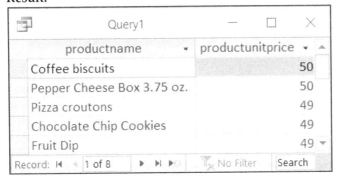

ATTENTION: Again, we need to be very careful when using TOP with percentages. TOP will provide accurate results when the values of the field used in the ORDER BY clause are unique. Any equal values will distort TOP results. For instance, in the products table we have 70 records and in our result set we should have had seven records since we are asking for 10%. However, we have eight. This is because the seventh record has a ProductUnitPrice of 48. However, the eighth record has a ProductUnitPrice of 48 as well. Since a ProductUnitPrice of 48 was included in the result set, all ProductUnitPrices of 48 will be included no matter if they are half the table!

149.   The TOP predicate with ORDER BY and text data

Select exactly 5 employees sorted by name

Discussion:

In this example, we use TOP in conjunction with ORDER BY to get the first five employees ordered by last name. Of course, the obvious question is: What is the difference with a simple SELECT and ORDER BY without the use of the TOP predicate? The answer is that with TOP we can define the exact number of employees to appear in the result set. The ASC keyword is not used with the ORDER BY clause here because it is assumed by default in Access.

Code:

```
SELECT TOP 5 lastname, firstname, title
FROM SalesReps
ORDER BY lastname
```

Result:

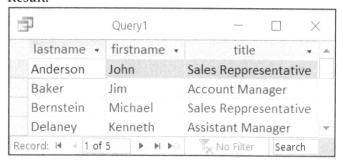

150. The TOP predicate with ORDER BY and dates

Find the 5 most recently hired employees

Discussion:

The TOP predicate is extremely useful when used with dates. In this example, we are looking for the five most recently hired employees in the corporation. We use the DESC keyword with ORDER BY to obtain this result. The DESC keyword will provide us with the latest dates. We could have used the ASC keyword to retrieve the 5 most senior employees of the corporation.

Code:

```
SELECT TOP 5 lastname, firstname, DateofHire
FROM SalesReps
ORDER BY DateofHire DESC
```

Result:

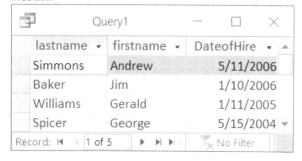

151. The TOP predicate with the GROUP BY clause

Retrieve the 10 largest orders from customers

Discussion:

Let us assume that our manager wants to see the 10 largest orders received from our customers. One somewhat crude way to prepare this report would be to calculate order subtotals (multiply the quantity of each product with its price) for all of the products contained in one order and do a GROUP BY on the orderid, followed by SORT DESC to get on top of the recordset of the largest orders. This way, we get what we need, but the whole affair is a mess. In addition, we get all of the orders we have, which might be a very long list for a printout.

Let us start by assuming that we only have two orders to work with (1 and 2 in the table below). We also notice that order number 1 contains three products, and order number 2 contains two products.

We also see the product quantities our customers ordered in the "Quantity" field, as well as the corresponding product prices that we extended to the customers. By the way, the product prices that we finally extended to the customers can be different from the prices in our catalog, which we store in the products table.

ProductsOrders			
OrderID	ProductID	UnitPrice	Quantity
1	1	15	2
1	2	12	3
1	3	18	5
2	1	15	2
2	3	18	8

Code:
SELECT orderid, Sum((([unitprice]*[quantity])) AS orderamount
FROM ProductsOrders
GROUP BY orderid
ORDER BY Sum((([unitprice]*[quantity])) DESC

When using the code above, the database will first multiply the UnitPrice with the Quantity for each product. This temporary calculation is shown in the table below so that you know how the database thinks.

ProductsOrders				
OrderID	ProductID	UnitPrice	Quantity	Temp
1	1	15	2	30
1	2	12	3	36
1	3	18	5	90
2	1	15	2	30
2	3	18	8	144

Then, the database calculates the total (SUM) for each order (this is due to the GROUP BY clause on the ORDERID). Since we have two orders, the grouping looks like the table below. The OrderAmount is an alias or a name that we gave to the calculated field.

OrderID	OrderAmount
1	156
2	174

Still however, we gave another command to the database: to ORDER BY the largest order. The database then shows the following result since 174 is larger than 156.

OrderID	OrderAmount
2	174
1	156

At this point, we are able to get a report of the biggest orders, but we still have a problem with the above code. All of the orders will appear. As you can see from the figure below, 919 orders appear even though we only need to see the 10 largest.

Result:

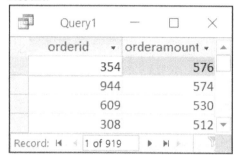

Let us see how we can quickly get the results we need by using the TOP clause.

Code:

```
SELECT TOP 10 orderid, Sum((([unitprice]*[quantity])) AS orderamount
FROM ProductsOrders
GROUP BY orderid
ORDER BY Sum((([unitprice]*[quantity])) DESC
```

Result:

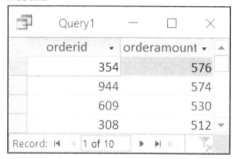

152. The TOP predicate with calculated fields and WHERE

Get the largest sales for a particular product

Discussion:

In this scenario, we have been asked to prepare a report that contains the 15 largest orders for a particular product—for example "Almonds, Roasted and Salted - 18 oz. Bag" (the product with productid = 2). As you can see from the code we use a calculated field by which we also sort results to get the top ten records we need.

Code:

```
SELECT TOP 10 orderid, productid, (unitprice*quantity) AS OrderAmount
FROM ProductsOrders
WHERE (productid=2)
ORDER BY (unitprice*quantity) DESC
```

Result:

orderid	productid	OrderAmount
764	2	90
379	2	90
314	2	90
978	2	90

Record: ◄ ◄ 1 of 14 ► ►I ►* | No Filter

CHAPTER 14 DISCUSSION QUESTIONS

1. What is the primary role of the TOP predicate?
2. What is the difference between TOP and TOP PERCENT?
3. What other predicates similar to TOP can be used to manipulate the number of rows retrieved?
4. Is TOP a required predicate or an optional one?
5. What is the default predicate if we do not specify one in the SQL statement?
6. Why TOP is not useful by itself?
7. What other SQL keywords can we use with TOP to retrieve useful results?
8. Where in the SELECT statement do we place the TOP predicate?
9. What do we need to pay attention to when using TOP?
10. What are some data types with which we can use TOP?

154. **CHAPTER 14 HANDS-ON EXERCISES**

Chapter 14 Case 1:

Create a new Access database and name it Chapter14_1.accdb. Copy the tables Customers, Orders, and Products from the PracticeDatabase.accdb and paste them to Chapter14_1.accdb.

1. The inventory people ask for a list of five products with the highest quantities per unit. Create a new query that includes the ProductName, QuantityPerUnit, and ProductUnitPrice fields and satisfies the inventory department request. Save the query as Qry1_QuantityPerUnit.

Your result should look like:

productname	QuantityPerUnit	ProductUnitPrice
Coconut Chocolate Chip Cookies	35	25
Chocolate Covered Cherries in 8 oz. Bag	35	37
Dark Chocolate Apricots in 20 oz. Bag	35	46
Dried Bluberries - 6oz.	35	26
Chocolate Chip Brownie	35	30
Roasted & Salted Almonds	35	19
Coconut Flavour Cream Wafers 10 oz.	35	38

Record: 1 of 7   No Filter   Search

2. The inventory people are back asking for a list that will display the top 15% of products with the highest product unit prices. Create a query that includes the ProductName, QuantityPerUnit, UnitsInStock, and ProductUnitPrice fields and satisfies the inventory request. Save the query as Qry2_ProductPrices.

Your result should look like:

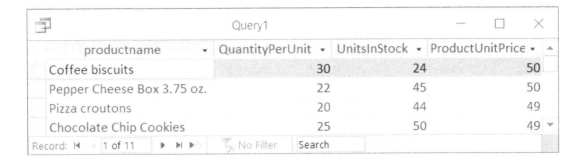

3. The marketing department is asking for a list of the 10 most recently placed orders. Create a query that includes the OrderID, CustomerID, OrderDate, and ShippingCost that satisfies this request and save it as Qry3_RecentOrders.

Your result should look like:

OrderID ▾	CustomerID ▾	OrderDate ▾	ShippingCost ▾
4	165	12/19/2019	48
874	159	12/16/2019	39
165	120	12/14/2019	52
881	167	12/12/2019	44

Record: ◄ ◄ 1 of 10 ▶ ▶ ▶ No Filter Search

4. The sales department is looking for a list of the top ten products sorted by ProductName. They have many typos in the printed catalog and they want to see the entries in the database. Create a query that includes the ProductName, QuantityPerUnit, UnitsInStock, and ProductUnitPrice fields and satisfies this request. Save it as Qry4_ProductNames.

Your result should look like:

ProductName ▾	QuantityPerUnit ▾	UnitsInStock ▾	ProductUnitPrice ▾
All-Purpose Marinade I	24	27	29
All-Purpose Marinade II	30	26	39
Almonds, Hickory Smoked - 1	12	40	35
Almonds, Roasted and Salted	12	32	22

Record: ◄ ◄ 1 of 10 ▶ ▶ ▶ No Filter Search

5. The marketing department is asking for a list of the ten orders with the highest shipping cost. Customers have complained about shipping charges and there is an internal review in place now. Create a query that includes the OrderID, CustomerID, ShippedDate, and ShippingCost fields and satisfies this request. Save it as Qry5_ShippingCost. Why do we get fifty seven records instead of ten?

Your result should look like:

Chapter 14 Case 2:

Create a new Access database and name it Chapter14_2.accdb. Copy the tables Orders, SalesReps, and ProductsOrders from the PracticeDatabase.accdb and paste them to Chapter14_2.accdb.

1. The HR department is looking for a list of the five most senior employees in the organization. Create a query that includes the FirstName, LastName, Title, and DateOfHire fields and satisfies this request. Save the query as Qry1_Employees.

    Your result should look like:

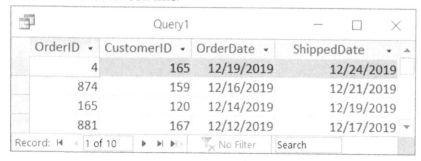

2. The sales department is looking for the ten most recently shipped orders. They have calls from customers that their orders have not arrived and they need to check shipments. Create a query that includes the OrderID, CustomerID, OrderDate, and ShippedDate fields and satisfies this request. Save it as Qry2_ShippedOrders.

    Your result should look like:

3. The marketing department has asked for a list of the 20 largest orders from our customers. Create a query that includes the OrderID, and a calculated field named OrderAmount and satisfies this request. Save the query as Qry3_20LargestOrders.

Your result should look like:

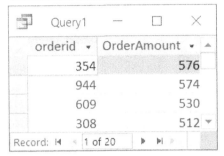

4. The marketing department is now asking for a report of the 20 largest orders for a particular product: California Original Pistachios - 1 lb. Bag. Create a query that includes the OrderID, the ProductID, and a calculated field named OrderAmount and satisfies this request. Save it as Qry4_CaliforniaPistachios.

Your result should look like:

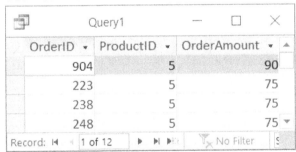

5. The HR department is preparing for the employee of the year event and has asked for a list of the 3 sales representatives with the most orders. Create a query that includes the SalesRepID field, and a calculated field using the count() function that satisfies this request. Save the query as Qry5_SalesReps.

Your result should look like:

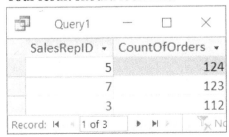

CHAPTER 15
CALCULATED FIELDS

Calculated fields are temporary columns created using arithmetic operators such as (+, *, -, /, ^, Mod). You can use calculated fields in tables, queries, forms, and reports. However, it is not a good practice to use calculated fields in tables. The third normal form rule of normalization says that all attributes should depend on the key. That is, all table fields need to be related to the entity they describe. That is, all customer fields need to be connected to the CustomerID PK field. A calculation used in a table is an ever changing attribute for the entity and this causes lot of trouble. In addition, a calculated field in a table cannot be indexed which creates additional problems by making the table slower. The most appropriate place for calculated fields are queries, not even forms or reports.

You can create calculated fields in a variety of ways. For instance, you can multiply a numeric field by a certain number or a certain percentage or you can multiply two numeric fields themselves. You can multiply two fields and divide the result by another field. You can also create calculated fields conditionally by using the iif() and switch() functions. You can also generate powerful pieces of information by using calculated fields with aggregate functions. Of course, you can use calculated fields in a query with the WHERE clause so that your calculations are applied only to a subset of records. You can also use calculated fields in the HAVING clause in a GROUP BY statement for filtering records after the aggregations from the GROUP BY clause are completed. Finally, you can use calculated fields with UPDATE statements to change hundreds or thousands of records instantly. The applications of calculated fields in databases are essential, and in this chapter, we will present you with multiple examples. However, we will deal with numeric calculations only. I have devoted two additional chapters on operations with dates and strings so that you can explore each in detail. The arithmetic operators available in Access appear in the following table:

Operator	Meaning
+	Addition
*	Multiplication
-	Subtraction
/	Division
^	Exponential
mod	Remainder

155.   Add a number to a numeric field
Create a product catalog with updated prices on the fly
Discussion:
The business goal here is to create a new product catalog that will appear on the corporate website for a promotional campaign. Management does not want the product prices in the underlying products table to change since this campaign will last only two weeks. We can create a query using the SQL code below to add $2 to the price of each product and use it as the data source for our web catalog.

Code:

SELECT productname, productunitprice + 2 AS ProductPrice
FROM Products

Result:

156.   Add a percentage to a numeric field

Update product prices on the fly by a certain percentage

Discussion:

This time, due to increased replenishment costs (receiving goods from suppliers), our manager tells us to add a 2% markup for the product catalog we are sending out this month.

Code:

SELECT productname, productunitprice * (1.02) as ProductPrice
FROM Products

Result:

157.   Add two numeric columns

Calculate product inventory quantities

Discussion:

Management is asking for a report of product inventory quantities. Specifically, they want to know not only what units we have in the warehouse but how many are on order as well. To answer this request, we create a new column named TotalUnits, which is simply the sum of the units that we have in stock and the ones we have on order that have not arrived yet.

Code:

SELECT productname, unitsinstock, unitsonorder,

(unitsinstock + unitsonorder)

AS TotalUnits

FROM products

Result:

productname	unitsinstock	unitsonorder	TotalUnits
California Original Pistachios - 1 lb. Bag	35	0	35
Choice Apricots - 16 oz. Bag	22	0	22
Cran Raisin Mix in 17 oz. Bag	24	0	24
Dried Blueberries - 1 lb. Bag	28	0	28

Query1 — Record: 1 of 70   No Filter   Search

158.   Multiply two columns and group their results

Calculate totals by order

Discussion:

The request this time is to calculate order totals for all of the orders that we have had to date. Each order might contain multiple products with multiple quantities for each product. We first need to multiply product prices with quantities for every product in each order and sum the results. Then, we need to group by OrderID so that we can obtain the total for every order. A sample data set on which to make these calculations appears below. The order with OrderID = 1, contains three different products with prices of 15, 12, and 18 and quantities of 2, 3, and 5 respectively. We need to first multiply the product unit price times the quantity for each product, get the subtotals, and sum up the results for each order.

ProductsOrders			
OrderID	ProductID	UnitPrice	Quantity
1	1	15	2
1	2	12	3
1	3	18	5
2	1	15	2
2	3	18	8

Code:

SELECT OrderID, Sum([UnitPrice]*[quantity]) AS OrderSubtotal

FROM ProductsOrders

GROUP BY OrderID

Result:

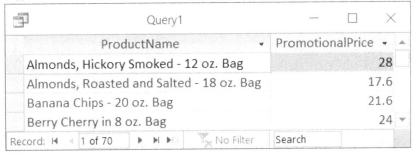

159. Subtract a percentage from a numeric column

Provide customers with a 20% discount on every product

Discussion:

Management decided to aggressively sell this month, and they have initiated a promotional campaign with a price discount of 20% for every product in the product catalog. We need to create a new product catalog, which the company wants to send out immediately. We can easily respond to this request using a calculated field as is shown in the code below:

Code:

```
SELECT ProductName, ProductUnitPrice * (1-0.2) as PromotionalPrice
FROM Products
```

Result:

ProductName	PromotionalPrice
Almonds, Hickory Smoked - 12 oz. Bag	28
Almonds, Roasted and Salted - 18 oz. Bag	17.6
Banana Chips - 20 oz. Bag	21.6
Berry Cherry in 8 oz. Bag	24

Record: 1 of 70 — No Filter — Search

160. Use calculated fields with the WHERE clause

Provide customers with a 20% discount on specific products

Discussion:

Since a 20% discount is too much to provide for every product, management has decided to apply it only on products from suppliers with SupplierID 1 and 4. We can quickly change the product catalog to:

Code:

```
SELECT ProductName, ProductUnitPrice * (1-0.2) as PromotionalPrice
FROM Products
WHERE supplierid = 1 or supplierid = 4
```

Result:

ProductName	PromotionalPrice
Almonds, Hickory Smoked - 12 oz. Bag	28
Almonds, Roasted and Salted - 18 oz. Bag	17.6
Banana Chips - 20 oz. Bag	21.6
Berry Cherry in 8 oz. Bag	24

Record: 1 of 16   No Filter   Search

161. Calculated fields with multiple conditions using switch()

Provide customers with different discounts based on the product supplier

Discussion:

The previous scenario of providing product discounts by filtering on supplier ids is fine for some cases, but it also has two major drawbacks. First, the same discount rate is applied to every supplier included in the WHERE clause. Second, discount rates can be applied only to suppliers included in the WHERE clause. In some cases, we might want to provide different discount rates for each supplier and include all products from all suppliers in the result set. Suppose we want to provide a 20% discount for products from SupplierID=1, 15% for those from SupplierID=2, 18% for those from SupplierID=3, and 25% for those from SupplierID=4. In addition, we might want to provide a 10% discount for all of the rest of the products regardless of supplier. The switch function comes to the rescue here, providing the flexibility to give us the results we need.

Code:

```
SELECT productname,
SWITCH(
SupplierID = 1,        ProductUnitPrice*(1-0.2),
SupplierID = 2,        ProductUnitPrice*(1-0.15),
SupplierID = 3,        ProductUnitPrice*(1-0.18),
SupplierID = 4,        ProductUnitPrice*(1-0.25),
TRUE,                  ProductUnitPrice*(1-0.1)
)
AS ProductPrice
FROM Products
```

Result:

productname	ProductPrice
Almonds, Hickory Smoked - 12 oz. Bag	28
Almonds, Roasted and Salted - 18 oz. Bag	17.6
Banana Chips - 20 oz. Bag	21.6
Berry Cherry in 8 oz. Bag	24

Record: 1 of 70   No Filter   Search

162.   How to use calculated fields with the iif() function
Determine employee bonus eligibility
Discussion:
In this example, we are looking for sales representatives who are eligible for a bonus. To be eligible for a bonus, a sales rep needs to have accumulated sales of $5,000 or more for the year. The SQL code in this example is long but easy. First, notice that we use three fields only: LastName, Bonus, and OrderDate. We use the OrderDate field to filter orders for 2014 only. Then, we use the lastname field with a GROUP BY clause to display results by employee name. The last field is that of the Bonus. Here, we use the iif() function with the syntax iif (expression, result if expression is true, result if expression is false) to actually make the calculations and determine bonus eligibility:

IIf(Sum([unitprice]*[quantity])>5000,"Bonus","No Bonus") AS Bonus

The iif() function above reads: If the total amount of orders serviced by the sales rep exceeds $5,000, give the sales rep a bonus. Otherwise, no bonus. The AS part means display this field name as "Bonus". Do not pay attention to the joins in this example since we only use them to get fields from three different tables. For a full overview of joins, see chapter 30.

Code:
```
SELECT SalesReps.LastName, IIf(Sum([unitprice]*[quantity])>5000,"Bonus","No Bonus") AS
Bonus
FROM
(SalesReps INNER JOIN Orders ON SalesReps.SalesRepID = Orders.SalesRepID) INNER
JOIN ProductsOrders ON Orders.OrderID = ProductsOrders.OrderID

WHERE (((Orders.OrderDate) Between #1/1/2017# AND #12/31/2017#))

GROUP BY SalesReps.LastName
```

Result:

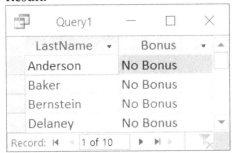

163.   Use calculated fields with GROUP BY and aggregate functions
Calculate total discount amounts by order
Discussion:
This time, we have a request to provide a report that will show the total discount amount for each order. Remember that each order might contain multiple products. In addition, for each product in the same order, we might have provided a different discount rate. Our goal is to calculate the discount amount for each product in each order and sum the results. To achieve this task, we will use the ProductsOrders table, which includes the unitprice (the one finally extended to the customer, not the

171

one in the products table used for the product catalog), the quantity of each product, and the discount rate for each product. A sample from the table with two orders appears below:

ProductsOrders				
OrderID	ProductID	UnitPrice	Quantity	Discount
1	1	15	2	20%
1	2	12	3	0
1	3	18	5	15%
2	1	15	2	10%
2	3	18	8	15%

For each product in an order, we need to multiply the unit price by the quantity to get the amount invoiced for that product. Then, we multiply the result by the discount rate to get the total discount for each product in each order. Then, we sum all of the discount amounts in each order. Finally, we group by OrderID so that we get the total discount amount by order.

Code:

```
SELECT OrderID, Sum((([UnitPrice]*[Quantity])*[Discount]) AS OrderDiscount
FROM ProductsOrders
GROUP BY OrderID
```

Result:

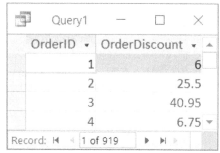

164. Use a calculated field with an aggregate function

Calculate the average discount amount for all orders

Discussion:

Our business goal is to find the average discount amount we have given away for all of our orders. Discounts are excellent, but we need to keep track of them and evaluate them on a continuous basis. Fortunately, we can do this in no time by simply using the AVG (average) function to get the average amount from all the orders.

Code:

```
SELECT Avg((([UnitPrice]*[Quantity])*[Discount]) AS AverageOrderDiscount
FROM ProductsOrders
```

Result:

Then, we can compare the above result with the actual average order amount using the code below. Now, we can make the conclusion that an average $9 discount for an average total order of $58 is an acceptable discount rate.

Code:
SELECT Avg([UnitPrice]*[Quantity]) AS AverageOrderAmount
FROM ProductsOrders

Result:

I know you noticed the number of decimals in the results above. We can decrease the number of decimals or eliminate them altogether by using a type conversion function. Actually, calculated fields are extensively used with type conversion functions to format numbers in the most appropriate way. Here, we use the cInt() function to convert the decimal number to an integer. For the full range of type conversion functions, read chapter 25, where they are explained in detail.

Code:
SELECT cInt(Avg([UnitPrice]*[Quantity])) AS AverageOrderAmount
FROM ProductsOrders

Result:

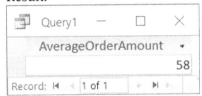

165. Use a calculated field with an aggregate function and WHERE

Calculate the average discount amount for specific orders

Discussion:

Knowing the average discount amount for all of our orders is excellent, but we might want to ask for the average discount amount provided for our customers in the city of Boston. We can easily isolate discount amounts for any city by using multi-table queries like the one below:

Code:

SELECT Avg((([UnitPrice]*[Quantity])*[Discount]) AS AverageOrderDiscount
FROM Customers
INNER JOIN (Orders INNER JOIN ProductsOrders ON Orders.OrderID =
ProductsOrders.OrderID) ON Customers.CustomerID = Orders.CustomerID
WHERE Customers.City='Boston'

Result:

AverageOrderDiscount ▾
7.60876288659794

Record: I◄ ◄ 1 of 1 ► ►I ▷

166. Storing the results of calculated fields with SELECT INTO

Storing total order amounts in a separate table

Discussion:

Sometimes, we might want to store the results of our calculations in a backup, archive, or temporary table. This is easy to achieve using SELECT INTO statements that were covered in the SELECT chapter. Storing results of calculated fields in production tables is not a good idea because these fields will interfere with normalization rules. However, for archiving purposes, we can go ahead.

In this example, we take the OrderID and OrderTotal fields from the ProductsOrders table and transfer their records in a new table named ArchivedOrders. Of course, the OrderTotal field is calculated from three different fields in the ProductsOrders table.

Code:

SELECT OrderID, SUM((unitprice*Quantity)*(1-Discount)) AS OrderTotal
INTO ArchivedOrders
FROM ProductsOrders
GROUP BY OrderID

Result:

The database will first ask you if you want to go ahead.

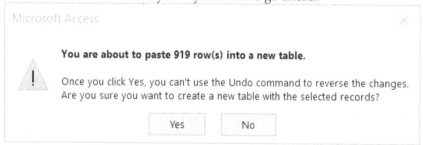

Microsoft Access ×

⚠ **You are about to paste 919 row(s) into a new table.**

Once you click Yes, you can't use the Undo command to reverse the changes.
Are you sure you want to create a new table with the selected records?

Yes   No

Then, in the objects pane, we can see the new table with a name exactly as we defined it in the SQL code.

167.   CHAPTER 15 DISCUSSION QUESTIONS

1. What is the goal of calculated fields in Access?
2. Is it a good idea to use calculated fields in tables? Why? Why not?
3. Why knowledge of the usage of calculated fields affects the design of the database?
4. What is the purpose of arithmetic operators in Access?
5. How many arithmetic operators do we have in Access?
6. What is the best object (table, query, form, report) in which to use calculated fields?
7. How can we create calculated fields conditionally?
8. What is the difference between the iif() and switch() functions?
9. Why does it make perfect sense to use calculated fields with UPDATE statements?
10. Can we use calculated fields with the WHERE and HAVING clauses? What is the difference?

168.   CHAPTER 15 HANDS-ON EXERCISES

Chapter 15 Case 1:

Create a new Access database and name it Chapter15_1.accdb. Copy the tables Products, Suppliers, and ProductsOrders from the PracticeDatabase.accdb and paste them to Chapter15_1.accdb.

1. The sales people embark on a sales effort for the next two days and they want all the product prices decreased by 20%. The new product catalog will be valid for only two days. Then, the prices will go back to normal. Create a new query that includes the ProductName and the new price field and satisfies the sales people request. Save the query as Qry1_Price20Percent.

Your result should look like:

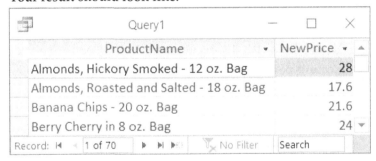

2. The accounts payable unit is conducting an internal audit and they are looking for product prices by item. That is, you need to divide the productunitprice by QuantityPerUnit to arrive at item prices so that accounts payable can better assess supplier prices. Create a new query that includes the ProductName, ProductUnitPrice, and QuantityPerUnit fields and satisfies the accounts payable request. Save the query as Qry2_AccountsPayable.

Your result should look like:

175

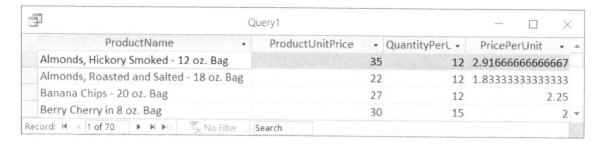

3. The marketing people need to print a new product catalog with prices decreased by 15% for the following suppliers: American Foods, LLC, Berkley Bakery Co., Nature's Food, Inc., and Old York Foods, Inc. Create a new query that includes the ProductName, ProductUnitPrice, and QuantityPerUnit fields and satisfies the marketing request. Hint: First identify the SupplierID from the suppliers table and then use the switch() function. The new report should contain the products from all suppliers. Save the query as Qry3_SpecificSuppliers. Sort results by ProductName ascending.

Your result should look like:

4. Accounts payable is back and they need to verify the payments they are supposed to extend to suppliers. They are asking for a report that includes all open requisitions. To achieve this you need to multiply UnitsOnOrder by ProductUnitPrice to find out how much we have to pay. Create a new query that includes the ProductName, ProductUnitPrice, QuantityPerUnit, and UnitsOnOrder fields and satisfies the accounts payable request. Save the query as Qry4_PendingPayments.

Your result should look like:

ProductName	ProductUnitPrice	QuantityPerUnit	UnitsOnOrde	OutstandingPayments
Almonds, Hickory Smoked - 12 oz. Bag	35	12	5	175
Almonds, Roasted and Salted - 18 oz. B	22	12	0	0
Banana Chips - 20 oz. Bag	27	12	0	0
Berry Cherry in 8 oz. Bag	30	15	0	0

Record: ◄ ◄ 1 of 70 ► ►► No Filter   Search

5. The order processing unit from the sales department is asking for a report that will list the total order amount by ProductID. Create a new query on the ProductsOrders table that contains the ProductID and a calculated field and satisfies the sales people request. Include the extended

discount in your calculations. Save the query as Qry5_OrderTotalsByProduct.

Your result should look like:

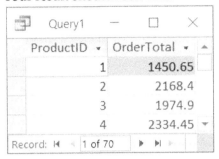

Chapter 15 Case 2:

Create a new Access database and name it Chapter15_2.accdb. Copy the tables Products, ProductsOrders, SalesReps, and Suppliers from the PracticeDatabase.accdb and paste them to Chapter15_2.accdb.

1. The inventory people need a list of products that shows the difference between the quantities of units in stock minus the reorder levels. They need to see if we have any negative amounts which mean we need to order new products. Create a new query that includes the ProductName field and a calculated field named "UnitStatus" that satisfies the inventory people request. Sort results by ProductName ascending. Save the query as Qry1_ReorderLevelCheck.

   Your result should look like:

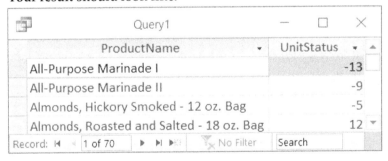

2. The inventory people responsible for replenishing are asking for a report that will show how many units they need to order for each product. Create a new query that includes the ProductName field and a calculated field named "UnitsToOrder" that satisfies the inventory people request. Sort results by ProductName ascending. Save the query as Qry2_UnitsToOrder.

   Your result should look like:

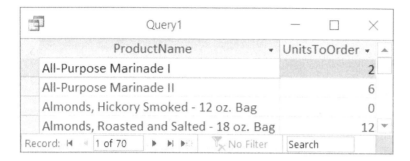

3. The marketing department is asking for a report of the total amount for each order (OrderTotal). Create a new query that includes the OrderID field and a calculated field named "OrderTotal" that satisfies the marketing people request. They want the discount given for each product to be taken into consideration for the total. Group orders by OrderID. Save the query as Qry3_OrderTotals.

    Your result should look like:

OrderID	OrderTotal
1	24
2	184.5
3	190.05
4	38.25

    Record: 1 of 919

4. The sales director feels the sales reps went over the limit in providing discounts for products in order to get the sale. So he wants a report that will ignore the sales people discount if it is more than 15% and replace it with a discount of exactly 15%. Create a new query that includes the fields OrderID, ProductID, and Discount from the ProductsOrders table as well as a logical calculated field named "AdjustedDiscount" that meets the sales director request. Name the query Qry4_AdjustedDiscount. Hint: Use the iff() function.

    Your result should look like:

OrderID	ProductID	UnitPrice	Discount	AdjustedDiscount
1	61	15	0.2	0.15
2	23	15	0.15	0.15
2	24	15	0.2	0.15
2	32	15	0	0

    Record: 1 of 2411

5. The marketing director wants to initiate a new campaign of generous discounts to customers. She just received a memo that the following suppliers have now discounted their products with the percentage shown: Home of Snacks, 25%, Mediterranean Foods, LLC, 20%, Nature's Food, Inc.,

30%, and Old York Foods, Inc., 30%. The marketing manager wants to pass 80% of the wholesale discount we received to the customers. For all other products, prices will remain the same. Create a new query that contains the productname field and a calculated field named "NewProductPrice" and satisfies the marketing director request. Name the query Qry5_ProductDiscounts. Hint: First identify the suppliers from the supplier table. Then calculate 80% of the supplier discount and finally use the switch() function.

Your result should look like:

productname	NewProductPrice
Almonds, Hickory Smoked - 12 oz. Bag	28
Almonds, Roasted and Salted - 18 oz. Bag	17.6
Banana Chips - 20 oz. Bag	21.6
Berry Cherry in 8 oz. Bag	24

Record: 1 of 70 No Filter Search

CHAPTER 16
CONCATENATED FIELDS

Concatenating fields means nothing more than displaying the contents of two or more columns in one. The operation of concatenation happens through a query on the fly, and the resulting column and its contents are not saved in the underlying table. There are no special arithmetical or logical calculations involved. Simply put, if we want a query or report to display the contents of the first and last name fields as one, we just concatenate the two fields. Though the concept sounds simple, its applicability in every day work tasks is indispensable.

Concatenation in databases can achieve much more than simply displaying the contents of two or more columns together. We can create mailing labels, write letters with the correct punctuation, combine field data with plain text, perform conditional concatenation based on the values of any field, and use string and other functions for truly powerful results.

To concatenate fields in MS Access, we can use the "&" character or the "+" character. Since the "+" character is the one used with most databases, we will be using this one for our examples.

169.   Column concatenation without spaces
Put all customer address information in one field
Discussion:
Suppose we have a job to create mailing labels for letters to our suppliers. My experience indicates that most people will go to Word, connect to Access or Excel, and go through multiple steps and a painful process to achieve this task. There is no need to go to this trouble since we can easily achieve this task using Access alone. There are two steps we need to follow: First, we create a query, namely qry_suppliers_labels, with a field that concatenates values from the address, city, state, and zip fields from the suppliers table. Second, we create a report based on this query to format our data to the label size we want. This is it—we are done forever.

Why? Because let's say in the future, we need to create mailing labels only for a subset of our suppliers in the city of Boston or in the state of California. We can just modify our qry_suppliers_labels and enter any criteria we need. Then, we can just run our report again. If we need to create labels of different sizes, it will take a few seconds to modify our report and get the label sizes we need.

We will see you how to use punctuation and spaces for formatting our concatenated columns so that we can do everything in Access. In this example, we create a simple concatenation of four fields. Using this code, there will be no spaces between the field values in the result set.

Code:
```
SELECT  (address+city+state+zip) AS FullAddress
FROM Customers
```

which is the same as

SELECT (address&city&state&zip) AS FullAddress
FROM Customers

Result:

As you can see, the four fields are concatenated into one. However, the data is cramped in a continuous string of characters. We need to add spaces between the fields so that we can easily read them and print the results in a way that will make sense to USPS.

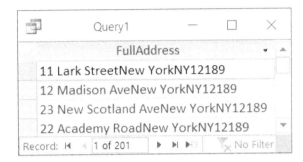

170. Column concatenation with spaces

Put all customer address information in one field with spaces between values

Discussion:

In this example, we just add spaces between the concatenated columns. We use single quotes with a space between them to achieve this output.

Code:

SELECT (address +' '+ city +' '+ state +' '+ zip) AS FullAddress
FROM Customers

Result:

171. Concatenation of columns and text

Writing customer letters in Access

Discussion:

What if we would like to write a letter using a database? We can indeed combine plain text with field data with enough flexibility to write automatic letters! There is a sample letter below. The SELECT statement is practically one field named "CustomerLetter".

Access Code:
SELECT 'Dear' + ' '+ (lastname + ' ' + firstname) +'.' + ' '+ 'It is our pleasure to announce that we reviewed your resume, and we have set up an interview time for you. Can you please verify that your address is' + ' ' + (address +' '+ City +' '+ State +' '+ Zip) + ' ' + 'to send you corporate policy details and directions?' AS CustomerLetter
FROM Customers

Result:

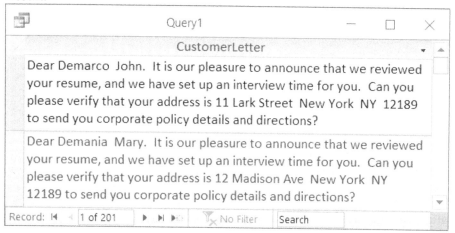

172.   Use the left() string function with concatenated fields
Displaying only the first letter from the customers' first names.
Discussion:

Let us assume we want to write a letter, but instead of using the complete first name of the customer, we only want the first letter to appear. We can achieve this result by using string (text) functions. In this example, we use the left() function, but we can use anyone that suits our needs. (There is a whole chapter on string functions to which you can refer for details). The left function in this example will extract the first character from the first name field.

Code:
SELECT 'Dear' + ' '+ (lastname + ' ' + left(firstname, 1)) +'.' + ' '+ 'Please complete the enclosed forms so that we can ship your order to your country.' AS CustomerLetter
FROM Customers

Result:

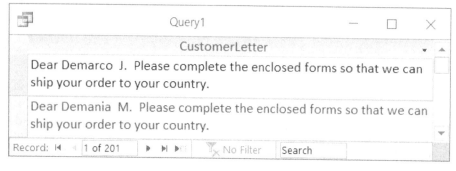

173.   Use the ucase() string function with concatenated fields

Uppercasing customer last names

Discussion:

This is an additional example of using a string function in conjunction with concatenated columns. Consult chapter 26 regarding text and string operations. Our goal here is to have the last name of our customers capitalized.

Code:

```
SELECT 'Dear' + ' '+ (ucase(lastname)) + ' ' + firstname +'.' + ' ' + "Please complete the enclosed
forms so that we can ship your order to your State." AS CustomerLetter
FROM Customers
```

Result:

174.   Use concatenated fields with criteria

Send letters to a select group of customers

Discussion:

The goal behind this example is to show that we can use additional fields in a query with concatenated fields to sort and filter data. This way, we have total control to retrieve exactly the records we want for concatenation. In this particular example, we restrict the output to customers from the city of Boston.

Code:

```
SELECT 'Dear' + ' '+ (ucase(lastname)) + ' ' + (ucase(firstname)) +'.' + ' ' + 'Please complete the
enclosed forms so that we can ship your order to your state.' AS CustomerLetter, city
FROM customers
WHERE city = 'Boston'
```

Result:

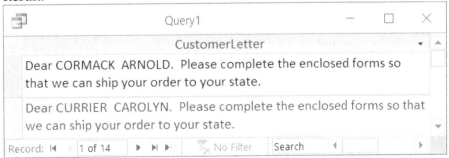

175. Using commas, periods, and other characters

Use correct punctuation with concatenated columns

Discussion:

Commas, periods, question marks, and other punctuation characters can become a pain when constructing concatenated fields. The answer is to enclose them in quotes. In addition, if they come right after or before the concatenated field, we need to use the + character as well. For example, notice the period, in both statements below at the end of the parenthesis of the first name.

This will work: SELECT (lastname) + ' ' + (firstname) + '.' FROM Customers

This will not work: SELECT (lastname) + ' ' + (firstname) '.' FROM Customers

Code:

SELECT (lastname) + ' ' + (firstname) + '.' AS CustomerName
FROM Customers

Result:

176. Conditional concatenation with the iif() function

Concatenating supplier fields using state as a condition

Discussion:

Sometimes, we do not apply the same concatenation rules for all of the records in the query. For example, we might want to create a certain label or letter for suppliers in NY and a different label or letter for everyone else, all in the same query. We can absolutely do this by using the iif() and switch() conditional functions. However, someone might ask why we need to do this and not use simple criteria in the query. First, in databases, we can achieve the same task in multiple different ways. There is always another less time-consuming and more effective way. Second, in this case, if we use a simple criterion such as (state = 'NY'), we only get the suppliers in NY. What we want is to send two different letters—one formatted for the state of NY and one for everyone else within the same query!

Using the iif(condition, true, false) function below, we tell the database to concatenate the CompanyName, ContacTtitle, and ContactName fields if the state is NY. If it is not, we tell the database to concatenate only the ContactTitle and ContactName fields. This way, we can create two different sets of labels in the same query.

Code:

```
SELECT iif((([State]='NY'),[Companyname]+' '+[ContactTitle]+' '+[Contactname],
[ContactTitle]+' '+[Contactname]) AS MailTo
FROM Suppliers
```

Result:

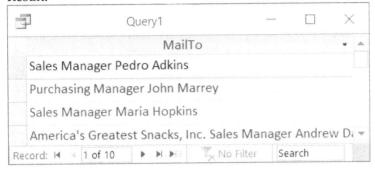

177.   More powerful conditional concatenation with the switch() function
Concatenating supplier columns different for each city
Discussion:

Now that we know conditional concatenation is possible, what if we want to create different letters for suppliers based on the city where they reside? Notice in the suppliers table that there are three cities: Boston, New York, and Dallas. Our task is to create a different letter for suppliers in each city using the same query. We can use the switch() function as shown below:

Code:

```
SELECT
SWITCH(
[city]= 'Boston',        'Dear' +' '+ [contactname]+',' +' '+ 'for our current sale we offer a 25%
discount in' +' '+ [city] ,
[city] ='Dallas',        'Dear' +' '+ [contactname]+',' +' '+ 'for our current sale we offer a 10%
discount in' +' '+ [city] ,
[city] ='New York',    'Dear' +' '+ [contactname]+',' +' '+ 'for our current sale we offer a 20%
discount in' +' '+ [city] ,
)
AS SupplierLetter
FROM suppliers
```

Result:

178.   Conditional concatenation with the switch(), left(), and instr() functions
Concatenate supplier fields conditionally for each city
Discussion:

In the previous example, we saw how to use the switch() function to create a different letter for suppliers based on the city where they reside. However, we used the full name of the supplier since the ContactName field in the suppliers table contains both the first and last names of the supplier. This time, we would like to send a more personal letter to them by using only the first name. This means that we need to extract the first name from the ContactName field. First, we use the instr() function to find the position of the space between the first and last name strings in the ContactName field. Then, we use the left function to extract the firstname characters from the beginning of the field up to the position of the space that we have identified using instr(). The whole SQL statement is shown below. As you can see in the result set, only the first names of the suppliers appear now.

Code:
```
SELECT
SWITCH(
[city]= 'Boston',        'Dear' +' '+ left(contactname, InStr(1,contactname," ")-1)
+',' +' '+ 'for our current sale we offer a 25% discount in' +' '+ [city] ,

[city] ='Dallas',        'Dear' +' '+ left(contactname, InStr(1,contactname," ")-1) +',' +' '+ 'for our
current sale we offer a 10% discount in' +' '+ [city] ,

[city] ='New York',    'Dear' +' '+ left(contactname, InStr(1,contactname," ")-1) +',' +' '+ 'for our
current sale we offer a 20% discount in' +' '+ [city] ,
)
AS SupplierLetter
FROM suppliers
```

Result:

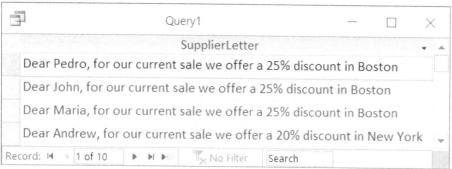

179. CHAPTER 16 DISCUSSION QUESTIONS

1. What is the goal of field concatenation?
2. How many fields can we concatenate? Two, three, or more?
3. What is the most common character for field concatenation in databases?
4. Is there any arithmetic involved in field concatenation?
5. In what Access objects is it a good idea to use concatenated fields?
6. Can we concatenate plain text with field data?
7. Could you name a few practical examples of field concatenation?
8. Why is it useful to use string functions with concatenated fields?
9. What do we need to pay attention to when we use commas, periods, and other characters with concatenated fields?
10. How many functions are available for conditional concatenation and what is the difference between them?

180. CHAPTER 16 HANDS-ON EXERCISES

Chapter 16 Case 1:

Create a new Access database and name it Chapter16_1.accdb. Copy the tables Customers and SalesReps from the PracticeDatabase.accdb and paste them to Chapter16_1.accdb.

1. The sales department is initiating a cross-selling campaign and is asking for mailing labels to send out to current customers. Create a new query that concatenates the FirstName, LastName, Address, City, State, and Zip fields from the customer table. Sort results by lastname ascending without including the lastname in the result set. Save the query as Qry1_MailingLabels.

   Your result should look like:

2. The sales department is asking again for mailing labels. This time they want only the first letter of the customer FirstName to appear in the label followed by a period. Create a new query that concatenates the FirstName, LastName, Address, City, State, and Zip fields from the customer table. Sort results by lastname ascending without including the lastname in the result set. Save the query as Qry2_MailingLabels_FirstCharacter.

187

Your result should look like:

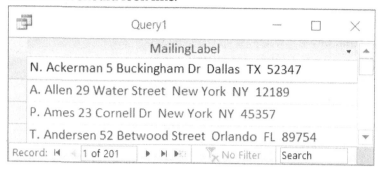

3. The HR department needs mailing labels to send out letters containing employee W-2s. Create a new query that concatenates the FirstName, LastName, Title, Address, City, State, and Zip fields from the SalesRep table. The FirstName, and LastName fields need to be capitalized. Sort results by lastname ascending without including the lastname in the result set. Save the query as Qry3_MailingLabels_Employees.

Your result should look like:

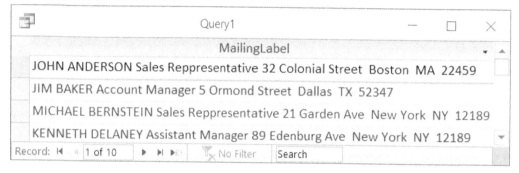

4. The marketing people want to send a mail card to customers announcing the availability of a new product line. The letter should be worded: Dear firstname, space lastname. Our company has just received a new line of products. If interested, please return this card and we will send you our new catalog at the following address (address space City space State space Zip). Create a new query that satisfies the request of the marketing people and sort results by lastname ascending without including lastname in the result set. Save the query as Qry4_CustomerLetter.

Your result should look like:

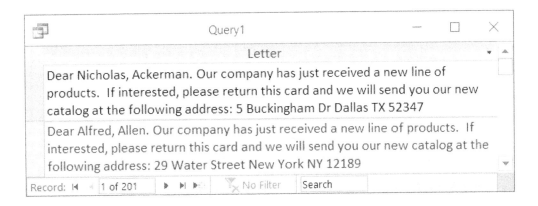

5. The sales people from the Boston office want to send a thank you letter to customers. For the customers in the city of Boston they want the mailing label to include the FirstName, Address, City, State, and Zip fields. For everyone else they want the label to include the FirstName, LastName, Address, City, State, and Zip fields. Create a new query that satisfies the marketing request. Sort results by lastname ascending without including the lastname in the result set. Save the query as Qry5_MailingLabelsCondition.

Your result should look like:

Chapter 16 Case 2:
Create a new Access database and name it Chapter16_2.accdb. Copy the tables Customers, SalesReps, and Suppliers from the PracticeDatabase.accdb and paste them to Chapter16_2.accdb.

1. The HR department needs mailing labels to send a letter to all employees in the organization. Create a new query that concatenates the Title, FirstName, LastName, Address, City, State, and Zip fields from the SalesReps table. Sort results by lastname ascending. Save the query as Qry1_MailingLabels.

Your result should look like:

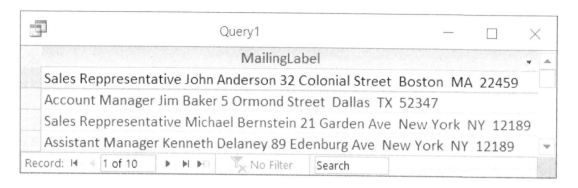

2. The director of inventory wants to send out a letter to suppliers asking for a reduction in their prices by 5%. The letter should be worded: "Dear [contactname], due to the recent downturn in the market we would like to ask for a 5% discount for the products we buy from you. Please let us know within the week if this is a possibility." Create a new query that satisfies the request of the inventory director, sort results by contactname ascending without including contactname in the result set. Save the query as Qry2_SupplierLetter.

Your result should look like:

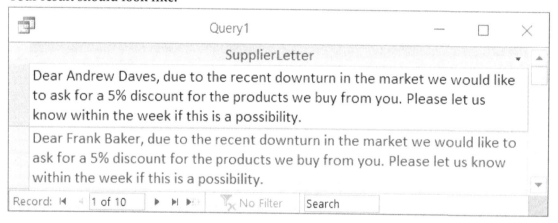

3. The president of the company wants to send out a letter of appreciation to employees hired before 12/31/2010 to invite them to a special evening dinner. The letter should be worded: "Dear [firstname], you are now working with us for more than ten years and the company highly appreciates your work and loyalty. You are invited to our family dinner this Friday night at 6:30 PM. Create a new query that satisfies the request of the president, sort results by lastname ascending without including lastname in the result set. Save the query as Qry3_SeniorEmployeeLetter.

Your result should look like:

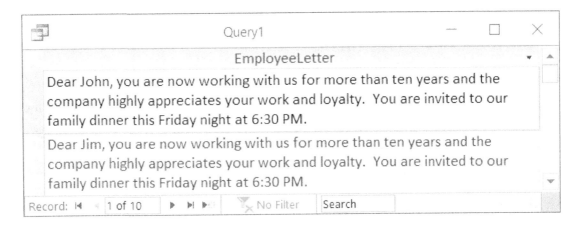

4. The sales director needs to send a letter to sales reps with information about upcoming events so that they can perform better in their sales quests. For each state the instructions are different but you need to create one SQL statement that contains all three letters. Specifically:

   a. For NY: Dear [firstname], Our major competitor cut prices by 15%. Cut our own prices by up to 20% but not more.

   b. For MA: Dear [firstname], Start introducing our new product immediately before any of our competitors enters the market with their own updated products.

   c. For TX: Dear [firstname], We were able to get significant discounts from our suppliers and as such try to increase market share by reducing our current price by 20% for the next two months.

   Create a new query that satisfies the request of the sales director, sort results by lastname ascending without including lastname in the result set. Save the query as Qry4_SalesRepsLetter.

   Your result should look like:

5. The marketing director wants to send a letter to customers announcing new discounts for next month. The letter should be worded: Dear [firstname], space [lastname]. For the next 30 days only, take the opportunity to obtain our product at the generous discount rate of [

   a. 15% for the customers in NY state

   b. 20% for the customer in Texas,

c. 25% for customers in Florida

d. 20% for California

].

Create a new query that satisfies the request of the marketing director and sort results by lastname ascending without including lastname in the result set. Limit the results of the query to contain only customers from the states of NY, TX, FL, and CA. Save the query as Qry5_CustomerDiscounts.

Your result should look like:

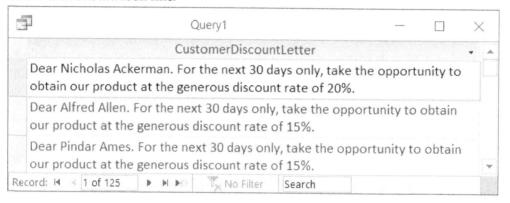

CHAPTER 17
THE GROUP BY CLAUSE

The GROUP BY clause is one of the foggiest keywords for both beginners and intermediate database professionals. Because of its intricacies, users and developers do not have a clear understanding of the circumstances when the GROUP BY clause is used. In this chapter, we have two goals: First, to understand in detail how and when the GROUP BY clause should be used, and second, to understand exactly what results to expect from it. The fundamental goal of the GROUP BY clause is to summarize data. The general syntax of the GROUP BY clause appears below but you do not need to memorize it since we will explore the role of each option in detail in the subsequent examples. Notice that in the statement below the WHERE, HAVING, and ORDER BY clauses are optional. However, we always need to use an aggregate function (sum, avg, min, max, etc.) in conjunction with the GROUP BY clause.

SELECT fields, aggregate function (field or calculated field)
FROM table
WHERE criteria (optional)
GROUP BY field(s)
HAVING criteria (optional)
ORDER BY field – (optional)

Before we do anything else, let's have a look at the table we prepared especially for this chapter. It is a simple table with only twelve records about customers and their orders. The goal is to run the GROUP BY examples on this table and give you the ability to do the calculations manually so that you know exactly how every result is obtained. The name of the table is tbls_customersgr.

LastName	OrderID	OrderDate	ProductName	UnitPrice	Quantity
Mahoney	502	8/3/2019	Roasted No-Salt Almonds	15	1
Mahoney	502	8/3/2019	Sesame Crackers in 20 oz. Pack	15	3
Mahoney	57	5/29/2017	Chocolate Chip Brownie	15	1
Mahoney	57	5/29/2017	Mushrooms Sauce	5	2
Mahoney	57	5/29/2017	Dark Chocolate Apricots in 20 oz. Ba	28	5
Martin	494	9/30/2018	Cream and honey biscuits	32	3
Martin	494	9/30/2018	Traditional Swedish Cookies, 5.25 oz	5	5
Riegert	1	11/6/2018	Dried Red Tart Cherries Gift Box - 6 (	15	2
Spicer	509	9/17/2018	All-Purpose Marinade II	15	2
Spicer	509	9/17/2018	Oatmeal Raisin Walnut Cookies	8	3
Spicer	509	9/17/2018	Corn Chips Bag	15	2
Spicer	509	9/17/2018	Dark Chocolate Apricots in 20 oz. Ba	28	3

Record: 1 of 12   No Filter   Search

First, notice that there are four customers in total. Second, Mr. Mahoney, ordered twice: orders 502 and 57. Third, the rest of the three customers have only one order each. Fourth, Mr. Riegert has one order with one product only, but he ordered two units of it. Fifth, orders 57, 494, 502, and 509 contain multiple products. Sixth, "Dark chocolate Apricots" is a product included in two orders (in 57 and 509). At this point, we are ready to go through our first example.

181.   The GROUP BY clause on one column and one aggregated field
Retrieve the total product units ordered by customer
Discussion:
In this scenario, the objective is to calculate the total product units ordered by each customer. There are only two fields used in the SQL code below. LastName is the field on which we apply the GROUP BY clause, and TotalUnits is the aggregated field that results from applying the sum() function on the Quantity column.

Code:
```
SELECT LastName, SUM(quantity) AS TotalUnits
FROM tbls_customersgr
GROUP BY LastName
```

Result:

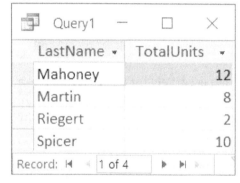

182.   The GROUP BY clause on one column and one aggregated-calculated field
Retrieve the total order amount by customer
Discussion:
In this scenario, we have a request from management to calculate the total order amounts by customer to create a list with our best customers. There are two fields used in the SQL code. LastName is the field on which we apply the GROUP BY clause. However, this time, the aggregation occurs on the result of the multiplication of unitprice * quantity to retrieve the total for each product in each order. Then we use the sum() function to present order totals by customer lastname.

Code:
```
SELECT LastName, SUM(unitprice*quantity) AS OrderTotal
FROM tbls_customersgr
GROUP BY LastName
```

Result:

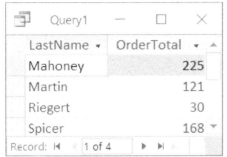

We see some interesting results here. First, since we grouped by customer last name, the result set produced four records, which is the exact number of unique customers we have in the tbls_customersgr table. We need to check the results to verify the database made the calculations correctly. We use Mahoney as an example.

LastName	Unit Price	Quantity	UnitPrice* Quantity
Mahoney	15	1	15
Mahoney	15	3	45
Mahoney	15	1	15
Mahoney	5	2	10
Mahoney	28	5	140
		SUM()	225

First, the database will do the multiplication of (unitprice * quantity) as we defined it in the calculated field named OrderTotal. This means that the database will multiply the price of each product ordered * its quantity ordered for all products in all orders for the particular customer. Then, it will simply SUM()results since we used the sum() function. Doing the calculations manually, we arrived at 225 for Mr. Mahoney, which is the same number the database produced for this customer.

183.   The GROUP BY clause on one column and two aggregated fields

Find total and average order amounts by customer

Discussion:

In this scenario, the goal is to produce a report that will show the total and average order amounts grouped by customer. There are three fields used in the SQL code: LastName, OrderTotal, and AvgOrder. The lastname is the field used with the GROUP BY clause. The fields OrderTotal and AvgOrder are the two aggregated fields.

Code:

```
SELECT lastname, SUM(unitprice*quantity) AS OrderTotal, AVG(unitprice*quantity) AS
AvgOrder
FROM tbls_customersgr
GROUP BY lastname
```

Result:

184. The GROUP BY clause on one column, one aggregated field, and WHERE

Find total order amounts for a subset of customers

Discussion:

Sometimes, we want to exclude certain records from our aggregate calculations. In these cases, we can use the WHERE clause to exclude records we are not interested in working with. Using WHERE, we exclude records before the GROUP BY clause takes effect. Therefore, if we have a source dataset with 3,000 records and use WHERE, the GROUP BY clause takes effect on the remaining records only. Later, you will learn the use of HAVING, which is a filtering statement like WHERE that takes effect after the GROUP BY calculates the summarized field values. Consequently, you need to know exactly what you want to do and use the appropriate filtering statement with GROUP BY.

In this example, we look for order totals by customer, but we want to exclude the orders from our customer Spicer. Mr. Spicer has only one order with orderid = 509. We use three fields in this SQL statement: Lastname, OrderTotal, and OrderID. LastName is the GROUP BY field, OrderTotal the aggregated field, and OrderID the filtering field.

Code:

```
SELECT LastName, SUM(unitprice*quantity) AS OrderTotal
FROM tbls_customersgr
WHERE orderid <> 509
GROUP BY LastName
```

Result:

LastName	OrderTotal
Mahoney	225
Martin	121
Riegert	30

Record: 1 of 3

185. The GROUP BY clause on one column, one aggregated field, and HAVING

Find customer orders with a total order amount exceeding $100

Discussion:

In this example, we want to exclude from the result set all customers whose order totals are less than $100. However, we do not know beforehand who these customers are. We need to run the GROUP BY clause, find the totals, and exclude those below $100. This is exactly the case in which HAVING is used. Using HAVING with GROUP BY is a powerful and flexible way to filter records. By the way, we use the HAVING clause only in conjunction with the GROUP BY clause. Looking at the result set, we can see that only three customers appear. The customer named Riegert does not appear because his order total is only 30.

Code:

```
SELECT LastName, SUM(unitprice*quantity) AS OrderTotal
FROM tbls_customersgr
GROUP BY LastName
HAVING SUM(unitprice*quantity)>100
```

Result:

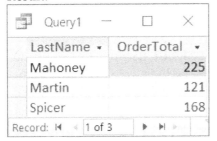

186. The GROUP BY clause on one column, one aggregated field, WHERE and HAVING

Obtain totals for orders above $100 excluding a subset of products

Discussion:

In this example, pay attention to the combined use of WHERE and HAVING. We want to calculate customer order totals, but we want to exclude from the result set customers whose order totals are less than $100. In addition, we want to exclude from the calculations the product "Chocolate Chip Brownie". Perhaps management wants to see how customer order amounts differ if this product is excluded from their orders. They are thinking of discontinuing this particular product.

In general, when it comes to filtering records in GROUP BY statements, we need to make some quick decisions: Do we need to use WHERE, HAVING, or a combination of the two? Your way of thinking should always be the same: Use the WHERE clause to exclude records that you do not want to be included in the aggregate calculations, and use HAVING to exclude values after the aggregations by GROUP BY are made. In this case, we use WHERE to exclude the product "Chocolate Chip Brownie" from the recordset, and we use GROUP BY to create the aggregations on whatever records remain. After the aggregations are made, the HAVING clause takes effect to exclude order totals less than $100. The bottom line is that in the SQL statement below, the WHERE clause will run first, the GROUP BY second, and the HAVING clause third.

Code:
SELECT LastName, SUM(unitprice*quantity) AS OrderTotal
FROM tbls_customersgr
WHERE productname <> "Chocolate Chip Brownie"
GROUP BY LastName
HAVING SUM(unitprice*quantity)>100

Result:

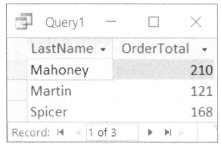

187. The GROUP BY clause with WHERE, HAVING, and ORDER BY
Sorting customer order totals
Discussion:
In this example, we put together all of the statements we learned about GROUP BY up to this point and introduce the ORDER BY clause. As you can see from the code, we first exclude from the result set the order with orderid=509 by using the WHERE clause. Then, the ORDER BY clause takes effect and calculates all the order totals by customer. Then, the HAVING clause excludes from the result set order totals less than $100. Finally, the ORDER BY clause will take effect on the remaining order totals sorting them descending so that the largest totals will appear first.

Code:
SELECT LastName, SUM(unitprice*quantity) AS OrderTotal
FROM tbls_customersgr
WHERE orderid <> 509
GROUP BY LastName
HAVING SUM(unitprice*quantity)>100
ORDER BY SUM(unitprice*quantity) DESC

Result:

188.   The GROUP BY clause with NULLS

Calculate average customer order amounts with and without nulls

Discussion:

For the purposes of this example, delete from the tbls_customersgr table the unit price for one of the products in Mahoney's order. Specifically, delete the unit price for Dark Chocolate Apricots. The idea is to demonstrate exactly what happens when nulls exist in data needed for calculations in GROUP BY clauses. Using 5 records in this table, you can check the results manually and learn so when you deal with 5,000 records, you know exactly what to do.

tbls_customersgr					
LastName	OrderID	OrderDate	ProductName	UnitPrice	Quantity
Mahoney	57	5/29/2017	Dark Chocolate Apricots in 20 oz. Bag		5
Mahoney	57	5/29/2017	Mushrooms Sauce	5	2
Mahoney	57	5/29/2017	Chocolate Chip Brownie	15	1

Let us run two pieces of code:

Code:

SELECT OrderID, Avg(([unitprice]*[quantity])) AS AverageOrderAmount

FROM tbls_customersgr

GROUP BY OrderID

Result with null values:

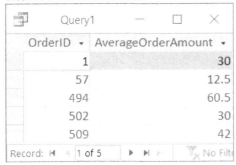

Now replace the deleted unit price for Dark Chocolate Apricots at $28 and run the SQL statement again:

Code:

SELECT OrderID, Avg(([unitprice]*[quantity])) AS AverageOrderAmount

FROM tbls_customersgr

GROUP BY OrderID

Result without null values:

OrderID	AverageOrderAmount
1	30
57	55
494	60.5
502	30
509	42

Record: ◄ ‹ 1 of 5 › ►► No Filt

As you can see from the first result set, all of the calculations look right except for orderid = 57. In this case, the database is giving us an average of 12.5. In other words, it takes into consideration only the two products in that order and leaves out the third—the one with the missing quantity. I will not express an opinion whether this is correct or not. I simply want you to know that when missing data exists, aggregate functions will ignore the missing values. Some people might argue that this is correct because if we do not have data for an item, it should not be included in the calculations. Others might say that when missing data exists, aggregate functions should take this into consideration.

We will not miss the forest for the tree in this case. Instead of becoming bogged down by database peculiarities, the most effective action when you make calculations like multiplications or when you use the GROUP BY clause is to first check your fields for missing data. It takes a few seconds to check for nulls (chapter 24), and you will not have to worry how aggregate functions will handle your data.

189. The GROUP BY clause on multiple columns
Find order totals grouped by customer and order number at the same time
Discussion:
Sometimes, you might want to retrieve more detailed information. For example, you might want to calculate order totals by customer and OrderID at the same time. You can easily achieve this with GROUP BY in Access. Since you grouped first by lastname and then by OrderID, orders will be totaled by last name first and then by OrderID for the same last name. As you can see from the result set below, for Mahoney, the order total is provided separately for his two orders while for the rest three of the customers the order total is provided in one line since they have only one order each. You can reverse the order of grouping or add more grouping fields according to the level of the detail you would like to see.

Code:
SELECT lastname, OrderID, SUM([unitprice]*[quantity]) AS OrderTotal
FROM tbls_customersgr
GROUP BY lastname, OrderID

Result:

Query1

lastname	OrderID	OrderTotal
Mahoney	57	165
Mahoney	502	60
Martin	494	121
Riegert	1	30
Spicer	509	168

Record: 1 of 5 No Filter

1.   What is the basic goal of the GROUP BY clause in relational databases?
2.   Are aggregate functions optional or required with the GROUP BY clause?
3.   Can we use multiple aggregate fields with the GROUP BY clause?
4.   Can we summarize values in multiple fields with the GROUP BY clause?
5.   What do we need to pay attention to when we have null values in the fields we use aggregate functions?
6.   How exactly the WHERE clause works with GROUP BY sql statements?
7.   What is the purpose of the HAVING clause in GROUP BY statements?
8.   Are the HAVING and WHERE clauses mandatory or optional with GROUP BY?
9.   On the other hand, can we use the HAVING clause without the GROUP BY clause?
10. Which one takes precedence? The WHERE clause or the HAVING clause?

Chapter 17 Case 1:

Create a new Access database and name it Chapter17_1.accdb. Copy the tables Customers and Orders from the PracticeDatabase.accdb and paste them to Chapter17_1.accdb.

1.   The inventory people are asking for a report that will provide the total shipping cost by ShipperID for all orders in the Orders table. Create a new query that satisfies the inventory people request. Save the query as Qry1_ShippingCostTotals.

Your result should look like:

2.   The marketing people are asking for a report that will provide the number of orders placed by CustomerID from the Orders table. Create a new query that satisfies the marketing people request. Save the query as Qry2_OrdersByCustomer.

Your result should look like:

3. The marketing people are now asking for a report that will provide the number of customers by zip code in the Customers table. Create a new query that satisfies the marketing people request. Save the query as Qry3_CustomersByZipCode.

Your result should look like:

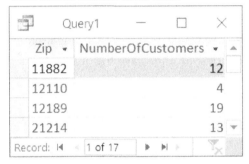

4. The marketing people became a pain in the neck and they are now asking for a report that will provide the average, minimum, and maximum shipping cost by CustomerID. Create a new query that satisfies the marketing people request. Save the query as Qry4_MinMaxAvgShippingCostByCustomer.

Your result should look like:

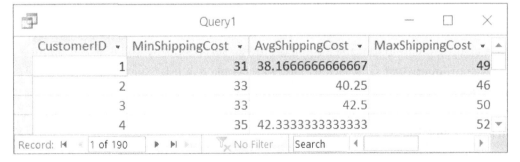

5. The marketing people are back and they now want the same report as in item number four (4) including however only customers with an average order shipping cost of less than 40. Create a new query that satisfies the marketing people request. Save the query as Qry5_ShippingCostBelow40.

Your result should look like:

CustomerID ▾	MinShippingCost ▾	AvgShippingCost ▾	MaxShippingCost ▾
1	31	38.1666666666667	49
5	32	39.25	45
7	32	39	46
10	35	37.6666666666667	42

Record: ◄ 1 of 60 ► ►► No Filter   Search

Chapter 17 Case 2:

Create a new Access database and name it Chapter17_2.accdb. Copy the tables ProductsOrders and Orders from the PracticeDatabase.accdb and paste them to Chapter17_2.accdb.

1. The sales department is asking for a report that will provide the total product quantity by productID for all order items in the table ProductsOrders. Create a new query that satisfies the sales people request. Sort results by TotalProductUnitsSold descending. Save the query as Qry1_ProductUnitTotals.

    Your result should look like:

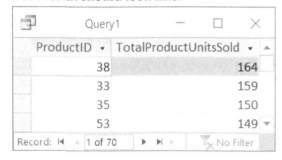

ProductID ▾	TotalProductUnitsSold ▾
38	164
33	159
35	150
53	149

Record: ◄ 1 of 70 ► ►► No Filter

2. The marketing people are asking for a report listing the most successful products in terms of overall sales. Specifically, they are asking for a report that will provide the total order amount by productID for all order items in the table ProductsOrders. Sort results by TotalOrderAmount DESC. Create a new query that satisfies the marketing people request. Save the query as Qry2_ProductTotals.

    Your result should look like:

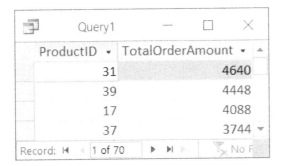

3. Accounts payable is asking for a report that will provide the min, average, and max shipping cost by ShipperID for all orders in the Orders table. Create a new query that satisfies the accounts payable request. Save the query as Qry3_ShippingCosts.

Your result should look like:

ShipperID	MinShippingCost	AvgShippingCost	MaxShippingCost
1	31	42.1402298850575	52
2	31	40.6766304347826	52
3	31	42.2142857142857	52

Record: 1 of 3 — No Filter — Search

4. The marketing people are again asking for a report that will provide the total order amount by ProductID for all order items in the table ProductsOrders. However, this time they want the products with ProductIDs 1,14,15, and 28 to be excluded from the results. They also want to see order totals above $2000. Create a new query that satisfies the marketing people request. Save the query as Qry4_ProductTotalsWithCriteria.

Your result should look like:

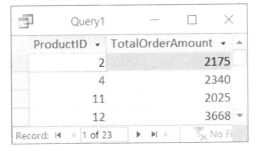

5. The marketing people need one additional report that will provide the total order amount for each product within each order in the ProductsOrders table. Consequently, this time you need the results aggregated by OrderID first and then by ProductID. Do not include any sorting in your query. Save the query as Qry5_TwoGroupings.

Your result should look like:

OrderID	ProductID	TotalOrderAmount
2	70	90
3	26	66
3	27	30
3	43	75

Record: ◄◄ ◄ 5 of 2411 ► ►► ▷ No Filter Sear

CHAPTER 18
AGGREGATE FUNCTIONS

Aggregate functions like sum(), avg(), count(), count(*), max(), and min() have the main goal of summarizing data and converting this data into useful pieces of information. Aggregate functions process values from a table column to produce a summary value, whether a summation, an average, or a maximum value.

With aggregate functions, you need to pay attention to any null values in your data. In this chapter, you will understand well the effect of null values on aggregate calculations. However, no matter how much knowledge you have regarding the behavior of aggregate functions with null values, you should have one goal in mind: To eliminate null values from the columns on which you conduct aggregations. In other words, you need to develop a habit to examine your data for nulls before you even use aggregate functions. Of course, advanced developers by design do not allow null values in their tables. They will use default values, constraints, or validation rules to avoid nulls altogether.

Aggregate functions can and are often used on calculated fields as well (chapter 15) which fields are themselves the result of the multiplication, summation, or division of two or more fields. Finally, aggregate functions are extremely useful when combined with the GROUP BY clause. We examined GROUP BY in the previous chapter and are now ready to go a step further, using it with aggregate functions to observe the power of the results obtained.

In this chapter, we will use aggregate functions with calculated fields, the GROUP BY clause, the WHERE clause, the HAVING clause, and a few operators so that you learn the combined use of aggregate functions—and not in isolation. For the purposes of this chapter, we have created a special table called tbls_customersag with only 20 records so that you can check the results against the dataset, make calculations manually, and fully understand the effects of aggregate functions. Before you start the examples in this chapter, open this table to understand its structure and have a look at its 20 records.

192.   The count() function
Count the number of orders
Discussion:
The count() function, used alone, will calculate the number of records in a dataset as soon as it is used on a field that contains no null values. In practice, the count() function is usually applied on the primary key of the table since it is the one field that is certain not to contain nulls. In this example, we use it on the OrderID field, which is not the primary key, but we will use it to show you the different results produced by count() in the subsequent examples. In this case, the count() function returned the number of records in the table, i.e. 20. We can be certain of one thing from this result: The OrderID field does not contain any null values since the number returned from the count() function is equal to the number of records in the table.

Code:

SELECT count(orderid) as NumberofOrders
FROM tbls_customersag

Result:

193.   The count() function with DISTINCT

Count the number of unique orders from customers

Discussion:

The previous example is fine, but what if we need to count the number of unique orders in this table? The proper way to accomplish this task in SQL is to use the COUNT and DISTINCT statements together:

SELECT Count (DISTINCT Orderid) as NumberofOrders FROM tbls_customersag

This is excellent, but our problem is that it does not work in Access. We need to deviate thematically for a second and use a subquery with DISTINCT to achieve the result we want (See chapter 31 on subqueries). From the result set below, notice that the number of orders produced by the count() function is now 15. This is actually the number of unique orders in the table, which is exactly what we need.

Code:

SELECT Count(*) AS NumberofOrders
FROM
(SELECT DISTINCT orderid FROM tbls_customersag)

Result:

194.   The count() function with the GROUP BY clause

Count the number of orders by customer

Discussion:

The question in this example is to count the number of orders by customer. We can provide an answer quickly by using the count() function with the GROUP BY clause. From the result set, you obtain two pieces of information. First, you know that you have 9 unique customers in the dataset and second, you have a count of the number of orders by each customer.

Code:

SELECT lastname, count(orderid) as NumberofOrders
FROM tbls_customersag
GROUP BY lastname

Result:

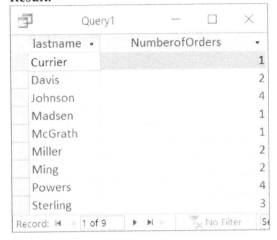

195.   The count() and count(*) functions in comparison

Count the number of records in a table using count(*)

Discussion:

In this scenario, the objective is to understand the difference between Count(), Count(*), and Count() DISTINCT so that you can take full advantage of them in your data tasks. For this purpose, let us temporarily delete the name of the customer Davis with OrderID = 4 from the table tbls_customersag. Now, we have 20 records in the table with the last name of a customer missing.

tbls_customersag					
PK	LastName	OrderID	ProductID	UnitPrice	Quantity
1		4	55	15	3
2	Sterling	60	56	12	5
3	Sterling	60	21	15	4

Let us start with the count() function on the lastname first. As you can see from the result set, the number returned is 19. This is because we used count() on the lastname field in which a value is missing. Consequently, while the table contains 20 records, we received only 19. You do not need to worry about these intricacies if you follow a simple piece of advice: Any time you work with aggregate functions, calculated fields, or GROUP BY, check your records for null values, and make the necessary edits and replacements (see chapter 24 for details on null values). Then, you do not need to worry about the intricacies of how aggregate functions behave with missing data.

Code:

SELECT count(lastname) as NumberofCustomers
FROM tbls_customersag

Result:

Now, let's use the count(*) function. As you can see from the result set, the count(*) function returned the correct result of 20 records in the table.

Code:

SELECT count(*) as NumberofCustomers
FROM tbls_customersag

Result:

Now, let's use count(*) with a subquery and DISTINCT. As you can see from the result set, the number of unique customers returned is 10. We know already, however, that we have 9 unique customers in the table. What happened? This time, the count(*) function returned 10 because it counted the "blank" customer as an additional unique customer.

Code:

SELECT Count(*) AS NumberofCustomers
FROM
(SELECT DISTINCT lastname FROM tbls_customersag)

Result:

Replace the deleted name "Davis" in the table.

196. The AVG() function

Calculate the average order amount by customer

In this example we calculate the number of orders and the average order amount by customer.

Code:

```
SELECT lastname, count(orderid) as NumberofOrders, AVG(unitprice*quantity)
AS AvgOrderAmount
FROM tbls_customersag
GROUP BY lastname
```

Result:

lastname	NumberofOrders	AvgOrderAmount
Currier	1	30
Davis	2	60
Johnson	4	18.75
Madsen	1	30
McGrath	1	10
Miller	2	25
Ming	2	60
Powers	4	31
Sterling	3	50

Record: 1 of 9   No Filter   Search

197. The avg() function with the WHERE clause

Calculate the number of orders and average order amounts for specific customers

Discussion:

We can use the WHERE clause with aggregate functions to manipulate the result set and retrieve the exact pieces of information we need. By using WHERE the database will first eliminate records as per the WHERE clause and perform any calculations on the remaining ones. In this particular example, we exclude two customers using the NOT IN operator.

Code:

```
SELECT lastname, count(orderid) as NumberofOrders, AVG(unitprice*quantity)
AS AvgOrderAmount
FROM tbls_customersag
WHERE lastname NOT IN ('Johnson', 'Madsen')
GROUP BY lastname
```

Result:

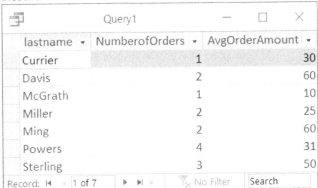

lastname	NumberofOrders	AvgOrderAmount
Currier	1	30
Davis	2	60
McGrath	1	10
Miller	2	25
Ming	2	60
Powers	4	31
Sterling	3	50

Record: 1 of 7   No Filter   Search

198.   The sum() function

Calculate the number of orders, average, and total order amounts by customer

Discussion:

Here, we add to the previous example the sum() function to calculate the total order amount by customer. Notice that the sum() function is applied on a calculated field.

Code:

```
SELECT lastname, count(orderid) as Num, avg(unitprice*quantity)
AS Avg, sum(unitprice*quantity) AS Total
FROM tbls_customersag
WHERE lastname NOT IN ('Johnson', 'Madsen')
GROUP BY lastname
```

Result:

lastname	Num	Avg	Total
Currier	1	30	30
Davis	2	60	120
McGrath	1	10	10
Miller	2	25	50
Ming	2	60	120
Powers	4	31	124
Sterling	3	50	150

Record: ◄◄ ◄ 1 of 7 ► ►► ►* No Filter

199.   The min() function

Calculate the minimum (lowest value) of customer orders

Discussion:

Let's assume we now have an additional request to find the minimum order amount for each customer. We can achieve this using the code below:

Code:

```
SELECT lastname, count(orderid) as Num, min(unitprice*quantity) AS Min,
avg(unitprice*quantity) AS Avg, sum(unitprice*quantity) AS Total
FROM tbls_customersag
WHERE lastname NOT IN ('Johnson', 'Madsen')
GROUP BY lastname
```

Result:

lastname	Num	Min	Avg	Total
Currier	1	30	30	30
Davis	2	45	60	120
McGrath	1	10	10	10
Miller	2	20	25	50
Ming	2	60	60	120
Powers	4	15	31	124
Sterling	3	30	50	150

Record: 1 of 7 ▶ ▶| No Filter Search

200. The max() function

Calculate the maximum value of customer orders

Discussion:

The max() function will calculate the value of the biggest order for each customer, and it will report just that in the result set.

Code:

```
SELECT lastname, count(orderid) as Num, min(unitprice*quantity) AS Min,
avg(unitprice*quantity) AS Avg, max(unitprice*quantity) AS Max, sum(unitprice*quantity)
AS Total
FROM tbls_customersag
WHERE lastname NOT IN ('Johnson', 'Madsen')
GROUP BY lastname
```

Result:

lastname	Num	Min	Avg	Max	Total
Currier	1	30	30	30	30
Davis	2	45	60	75	120
McGrath	1	10	10	10	10
Miller	2	20	25	30	50
Ming	2	60	60	60	120
Powers	4	15	31	45	124
Sterling	3	30	50	60	150

Record: 1 of 7 ▶ ▶| No Filter Search

201. The Standard Deviation and Variance functions

Calculate the standard deviation and variance of customer order amounts

Discussion:

Using SQL, we can do much more than the usual arithmetic calculations. Actually, we can even perform some statistical analysis. In this example, we are looking for the standard deviation and variance of order amounts for each customer. We used the cint() conversion function to avoid multiple decimals for the standard deviation column (chapter 25). In the result set, Currier and McGrath have

213

only one order and, as it is logical, no variance and standard deviation can be calculated. From a business point of view, customers Davis, Sterling, and Powers are prone to making orders that vary a lot in size.

Code:

```
SELECT lastname, count(orderid) as Num, min(unitprice*quantity) AS Min,
avg(unitprice*quantity) AS Avg, max(unitprice*quantity) AS Max, sum(unitprice*quantity)
AS Total, cint(stdev(unitprice*quantity)) As stdev, var(unitprice*quantity) as var
 FROM tbls_customersag
WHERE lastname NOT IN ('Johnson', 'Madsen')
GROUP BY lastname
```

Result:

lastname	Num	Min	Avg	Max	Total	stdev	var
Currier	1	30	30	30	30	#Error	
Davis	2	45	60	75	120	21	450
McGrath	1	10	10	10	10	#Error	
Miller	2	20	25	30	50	7	50
Ming	2	60	60	60	120	0	0
Powers	4	15	31	45	124	15	218
Sterling	3	30	50	60	150	17	300

Record: ◄ ◄ 1 of 7 ► ►► No Filter   Search

202.   Aggregate functions with GROUP BY and HAVING

Calculate order amounts and filter records based on results of aggregate functions

Discussion:

This time, our manager wants a report that shows the number of orders, minimum, average, maximum, and total order amounts calculated by customer. In addition, he wants products with ProductID 13, 56, and 30 to not participate in the calculations. He also wants us to exclude from the result set any customers with total order amounts of less than $100 and any customers with average order amounts of less than $40. Finally, he wants us to exclude from the calculations any customers with a standard deviation in their order amounts of 20 and above, but the standard deviation calculation should not appear in the result set.

The above sounds complicated, and it is complicated to a degree. Still, it is not difficult to achieve. I would like you to learn to follow a process when it comes to complicated SQL statements. This process involves the incremental building of the SQL statement instead of trying to think about everything at once. Essentially, we will build the solution one step at a time.

Our first step in any complicated problem involving SQL is to try to identify the fields. In this example, we need seven fields to do our job, and this step is straightforward. The SELECT statement with the seven fields appears below. We include the type conversion function cint() so that we restrict the number of decimals for the standard deviation field.

SELECT lastname, count(orderid) as Num, min(unitprice*quantity) AS Min, avg(unitprice*quantity) AS Avg, max(unitprice*quantity) AS Max, sum(unitprice*quantity) AS Total, cint(stdev(unitprice*quantity)) As stdev
FROM tbls_customersag
GROUP BY lastname

Our next step is to exclude products with productID 13, 56, and 30. For this task, we make use of the WHERE clause with the NOT IN operator (chapter 12) as it appears below:

SELECT lastname, count(orderid) as Num, min(unitprice*quantity) AS Min, avg(unitprice*quantity) AS Avg, max(unitprice*quantity) AS Max, sum(unitprice*quantity) AS Total, cint(stdev(unitprice*quantity)) As stdev
FROM tbls_customersag
WHERE productID NOT IN (13,56,30)
GROUP BY lastname

The next step is to exclude from the result set any customers with total order amounts of less than $100 and any customers with average order amounts of less than $40. For cases like this one, we make use of the HAVING clause, which is the filtering clause you can use to filter records after aggregate calculations have been performed. The code will now look like this:

SELECT lastname, count(orderid) as Num, min(unitprice*quantity) AS Min, avg(unitprice*quantity) AS Avg, max(unitprice*quantity) AS Max, sum(unitprice*quantity) AS Total, cint(stdev(unitprice*quantity)) As stdev
FROM tbls_customersag
WHERE productID NOT IN (13,56,30)
GROUP BY lastname
HAVING sum(unitprice*quantity) > 100 AND avg(unitprice*quantity) > 40

The final step in building the SQL statement is to exclude from the calculations any customers with a standard deviation in their order amounts of 20 and above but without including the standard deviation calculation in the result set. In the SQL code below, we took out the expression cint(stdev(unitprice*quantity)) from the SELECT statement and put it in the HAVING clause. This way, the filtering happens, but the standard deviation calculations do not appear in the result set.

Code:
SELECT lastname, count(orderid) as Num, min(unitprice*quantity) AS Min, avg(unitprice*quantity) AS Avg, max(unitprice*quantity) AS Max, sum(unitprice*quantity) AS Total FROM tbls_customersag
WHERE productID NOT IN (13,56,30)
GROUP BY lastname
HAVING sum(unitprice*quantity) > 100 AND avg(unitprice*quantity) > 40 AND cint(stdev(unitprice*quantity)) < 20

After all of the filtering, one customer out of nine satisfied all of the criteria.

Result:

lastname	Num	Min	Avg	Max	Total
Ming	2	60	60	60	120

CHAPTER 18 DISCUSSION QUESTIONS

1. What is the main goal of aggregate functions?
2. Name two aggregate functions and their corresponding roles.
3. Can we use aggregate functions with calculated fields?
4. What is the clause that greatly enhances the usefulness of aggregate functions?
5. Why do we need to pay attention to null values when using aggregate functions?
6. How can we avoid null values by design?
7. What is the difference between the Count() and Count(*) aggregate functions?
8. What solution do we need to employee to count distinct records in a table?
9. What other clauses can we use with aggregate functions to greatly improve their usefulness?
10. What statistical functions can we use in Microsoft Access?

204.   CHAPTER 18 HANDS-ON EXERCISES

Chapter 18 Case 1:

Create a new Access database and name it Chapter18_1.accdb. Copy the table Customers from the PracticeDatabase.accdb and paste it to Chapter18_1.accdb.

1. The sales people are asking for the total number of customers in the customer table. Create a new query that satisfies the sales people request. Save the query as Qry1_NumberOfCustomers.

   Your result should look like:

   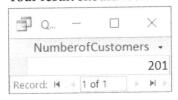

2. The sales people are back asking for a report that will display the number of customers by city. Create a new query that satisfies the sales people request and sort results by number of customers descending. Save the query as Qry2_NumberOfCustomersByCity.

   Your result should look like:

   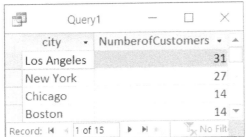

3. The sales people are now asking for a report that will display the number of customers by city excluding customers from NY State. Create a new query that satisfies the sales people request and sort results by number of customers descending. Save the query as Qry3_NumberOfCustomersByCityNoNY.

Your result should look like:

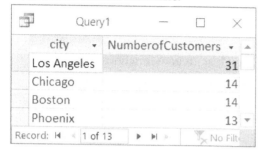

4. The sales people are asking for a report that will display the number of customers by city excluding customers from NY State. In addition, the report should exclude any cities with less than 10 customers. Create a new query that satisfies the sales people request and sort results by number of customers descending. Save the query as Qry4_NumberCustomersByCityNoNYUp10.

Your result should look like:

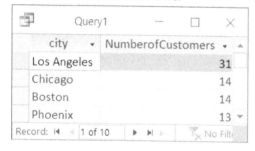

5. The sales people are now asking for a report that will display the number of customers by zip code excluding customers from NY State. In addition, the report should exclude any zip codes with less than 10 customers. Create a new query that satisfies the sales people request and sort results by number of customers descending. Save the query as Qry5_NumberCustomersByZipNoNYUp10.

Your result should look like:

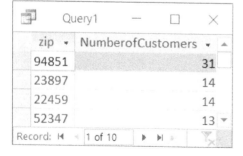

Chapter 18 Case 2:

Create a new Access database and name it Chapter18_2.accdb. Copy the table ProductsOrders from the PracticeDatabase.accdb and paste it to Chapter18_2.accdb.

1. The sales department is asking for a report that will provide the total number of distinct products within all the orders in the ProductsOrders table. Create a new query that satisfies the sales people request. Save the query as Qry1_DistinctProductsInOrders. Hint, look at chapter 15, example 145.

    Your result should look like:

2. The marketing department is asking for a report that will provide the minimum, average, maximum, and total product units sold. Create a new query that satisfies the marketing people request. Save the query as Qry2_QuantityStatistics.

    Your result should look like:

3. The marketing department is again asking for a report that will provide the minimum, average, maximum, and total product units sold but grouped by ProductID this time. Sort results by ProductID ascending. Create a new query that satisfies the marketing people request and save it as Qry3_QuantityStatisticsGroup.

    Your result should look like:

    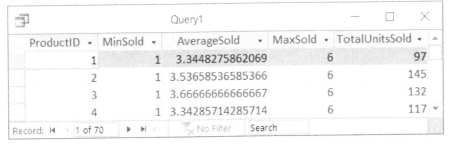

4. The marketing department is now asking for a report that will provide the minimum, average, maximum, and total product units sold grouped by ProductID. In addition, results should exclude products with product IDs in the range 35 to 70. Sort results by ProductID ascending. Create a new

query that satisfies the marketing people request and save it as
Qry4_QuantityStatisticsExcludeProductIDs.

Your result should look like:

ProductID ▾	MinSold ▾	AverageSold ▾	MaxSold ▾	TotalUnitsSold ▾
1	1	3.3448275862069	6	97
2	1	3.53658536585366	6	145
3	1	3.66666666666667	6	132
4	1	3.34285714285714	6	117

Record: 1 of 34   No Filter   Search

5. The marketing department is finally asking for a report that will provide the minimum, average, maximum, and total product units sold grouped by ProductID. In addition, results should exclude products with product IDs in the range 35 to 70. Moreover, the query should exclude Products with total units sold less than 100. Sort results by ProductID ascending. Create a new query that satisfies the marketing people request and save it as Qry5_QuantityStatisticsAbove100.

Your result should look like:

ProductID ▾	MinSold ▾	AverageSold ▾	MaxSold ▾	TotalUnitsSold ▾
2	1	3.53658536585366	6	145
3	1	3.66666666666667	6	132
4	1	3.34285714285714	6	117
6	1	3.025	6	121

Record: 1   No Filter   Search

CHAPTER 19
CROSSTAB QUERIES

Crosstab queries have a reputation of being complicated and intricate objects. This should not be the case. We can really work efficiently with crosstab queries once we recognize their basic structure. In essence, to create a crosstab query, we use three fields only. One field will function as the column heading, the second as the row heading, and the third as the value field. The value field is the actual field on which calculations occur using aggregate functions like sum(), avg(), count(), count(*), max(), and min().

Let us suppose we want to calculate order totals by state and year. In other words, we would like to know how much we sold in every state in every year. Since we know already that to create a crosstab query, we need to have a field as a column heading, a field as a row heading, and a value field, our query will look like this in its basic design:

	Year
State	Value

When we run the query, since we have multiple states and years in our data, our result set will look like this:

	Year1	Year2	Year3
State1	Value	Value	Value
State2	Value	Value	Value
State3	Value	Value	Value

The state row field will expand automatically to include data for as many states as we have in our database. The year field will expand to include as many columns as the number of years we have in our data. The value field will present the sum of order amounts for all of the combinations of year and state.

The above diagram represents the basic structure of a crosstab query in Access. However, you have a couple of bonuses at this point. Once you understand how crosstab queries work in Access, you also understand how pivot tables work in Excel, how pivot charts summarize their data, how OLAP cubes work, how data visualization software like Tableau works, and you definitely have an advantage over someone who creates pivot tables and charts without full knowledge of data summaries under the hood. In the following examples, we start with basic crosstab queries and incrementally add techniques that will make our crosstab queries powerful tools for our work.

Working with crosstab queries usually involves the joining of multiple tables. We might need a field from the customers table, a field from the orders table, and a field from the products table. Since joins are not the focus of this chapter, I would like to spare you the intricacies of joining tables and focus on the actual crosstab queries themselves. That is why the examples in this chapter are based on a query purposely made for this chapter. Its name is "Qry_Crosstab_Base" from which we will take all of the fields we need to work with. Of course, we also provide chapter 30 toward the end of the book to explain joins inside out so that you can professionally and easily work with joined tables.

205.   A crosstab query with three fields - example 1
Find total sales by state and year
Discussion:
As you can see from the SQL code, we use three fields to create this very informative crosstab query. The first is the state field, which we use for row headings. The second is the OrderDate field, which we use for column headings. For the OrderDate field there is a catch: We use the year() function to extract the year out of the order dates we have in the database. The third field is the value field, which we call OrderTotal. This is a calculated field that sums the unitprice * the quantity of each product for each of our customer orders.

When you look at the SQL code, you will notice the use of a new statement called TRANSFORM. The TRANSFORM statement relates to the value field in a crosstab query, and it always precedes the SQL statement. Additionally, it is always followed by the aggregate function used for the value field, which in this case is sum(Quantity * UnitPrice). Below is the SQL code for the crosstab query explaining it step by step:

TRANSFORM Sum([unitprice]*[quantity]) AS Ordertotal
The TRANSFORM statement is used for the value field in a crosstab query.

SELECT State FROM Qry_Crosstab_Base
The SELECT statement is used for the row-heading field of the crosstab query.

GROUP BY State
The GROUP BY clause follows next, and it is applied on the same field used in the SELECT statement. Since we used State for the SELECT statement, we use State for the GROUP BY clause as well.

PIVOT Year([OrderDate])
The PIVOT statement is the last one used in a crosstab query, and it is applied on the column-heading field.

Below is the general structure of a crosstab query in SQL code.

```
TRANSFORM ValueField
SELECT ColumnField
FROM DataSource
GROUP BY ColumnField
PIVOT RowField
```

Code:

```
TRANSFORM sum([unitprice]*[quantity]) AS Ordertotal
SELECT CustomerState
FROM Qry_Crosstab_Base
GROUP BY CustomerState
PIVOT Year([OrderDate])
```

Looking at the results below, we can quickly understand and compare sales volumes by each state and each year. For example, the biggest sales revenues come from California, and they grow year by year. In Florida, we need to have a look at what is happening because sales dropped a lot for 2019. This is the power of crosstab queries. We get summarized results in seconds. We also notice an amount of $202 without an associated year. This means right away that we have an order or orders without date values in the OrderDate field which means we have null values in our data. As we have said multiple times before, null values always interfere with calculations and they need to be dealt with. See chapter 24 for an in depth look on null values.

Result:

CustomerState	<>	2017	2018	2019
AZ		2849	2386	3460
CA		12216	13364	14919
CO		1961	3326	1937
DC		3020	3351	3102
FL		4439	4736	3413
MA		1999	2020	859
NY		8584	6089	7188
OH	202	2151	4924	3076
PA		1525	1781	1738
TX		5284	9187	5310

Record: ◄ ◄ 1 of 10 ► ►► No Filter | Search

206.   A crosstab query with three fields—example 2

Find total sales by city and year

Discussion:

Our business manager is very happy with the comprehensive sales report we provided by state and year. Now that she knows what our database can do, she asks for an additional report that will show sales volumes by city and year. In about three seconds we replace the state field with the city field in our query, and our new crosstab query is ready!

Code:

```
TRANSFORM Sum([unitprice]*[quantity]) AS Ordertotal
SELECT CustomerCity
FROM Qry_Crosstab_Base
GROUP BY CustomerCity
PIVOT Year([OrderDate])
```

Result:

CustomerCity ▾	<> ▾	2017 ▾	2018 ▾	2019 ▾
Albany		1199	1214	1356
Boston		1999	2020	859
Chicago	202	2151	4924	3076
Dallas		2691	4174	3292

Record: ◄ ◄ 1 ► ►► ▼ No Filter   Search

207. The issue of uniqueness of values in crosstab queries

Find total sales by customer and year

Discussion:

Now, our supervisor asks for additional detail. Specifically, he wants a sales report by customer and year. Again, in a few seconds, we replace the city field from the previous example with lastname and presumably, we are done!

Unfortunately, that isn't the case this time! Our problem is that multiple customers might have the same last names. Since we are grouping on the last name field, all of the customers with the same lastname will be grouped together! This is a very common problem in crosstab queries and when using the GROUP BY clause. Consequently, I would like you to develop a process to think thoroughly about the uniqueness of values when using the GROUP BY clause. For instance, you should think about the possibility of having the same last name in your data for multiple customers. The same is true for city fields since the same city name might refer to multiple distinct cities, as is the case with Portland, Oregon and Portland, Maine. In the next example, we solve this problem using concatenated fields.

Also, notice that in the result set that there are some blank values. For example, there are blank values for Ames in 2017 and 2018. These blanks mean that Ames has not placed any orders in 2017 and 2018 respectively.

Code:

```
TRANSFORM sum([unitprice]*[quantity]) AS Ordertotal
SELECT Customerlastname
FROM Qry_Crosstab_Base
GROUP BY Customerlastname
PIVOT year([OrderDate])
```

Result:

Customerlastname	<>	2017	2018	2019
Ackerman		120	32	207
Ames				871
Andersen		350		393
Anderson		965	924	1434

Record: ◄ ◄ 1 ► ►► ► 🦅 No Filter   Search

208. Crosstab queries with concatenated fields

Find total sales by customer and year displaying full customer names

Discussion:

In the previous example, the results of the crosstab query were questionable because multiple customers might have the same last name. In this example, we need to make sure to summarize sales volumes by unique customers. The knowledge acquired from the concatenated fields chapter (chapter 16) comes in handy here. In this example, we will GROUP BY the field resulting from the concatenation of the last and first name fields of the customers to obtain accurate results.

I know what you are thinking: What if there are customers with the same last and first names? This is a possibility, after all. We have three ways to solve this problem depending on its nature. First, if two customer entries pertain to the same customer, that is we have duplicated records in the data set, read chapter 23 on duplicate and orphaned records to explore a range of solutions.

Second, if the two customer entries pertain to two different customers, we can add middle names, zip codes, and even part of the address information to the concatenated expression to obtain unique results.

Third, to avoid this problem in its conception, we can add to the customer table a unique multiple-field index on the last and first name fields so that values of customers with the same last and first names are not accepted at all in the table. See chapter 3 for the exact syntax of multiple-field unique indexes.

I have created an additional problem on purpose: When you look at the result set in this example, you will notice that the first record is blank! If this is the case, go immediately to your record set, and check the values of the fields you use in the concatenated expression for blanks. You will notice that customer "Corelli" does not have a first name entry! If you add a first name for this customer, your blank record will disappear when you run your crosstab again.

Code:
```
TRANSFORM Sum([unitprice]*[quantity]) AS Ordertotal
SELECT (CustomerLastname+' '+CustomerFirstName) AS Customer
FROM Qry_Crosstab_Base
GROUP BY (CustomerLastname+' '+CustomerFirstName)
PIVOT Year([OrderDate])
```

Result:

Customer	<>	2017	2018	2019
		90	1131	240
Ackerman Nicholas		120	32	207
Ames Pindar				871
Andersen Thomas		350		393
Anderson Joseph		110	575	477
Anderson Paul		371	72	513

Record: 1 — No Filter — Search

209. Display column totals in crosstab queries

Calculate order totals by state and year and provide grand totals for the year columns

Discussion:

There are two types of grand totals in crosstab queries. The first are column grand totals. For example, the grand totals of orders in all states for 2017, 2018, and 2019. To achieve this task let us run this crosstab query first.

Code:

```
TRANSFORM sum([unitprice]*[quantity]) AS Ordertotal
SELECT CustomerState
FROM Qry_Crosstab_Base
GROUP BY CustomerState
PIVOT Year([OrderDate])
```

Result:

CustomerState	<>	2017	2018	2019
AZ		2849	2386	3460
CA		12216	13364	14919
CO		1961	3326	1937
DC		3020	3351	3102
FL		4439	4736	3413
MA		1999	2020	859
NY		8584	6089	7188
OH	202	2151	4924	3076
PA		1525	1781	1738
TX		5284	9187	5310

Record: 9 of 10 — No Filter — Search

Then, we use the $\sum$ command on the ribbon. We can find it at the "Home" tab in the "Records" group. By clicking on $\sum$, an additional row will become available at the bottom of the crosstab query grid where we can select any grand total calculations we want as the following figure shows:

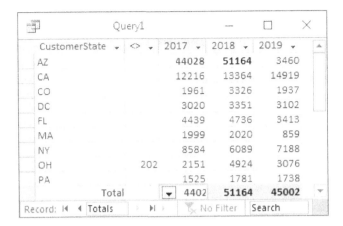

210.   Display row totals in crosstab queries

Calculate order totals by state and year and provide grand totals for the state rows

Discussion:

In this example, we calculate order grand totals for the state rows in the crosstab query. To accomplish this task, the only thing we need to do is to add the value field expression Sum([unitprice]*[quantity]) AS GrandTotal in the SELECT line of the SQL statement as it appears below:

Code:

```
TRANSFORM Sum([unitprice]*[quantity]) AS Ordertotal
SELECT CustomerState, Sum([unitprice]*[quantity]) AS GrandTotal
FROM Qry_Crosstab_Base
GROUP BY CustomerState
PIVOT Year([OrderDate])
```

Result:

CustomerState	GrandTotal	<>	2017	2018	2019
AZ	8695		2849	2386	3460
CA	40499		12216	13364	14919
CO	7224		1961	3326	1937
DC	9473		3020	3351	3102
FL	12588		4439	4736	3413
MA	4878		1999	2020	859
NY	21861		8584	6089	7188
OH	10353	202	2151	4924	3076
PA	5044		1525	1781	1738
Total			44028	51164	45002

Record: I◄ 1 of 10 ► ►I   No Filter   Search

211.   Limit the number of rows in crosstab queries using WHERE

Find total sales by product and year for certain products only

Discussion:

All of the crosstab queries we have examined to this point produce summaries counting every record in the underlying database table. Experience shows, however, that in the vast majority of cases, we will make calculations on a subset of data. We can use the WHERE clause to filter the data we want to cross tabulate. The WHERE clause always affects the number of records returned from a query whether this query is a simple SELECT or a crosstab one. In this specific example, the goal is to provide sales volumes by product and year, excluding some products from the calculations. Specifically, the products 'Chocolate Chip Cookies' and 'Chocolate Fudge' should be excluded from the calculations. We can use the WHERE clause in conjunction with the NOT IN operator to get exactly the results we need.

Code:
```
TRANSFORM Sum([unitprice]*[quantity]) AS Ordertotal
SELECT ProductName
FROM Qry_Crosstab_Base
WHERE Productname NOT IN ('Chocolate Chip Cookies','Chocolate Fudge ')
GROUP BY ProductName
PIVOT Year([OrderDate])
```

Result:

ProductName	<>	2017	2018	2019
All-Purpose Marinade I	42	350	560	560
All-Purpose Marinade II		915	750	255
Almonds, Hickory Smoked - 1		600	180	675
Almonds, Roasted and Saltec		660	975	540

Record: 1 of 65   No Filter   Search

212. Limit the number of columns in crosstab queries
Find total sales by product and year for specific years
Discussion:
Let us assume that our dataset contains sales data for the last ten years and we do not want to include all of them in our crosstab results. We might want to see only the last two or three years. In this scenario, we are looking to control the number of columns appearing in the crosstab results. To achieve this task, we can use the IN operator in the PIVOT statement. In this particular example, we only want to see sales volumes for the years 2018 and 2019.

Code:
```
TRANSFORM Sum([unitprice]*[quantity]) AS Ordertotal
SELECT productname
FROM Qry_Crosstab_Base
GROUP BY productname
PIVOT Year([OrderDate]) IN (2018,2019)
```

Result:

productname	2018	2019
All-Purpose Marinade I	560	560
All-Purpose Marinade II	750	255
Almonds, Hickory Smoked - 1	180	675
Almonds, Roasted and Saltec	975	540

Record: 1 of 67   No Filter   Sea

213.   Filter crosstab queries using any field for criteria

Find total sales by product and year in AZ, CA, and OH

Discussion:

In the previous two examples of filtering crosstab queries, we used the WHERE clause on the productname field to limit the number of rows and the PIVOT IN on the Orderdate field to limit the number of columns. Both of these fields are part of the crosstab query. The productname field is used for rows, and the orderdate field for columns. However, we can use any field in our dataset to filter records in a crosstab query without this field being an integral part of the crosstab query. We simply designate it as a field in the WHERE clause as it appears in the SQL code. The state field, used as a "WHERE" field in this example, will not appear in the result set.

Code:

```
TRANSFORM Sum([unitprice]*[quantity]) AS Ordertotal
SELECT ProductName
FROM Qry_Crosstab_Base
WHERE CustomerState IN ('AZ','CA','OH')
GROUP BY ProductName
PIVOT Year([OrderDate])
```

Result:

ProductName	<>	2017	2018	2019
All-Purpose Marinade I	42	140	70	238
All-Purpose Marinade II		450	360	120
Almonds, Hickory Smoked - 1		360	45	495
Almonds, Roasted and Saltec		225	615	315
Apple Cinnamon Raisin Cook		180	108	276

Record: 1 of 67   No Filter   Search

214.   Using parameters with crosstab queries

Find sales by customer and year using state as a parameter

Discussion:

Now, we have a new situation. Corporate managers are ecstatic about our ability to produce such useful results with crosstab queries. However, they call on us constantly to design the queries they need, and we spend a lot of time defining simple criteria. To solve this problem, we can use parameters with crosstab queries. The items to notice in the SQL code below are the PARAMETERS statement in the first line and the WHERE clause. Notice that the WHERE clause is waiting for a value from the PARAMETERS statement. (For a detailed analysis on parameters, see chapter 20).

Code:

```
PARAMETERS [Enter CustomerState:] Text ( 255 );
TRANSFORM Sum([unitprice]*[quantity]) AS Ordertotal
SELECT (CustomerLastname+' '+CustomerFirstName) AS Customer
FROM Qry_Crosstab_Base
WHERE Qry_Crosstab_Base.CustomerState=[Enter CustomerState:]
```

GROUP BY (CustomerLastname+' '+CustomerFirstName)
PIVOT Year([OrderDate])

Result:
The result set produced in this example is for the state of NY.

Customer	2017	2018	2019
Ames Pindar			871
Anderson Peter	484	277	444
Anthopolis Ricky	220	240	48
Aversa Scott	469		
Carr Edward	301	541	

Record: 1 of 29   No Filter

215.   Conditional processing of crosstab queries using the iif() function
Calculate discounted sales volumes depending on revenue volumes
Discussion:
Our business assignment in the first example of this chapter was to give our manager a report of sales totals by state and year. We were able to do that successfully and in no time. Now, however, our task is a little bit more complicated. Management wants to know the resulting sales volumes if they gave a 10% discount to customers in states with total sales of more than $10,000. In addition, they want to know the sales volumes if they gave a discount of 5% to customers in states with total sales of less than $10,000. And they want to see all results in one report.

This is not a problem at all. The key here is to use the iif() function with the crosstab query. The expression for the value field in the crosstab query is the expression shown below. We ask the database to apply a 10% discount if total sales are higher than $10,000 or to apply a 5% discount if total sales are less than $10,000. For a detailed overview of conditional statements in Access see chapter 21.

Code:
```
TRANSFORM Sum(iif([unitprice]*[quantity]>10000, ([unitprice]*[quantity])*(0.9),
([unitprice]*[quantity])*(0.95))) AS Ordertotal
SELECT CustomerState
FROM Qry_Crosstab_Base
GROUP BY CustomerState
PIVOT Year([OrderDate])
```

Result:

CustomerState	<>	2017	2018	2019
AZ		2706.55	2266.7	3287
CA		11605.2	12695.8	14173.05
CO		1862.95	3159.7	1840.15
DC		2869	3183.45	2946.9
FL		4217.05	4499.2	3242.35

Record: 1 of 10   No Filter   Search

216. Format output in crosstab queries

Find total sales by product and year and show results as currency

Discussion:

There might be some instances in which we would like to format the results of the value field of a crosstab query as currency so that the dollar sign appears in front of the numbers. This can be accomplished by using the format() function right in the TRANSFORM statement as it appears below.

Code:

```
TRANSFORM Format(Sum([unitprice]*[quantity]), 'Currency') AS Ordertotal
SELECT ProductName
FROM Qry_Crosstab_Base
GROUP BY ProductName
PIVOT Year([OrderDate])
```

Result:

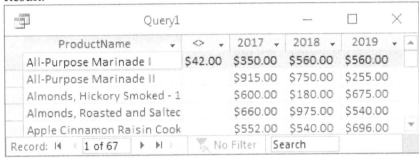

217. Using the nz() function in crosstab queries

Find total customer orders by customer and year

Discussion:

In the cross-tabbed results below, the many blanks in the grid are immediately noticeable and do not appear very professional.

Code:

```
TRANSFORM Sum([unitprice]*[quantity]) AS Ordertotal
SELECT (CustomerLastname + ' ' + CustomerFirstName) AS customer
FROM Qry_Crosstab_Base
WHERE ((CustomerState) In ('AZ','CO','MD'))
GROUP BY (CustomerLastname + ' ' + CustomerFirstName)
PIVOT Year([OrderDate])
```

Result:

customer	2017	2018	2019
Cutillo Paul		377	120
Darek Matthew		1172	286
Datek Jason	286	145	
Edwards Jim	75		216
Lanci Christine	378		

Record: ◄ ◄ 1 of 24 ► ►► ⌦ No Filter S

There is a way to replace these blank values with zeros using the nz() function. Notice how we use three functions in the TRANSFORM line to obtain the results we need.

Code:

```
TRANSFORM Ccur(Nz(Sum([unitprice]*[quantity]))) AS Ordertotal
SELECT (CustomerLastname + ' ' + CustomerFirstName) AS customer
FROM Qry_Crosstab_Base
WHERE ((CustomerState) In ('AZ','CO','MD'))
GROUP BY (CustomerLastname + ' ' + CustomerFirstName)
PIVOT Year([OrderDate])
```

Result:

customer	2017	2018	2019
Cutillo Paul	$0.00	$377.00	$120.00
Darek Matthew	$0.00	$1,172.00	$286.00
Datek Jason	$286.00	$145.00	$0.00
Edwards Jim	$75.00	$0.00	$216.00
Lanci Christine	$378.00	$0.00	$0.00

Record: ◄ ◄ 1 of 24 ► ►► ⌦ No Filter Sea

218. Conditional crosstab queries with the switch() function

Calculate sales totals for "expensive" and "inexpensive" products

Discussion:

This time, management wants to know the contribution to the total sales volume of products selling above $25 per unit and the contribution of products selling below $25 per unit. Depending on the results we give them, they will change their sales priorities to focus more on products that will generate the most sales for the company. In addition, they would like to have the results by year so that they can also distinguish any trends in sales volumes. We can use the switch function right in the PIVOT statement to create product categories exactly the way management has asked.

Code:

```
TRANSFORM Sum([unitprice]*[quantity]) AS Ordertotal
SELECT Year([OrderDate]) As Year
FROM Qry_Crosstab_Base
GROUP BY Year([OrderDate])
PIVOT
SWITCH(
unitprice >= 25 ,      'ExpensiveProducts',
unitprice < 25,        'InexpensiveProducts'
)
```

Result:

Year	ExpensiveProducts	InexpensiveProducts
	160	42
2017	12184	31844
2018	15256	35908
2019	11844	33158

Record: I◄ ◄ 1 of 4 ► ►I ► | No Filter | Search

219. CHAPTER 19 DISCUSSION QUESTIONS

1. How many fields do we need for a basic crosstab query?
2. What is the purpose of the TRANSFORM statement in crosstab queries?
3. What is the purpose of the PIVOT statement in crosstab queries?
4. What is the purpose of the GROUP BY clause in cross tab queries?
5. Why do we need to pay attention to the uniqueness of values in the GROUP BY field?
6. What is the meaning of blank values in the results of crosstab queries? Is this a database issue or a business fact?
7. How do we calculate totals for columns and rows in crosstab queries?
8. How do we limit the number of rows in crosstab queries?
9. How do we limit the number of columns in crosstab queries?
10. Why do we use the nz() function in crosstab queries?

220. CHAPTER 19 HANDS-ON EXERCISES

Chapter 19 Case 1:

Create a new Access database and name it Chapter19_1.accdb. Copy the table tbls_crosstab from the PracticeDatabase.accdb and paste it to Chapter19_1.accdb.

1. The management of the company needs a report that will provide the total number of orders by city and year. Create a new query that satisfies the managerial request and name it Qry1_CityYear.

Your result should look like:

CustomerCity ▾	<> ▾	2017 ▾	2018 ▾	2019 ▾
Albany		20	22	23
Boston		37	37	23
Chicago	2	44	88	53
Dallas		45	71	55
Denver		33	60	35

Record: I◄ ◄ 1 of 15 ► ►I ►   No Filter   Search

2. The management of the company is now asking for a report that will provide the total number of orders by state and year. Create a new query that satisfies the managerial request and name it Qry2_StateYear.

Your result should look like:

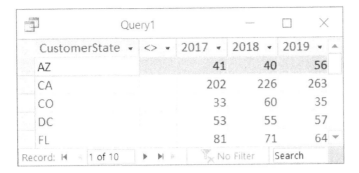

3. The management is really very happy with all the useful information. They now want the report you created in question 2 to exclude the states of California and New York. Create a new query that satisfies the managerial request and name it Qry3_StateYear_LimitRows

   Your result should look like:

CustomerState	<>	2017	2018	2019
AZ		41	40	56
CO		33	60	35
DC		53	55	57
FL		81	71	64
MA		37	37	23

   Record: 1 of 8   No Filter   Search

4. The management now wants a report like the one you created in question 3 but to exclude the year of 2017. Create a new query that satisfies the managerial request and name it Qry4_StateYear_LimitColumns.

   Your result should look like:

   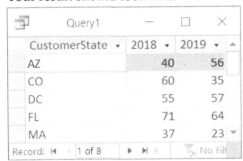

CustomerState	2018	2019
AZ	40	56
CO	60	35
DC	55	57
FL	71	64
MA	37	23

   Record: 1 of 8   No Filt

5. Finally, the management requests a report like the one you created in step 4 but which calculates the total shipping cost by state instead of the total number of orders. All the other criteria they want to remain the same. Create a new query that satisfies the managerial request and name it Qry5_StateYear_ShippingCost.

   Your result should look like:

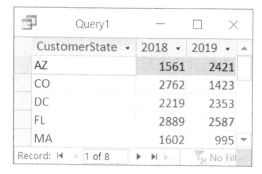

Chapter 19 Case 2:

Create a new Access database and name it Chapter19_2.accdb. Copy the table tblS_Crosstab from the PracticeDatabase.accdb and paste it to Chapter19_2.accdb.

1. The marketing department is asking for a report that will provide the total order amount by customer state and year. Create a new query that satisfies the marketing people request. Do not forget to deduct the given discounts from the calculations. Save the query as Qry1_StateYear.

Your result should look like:

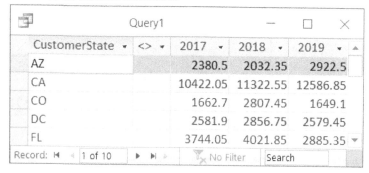

2. The sales people are asking for a report that will provide the total order amount by customer name and year. To avoid any potential issues with duplicates they are asking you to provide the report by concatenating the customer first name with the customer last name. Create a new query that satisfies the sales people request. Save the query as Qry2_CustomerName_Year.

Your result should look like:

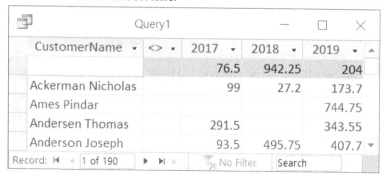

3. The sales people are happy with the very useful report you created for them in question 2. They are now asking you for the same report but limiting the customers to those in the states of Florida and California only. Create a new query that satisfies the sales people request. Save the query as Qry3_SpecificStates.

Your result should look like:

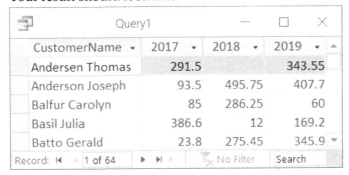

CustomerName ▾	2017 ▾	2018 ▾	2019 ▾
Andersen Thomas	291.5		343.55
Anderson Joseph	93.5	495.75	407.7
Balfur Carolyn	85	286.25	60
Basil Julia	386.6	12	169.2
Batto Gerald	23.8	275.45	345.9

Record: ◄ 1 of 64 ► ►| No Filter Search

4. The sales people are now asking if it is possible to add customer grand totals. Create a new query that satisfies the latest sales people request. Save the query as Qry4_Totals.

Your result should look like:

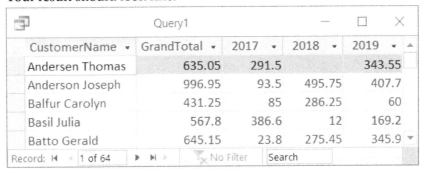

CustomerName ▾	GrandTotal ▾	2017 ▾	2018 ▾	2019 ▾
Andersen Thomas	635.05	291.5		343.55
Anderson Joseph	996.95	93.5	495.75	407.7
Balfur Carolyn	431.25	85	286.25	60
Basil Julia	567.8	386.6	12	169.2
Batto Gerald	645.15	23.8	275.45	345.9

Record: ◄ 1 of 64 ► ►| No Filter Search

5. At this point the management asks for a report showing the contribution of products to sales based on their sales price. Specifically, the management wants to see what is the total revenue from products within the 10-20 price range, including the boundaries (that is those with the price of 10 and those with the price of 20), from products with prices between 21 and 30 including boundaries, and 31 to 40 including boundaries. Total contributions need to be reported by year. In addition, your report should leave out any products with prices less than 10 or more than 40. Create a new query that satisfies the management request and save it as Qry5_ProductPriceRanges.

Your result should look like:
We see right away that products in the 10-20 range account for the vast majority of our business for

all years.

Year	10_20	21_30	31_40
	35.7		136
2017	22751.8	7924.2	4940.8
2018	26772.4	9840.7	5110.4
2019	24237.5	8299.2	3604.8

Record: ◄ ◄ 1 of 4 ► ►► No Filter

CHAPTER 20
PARAMETER QUERIES

The primary goal of a parameter query is to provide flexibility in criteria expressions. Instead of hard coding criteria values in the query code, it provides users the capability to supply the values they want to work with. For example, instead of hard coding the value "NY" for the state field, a parameter query allows users to enter any state and get the corresponding results.

Parameter queries in their simplest form will include one or two parameterized fields but they can become more complex with wildcard characters, operators, equality and inequality predicates, and even functions. We will go through examples of all the above in this chapter so that you can make full use of the power and flexibility of parameter queries.

221.   Creating a query with one parameter field
Retrieve order information using state as a parameter
Discussion:
The simplest form of a parameter query is one with a single parameter field. The parameter field always appears in the WHERE clause of the query and its parameter prompt is enclosed in brackets. In this example, the parameter field is "state", and its prompt will appear as [Enter State:]. The colon at the end of the prompt is optional, and you can omit it if you want. In this specific example, we used the equality predicate "=" in the expression ((State)=[Enter State:]). This is because the parameter in this query is waiting for complete state values like "NY", "AZ", "FL", or "CA". However, you are not restricted to equality or inequality predicates such as (=, <>, <, <=, >, =>). Later, you will learn how you can enter only part of the value you are looking for, in which case you can use an operator such as LIKE. You could also use the BETWEEN operator or even wildcard characters and functions as you will see in this chapter.

Code:
SELECT OrderID, OrderDate, City, State
FROM Qry_Parameters_Base
WHERE State=[Enter State:]

Parameter Prompt:

Result:

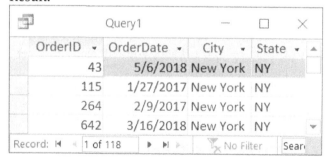

222. Creating a query with two parameter fields

Retrieve order information using state and city as parameters

Discussion:

Creating multi-field parameter queries is a possibility in Access. In this example, we use the state and city as parameter fields using the AND operator. This means that we force our users to select a state first and then, a city within that state. In this example, we select "NY" and then "New York". We can just as easily use the OR operator so that our users can select any state and any city they want.

Code:

```
SELECT OrderID, OrderDate, City, State
FROM Qry_Parameters_Base
WHERE State=[Enter State:] AND City=[Enter City:]
```

Result:

OrderID	OrderDate	City	State
43	5/6/2018	New York	NY
115	1/27/2017	New York	NY
264	2/9/2017	New York	NY
642	3/16/2018	New York	NY

Record: 1 of 118   No Filter   Sear

223. Creating a query with three parameter fields, one of them an expression

Retrieve order information using state, city, and ordertotal as parameters

Discussion:

In this example, we use three parameters for the State, City, and TotalOrder fields. Notice the third parameter ">[Enter Amount Bigger Than:]" for the TotalOrder field. Here, we use the ">" greater than inequality predicate to retrieve orders from "NY" state and "New York" city, which are bigger than $200 in this example. Equality and inequality predicates allow amazing flexibility in parameter queries. For a review of equality and inequality predicates, review chapter 10.

Code:
SELECT OrderID, OrderDate, City, State
FROM Qry_Parameters_Base
WHERE State=[Enter State:] AND City=[Enter City:] AND totalorder>[Enter Amount Bigger Than:]

Result:

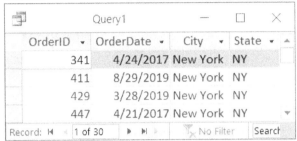

224. Define the order of the parameter prompts

Retrieve order information using orderdate, state, and ordertotal as parameters

Discussion:

Using multiple parameters might present a problem if we enter them directly in the query design grid in Access. In this case, Access will present the parameters from left to right according to the lineup of the columns in the grid. Some sources suggest entering parameters in the "Parameters" sheet in the "Show/Hide" group of the "design" tab to force order. It is really not necessary to type our parameters a second time. In our SQL statement, we just type our parameters in the order we would like them to appear. However, always think about the logic behind the parameter lineup. In this example with the AND operator, the order will not make a difference in the result set since all three parameter values will apply concurrently on the fields for which they are specified. However, there might be cases in which we want a certain date range to be specified first and then, use operators to search for data within that range using operators different from AND.

In this example, the parameters are: NY, 1/1/2017, and $200.

Code:
SELECT OrderID, OrderDate, City, State
FROM Qry_Parameters_Base
WHERE State=[Enter State:] AND orderdate>[Enter Date Later Than:] AND totalorder>[Enter Amount Bigger Than:]

Result:

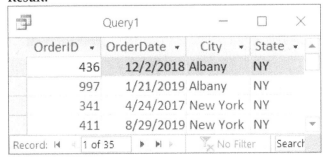

225.   How to retrieve records by providing only part of the parameter value
Find customers by supplying only part of the name
Discussion:

We want to give our users the ability to search orders by customer name without remembering the exact last name of the customer. In this example, we use the * wildcard character and lastname as the parameter field. Of course, we can use our creativity and employ any wildcard character we want (see chapter 8) with any kind of equality or inequality predicates to achieve amazing results. In this example, we will look for all customer names starting with "Ba". As you might expect, the same customer will come up multiple times since each customer might have multiple orders. That is why the name Balfur appears multiple times.

Code:
```
SELECT lastname, firstname, city, state
FROM Qry_Parameters_Base
WHERE lastname LIKE [Enter last name:] + "*"
```

Result:

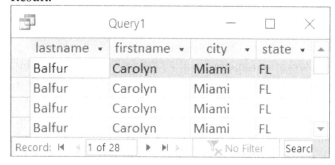

226.   Using numeric ranges in parameter queries
Find sales volume ranges from customer orders
Discussion:

In this example, we enable managers to retrieve order records using any order total boundaries they want. For instance they might want to retrieve orders with total order amounts between $200 and $300. To achieve this, we use the "<" and ">" inequality predicates because we do not want the lower and upper limits of our boundaries ($200, $300) to appear in the result set. If we used BETWEEN (chapter 11), which is inclusive, the boundaries would have been included in the result set. The same would happen if we used the "<=" and "=>" inequality predicates. As you can see from the result set, there are 159 orders between $200 and $300.

Code:
```
SELECT OrderID, OrderDate, City, State, TotalOrder
FROM Qry_Parameters_Base
WHERE TotalOrder>[Enter Min Order Amount:] AND totalorder<[Enter Maximum Order Amount:]
```

Result:

OrderID ▾	OrderDate ▾	City ▾	State ▾	TotalOrder ▾
507	5/2/2018	Houston	TX	225
517	7/5/2019	Houston	TX	240
508	10/21/2019	Orlando	FL	211
96	3/6/2018	Washington	DC	202

Record: ◄ ‹ 1 of 159 ► ►► › ⊽✗ No Filter | Search

227. Using date ranges in parameter queries

Find total order amounts between specific dates

Discussion:

This time, our goal is to retrieve order records between specific order dates. We might want to retrieve sales volumes only for a period of five days, ten days, a few months, or years. In this example, we are looking for orders between 1/1/2018 and 1/15/2018.

Code:

```
SELECT OrderID, OrderDate, City, State, TotalOrder
FROM Qry_Parameters_Base
WHERE OrderDate>[Enter Min Date:] AND OrderDate<[Enter Max Date:]
```

Result:

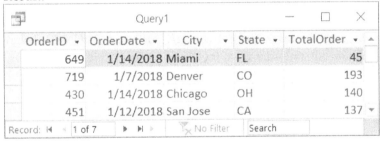

OrderID ▾	OrderDate ▾	City ▾	State ▾	TotalOrder ▾
649	1/14/2018	Miami	FL	45
719	1/7/2018	Denver	CO	193
430	1/14/2018	Chicago	OH	140
451	1/12/2018	San Jose	CA	137

Record: ◄ ‹ 1 of 7 ► ►► › ⊽✗ No Filter | Search

228. Using functions in parameter queries

Find orders for a specific month for any range of years

Discussion:

Now, we have a very peculiar request from our company. Management wants to do some decision-making, and they have asked us for a way to run multiple scenarios such as: What were the sales volumes in the months of May for the last two years? Or for the month of June in the last three years? Or for any month for any range of years? They want to be able to perform these scenarios at will. To achieve this goal, we use the month() function to extract the month out of the OrderDate field, the year() function to extract years out of the OrderDate field, and the BETWEEN operator!

In this example, we used May (enter 5 in the prompt) for the month and 2017 to 2018 for the year range. As you can see from the result set, we indeed only retrieved orders for May 2017 and May 2018.

Code:

```
SELECT OrderID, OrderDate, City, State, TotalOrder
FROM Qry_Parameters_Base
WHERE Month(OrderDate)=[Enter Month Number:] AND Year(OrderDate) BETWEEN [
Enter Min Year:] And [Enter Max Year:]
```

Result:

OrderID	OrderDate	City	State	TotalOrder
507	5/2/2018	Houston	TX	225
378	5/4/2017	Washington	DC	156
43	5/6/2018	New York	NY	150
112	5/2/2018	Phoenix	AZ	100

Record: 1 of 59   No Filter   Search

229. Calculations and functions in parameter queries

Find fulfillment cycle times for customer orders for specific periods

Discussion:

Management now wants to find fulfillment cycle times for customer orders for internal efficiency indicators. Practically, they are looking to retrieve the amount of time it takes to ship an order from the time it is received. To achieve this, we first use the day() function twice to construct a calculated field (lagTimesInDays) to measure the difference between ShippedDate and OrderDate in days. Second, we use two parameters on the OrderDate field so that managers can enter the time period they desire. In this example, we measure the lag time in days for the period between 1/1/2018 and 1/30/2018. As you see from the result set, it takes us five days to ship an order from the time we received it.

Code:

```
SELECT OrderID, (day(ShippedDate) - day(OrderDate)) AS LagTimeInDays, TotalOrder
FROM Qry_Parameters_Base
WHERE OrderDate>[Enter Min Date:] AND OrderDate<[Enter Max Date:]
```

Result:

OrderID	LagTimeInDays	TotalOrder
649	5	45
317	5	30
599	5	228
624	5	45

Record: 1 of 19   No Filter   Sear

CHAPTER 20 DISCUSSION QUESTIONS

1. What is the primary goal of parameter queries?
2. Why do parameter queries save time?
3. Can we use multiple parameters in a parameter query?
4. Are parameters restricted to certain data types?
5. Can we use wildcard characters in parameters?
6. Can we use operators in parameters?
7. Can we use functions to construct parameters in parameter queries?
8. Can we define the order of the parameter prompts? Why is this useful?
9. How can we use numeric ranges as parameters in parameter queries?
10. How can we use date ranges as parameters in parameter queries?

231.   CHAPTER 20 HANDS-ON EXERCISES

Chapter 20 Case 1:

Create a new Access database and name it Chapter20_1.accdb. Copy the tables Customers and Orders from the PracticeDatabase.accdb and paste them to Chapter20_1.accdb.

1. The inventory people are asking for a list of customers they can dynamically generate by entering any state they need. Create a new query that includes the fields FirstName, LastName, City, State, and Zip from the customer table and satisfies the inventory people request. Use "NY" as the parameter. Order the results by state and then city ascending. Save the query as Qry1_State.

    Your result should look like:

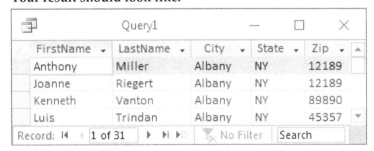

2. The inventory people are asking again for a list of customers which they can dynamically generate by entering any state and city they need. Create a new query that includes the fields FirstName, LastName, City, State, and Zip from the customer table and satisfies the inventory people request. Use "NY" and "Albany" as parameters. Order the results by lastname ascending. Save the query as Qry2_StateCity.

    Your result should look like:

245

3. The inventory people are now asking for a list of customers which they can dynamically generate by entering any state, city, and zip they need. Create a new query that includes all fields from the customer table and satisfies the inventory people request. Use "NY", "Albany", and "12189" as parameters. Order the results by lastname ascending. Save the query as Qry3_StateCityZip.

    Your result should look like:

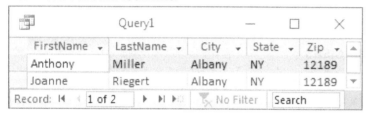

4. The sales people are asking for a list of orders which they can dynamically generate by entering any orderdate period they need. Create a new query that includes all fields from the orders table and satisfies the sales people request. Order the results by orderdate so that the latest dates appear first in the result set. Use "1/1/2018" and "1/31/2018" as parameters. Save the query as Qry4_OrderDate.

    Your result should look like:

OrderID	CustomerID	SalesRepID	ShipperID	OrderDate
551	18	6	1	1/31/2018
124	182	1	3	1/30/2018
206	174	2	2	1/28/2018
624	13	7	2	1/26/2018

Record: 1 of 24 — No Filter — Search

5. The sales people are now asking for a list of orders which they can dynamically generate by entering any shipping cost range they need. Create a new query that includes the OrderID, SalesRepID, OrderDate, and ShippingCost fields from the orders table and satisfies the sales people request. Use "30" and "50" as parameters. Order the results by shipping cost so that higher shipping costs appear first. Save the query as Qry5_OrderShippingCost.
    Your result should look like:

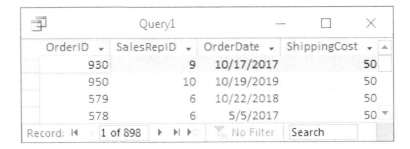

Chapter 20 Case 2:

Create a new Access database and name it Chapter20_2.accdb. Copy the tables Customers, Orders, and Products from the PracticeDatabase.accdb and paste them to Chapter20_2.accdb.

1. The marketing people are asking for a list of orders which they can dynamically generate by entering any specific order date they need. Create a new query that includes all fields from the orders table and satisfies the marketing people request. Use "5/22/2019" as the parameter. Order the results by OrderDate so that the latest orders appear first. Save the query as Qry1_OrderDate.

Your result should look like:

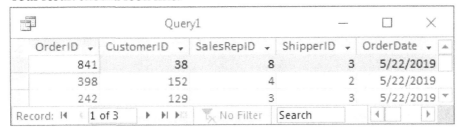

2. The marketing people are now asking for a list of orders which they can dynamically generate by entering the year and the month. Create a new query that includes the OrderID, SalesRepID, and OrderDate fields from the orders table and satisfies the marketing people request. Hint: (When you run the query, enter months in number format like 4 for April, 5 for May). Use "5" for May and "2019" as the parameters. Order the results by OrderDate so that the latest orders appear first. Save the query as Qry2_OrderYearMonth.

Your result should look like:

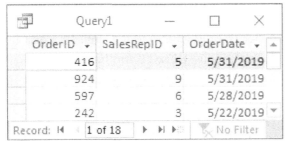

3. The inventory people are asking for a list of products which they can dynamically generate by entering minimum and maximum UnitsInStock quantities. Create a new query that includes the ProductID, ProductName, ProductUnitPrice, and UnitsInStock fields from the products table and satisfies the inventory people request. Use "20" and "50" as parameters. Order results by UnitsInStock so that biggest quantities appear first. Save the query as Qry3_UnitsInStock.

Your result should look like:

ProductID	ProductName	ProductUnitPrice	UnitsInStock
4	Berry Cherry in 8 oz. Bag	30	50
46	Artichokes in white sauce	22	50
47	Chocolate Chip Cookies	49	50
69	Salsa Verde	35	49

Record: 1 of 64 — No Filter — Search

4. The marketing people are asking for a list of customers which they can dynamically generate by entering any customer last name they need. However, they also want the query to provide results even if they do not remember the full last name of the customer and they enter part of it. Create a new query that includes all fields from the customers table and satisfies the marketing people request. Use "Da" as the parameter. Order the results by lastname ascending. Save the query as Qry4_Customers.

Your result should look like:

CustomerID	FirstName	LastName	Address	City
144	Janet	Dalton	102 Gumey street	New York
196	Matthew	Darek	78 Unity Street	Denver
110	Diane	Darek	9 North Bridge Dr	San Jose
197	Jason	Datek	19 Paul Street	Denver

Record: 1 of 6 — No Filter — Search

5. The inventory people need a list of products for which they need to order additional units for inventory. Create a calculated field, UnitsToOrder, which will be the result of the sum of the reorder level, the current units in stock, and the current units on order. The inventory people want to select the supplierID dynamically and get the results for the UnitsToOrder associated to that supplier. Create a new query that includes the SupplierID, ProductID, and the UnitsToOrdser field from the products table and satisfies the inventory people request. Use "1" for the SupplierID parameter value. Order the results by UnitsToOrder so that the biggest quantities appear first. In addition, include in the query only UnitsToOrder quantities that are equal to or higher than zero. Save the query as Qry5_UnitsToOrder.

Your result should look like:

SupplierID	ProductID	UnitsToOrder
1	6	3
1	8	2
1	7	1
1	1	0

Query1

Record: 1 of 4   No Filter   Sea

CHAPTER 21
CONDITIONAL DATA MANIPULATION

The iif(), switch(), and partition() functions are the most useful and practical functions for conditional data manipulation in Access. Keep in mind that CASE does not work in Access, so do not bother wasting your time looking for it.

What exactly do we mean by conditional data processing? Let's assume we have a customer database we use for promotional campaigns. We might decide we want to provide different discount levels for customers in the Northeast, Midwest, West, Southeast, and Southwest states. Since we do not have region information in our database, we need to create multiple SELECT queries for these categories and apply the appropriate discount for each region. Using conditional data processing, on the other hand, will enable us to do our job in just one query.

You might be thinking at this point that it does not bother you to create four queries to do your job. What matters in the end is getting the job done. I totally agree. However, what will happen after a couple of years at work is that you will end up with several hundred queries. In the end, you will not remember what was what, and you will be afraid to delete even one of them since you no longer know what it was used for. During the last 20 years, I have seen this happen countless times with departmental databases.

To encourage you to use conditional processing, let me give you another example. Let's say we have a database in which we store our products, along with the corresponding suppliers. Every now and then, our suppliers send us updated prices, and we need to update our own product catalog as well. We have only 20 suppliers and 200 products in our database, and we need to update our prices every few weeks.

Of course, thinking logically, suppliers will provide us with different price updates. Some of them will increase their prices by 3%, some by 5%, some by 3.5%, some by 4%, ending up with four clusters in this example. Still, we will have to create four update queries and include the specific calculated fields for the updates and specific criteria so that the appropriate supplier products are updated and with the correct percentages.

Furthermore, every time we have price updates, we will need to modify our current update queries, create new ones, modify their criteria, and calculate new prices for the updates. We will end up with an unmanageable number of queries even for this simple scenario. Using conditions, on the other hand, we can do the job very effectively using just a single query!

A final point on conditional statements: Those who understand conditional statements will produce much better database designs and entity relationship diagrams since they know in advance what needs to be stored and what can be produced automatically by the database.

232.   Using the iif() and switch() functions with two simple conditions

Produce a product catalog with special discounts for one product only

Discussion:

We received an urgent message from the inventory department saying we have a large quantity of Chocolate Fudge which needs to go out into the market fast. We only have a few hours to produce a new product catalog for this week and send it to our customers. All of the product prices in the catalog should remain the same except for Chocolate Fudge, which will be reduced by 50%. We must not make this percentage change right in the table because this price will be valid only for a week.

Solution 1: using the iif() function

We can solve this problem using an iif() conditional function. The translation of the iif() function in this example says: For the product with ProductID = 14, reduce the value of the field ProductUnitPrice by 50%, and for the rest of the products in the catalog, leave the price as is in the table. In addition, notice that a second function is used, cCur(), to display numbers with the dollar sign in front of them. Notice also that we changed the title of the ProductUnitPrice field to appear as "ProductPrice" in this week's catalog. Finally, notice in the result set that the price of Chocolate Fudge is now $20.50 in the query, while it remains $41 in the products table.

Code:

```
SELECT ProductID, ProductName, QuantityPerUnit,
cCur(iif([productid]=14,[productunitprice]*0.5,[productunitprice])) AS ProductPrice
FROM Products
```

Result:

ProductID	ProductName	QuantityPerUnit	ProductPrice
4	Berry Cherry in 8 oz. Bag	15	$30.00
5	California Original Pista	15	$29.00
6	Choice Apricots - 16 oz. B	25	$32.00
7	Cran Raisin Mix in 17 oz.	12	$31.00

Record: 1 of 70   No Filter   Search

Solution 2: using the switch() function

There is no need to use the switch function in this case since the conditions are very simple. However, we would like to know its syntax and how it works with respect to an iif() function. In this example, we again used the Ccur() function in front of the switch function to obtain the dollar sign in front of the product prices. We also change the price of the product when the ProductID = 14 and we leave the price unchanged when the ProductID is different than 14. There is no doubt that the switch() function is much cleaner and comprehensible than the iif() function. This becomes more evident as the number of conditions goes up.

Code:
SELECT ProductID, ProductName, QuantityPerUnit,
SWITCH(
productid = 14,   productunitprice*0.5,
productid <>14,   productunitprice
)
AS ProductPrice
FROM Products

Result:

ProductID ▾	ProductName ▾	QuantityPerUnit ▾	ProductPrice ▾
4	Berry Cherry in 8 oz. Bag	15	$30.00
5	California Original Pista⟨	15	$29.00
6	Choice Apricots - 16 oz. B	25	$32.00
7	Cran Raisin Mix in 17 oz.	12	$31.00

Record: I◀ 1 of 70 ▶ ▶I ▶⁕ 🔽 No Filter Search

233.   Using the iif() and switch() functions with two conditions but multiple criteria
Provide custom discounts for customers in NY, TX, and CA
Discussion:
This time, management initiates a new promotional campaign. They want to offer a 20% discount to customers in large states such as NY, TX, and CA and 10% to everyone else around the country. They want a list of customers and their corresponding discount rates for review.

Solution 1: using the iif() function
Using the iif() function becomes a bit more complicated this time and requires two OR operators. The iif() function translates to: If the customer is in NY, CA, or TX, provide him or her with a discount of 20%. Otherwise, provide the customer with a discount of 10%.

Code:
SELECT State, lastname, firstname, OrderTotal,
IIf([state]= 'NY' Or [state]= 'CA' Or [state]= 'TX','20%','10%')
AS Discount
FROM Qry_Conditions

Solution 2: using the switch() function
The use of the switch function with two conditions and multiple criteria is again more legible than using the iif() function and, therefore, easily editable if we need to update our criteria later on.

Code:

```
SELECT State, lastname, firstname,  OrderTotal,
SWITCH(
[state]= 'NY' Or [state]= 'CA' Or [state] = 'TX',      '20%',
[state] <> 'NY' Or 'CA' Or 'TX',                       '10%'
)
AS Discount
FROM Qry_Conditions
```

Result:

State	lastname	firstname	OrderTotal	Discount
NY	Riegert	Joanne	30	20%
DC	Read	Lisa	210	10%
AZ	Moore	Gerald	231	10%
MA	Davis	Catherine	45	10%

Record: ◀ 1 of 919 ▶ ▶│   No Filter   Search

234.   Working with multiple conditions and criteria

Calculate discount amounts based on customer sales volumes

Discussion:

Our sales manager wants to provide order discounts to customers based on their historical sales volume with the company. Thus, if a customer has a certain recorded sales volume, the next time she orders, she will get a predetermined discount rate regardless of her new order amount.

If the total order amount for a customer is less than $200, that customer will receive no discounts. If it is between $200 and $300, the customer will get a 5% discount. If it is between $300 and $500, the customer will get a 10% discount. For anything above that, our manager will offer a generous 25% discount to the customer. Our job is to create a report that will list our customers and their corresponding discount rate.

Solution 1: using nested iif() functions

Our first option is to use a series of nested iif() functions as shown below—four iif() functions, one inside the other to accomplish our goal. However, the use of nested iif() functions is a convoluted process. In addition, if we need to change the business logic behind our statement by adding additional categories, the task is not a clear and clean preposition. The problem originates from the fact that the iif() function takes only two arguments. For more outcomes or categories, we need to nest, which results in complicated statements.

Code:

```
SELECT lastname, firstname, OrderTotal, IIf([ordertotal]<200,0,IIf([ordertotal]>=200 And
[Ordertotal]<300,'5%',IIf([ordertotal]>=300 And
[ordertotal]<500,'10%',IIf([ordertotal]>500,'25%')))) AS Discount
FROM Qry_Conditions
```

Solution 2: using the switch() function

In this example, the first observation is that the switch() function does not limit the number of expressions we can use, so we need no nesting. In addition, our logic becomes immediately apparent to us and anyone else who will need to edit the SQL statement later on. The cleanliness of the SQL statement is obvious:

Code:

```
SELECT lastname, firstname, ordertotal,
SWITCH(
ordertotal < 200,                        '0',
ordertotal>= 200 and ordertotal < 300,   '5%',
ordertotal> 300 and ordertotal <= 500,   '10%',
ordertotal> 500 ,                        '25%'
)
AS Discount
FROM qry_conditions
```

Result:

lastname	firstname	ordertotal	Discount
Riegert	Joanne	30	0
Read	Lisa	210	5%
Moore	Gerald	231	5%
Davis	Catherine	45	0

Record: 1 of 919   No Filter   Search

235. An effective trick with the switch() function

Calculate customer discounts based on location

Discussion:

This time, the task is to provide discounts for customers in five specific states. At the same time, a general discount percentage should be extended to all customers in states not included in the specific state list. We can achieve this task by using the TRUE keyword as part of the last expression in a switch() function. This last expression will evaluate true for every state not included in the specific state list, and we will extend the 10% discount to all of the customers in states different from NY, AZ, CO, FL, and MA.

Code:
```
SELECT State, lastname, firstname, OrderTotal,
SWITCH(
[state]= 'NY',   '20%',
[state] ='AZ',   '15%',
[state] ='CO',   '12%',
[state] ='FL',   '18%',
[state] ='MA',   '18%',
TRUE,            '10%',
)
AS Discount FROM Qry_Conditions
```

Result:

236.   Using switch() with WHERE, IN, and ORDER BY

Calculate order totals based on customer sales volumes

Discussion:

Our goal now is to estimate what would have been the total sales by customer if we have provided them with discounts. We create our analysis by offering various discount levels to customers with order totals between $200 and $500 only. We extend these discounts to customers in AZ, CO, TX, and FL only. After the switch function, we use the WHERE clause with the IN operator to define the exact records for which our calculations will apply.

Code:
```
SELECT OrderID, lastname, firstname, State,
SWITCH(
ordertotal>= 200 and ordertotal < 300,   Ordertotal*(1-0.1) ,
ordertotal> 300 and ordertotal <= 500,   OrderTotal*(1-0.15) ,
ordertotal> 500 ,                         OrderTotal*(1-0.2),
TRUE,                                     OrderTotal
)
as DiscountedOrders
FROM qry_conditions
WHERE state in ('AZ', 'CO', 'TX', 'FL')
ORDER BY ordertotal DESC
```

Result:

OrderID	lastname	firstname	State	DiscountedOrder
944	Corelli		TX	459.2
308	Darek	Matthew	CO	409.6
404	Crandil	Joseph	TX	408
932	Weinberger	Fred	FL	386.75

Record: 1 of 301 — No Filter — Search

237. Using switch() with calculated fields
Produce product categories based on product prices
Discussion:

This time, the request we have from management is to provide a product list categorized arbitrarily by price. They want to see a product list that specifies each product as "economical", "moderate", and "expensive" based on its price. Although we carry no such field in the database, we can absolutely create the list in seconds by using the switch() function with calculated fields. In essence, we calculate the unit price times its quantity per unit to get the total price for the product, and we then assign categories based on price. For instance, if the price falls between $500 and $1000, we designate these products as "moderately" priced. We can save this query and update it at will if management wants more, less, or otherwise defined categories.

Code:
```
SELECT ProductName, UnitsInStock, UnitsOnOrder,
SWITCH(
ProductUnitPrice*QuantityPerUnit < 500,     'Economical',
ProductUnitPrice*QuantityPerUnit >= 500 AND ProductUnitPrice*QuantityPerUnit<1000,
'Moderate',
ProductUnitPrice*QuantityPerUnit >= 1000, 'Expensive',
)
as PricingCategory
FROM Products
ORDER BY  ProductUnitPrice*QuantityPerUnit DESC
```

Result:

ProductName	UnitsInStock	UnitsOnOrder	PricingCategory
Chocolate Chunk Cooki	15	20	Expensive
Dark Chocolate Apricot	38	0	Expensive
Buttermilk Muffins	31	0	Expensive
Coffee biscuits	24	0	Expensive

Record: 1 of 70 — No Filter — Search

238.   Using switch() with aggregate functions

Calculate employee commissions and bonuses based on their sales volume

Discussion:

There are multiple tasks in this example. First, we need to calculate employee commissions as a percentage of their sales. Second, we need to calculate employee bonuses based again on sales volumes. Third, we need to add commission and bonus amounts. Fourth, we need to make these calculations only for 2014. Fifth, we need to present the results as currency.

Do not be intimidated by the long SQL statement. It is long but not as tough as it looks. In two minutes, you will have a total grasp of it. First, notice we use only three fields in this SQL statement: lastname, orderdate, and CommissionAndBonus. We use the lastname field as is. For the orderdate field, we use the function year() to extract the year part of the date. The CommissionAndBonus field will be the result of the switch function calculations.

Next, notice that we use three functions, sum(), Ccur(), and switch(), one after the other. We use the sum() function to obtain the total order amounts sold by our salesperson. Since we do not have a field for order totals in the database (correctly, since we can calculate them), we need to multiply the quantity of each product sold by its price in every order and sum() the results. Then, we use the Ccur() function to convert the data type of the CommissionAndBonus field to appear as currency. Finally, we use the switch function to assign commissions and bonuses according to sales volumes.

Next, we have a FROM statement but do not pay attention to the joins since Access will create the joins automatically when we paste this code in a query and look at its design. We devote a whole chapter on joins (chapter 30).

In the final part of the SQL statement, we group by employee and year since we need to have commissions and bonuses shown by employee. We filter the year by using the HAVING clause as we examined in our "GROUP BY" chapter.

In the end, the whole query is reduced to three fields: lastname and year by which we group by and the commissionandbonus field on which we apply the sum() aggregate function.

Code:

```
SELECT LastName,  Year([OrderDate]) AS [Year],

SUM(CCur(SWITCH(
([UnitPrice]*[quantity]) < 5000,          ([UnitPrice]*[quantity])*(0.1) + 500 ,
([UnitPrice]*[quantity]) >= 5000 and  ([UnitPrice]*[quantity]) <10000,
([UnitPrice]*[quantity])*(0.15) + 1000,
([UnitPrice]*[quantity]) >= 10000 and  ([UnitPrice]*[quantity]) <15000,
([UnitPrice]*[quantity])*(0.2) + 3000,
([UnitPrice]*[quantity]) >= 15000 ,       ([UnitPrice]*[quantity])*(0.25) + 5000,
)))
as CommissionAndBonus

FROM SalesReps INNER JOIN (Orders INNER JOIN ProductsOrders ON Orders.OrderID =
ProductsOrders.OrderID) ON SalesReps.SalesRepID = Orders.SalesRepID

GROUP BY LastName, Year([OrderDate])
HAVING Year([OrderDate])=2017
ORDER BY Sum([UnitPrice]*[quantity]) DESC
```

Result:

LastName	Year	CommissionAndBonus
Zensons	2017	$47,092.40
Spicer	2017	$46,563.40
Anderson	2017	$39,988.80
Baker	2017	$44,976.60

Record: 1 of 10   No Filter   Search

239.   Using partition() for data visualization

Create intervals on sales volumes and count orders included

Discussion:

What if we encounter a request for a visualization of the distribution of our orders? For example, we would want to know how many orders fall between 0 and $50, how many between $50 and $100, how many between $100 and $150, etc. We can provide an answer using the partition() function.

The partition() function has the syntax:

Partition(field, beginning number, ending number, interval)

For instance, if we want to categorize orders in $50 increments starting at $0 and ending at $500, we can write: Partition(ordertotal, 0, 500, 50).

In this example, we use two fields: "Range" and "Count". Both of these fields are calculated fields. The contents of the Range field are produced by the partition function, and the contents of the Count field are produced by counting the number of orders in each partition according to their order total amount. We can change the parameters of the partition function at will to produce any intervals we want.

In this example, we defined the boundaries between $0 and $500 with intervals of $50. This does not mean that the partition function will stop at $500. It will stop producing intervals at $500, and from $501 and above, it will put all remaining orders in the same category. We will still know how many orders we have above $501.

Code:
SELECT DISTINCTROW Partition([ordertotal],0, 500, 50) AS Range,
Count(ordertotal) AS Count
FROM Qry_Conditions
GROUP BY Partition([ordertotal],0, 500, 50)

Result:

Range	Count
0: 49	138
50: 99	188
100:149	194
150:199	144
200:249	94
250:299	70
300:349	49
350:399	17
400:449	16
450:499	4
501:	5

Record: 1 of 11

240. Using switch() with update queries
Update multiple product prices from multiple suppliers conditionally
Discussion:
Now, this is an occasion where a switch() function will show its true and unique power. When we combine it with update statements, we can produce highly effective updates that otherwise would have required multiple update queries to obtain.

In this example, we want to update 70 products from ten suppliers, and for each supplier, we apply different update percentages. Those percentages start from 2% all the way up to 11%, as you can see from the SQL code below. By combining the switch() function with the UPDATE statement, we can do everything in one single query. We can save this query and use it every time we need to update our prices.

Code:

```
UPDATE tbls_Products_Upd
SET ProductUnitPrice =
SWITCH (
supplierid=1,    ProductUnitPrice*(1.1) ,
supplierid=2,    ProductUnitPrice*(1.08),
supplierid=3,    ProductUnitPrice*(1.07) ,
supplierid=4,    ProductUnitPrice*(1.05) ,
supplierid=5,    ProductUnitPrice*(1.03) ,
supplierid=6,    ProductUnitPrice*(1.02) ,
supplierid=7,    ProductUnitPrice*(1.03) ,
supplierid=8,    ProductUnitPrice*(1.07) ,
supplierid=9,    ProductUnitPrice*(1.11) ,
supplierid=10,   ProductUnitPrice*(1.08) ,
)
```

Result:

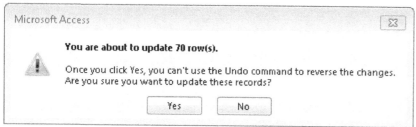

Microsoft Access

You are about to update 70 row(s).

Once you click Yes, you can't use the Undo command to reverse the changes. Are you sure you want to update these records?

[Yes]   [No]

241.   Using switch() with crosstab queries

Create a crosstab query that calculates order totals for "big" and "small" cities

Discussion:

This time, we have a request from management to calculate sales volumes by year and, at the same time, categorize results by small and big cities in the country. They told us specifically that they want to see combined sales volumes for big cities like New York and Los Angeles and combined sales volumes for every other city in which we do business. This is an excellent occasion to combine the power of the switch function with the flexibility of crosstab queries. Instead of pivoting by the city field as we did in the crosstab queries chapter, we use the switch function right in the PIVOT statement to create city categories of our own imagination and creativity!

Code:

```
TRANSFORM Sum([unitprice]*[quantity]) AS Ordertotal
SELECT Year([OrderDate]) As Year
FROM Qry_Crosstab_Base
GROUP BY Year([OrderDate])
PIVOT
SWITCH(
[CustomerCity]= 'New York' Or [CustomerCity]= 'Los Angeles' ,       'BigCities',
[CustomerCity] <> 'New York' Or 'Los Angeles',              'SmallCities'
)
```

Result:

Year	BigCities	SmallCities
		202
2017	13110	30918
2018	13445	37719
2019	15950	29052

Record: 1 of 4   No Fil

Why do we see a blank row for "Year" and "BigCities" with a corresponding sales volume of 202 in the result figure above? This is because we have two records with blank OrderDates that do not allow the classification of those orders to any particular year. To verify that yourselves open the query "Qry_Crosstab_Base" and sort its records by OrderDate ascending. You will see the two blank order dates right away. Also, notice that the associated city for both these records is Chicago which is considered a small city for the classification in this example. That is why you see a number for the SmallCities and nothing for the BigCities for the blank year row in the result above.

CHAPTER 21 DISCUSSION QUESTIONS

1. What are the goals of conditional data manipulation?
2. Which are the basic three functions for conditional data manipulation?
3. Does the CASE() function work in Access?
4. Why the understanding of conditional statements leads to better entity relationship diagrams?
5. How many conditions can we process with an iif() function?
6. How many conditions can we process with a switch() function?
7. Can we process multiple conditions with iif() functions? How?
8. What is the purpose of the "TRUE" keyword in a switch function?
9. Can we use calculated fields within the switch function?
10. How is the partition function different than the iif() and switch() functions?

243. CHAPTER 21 HANDS-ON EXERCISES

Chapter 21 Case 1:

Create a new Access database and name it Chapter21_1.accdb. Copy the tables Customers, Products, and sales reps from the PracticeDatabase.accdb and paste them to Chapter21_1.accdb.

1. The marketing department initiates a new campaign to provide customers with discount coupons. The customers in NY and CA will receive 20% discounts while the customers in the rest of the country 25%. Create a query that will contain the firstname, lastname, and city fields from the customer table. In addition you need to include a field that will show the actual discount the customer will get. Name the new field CouponDiscount. You must use the iif() function to get your result. Save the query as Qry1_CustomerCoupons_a.

Your result should look like:

2. Create the same outcome as in number 1 but using the switch function this time. Save the query as Qry1_CustomerCoupons_b.

Your result should look like:

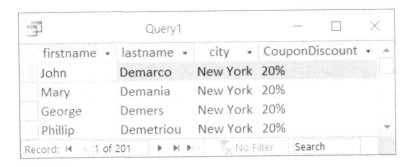

3. The management wants to extend a special bonus to employees based on seniority. Employees with 5 years or less in the company will receive $2500, between five and ten years $5,000, and beyond 10 years $7500. Create a new query that includes the firstname, lastname, dateofhire, as well as one additional field to show the associated bonus. Save the query as Qry3_EmployeeBonuses. HINT: use the datediff() function in the following way datediff("yyyy", [dateofhire], date()) to find the difference in years between today's date and the date the employee was hired. See chapter 27 for more information on date functions.

Your result should look like:

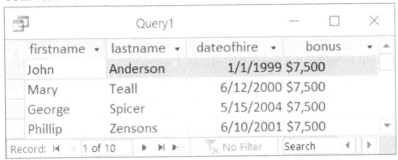

4. The marketing department is asking for a report that will list the number of customers in "big" and "small" cities. "Big" cities are considered to be the cities of New York, Los Angeles, and Houston. Every other city is considered to be a "small" city. The results need to be crosstabbed by state. In addition, results should be limited to the states of NY, CA, and TX only. Create a new query that satisfies the marketing people request and save it as Qry4_BigSmallCities.

Your result should look like:

5. The inventory director needs a report that will list the number of products within certain price ranges. Specifically, he needs the number of products in the price ranges of 0-10, 10-20, 20-30, 30-

40, and 40-50. Create a new query that satisfies the inventory director's request and save it as Qry5_ProductPriceRanges. You must use the partition() function to produce your results.

Your result should look like:

Chapter 21 Case 2:

Create a new Access database and name it Chapter21_2.accdb. Copy the table Products from the PracticeDatabase.accdb and paste it to Chapter21_2.accdb.

1. For the next couple of days the products California Original Pistachios - 1 lb. Bag, Choice Apricots - 16 oz. Bag, and Cran Raisin Mix in 17 oz. are on sale with a generous discount of 20%. The sales people are asking for a new product catalog to reflect these discounts which will be valid for only two days. Create a new query that includes the fields ProductID, ProductName, ProductUnitPrice, and a calculated field, named ProductPrice, from the products table and satisfies the sales people request. Order the results by ProductID ascending. Save the query as Qry1_20Percent. You must use a logical iif() function. Hint: use the IN operator within the iif() function.

Your result should look like:

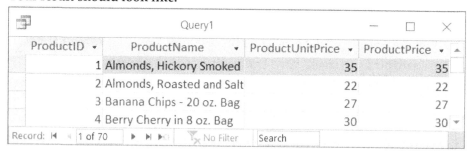

2. Achieve the exact same results as in number one (1) by using the switch() function this time. Save the query as Qry2_20PercentSwitch.

Your result should look like:

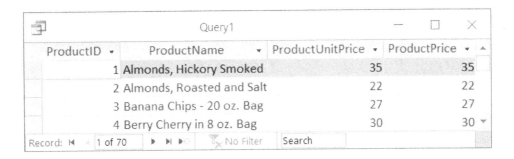

3. The marketing people are initiating a new campaign so that the company can get rid of high inventory items. In this respect create a new product catalog with the following discounts: 20% discount for products with units in stock below 20, 25% discount for products with units in stock greater than 20 and less than 30, 30% discount for products with units in stock greater than 30 and less than 40, and 35% discount for products with units in stock greater than 40. Create a new query that includes the fields ProductName, UnitsInStock, ProductUnitPrice, and a calculated field, named NewPrice, from the products table and satisfies the marketing people request. Order the results by ProductName ascending. Save the query as Qry3_MultipleDiscounts.

Your result should look like:

ProductName	UnitsInStock	ProductUnitPrice	NewPrice
All-Purpose Marinade I	27	29	21.75
All-Purpose Marinade II	26	39	29.25
Almonds, Hickory Smoked	40	35	22.75
Almonds, Roasted and Salt	32	22	15.4

Record: ◄ ◄ 1 of 70 ► ►► No Filter   Search

4. The marketing people are amazingly happy from your report in question three. However, someone from replenishment pointed out that the report in question three though amazing does not solve the problem with highly inventoried items. They propose to add to the units in stock the units on order to arrive at what we actually have in inventory even though the units on order are not physically in yet. Consequently, recreate the query in step three (3) taking into consideration the sum of units in stock and units on order to provide the corresponding discounts. The new query should include the fields ProductName, UnitsInStock, UnitsOnOrder, ProductUnitPrice, and a calculated field, named NewPrice, from the products table and satisfies the replenishing people request. Save the query as Qry4_MultipleDiscountsSum.

Your result should look like:

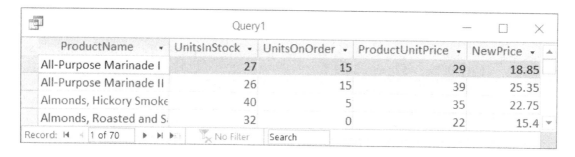

ProductName	UnitsInStock ▾	UnitsOnOrder ▾	ProductUnitPrice ▾	NewPrice ▾
All-Purpose Marinade I	27	15	29	18.85
All-Purpose Marinade II	26	15	39	25.35
Almonds, Hickory Smoke	40	5	35	22.75
Almonds, Roasted and S.	32	0	22	15.4 ▾

Record: I◄ ◄ 1 of 70 ► ►I ►⁺ ⊽× No Filter   Search

5. The management of the company is asking for a report identical to that of item four (4). However, this time they want to see the actual discount extended (for example 20%, 25%, 30%) for each product instead of the new price of the product. Create a new query that satisfies the management's request and save it as Qry5_DiscountExtended.

Your result should look like:

ProductName	UnitsInStock ▾	UnitsOnOrder ▾	ProductUnitPrice ▾	DiscountExtend ▾
All-Purpose Marinade I	27	15	29	35%
All-Purpose Marinade II	26	15	39	35%
Almonds, Hickory Smoke	40	5	35	35%
Almonds, Roasted and S.	32	0	22	30%

Record: I◄ ◄ 1 of 70 ► ►I ►⁺ ⊽× No Filter   Search

CHAPTER 22
UNION OPERATIONS

The primary goal of the UNION statement is to combine records from multiple data sets. In this respect, you can merge records from two or more SQL statements, from a SQL statement and a table, or from two or more tables. In contrast to popular belief, you can combine records with fields of different data types and sizes in Access. In addition, the fields do not have to be similar in content or name! The number of fields, however, does need to be the same. The UNION operator will return no duplicate records, while the UNION ALL operator will return all records from the combined data sets.

The UNION operator is not just a dull SQL statement that we use to combine records. We will see throughout this chapter that we can use it with clauses like WHERE, ORDER BY, and GROUP BY, operators like IN, NOT IN, and BETWEEN, and even subqueries for powerful results. Understanding the UNION operator will enable us to perform operations and achieve results that other database users could not even imagine possible.

In this chapter, we will work with two customer tables under the assumption that we have two distribution centers with one as our main center and the other as a regional center. For the most part, customers order from one of the two distribution centers. However, just to complicate our scenario a bit, we do have customers who will order from both. Consequently, we need to pay attention to how customer records are merged in order to exclude duplicate ones.

We will use two tables: The customers table with 201 records and the tbls_customers_un table with 20 records. Fourteen of the customers in the tbls_customers_un table are identical to the customers table, while six are different. The similarities or dissimilarities of data among tables are important for UNION statements, as we shall see in a second.

244.   The UNION operator with similar fields
Combine unique customer records from two datasets
Discussion:
In this example, we use a simple UNION statement to combine customer records from the two distribution centers. Notice that the number of customers returned is 207. This is because we combined 201 customers from the first table and 20 from the second. Since 14 customers are identical in both tables, and we use the UNION operator, we will only get 207 unique customers. If we used the UNION ALL operator, we would get 221 records.

Code:
```
SELECT lastname, firstname, city, state, zip
FROM customers
UNION
SELECT lastname, firstname, city, state, zip
FROM tbls_customers_un
```

Result:

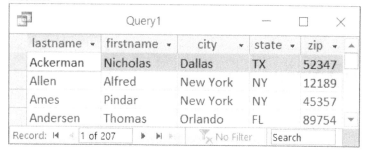

245.   The UNION operator with dissimilar fields

Combine customer and supplier records from two different tables

Discussion:

Here, we demonstrate the ability of the UNION statement to combine data from two dissimilar tables. Notice the different field names from the customer and supplier tables. In addition, check the numbers. We get all of the customers from the customers table (201) and all of the suppliers (10) from the suppliers table for a total of 211 records.

Code:

SELECT lastname, firstname, city, state, zip

FROM customers

UNION

SELECT companyname, contactname, city, state, zip

FROM suppliers

Result:

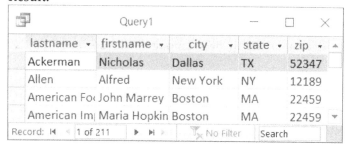

246.   The UNION operator with tables and SQL statements

Combine all customer records from a table and some from a SQL statement

Discussion:

In this example, we will combine all of the records from the customers table with some of the records from the tbls_customers_un table. Essentially, we merge a table and a SQL statement. Notice the absence of a SELECT statement for the customers table and the use of the WHERE clause in the code below:

Code:

TABLE [customers]

UNION

SELECT *

FROM tbls_customers_un
WHERE state='TX'

Result:

CustomerID	FirstName	LastName	Address	City	State	Zip
1	John	Demarco	11 Lark Street	New York	NY	1218
2	Mary	Demania	12 Madison Ave	New York	NY	1218
3	George	Demers	23 New Scotlan	New York	NY	1218
4	Phillip	Demetriou	22 Academy Ro	New York	NY	1218

Record: 1 of 208 — No Filter — Search

247. Using multiple UNION operators

Combine records from two customer tables and a supplier table

Discussion:

We can use UNION to merge records from multiple data sources. In this example, we employ two UNION statements to merge data from three data sources. Notice that while the first two SELECT statements contain identical fields, the third one uses different ones. Also, we must pay attention to our numbers. The first table (customers) contains 201 records, the second (tbls_customers_un) 20, and the third (suppliers) 10. We have a total of 231 records, but our result set contains only 217. This is correct since we have 14 identical records in the customers and tbls_customers_un tables. Consequently, the final result is 231-14 = 217 records.

Code:

```
SELECT lastname, firstname, city, state, zip
FROM customers
UNION
SELECT lastname, firstname, city, state, zip
FROM tbls_customers_un
UNION
SELECT companyname, contactname, city, state, zip
FROM suppliers
```

Result:

lastname	firstname	city	state	zip
Ackerman	Nicholas	Dallas	TX	52347
Allen	Alfred	New York	NY	12189
American Foods,	John Marrey	Boston	MA	22459
American Import	Maria Hopkin	Boston	MA	22459

Record: 1 of 217 — No Filter — Search

248.   The UNION ALL operator

Combine customer records from two data sources and allow duplicates to appear

Discussion:

The UNION operator will exclude duplicate records. If we need to combine two lists, but we also want to include duplicates, then we will use the UNION ALL operator. Have a look at the number of records returned. In this case, it should be 201 + 20 for a total of 221, and this is exactly what we get. (Remember we have 201 records in the customer table and 20 in the tbls_customers_un).

Code:

SELECT lastname, firstname, city, state, zip

FROM customers

UNION ALL

SELECT lastname, firstname, city, state, zip

FROM tbls_customers_un

Result:

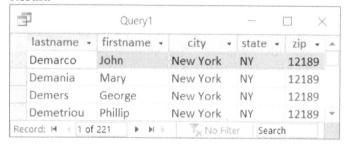

249.   Using UNION with ORDER BY

Sort customer records correctly when using UNION

Discussion:

The ORDER BY clause should be used at the end of the whole SQL statement when using UNION operators, not after the individual SQL statements.

Code:

SELECT lastname, firstname, city, state, zip

FROM customers

UNION

SELECT lastname, firstname, city, state, zip

FROM tbls_customers_un

ORDER BY lastname

Result:

250. Using UNION with WHERE

Create customer lists with criteria using WHERE

Discussion:

In this example, notice the use of the WHERE clause in each individual SELECT statement. We can absolutely use multiple WHERE clauses to get exactly what we need from the individual data sets. In this example, we wanted to get only customers from New York from the first and customers from Texas from the second.

Code:

```
SELECT lastname, firstname, city, state, zip
FROM customers
WHERE state = 'NY'
UNION
SELECT lastname, firstname, city, state, zip
FROM tbls_customers_un
WHERE state ='TX'
ORDER BY state
```

Result:

251. Using UNION with IN and NOT IN

Create customer lists with filtering criteria using IN and NOT IN

Discussion:

We can perform detailed filtering using the WHERE clause and the IN or NOT IN operators within each individual SELECT statement in this UNION operation. Notice we can apply criteria with different operators on different fields. We might have used the WHERE clause with the AND operator in the first SELECT and the IN operator in the second. In addition, we could have applied some criteria on the city field in the first SELECT and some criteria on the state field in the second.

Code:

```
SELECT lastname, firstname, city, state, zip
FROM customers
WHERE city IN('New York', 'Los Angeles')
UNION
SELECT lastname, firstname, city, state, zip
FROM tbls_customers_un
WHERE city IN('Dallas', 'Miami', 'Orlando', 'Ontario')
ORDER BY lastname
```

Result:

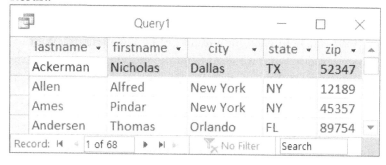

lastname	firstname	city	state	zip
Ackerman	Nicholas	Dallas	TX	52347
Allen	Alfred	New York	NY	12189
Ames	Pindar	New York	NY	45357
Andersen	Thomas	Orlando	FL	89754

Record: 1 of 68   No Filter   Search

252.   Using UNION with BETWEEN

Find customers in a certain zip code range who ordered from multiple distribution centers

Discussion:

We can use the BETWEEN clause to filter results in UNION statements. As soon as we satisfy the basic requirements of a UNION statement, we can filter records as we please using any filtering clauses such as LIKE, "=", or BETWEEN. Notice in this example that we must use the cLng() number conversion function (chapter 25) to convert zip codes to numbers since in the original table, they are stored as text. Otherwise, the BETWEEN operator will not work since it cannot find text ranges. We can use any conversion functions we want in UNION statements.

Code:

```
SELECT lastname, firstname, city, state, zip
FROM customers
WHERE cLng(zip) BETWEEN 12000 AND 12999
UNION
SELECT lastname, firstname, city, state, zip
FROM tbls_customers_un
WHERE cLng(zip) BETWEEN 12000 AND 12999
ORDER BY lastname
```

Result:

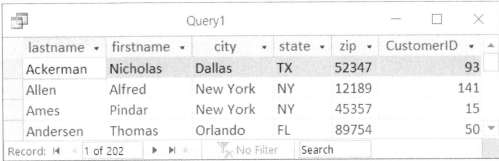

lastname ▾	firstname ▾	city ▾	state ▾	zip ▾
Allen	Alfred	New York	NY	12189
Anderson	Peter	New York	NY	12189
Anthopolis	Ricky	New York	NY	12189
Aversa	Scott	New York	NY	12189

Record: I◄ 1 of 27 ► ►I ▾ No Filter   Search

253. A trick with UNION and the aggregate function count()

Display total customer numbers dynamically

Discussion:

Here, we use a trick to display all of the customer records from the customers table and a total row at the end of the recordset. We can do this by using a single SQL statement and UNION. Notice in the second SQL statement we use quotes instead of fields to satisfy the UNION requirement of same field numbers in both statements. In addition, notice that we start the name of the first field of the second SQL statement with a "z", which has no other meaning but to force the total row to appear last in the recordset. Finally, for our trick to succeed, we need to use the ORDER BY clause on the first field of the first SQL statement.

Code:

```
SELECT lastname, firstname, city, state, zip, CustomerID
FROM customers
UNION
SELECT
'zTotal customer count', '', '', '', '', Count(CustomerID)
FROM customers
ORDER BY lastname ASC
```

Result:

lastname ▾	firstname ▾	city ▾	state ▾	zip ▾	CustomerID ▾
Ackerman	Nicholas	Dallas	TX	52347	93
Allen	Alfred	New York	NY	12189	141
Ames	Pindar	New York	NY	45357	15
Andersen	Thomas	Orlando	FL	89754	50

Record: I◄ 1 of 202 ► ►I ▾ No Filter   Search

254. Using UNION with SELECT INTO

Combine customer data from multiple tables and save the combined dataset dynamically in a different table

Discussion:

This is a useful trick to get data from multiple data sources and save it in a different table. We can use SELECT INTO to pull this off, but we must pay attention! The first of the following two SQL statements may naturally come to mind, but it will not work. We need to use a subquery (chapter 31) as can be seen in the second SQL statement. Pay attention to the number of records. It has to be 207 (201 from the first table and 6 from the second) since we are asking for unique records to be moved. If we want to move everything, we can use UNION ALL.

Code: (Will not work)
SELECT lastname, firstname, city, state, zip INTO UnionTable
FROM customers
UNION
SELECT lastname, firstname, city, state, zip
FROM tbls_customers_un

Code: (Will work)
SELECT lastname, firstname, city, state, zip INTO tempTable
FROM
(SELECT lastname, firstname, city, state, zip
FROM customers
UNION
SELECT lastname, firstname, city, state, zip
FROM tbls_customers_un
)

Result:

255.   Using UNION with INSERT INTO
Combine records from multiple data sources, filter them, and append them into an existing table
Discussion:

There are occasions in which we need to combine data from multiple tables and append it in an existing table. We can use INSERT INTO and UNION to accomplish these tasks. The table "tbls_Union_Insert" used in this example needs to exist before we run the SQL statement. Also, notice the use of the WHERE clause through which we can transfer the records we want.

Code:

```
INSERT INTO tbls_Union_Insert (lastname, firstname, city, state, zip)
SELECT lastname, firstname, city, state, zip
FROM
(SELECT lastname, firstname, city, state, zip
FROM customers
WHERE state = 'NY'
UNION
SELECT lastname, firstname, city, state, zip
FROM tbls_customers_un
WHERE state = 'NY'
)
```

Result:

256.   Using UNION with GROUP BY within each SELECT statement

Combine customer data from the two distribution centers, count the totals, and show in the query the center they came from

Discussion:

The business goal in this example is to calculate the number of customers for the "Main" and "Regional" centers in each state. Practically, we would like to know how many customers buy from the main center and how many from the regional one. We use a number of tricks and functions to arrive at the result we need. First, notice we use a GROUP BY clause in both SQL statements in the query. Second, we use the count() function to get the number of customers by state. Third, we create a field of our own ("Main" and "Regional") in the beginning of each of the two SQL statements to display customer numbers according to distribution center. Finally, we use the ORDER BY clause to present results by state for easy comparison of numbers. Some states appear only once because they have just one distribution center.

Code:

```
SELECT "Main" As DisCenter, state, count(CustomerID) AS Customers
FROM customers
GROUP BY state
UNION
SELECT "Regional" As Center, state, Count(CustomerID) AS Customers
FROM tbls_customers_un
GROUP BY state
ORDER BY STATE
```

Result:

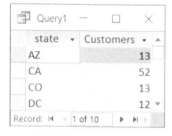

DisCenter	state	Customers
Main	AZ	13
Main	CA	48
Regional	CA	4
Main	CO	13
Main	DC	12

Record: ◄ ◄ 1 of 14 ► ►I ► 🏷 No Fil

257. Using UNION with GROUP BY outside each SELECT statement

Combine customer data from all distribution centers, count the totals, and group results by state

Discussion:

In this example, the GROUP BY clause produces combined results from each state regardless of distribution center. Unlike what we did in the previous example, we first combine the data and then we use the GROUP BY clause. Notice the use of the subquery with the UNION operator that enables us to GROUP results from the two data sets.

Code:

```
SELECT state, count(customerid) as Customers
FROM

(SELECT state, CustomerID
FROM customers
UNION
SELECT state, CustomerID
FROM tbls_customers_un
)

GROUP BY state
ORDER BY STATE
```

Result:

state	Customers
AZ	13
CA	52
CO	13
DC	12

Record: ◄ ◄ 1 of 10 ► ►I ►

258. Using UNION with two subqueries to filter records for aggregations

Compare customer data from two tables only for states existing in both tables

Discussion:

Our goal this time is to present customer numbers for states with two distribution centers. If a state has just one distribution center, it will not appear in the result set. We need a subquery in the first SELECT statement to achieve the desired output. This subquery will search for matching records in the table in the second SELECT statement and limit the output of the first SELECT statement only for common states between the "customers" and tbls_customers_un" tables.

Code:
SELECT "Main" As DisCenter, state, count(CustomerID) AS Customers
FROM customers
WHERE State in (SELECT state from tbls_customers_un)
GROUP BY state
UNION
SELECT "Regional" As Center, state, Count(CustomerID) AS Customers
FROM tbls_customers_un
GROUP BY state
ORDER BY STATE

Result:

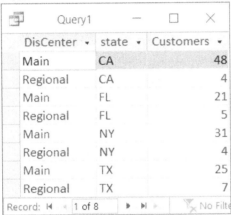

1.   What is the fundamental goal of the UNION operator?

2.   Can we combine the records of a table with those of a query using the UNION operator?

3.   When using the UNION operator to combine two or more tables, do we need to have the same number of fields?

4.   When using the UNION operator to combine two or more tables, do we need to have the same data types and sizes of the fields in both tables?

5.   Which operator returns duplicate values? UNION or UNION ALL?

6.   Can we use the ORDER BY clause with UNION and multiple SQL statements? Where should we place it in the SQL statement?

7.   Can we use the WHERE clause with UNION and multiple SQL statements? Where should we place it in the SQL statement? How many WHERE clauses can we use within a UNION statement?

8.   Can we use different criteria for each of the WHERE clauses used in the SQL statements combined with the UNION operator?

9.   How can we show the total number of records from a recordset using the UNION operator?

10. What difference it will make if we use the GROUP BY clause within each SQL statement with the UNION operator or if we use the GROUP BY clause outside all SQL statements with a UNION operator?

260.   CHAPTER 22 HANDS-ON EXERCISES

Chapter 22 Case 1:

Create a new Access database and name it Chapter22_1.accdb. Copy the tables Products and tbls_ProductsUnion from the PracticeDatabase.accdb and paste them to Chapter22_1.accdb. Notice that the Products table has seventy (70) records while the tbls_ProductsUnion has ten (10) records.

1.   The sales people are asking for a new product catalog that will combine the Products and tbls_ProductsUnion tables. They want the new catalog to contain only the ProductName field. Create a new query that satisfies the sales people request and save it as Qry1_CombinedCatalog. Why do you think the resulting recordset contains 76 records?

Your result should look like:

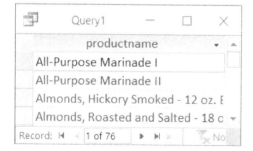

2. The sales people are back asking for a new report that will again combine the Products and tbls_ProductsUnion tables. They want the new report to contain the ProductName, SupplierID, and ProductUnitPrice fields. Create a new query that satisfies the sales people request and save it as Qry2_CombinedProductInfo. Why do you think the resulting recordset contains 80 records?

Your result should look like:

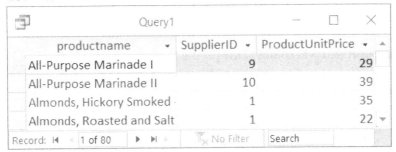

3. After your explanation from question 2, the sales people are explicitly asking for a new report that will combine ALL the products in the Products table with ALL the products in the tbls_ProductsUnion table. They want the new report to contain the ProductName field only. Create a new query that satisfies the sales people request and save it as Qry3_AllCombinedProducs. Compare the result with question 1.

Your result should look like:

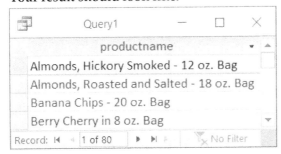

4. The sales people are really happy with your ability to provide them with combined information. Now, they are asking for a report that will combine the products from suppliers 1, 2, and 3 from the Products table and suppliers 2, 5, and 10 from the tbls_ProductsUnion table. They want the new report to contain the ProductName, ProductUnitPrice, and SupplierID fields. They also need the report to be sorted by ProductName ascending. Create a new query that satisfies the sales people request and save it as Qry4_SpecificSuppliers.

Your result should look like:

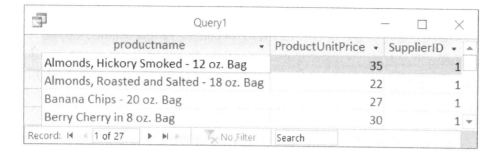

5. The sales people now need a report that will combine the products from suppliers 1 through 5 from the Products table and suppliers 1 through 5 from the tbls_ProductsUnion table. They want the new report to contain the ProductName, ProductUnitPrice, and SupplierID fields. They also need the report to be sorted by ProductName ascending. Create a new query that satisfies the sales people request and save it as Qry5_SpecificSupplierRange.

Your result should look like:

productname	SupplierID	ProductUnitPrice
Almonds, Hickory Smoked - 12 oz. Bag	1	35
Almonds, Roasted and Salted - 18 oz. Bag	1	22
Banana Chips - 20 oz. Bag	1	27
Banana Glazed Chips 35 lb. bag	1	30

Record: ◄ ◄ 1 of 44 ► ►► No Filter   Search

Chapter 22 Case 2:

Create a new Access database and name it Chapter22_2.accdb. Copy the tables Customers, SalesReps, Suppliers, Products_Local, and Products_Regional from the PracticeDatabase.accdb and paste them to Chapter22_2.accdb.

1. The marketing people are asking for a list of contact information from Customers, Suppliers, and SalesReps so they can send out an end of the year thank you note. Create a new query that includes the fields lastname, firstname, city, state, zip from the Customers and SalesReps tables and the fields companyname, contactname, city, state, zip from the Suppliers table. Save the query as Qry1_AllNames.

Your result should look like:

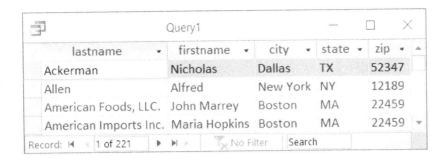

2. The marketing people are back asking you to create a new table that contains all the people records from question 1. Create a new query which when executed it creates a new table with all the records from the Customers, Suppliers, and SalesReps tables and the fields specified in question 1. Save the query as Qry2_MakeTable.

Your result should look like:

3. The inventory department asks for a report that will list the number of products by stock keeping unit (sku) for all products in the Products_Local and Products_regional tables. They want the report to contain numbers from both tables but differentiate between product units in the local warehouse and the regional warehouse. Create a new query that satisfies the inventory people request and save it as Qry3_Skus.

Your result should look like:

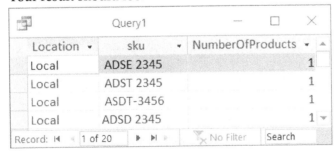

4. The inventory people really liked the report you created for them in question 3. Now, they want the same report of product units by sku without however differentiating between local and regional warehouses. Create a new query that satisfies the inventory people request and save it as Qry4_Skus_Combined.

Your result should look like:

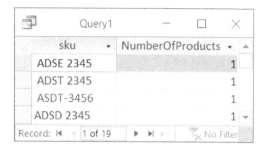

5. The inventory people are super happy with the reports you provided. They have a final request. They need a report identical to the one in question 4 with the following additions: First, they need to include only products with ProductUnitPrices between $20 and $35. Second, they want to include products with a total count by sku of more than 1. Create a new query that satisfies the inventory people request and save it as Qry5_Skus_Criteria.

Your result should look like:

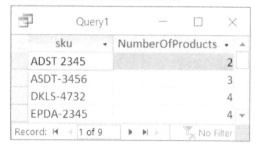

CHAPTER 23
DUPLICATE, ORPHANED, and UNRELATED RECORDS

This chapter focuses on four learning goals: The identification of duplicate, orphaned, related, and unrelated records. Orphaned and duplicate records will affect your database integrity, while related and unrelated records will affect your business decisions.

Orphaned records occur when there are no primary key values for corresponding foreign key values in a one-to-many relationship. For example, in a relationship between customers and orders, you might have orders without corresponding customers. This scenario can occur if referential integrity for this relationship is off (chapter 4). This will allow a user to delete a customer without any warning that there are existing orders for this customer. Alternatively, it might allow a user to enter an order without first entering a customer.

We need to have referential integrity on in order to avoid the occurrence of orphaned records. Yet, what happens when we already have orphaned records in the database? There are two solutions with orphaned records. The first is to delete orphaned records from the database. However, to eliminate orphaned records, we first need to find them. In this chapter, there will be plenty of examples to locate orphaned records.

The second solution is to keep orphaned records such as orders in the database, but in this case, we need to enter their corresponding customer information. In any case, we must be able to identify the orphaned records in a table.

A second common occurrence in business databases is duplicate records. In this chapter, you will learn several techniques to identify and deal with duplicate records, which are not, by the way, synonymous with identical records. Two customer records might be duplicates even if they have the same name but different address information. So, you will learn how to find duplicate records based on the values of one, two, or multiple fields.

A third case involves unrelated records. For example, we might have customers in the database who have not placed an order for quite some time. This is a business and not a database problem. However, we need to act, and we have two choices for inactive customers. The first is to use a marketing campaign to entice them to start buying again. If this is not feasible, we might want to delete them from the database or move them to a historical customer table. To delete or move these records, we need to be able to find them first and this is exactly what we do in this chapter.

The fourth scenario is related records. We might want to know how many customers placed orders over a period of a year, month, or quarter. In other words, we want to know how many customers have related orders in the orders table. In this chapter, you will learn how to quickly identify these customers to increase the effectiveness of your business operations.

Finally, so that you can check your numbers, you will use the table named tbls_orders, which contains a number of orphaned and duplicate records. Specifically, the records with OrderID = 8, 45, 254, 820, 993 are duplicate records. In addition, there are two records with null OrderIDs, which I put in to make our work a bit more complicated.

SECTION 1 – DUPLICATE RECORDS

261.   Find duplicate records in a table based on the values of one field

Find duplicate orders based on the value of the orderID

Discussion:

In this example, we are looking for records in the tbls_Orders table that have the same value for the OrderID field. We can use the code below to look for duplicate values for any field. We will just replace the OrderID field with the field on which we want to search for duplicate values. Remember that this example will give us duplicate field values and not necessarily duplicate records. Though the OrderID values are the same, the rest of the fields in the returned records might have different values. Still, it is very useful to know how to search for duplicate values on one field. We also use the count(*) function to calculate the number of duplicate records. As you can see from the result set, two records have null values for the blank OrderID. In addition, there are two instances of duplicate records for OrderIDs with values 8, 45, 254, and 820. Finally, the OrderId with value 993 appears in three records in the table.

Code:

```
SELECT OrderID, Count(*) AS NumberofDuplicates
FROM tbls_Orders
GROUP BY OrderID
HAVING count(*)>1
```

Result:

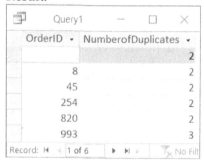

262.   Find duplicate records in a table based on the values of two fields

Find duplicate customer orders based on the values of OrderID and CustomerID

Discussion:

In this example, we are looking for duplicate records based on the values of OrderID and CustomerID. If the values of the OrderID and CustomerID are the same for at least two records, they will appear in the result set as duplicates. In addition, the count(*) function is used to calculate the number of records with identical OrderID and CustomerID values. Keep in mind that while two records might have matching values for two fields, this does not necessarily mean that they have identical values for the rest of their fields. This code will allow us to locate potential duplicate records based on the values of two fields. We need to examine the individual records to verify that they are indeed duplicates.

Code:
SELECT OrderID, CustomerID, Count(*) AS NumberofDuplicates
FROM tbls_Orders
GROUP BY OrderID, CustomerID
HAVING count(*)>1

Result:

OrderID	CustomerID	NumberofDuplicates
8	71	2
45	93	2
254	198	2
820	46	2
993	99	3

Record: 1 of 5 — No Filter — Search

263. Find duplicate records in a table based on the values of multiple fields

Find duplicate customer orders based on the values of multiple fields

Discussion:

In this example, we are looking for duplicate records based on the values of eight fields. In other words, if the values of eight fields of at least two records are identical, those records will appear as duplicates. Notice that there are two identical records for each OrderID with values 8, 45, 254, and 820, while there are three identical records with OrderID = 993.

Code:
SELECT Count(*) AS NumberofDuplicates, OrderID, CustomerID, SalesRepID, ShipperID, OrderDate, RequiredDate, ShippedDate, ShippingCost

FROM tbls_Orders

GROUP BY OrderID, CustomerID, SalesRepID, ShipperID, OrderDate, RequiredDate, ShippedDate, ShippingCost
HAVING count(*)>1

Result:

NumberofDuplicates	OrderID	CustomerID	SalesRepID	ShipperID
2	8	71	3	1
2	45	93	1	3
2	254	198	3	2
2	820	46	8	1
3	993	99	10	2

Record: 1 of 5 — No Filter — Search

264. Find and display all duplicate records in a table

Find and display all duplicate records in the Orders table
Discussion:
In the previous examples, we were able to find duplicate records in the table but display only one instance from each in the result set. There are cases, however, in which we will want to display all instances from all duplicate records. We can achieve this goal by using a subquery. In this example, we will display all instances of all duplicate records based on the values of the OrderID field, or put another way, based on the values of one field.

Code:
```
SELECT *
FROM tbls_Orders WHERE OrderID IN(
SELECT OrderID
FROM tbls_Orders
GROUP BY OrderID
HAVING count(*)>1)
ORDER BY OrderID
```

Result:

OrderID	CustomerID	SalesRepID	ShipperID	OrderDate
8	71	3	1	4/1/2019
8	71	3	1	4/1/2019
45	93	1	3	10/23/2017
45	93	1	3	10/23/2017
254	198	3	2	7/15/2017

Record: 1 of 11   No Filter   Search

SECTION 2 – ORPHANED RECORDS

265. What are orphaned records and how to deal with them

In the figure below, there are five orders in the Orders table with OrderIDs from 1 to 5. For the first four orders, there are corresponding customers in the Customers table. For orders with OrderID=5, there does not exist a corresponding customer in the database. This is an order that belongs to no one. The record in the Orders table with OrderID=5 is called an orphaned record.

CUSTOMERS		ORDERS		
CustID	Name	OrderID	CustID	OrderDate
1	John	1	2	9/10/2018
2	Mary	2	2	10/10/2019
3	George	3	1	11/10/2019
4	Stacy	4	3	11/11/2019
		5	7	11/15/2019

A reason for this might be that when the database was created and relationships established, referential integrity was not turned on. The immediate consequence is that a user of the database deleted the customer with CustomerID=7 either by mistake or on purpose. Although the customer record is gone, his or her orders are still in the database, useless and compromising data integrity. Another reason might be that a user received an order from a new customer. The correct process would have been to check if the customer existed and then enter the order. If referential integrity is off a representative can enter an order without an existing customer. To avoid orphaned records, referential integrity should be turned on for a relationship between two tables.

266. Find orphaned records using a subquery

Find orders for which there are no customers using a subquery

Discussion:

Let us assume that we want to turn on referential integrity for the relationship between the Customers and Orders tables. If Access does not allow us to do this, our first action should be to look for orphaned records in the Orders table or in the table in the many side of the relationship. We can use the code below to do just that. In this example, we use the tbls_Orders table since in the original Orders table, there are no orphaned records. As you can see in the result set, there are three orders (OrderID= 1500, 1501, and 1502) that came up as orphaned records. This in turn means that the customers with CustomerID values of 250, 251, and 252 do not exist in the Customers table. If we open the customers table, we will not find any customers with these CustomerID values.

Code:

```
SELECT *
FROM tbls_Orders
WHERE CustomerID
NOT IN (SELECT CustomerID from Customers)
```

Result:

OrderID	CustomerID	SalesRepID	ShipperID	OrderDate
1500	250	11	2	1/20/2017
1501	251	12	2	11/18/2017
1502	252	14	3	2/5/2018

Record: 1 of 3   No Filter   Search

267. Find orphaned records using a join

Find orders for which there are no customers using a join

Discussion:

There is a second and faster way to locate orphaned records in a table. Specifically, we can use a LEFT join (chapter 30) between Customers and tbls_Orders to locate any orphaned records in the tbls_Orders table. As you can see, the result set is identical to the one using a subquery in the previous example.

Code:
```
SELECT *
FROM tbls_Orders
LEFT JOIN Customers ON tbls_Orders.[CustomerID] = Customers.[CustomerID]
WHERE Customers.CustomerID Is Null
```

Result:

OrderID ▾	tbls_Orders.(▾	SalesRepID ▾	ShipperID ▾	OrderDate ▾
1500	250	11	2	1/20/2017
1501	251	12	2	11/18/2017
1502	252	14	3	2/5/2018

Record: ◄ ◄ 1 of 3 ► ►► No Filter   Search

268.   Delete orphaned records using a subquery

Delete orders for which there are no customers using a subquery

Discussion:

We can use a subquery to find and delete orphaned records in one step. In the code below, we use the DELETE statement to delete orders in the tbls_Orders table for which there are no customers in the customers table. The subquery will isolate CustomerID values in the tbls_Orders table for which there are no corresponding CustomerID values in the Customers table. Notice that the CustomerID is the primary key in the Customers table and the foreign key in the tbls_Orders table.

Code:
```
DELETE
FROM tbls_Orders
WHERE CustomerID
NOT IN (SELECT CustomerID FROM Customers)
```

Result:

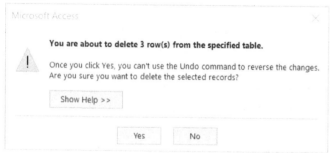

Microsoft Access

You are about to delete 3 row(s) from the specified table.

Once you click Yes, you can't use the Undo command to reverse the changes. Are you sure you want to delete the selected records?

Show Help >>

Yes   No

269.   Delete orphaned records using a join

Delete orders for which there are no customers using a join

Discussion:

We can also use a LEFT join to isolate and delete orphaned records in the tbls_Orders table. Notice the WHERE clause in the code below which looks for CustomerID values in the LEFT JOIN with a null value, i.e. CustomerID or foreign key values in the tbls_Orders table for which no primary key values exist in the customers table. Joins work faster than subqueries especially on indexed fields, and while
288

they are more complicated, their use might well be justified in cases with many records. However, this does not mean that a join will always be faster than a subquery. The bottom line is that we have the option to isolate and delete orphaned records using joins.

Code:
```
DELETE  tbls_Orders.*
FROM tbls_Orders
LEFT JOIN Customers ON tbls_Orders.[CustomerID] = Customers.[CustomerID]
WHERE Customers.CustomerID Is Null
```

Result:

Microsoft Access

You are about to delete 3 row(s) from the specified table.

Once you click Yes, you can't use the Undo command to reverse the changes. Are you sure you want to delete the selected records?

Show Help >>

Yes   No

SECTION 3 – UNRELATED RECORDS

The knowledge to locate unrelated records is fundamental in database applications. It allows us to reply to questions such as: How many customers have not placed any orders? How many students have not taken classes this semester? What sales reps did not have sales last week? So, we are looking for customers who have no orders (maybe over a period of time) knowing that there is a one-to-many relationship between customers and orders. Keep in mind that finding customers without orders is not a problematic situation when it comes to database integrity; it is simply a business fact. However, finding orders without customers represents a database integrity problem, and we call these orphaned records.

270.   Find unrelated records using a subquery

Find customers for whom there are no orders using a subquery

Discussion:

In this example, we use a subquery with the NOT IN operator to find customers who do not have any orders. We are looking for records in the customers table that have no related records in the Orders table. In other words, we are looking for primary key values (CustomerID) in the customers table with no corresponding foreign key values (CustomerIDs) in the Orders table. The code appears below:

Code:
```
SELECT *
FROM Customers
WHERE CustomerID
NOT IN (SELECT CustomerID from tbls_Orders)
```

Result:

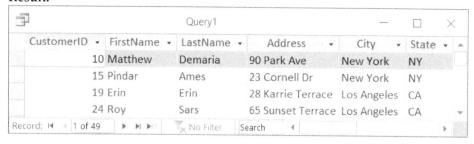

271. Find unrelated records using a subquery and date criteria

Find customers for whom there are no orders using date criteria

Discussion:

In the previous example, you learned how to identify customers without orders for all sales years in the database. This is excellent knowledge, but in actual business practice, you will need some additional criteria to derive insightful pieces of information. For example, we might want to know what customers have not placed any orders in the last year, quarter, month, or even week. Alternatively, we might want to know what customers from NY have not placed any orders in the last two months. We can extract these amazing pieces of information using date criteria. In this example, we are looking for customers who have not placed any orders in 2017. As you can see from the result set, we have 49 such customers. Of course, we can use the vast arsenal of date functions in chapter 27 to extract any period we feel we need to look into.

Code:
```
SELECT *
FROM Customers
WHERE CustomerID NOT IN
(SELECT CustomerID
FROM tbls_Orders
WHERE OrderDate BETWEEN #1/1/2017# AND #12/31/2017#)
```

Result:

CustomerID	FirstName	LastName	Address	City	State
10	Matthew	Demaria	90 Park Ave	New York	NY
15	Pindar	Ames	23 Cornell Dr	New York	NY
19	Erin	Erin	28 Karrie Terrace	Los Angeles	CA
24	Roy	Sars	65 Sunset Terrace	Los Angeles	CA

Record: 1 of 49 — No Filter — Search

SECTION 4 – RELATED RECORDS

272. Find related records using a subquery

Find customers who placed orders

Discussion:

There will be occasions in your work in which you will need to find related records. In other words, you might want to find customers who placed orders, suppliers who sent raw materials, or products that sold some units. In this example, we are looking for customers who actually placed orders. Since we know from previous examples that out of the 201 customers, 11 never placed any orders, we would expect to retrieve 190 records. This is exactly the result from the following code. Remember that we can add additional criteria to identify customers who placed orders in certain periods such as years, quarters, or months, as we shall see in the next example.

Code:

SELECT *
FROM Customers
WHERE CustomerID
IN (SELECT CustomerID from tbls_Orders)

Result:

273. Find related records using a subquery and criteria

Find customers who placed orders during a specific date interval

Discussion:

In this scenario, we are looking for customers who placed orders in the 4th quarter of 2017. Notice that we use two date functions, datepart() and year(), to extract the quarter and year out of the OrderDate field respectively. Using the subquery and the two date functions, we are able to extract exactly the information we need for our customers. This list of customers can definitely help in our marketing and promotional campaigns, and we can retrieve it in seconds.

Code:

SELECT *
FROM Customers
WHERE CustomerID
IN (SELECT CustomerID from tbls_Orders
WHERE DatePart('q',[OrderDate]) = 4 AND year(OrderDate) = 2017)

Result:

CHAPTER 23 DISCUSSION QUESTIONS

1. How do we call the records for which there are no primary key values for corresponding foreign key values?
2. How do we call the records for which there are no foreign key values for corresponding primary key values?
3. When referential integrity is off what kind of risk do we incur?
4. If referential integrity is on can we still end up with duplicate records in the database? Why yes or why not?
5. What techniques can we use to identify orphaned records in the database?
6. What do we mean by duplicate records? For two records to be duplicates do they need to have identical data?
7. If we have customers without orders, is this a database integrity problem or a business problem?
8. If we have orders without customers, is this a database integrity problem or a business problem?
9. What kind of action do we need to take when we find orphaned records in the database?
10. What kind of action do we need to take when we find unrelated records in the database?

275. **CHAPTER 23 HANDS-ON EXERCISES**

Chapter 23 Case 1:

Create a new Access database and name it Chapter23_1.accdb. Copy the tables SalesReps and tble_Orders from the PracticeDatabase.accdb and paste them to Chapter23_1.accdb.

1. The accounts department has notified IT that something is not right with the orders presented for payment. It looks like some of them are repeated entries and we risk paying them twice. They are asking you to find duplicate records in the table tble_Orders based on the values of the fields CustomerID, SalesRepID, and ShipperID. Your report should also include the number of instances of duplicated records. Create a new query that includes the above fields from the tble_Orders table and satisfies the accounts receivable request. Save the query as Qry1_DuplicateRecords.

Your result should look like:

NumberofDuplicates	CustomerID	SalesRepID	ShipperID
2	1	4	1
2	3	4	1
2	8	5	2
2	9	7	2

Record: 1 of 94   No Filter   Search

2. The accounts receivable people are happy with your report but they want to make sure that what they do makes business sense. In this respect, it might be natural for the same customer to have

ordered through the same sales person, and used the same shipping company multiple times. To account for this fact and make sure they identify only duplicate records they are asking you to find duplicate records in the table tble_orders based on the values of all fields. Your report should also include the number of instances of repeated records. Create a new query that includes all fields from the tble_Orders table and satisfies the accounts receivable request. Save the query as Qry2_IdenticalRecords. (Hint: Do not include the OrderID in the list of fields in your code since it is the primary key and it will always have a unique value.)

Your result should look like:

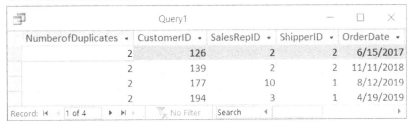

3. Human Resources called in and they say they are trying to calculate commissions for sales people but some orders refer to sales reps they cannot find in the database. Check to see why the HR people cannot find in the SalesReps table the sales representatives appearing as processing the orders in the tble_Orders table. Make a list of all orders for which no sales people exist in the SalesReps table. Create a new query that includes all fields from the tble_Orders table and satisfies the HR people request. Save it as Qry3_MissingSalesPeople.

Your result should look like:

4. The sales director thinks that some of the sales people are not very aggressive in the market with the result for them missing commissions and the company sales. He asks for a report that lists the sales people without sales for the year 2017. Create a new query that includes all fields from the SalesReps table and satisfies the sales director request. Save it as Qry4_SalesPeopleNoSales.

Your result should look like:

5. The sales director is now asking for a report of sales people who actually had sales in the year of 2017.   Create a new query that includes all fields from the SalesReps table and satisfies the sales director request. Save it as Qry5_SalesPeopleWithSales.

Your result should look like:

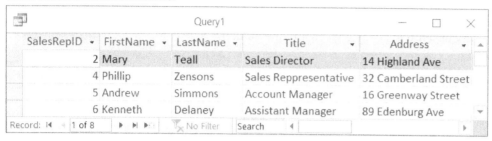

Chapter 23 Case 2:

Create a new Access database and name it Chapter23_2.accdb. Copy the tables ShippingCompanies and tble_Orders from the PracticeDatabase.accdb and paste them to Chapter23_2.accdb.

1. The sales people are asking for a list of any orders without a shipping company. Create a query that includes all fields from the tble_Orders table that satisfies the sales people request. Name the query as Qry1_OrdersNoShippers.

Your result should look like:

2. The sales people are back asking for a report that will list any shipping companies that have not been used in the shipping of our orders for the first six months of 2017. Create a query that includes all fields from the ShippingCompanies table and satisfies the sales people request. Name the query as Qry2_ShippersNoOrdersCriteria.

Your result should look like:

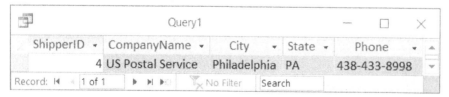

3. The sales people are back asking for a report that will list any shipping companies that have not been used at all in the shipping of our orders. Create a query that includes all fields from the ShippingCompanies table and satisfies the sales people request. Name the query as Qry3_ShippersNoOrders.

Your result should look like:

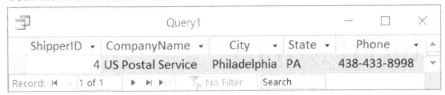

4. The sales people want a report that will list all shipping companies that shipped at least one order for us. Create a query that includes all fields from the ShippingCompanies table and satisfies the sales people request. Name the query as Qry4_ShippersWithOrders.

Your result should look like:

5. Finally, the sales people want a report that will list all the shipping companies that participated in the shipping of our orders in the first five days of June 2017. Create a query that includes all fields from the ShippingCompanies table and satisfies the sales people request. Name the query as Qry5_ShippersWithOrdersCriteria. Hint: use the BETWEEN operator for the date interval.

Your result should look like:

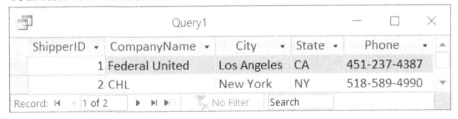

CHAPTER 24
WORKING WITH NULLS

There are three concepts to know to understand null values in full: First, a zero (0) value is not a null value. It means that there is a value, and it is zero. Second, a zero-length string, also called an empty string, is not a null value. It means that there should be a value, but there is none. In Access we designate an empty string by typing two double quotation marks with no space between them (""). Third, a null value means that we do not know whether there should be a value or not.

Zero-length strings and null values appear as empty cells in Access. We have no way of distinguishing which cell actually has a null value and which one has an empty string in it; they both appear empty. Do not be concerned about this because in our examples, we will see how to take care of this situation. The best way to avoid tricky and problematic situations with nulls and zero-length values is to avoid them altogether. When designing a new database, we can assign default values to fields that users might leave blank. For example, for a customer middle name, we can set a default value of "NA" when none is entered. For existing databases, we can run effective update statements (chapter 28 in this book) to replace null and empty string values with default values.

Null values will affect your calculations in aggregate functions, searching expressions, union operations, and will leave doubts about the validity of your results. Let us explore in detail all of the scenarios around nulls and the ways to eliminate them. For this chapter, so that you can verify the effects of null values and zero-length strings, we have created a table called "tbls_ProductsN" which contains only ten records. Using these ten records, you will be able to verify your calculations and learn to work with nulls effectively.

276. Looking for nulls using criteria
Find products whose stock keeping unit codes (SKUs) are null
Discussion:
Our task is to find all products for which the SKU code is missing. Of course, with only ten products, we can just eye the table and tell right away that there are four SKU codes missing. Let us try to write the code to retrieve them and see if the database agrees. In this example, we are looking for null values using the criterion "is null" in the WHERE clause, and as you can see, the SQL statement returned four records.

Code:
SELECT productID, productname, productunitprice, SKU
FROM tbls_ProductsN
WHERE SKU IS NULL

Result:

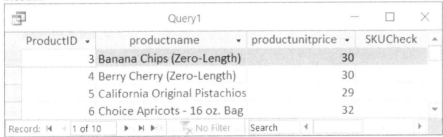

277.   Looking for nulls using the IsNull() function

Display all products whose SKU is null

Discussion:

The isnull() function provides us with additional functionality in looking for nulls. Specifically, it will produce a true or false value for all of the entries in the field we are inspecting. In this example, we use isnull() to check the SKU field for nulls. For every value in the SKU field, we will get a true or false response from the database. In Access, the value 0 means false, and the value -1 means true. In the following datasheet, we will get -1 for the four records with null values.

Code:

SELECT ProductID, productname, productunitprice, IsNull(SKU) AS SKUCheck
FROM tbls_ProductsN

Result:

ProductID	productname	productunitprice	SKUCheck
3	Banana Chips (Zero-Length)	30	
4	Berry Cherry (Zero-Length)	30	
5	California Original Pistachios	29	
6	Choice Apricots - 16 oz. Bag	32	

Record: ◄ ◄ 1 of 10 ► ►I ►▪ No Filter   Search

278.   Looking for nulls using the iif() function

Display the word "null" for products with null SKUs

Discussion:

You can use the iif() function to search for nulls in a field and obtain more readable results. The iif() function in this example will display the word "null" for every null value it finds in the SKU field and if there is no null value, it will display the actual SKU value.

Code:

SELECT ProductID, productname, productunitprice, IIf(IsNull([SKU]),"NULL", [SKU]) AS
SKUCheck
FROM tbls_ProductsN
ORDER BY SKU

Result:

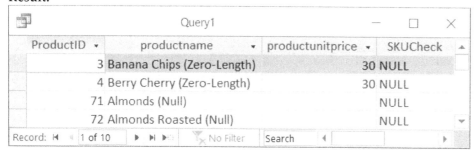

279.   Calculations with nulls

Calculate product inventory subtotals where some values are nulls

Discussion:

In this example, we want to multiply the ProductUnitPrice with the QuantityPerUnit to calculate the value of our inventory by product. In the ProductsN table, there are blank values for both the ProductUnitPrice and the QuantityPerUnit fields. Let's see how our result set will come up.

Code:

SELECT productname, productunitprice, quantityperunit, (productunitprice*quantityperunit) As Subtotal

FROM tbls_ProductsN

ORDER BY (productunitprice*quantityperunit) DESC

Result:

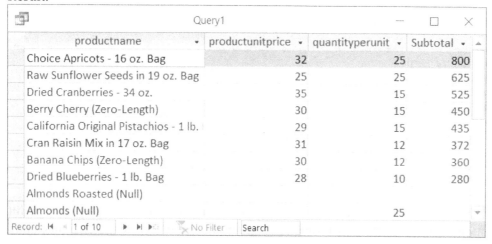

As you can see, for the records with null values for either one of the two multiplied fields, there will be no result. This will have consequences in our inventory results since at least for the product "Almonds" in record 10, we know that we have a value of 25 for quantity per unit. Since their price is missing, the inventory report will be erroneous. To avoid this situation, we need to make it a habit to look for nulls before we do any calculations.

280. Using sum() with null values

Calculate the total inventory value of our products

Discussion:

The situation becomes even worse when we use aggregate functions to summarize data since we cannot see the empty field values to realize we have missing data. When aggregate functions encounter null values, they will leave them out of the calculations altogether and report only on known values.

In this case, products with productID 71 and 72 will be missing from the calculations. For productid=72, we have no quantity or price data. For productid=71, we know that we have a quantity on hand = 25 but no price, and our results are definitely wrong. The best way to avoid the above situations is to check the data for nulls and make every effort to fill in the missing values.

Code:

```
SELECT SUM(productunitprice*quantityperunit) As Total
FROM tbls_ProductsN
```

Result:

281. Using count() with nulls

Count the number of products in the inventory correctly

Discussion:

As we have mentioned countless times in this book, our primary goal is to rid the database of nulls by replacing them with concrete values in our tables such as "NA" for text fields or zeros for numeric ones. Now, our goal is to calculate the number of products in our inventory table. If we apply the count() function on the SKU field, we will get six records. This is because the four null values in the SKU field have not been counted!

Code:

```
SELECT Count(SKU) As CountSKUs
FROM tbls_ProductsN
```

Result:

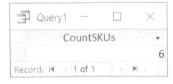

Discussion:

The solution to this problem is to use count() on fields that, by default, do not allow nulls in their values such as the ProductID field which is the primary key of the table.

Code:

SELECT Count(ProductID) As CountSKUs

FROM tbls_ProductsN

Result:

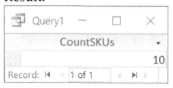

Discussion:

Another solution for correct counts is to use the count(*) function, which will return the actual number of records in the table independently of any null values in any field.

Code:

SELECT Count(*) As CountRecords

FROM tbls_ProductsN

Result:

282.   Leaving nulls out of the result set

Find products for which the SKU code is not null

Discussion:

We can obtain a list of products that do not contain null values in the SKU field by using the IS NOT NULL clause. The IS NOT NULL clause is not a panacea however to null values problems. The real solution would be to use UPDATE statements to replace null values with concrete values such as "NA" for text or zeros for numeric fields. As we expected, the SQL statement returned six records with non-null values for the SKU field.

Code:

SELECT productID, productname, productunitprice, SKU

FROM tbls_ProductsN

WHERE SKU IS NOT NULL

Result:

productID ▾	productname ▾	productunitprice ▾	SKU ▾
5	California Original Pistachios - 1 lb. Bag	29	PDK-2347
6	Choice Apricots - 16 oz. Bag	32	PDK-2347
7	Cran Raisin Mix in 17 oz. Bag	31	PDKLS-1889
8	Dried Blueberries - 1 lb. Bag	28	PDKLS-1889
9	Dried Cranberries - 34 oz.	35	PDK-2347
10	Raw Sunflower Seeds in 19 oz. Bag	25	PDKLS-1889

Record: ◄ ◄ 1 of 6 ► ►I ►⃰ No Filter Search

283. Using the NZ() function to deal with null values

Calculate inventory replenishment amounts

Discussion:

Our task this time is to replenish our inventory. We need to know how many units of a product we need to have so that we will have enough to operate. We must take into consideration the units we have on hand, how many we have already ordered, and the reorder level that will trigger more orders. All of this information is available in the "tbls_ProductsN" table.

We need to add the units in stock to the units we have already ordered and subtract the result from the reorder level amount which is preset. This is easier said than done because the awful null values will get in the way again. Of course, with ten records in the table, we can easily check for null values, but with 10,000 product records, we will not be able to tell. If we try to do the calculations while ignoring the presence of nulls, we will end up with the database unable to produce results for 40% of our products—four out of ten!

Code:

```
SELECT ProductID, (ReorderLevel-(UnitsInstock+UnitsOnOrder)) AS UnitsToOrder
FROM tbls_ProductsN
```

Result:

ProductID ▾	UnitsToOrder ▾
3	5
4	5
5	
6	3
7	
8	2
9	
10	3
71	21
72	

Record: ◄ ◄ 1 of 10 ► ►I ►⃰

Some people resort to sorting as a way of identifying with null values. This is an impractical method and it constitutes an obstacle to automation. Even if they find them, what are they going to do with them? Thankfully, in Access, there is a function for situations like this one, and it is called the nz() function. The nz() function has two arguments as shown below:

Nz(field, value of field if it is null)

For the "value of field if it is null" argument, we can put any value we want to like 0, 1, 2, etc. for numeric fields or "hi my name is John" for text fields. In this particular example, the nz() function will replace the null values of the fields unitsinstock and unitsonorder with zeros so that the calculations can go ahead. Please notice from the result set that the database was now able to produce results for 100% of our records.

Code:
```
SELECT ProductID, (ReorderLevel-(nz(UnitsInstock,0)+nz(UnitsOnOrder,0))) AS
UnitsToOrder
FROM tbls_ProductsN
```

Result:

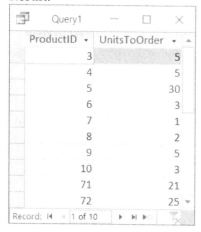

ProductID	UnitsToOrder
3	5
4	5
5	30
6	3
7	1
8	2
9	5
10	3
71	21
72	25

Record: 1 of 10

284. Permanently replace nulls using an update statement
Use UPDATE to replace null values in the SKU field
Discussion:
We can replace the null values in the SKU field by using the UPDATE statement with the WHERE clause and the IS NULL expression. As you can see from the result set, the database is asking to replace the four existing null values in the SKU field. (Check chapter 28 for an in depth look at the update statement).

Code:
```
UPDATE tbls_ProductsN
SET SKU = "NA"
WHERE SKU IS NULL
```

Result:

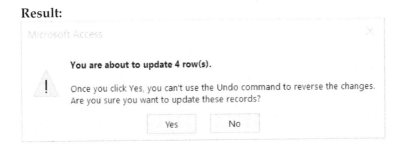

285.   CHAPTER 24 DISCUSSION QUESTIONS

1.   What do we mean by a null value in a table cell?
2.   Is a null value the same as a zero (0) value?
3.   Is a null value the same as a zero length string? What is the difference?
4.   How can we designate a zero length string in Access?
5.   If we look at data in an Access table can we distinguish which cells contain zero length strings and which ones null values?
6.   What is the best strategy to avoid problematic situations with null values?
7.   How can we avoid the presence of null values when we design a new database?
8.   How can we eliminate null values from an existing database?
9.   How do null values affect calculations with aggregate functions?
10. Why is it a good idea to use the IsNull() function in Access? What kind of results does it produce?

286.   CHAPTER 24 HANDS-ON EXERCISES

Chapter 24 Case 1:

Create a new Access database and name it Chapter24_1.accdb. Copy the table tble_CustomersN from the PracticeDatabase.accdb and paste it to Chapter24_1.accdb.

1.   The marketing people have initiated a marketing campaign which includes regular written letters to customers. They have many of those letters coming back with an "undeliverable" notice. It looks like the state is missing from many of the addresses they have in their database. They are asking you to help them identify who are the customers with missing states. Create a new query that includes all the fields from the tble_CustomersN table and satisfies the marketing people request. Save the query as Qry1_CustomersWithoutStates.

Your result should look like:

2.   The marketing people are now asking for a list of customers with the following fields: CustomerID, lastname, firstname, city, StateCheck, and zip. For the stateCheck field, whenever there no state value they want the following expression to appear: "NA". Create a new query that satisfies the marketing people request and name it Qry2_ConditionalEntries. Hint: you need to use an iif() function.

Your result should look like:

3. The marketing people need some statistics on the number of bad records they have. Specifically they need to know how many states actually have values in the table. Use the count() function on the state field to provide them with an answer. Create a new query that satisfies this request and save it as Qry3_NumberOfStates.

    Your result should look like:

4. The marketing people need the number of the total records they have in the table. Use the count(*) function on the state field to provide them with an answer. Create a new query that satisfies this request and save it as Qry4_NumberOfRecords. Why are the answers different between questions 3 and 4?

    Your result should look like:

    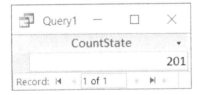

5. The marketing people need a list of customers for which the state field is null. Create a new query that includes all the fields from the tble_CustomersN table and satisfies the marketing people request. Save it as Qry5_CustomersWithStates.

Your result should look like:

Chapter 24 Case 2:

Create a new Access database and name it Chapter24_2.accdb. Copy the table tble_ProductsOrdersN from the PracticeDatabase.accdb and paste it to Chapter24_2.accdb.

1. The inventory people are asking for some analytics to better plan for inventory replenishment. Specifically, they need your help for a report that will provide them the total number of orders, the total order amount, and the average order amount by ProductID. Create a new query that satisfies the inventory people request and save it as Qry1_ProductAggregations.

Your result should look like:

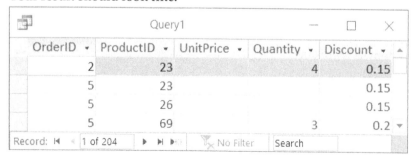

2. The inventory people are back and are very politely indicating to you that the numbers you provided appear to be off according to some written records they have. Your mind immediately goes to null values. Check to see if there are any null values for the fields UnitPrice or Quantity. Create a new query that includes all fields from the tble_ProductsOrdersN table and shows the records with null values for the UnitPrice or Quantity fields. Save the query as Qry2_EntriesWithNulls.

Your result should look like:

3. Now that you know you have 204 records with null values for the UnitPrice or Quantity fields, you need to recreate the report requested by the inventory people in question 1. However, this time you need to make sure you leave out any null values from your calculations. Create a new query that satisfies the inventory people request and save it as Qry3_ProductAggregationsNoNulls. Why are the numbers the same with question 1? Why the results from both question 1 and question 3 are problematic?

   Your result should look like:

   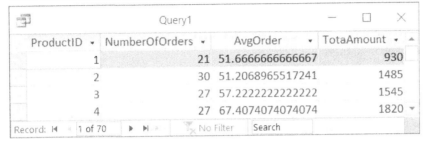

4. Create a new query that includes the fields ProductID, OrderID, UnitPrice, and Quantity from the table tble_ProductsOrdersN. Use the nz function on the fields UnitPrice and Quantity. Save the query as Qry4_nzValues.

   Your result should look like:

   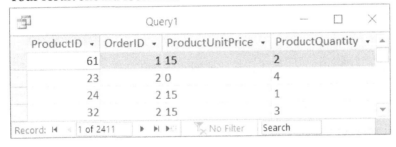

5. Create the same summary statistics (total number of orders, total order amount, and the average order amount by product) as in question 1 but this time use the query Qry4_nzValues as your data source. Save the query as Qry5_ ProductAggregationsNZ. Compare the results from question 5 with those of questions 1 and 3. What are your conclusions?

   Your result should look like:

CHAPTER 25
TYPE CONVERSION FUNCTIONS

Type conversion functions are an excellent tool in the arsenal of the database power user and developer. Unfortunately, they usually go underneath the radar screen of even advanced users because their functionality is not apparent or because they use other methods to accomplish the same result. For instance, to convert a column from a text data type to number data type, some users go to the table design view and force a change there.

There are three problems with this approach: First, by changing the field data type forcefully, data might be lost. Second, if something goes wrong, there is no turning back to the original data. Third, Access might function as the front-end to enterprise databases like MSSQL, Oracle, or IBM DB2, in which case the administrators will not allow a change to the design of the back-end database. The solution is to use type conversion functions to change data types on the fly without affecting table design. In Access, the type conversion functions at our disposal are:

FUNCTION	RETURN TYPE	RANGE FOR *EXPRESSION* ARGUMENT
CBool	Boolean	Any valid **string** or numeric expression.
CByte	Byte	0 to 255.
CCur	Currency	-922,337,203,685,477.5808 to 922,337,203,685,477.5807.
CDate	Date	Any valid date expression.
CDbl	Double	-1.79769313486231E308 to -4.94065645841247E-324 for negative values; 4.94065645841247E-324 to 1.79769313486232E308 for positive values.
CDec	Decimal	+/-79,228,162,514,264,337,593,543,950,335 for zero-scaled numbers, that is, numbers with no decimal places. For numbers with 28 decimal places, the range is +/-7.9228162514264337593543950335. The smallest possible non-zero number is 0.0000000000000000000000000001.
CInt	Integer	-32,768 to 32,767; fractions are rounded.
CLng	Long	-2,147,483,648 to 2,147,483,647; fractions are rounded.
CSng	Single	-3.402823E38 to -1.401298E-45 for negative values; 1.401298E-45 to 3.402823E38 for positive values.
CStr	String	Returns for CStr depend on the *expression* argument.
CVar	Variant	Same range as **Double** for numerics. Same range as **String** for non-numerics.

Source: msdn.microsoft.com

http://msdn.microsoft.com/en-us/library/office/gg278896(v=office.15).aspx

We will start by examining the conversion functions CByte(), CInt(), CLng(), CSng(), and CDbl(). All of these functions relate to the number data type in Access, and we use them for two purposes: First, to change numeric data from one format to another such as to change a numeric field from an integer to a double size. Second, to convert text data to numeric data. For instance, suppose a developer created a table and assigned the "Quantity" as a text field. If we later need to make calculations on this field, we first need to convert it to a numeric data type.

Let's say we have a table field called "PartWeight": Although the data type is number, you can see from the figure below that you have various choices for its size. Shifting dynamically between these choices of Byte, Integer, Single, Double, or Decimal is exactly the job of conversion functions like CByte(), CInt(), CLng(), CSng(), and CDbl().

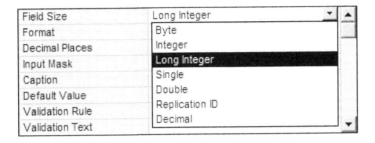

287. The CByte() function
Convert numbers to the size of a byte
Discussion:
The CByte() function will convert any numbers, such as those with decimals, to a number between 0 and 255, which is one byte according to extended ASCII. Let us suppose we have a column or a number that we want to convert to a byte.

Code:
SELECT cbyte(245.2346) as Number_Byte

Result:

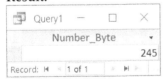

If we try to use cbyte() on a number bigger than 255, we get an overflow error, and the conversion is not possible.

Code:
SELECT cbyte(289.2346) as Number_Byte

Result:

Finally, we can dynamically use the cbyte() function on a column without affecting the table design as per the code below:

Code:

SELECT cbyte(unitprice) as ByteNumber
FROM ProductsOrders

Result:

288.   The CInt() function

Convert numbers to an integer size

Discussion:

An integer number size will hold numbers between -32,768 to 32,767 and with no decimals. Consequently, if we want to convert the number 3900.2345 to an integer value, we can write:

Code:

SELECT cint(3900.2345) as Number_Integer

Result:

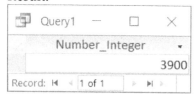

289.   The CLng() function

Convert expressions to long integer numbers

Discussion:

A long integer number size will hold numbers between -2,147,483,648 to 2,147,483,647 with no decimals. If we want to convert the number 50,234.2345 to a long integer value, we will write clng(50234.2345). Notice that we cannot convert to a simple integer in this case since this number exceeds the integer's capabilities.

Code:

SELECT clng(50234.2345) as Number_Long

Result:

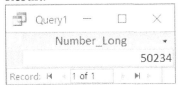

290.   The CSng() and CDbl() functions

Convert numbers to Single or Double sizes

Discussion:

We can use the Single and Double number sizes when working with high precision floating numbers. Both single and double sizes are high precision field sizes, and we can store a lot of detail using them. Specifically, we can use the Single size for floating values between -3.4×10^{38} and $+3.4 \times 10^{38}$. Single number field sizes can have up to 7 digits. We can use the double size for floating values between -1.797×10^{308} and $+1.797 \times 10^{308}$. Double number field sizes can have up to 15 digits. Let us go through two examples working with the number 1500345.45349345. Notice this number has 15 digits in total.

If we convert it to a single number, we write:

Code:

SELECT csng(1500345.45349345) as Number_Single

Result:

Notice the resulting number contains only 7 digits, and the decimal has been rounded to one digit.

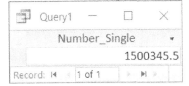

If we convert the same number to a double, we write:

Code:

SELECT cdbl(1500345.45349345) as Number_Double

Result:

As you can see, converting to a double number, we have not lost any of the digits either before or after the decimal since double numbers can hold up to fifteen digits.

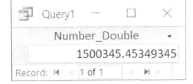

311

291.   The CBool() function

Compare customer first and last name values

Discussion:

The cbool() function will return a true or false value. To demonstrate its usefulness, let us assume that a coworker comes to our office and says that something is wrong with the mailing labels they are producing. On certain occasions, the last and first name fields print the same. Obviously, someone typed in the same value as both first and last name in the database. We can use the cbool() function to find the records for which this occurs.

Code:

```
SELECT CustomerID, cbool([lastname]=[firstname]) As TrueFalse
FROM customers
```

Result:

Whenever you see 0 in Access, this means the result is false, or, in other words, the last and first names have different values since you checked for equality. If you see -1, the result is true, which means that the first and last names have identical values. As you scroll through the records, you will notice that you get a -1 for customerid = 19 and an error for 106.

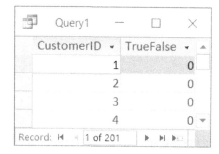

This is cause for investigation. For record 19, the last and first names are the same, while for record 106, the first name is missing! Consequently, with one function, we found two errors that would mess up our coworker's job.

292.   The cCur() function

Convert numbers to currency

Discussion:

If we open the ProductsOrders table in design view, we will notice that the UnitPrice and Quantity fields are of the number data type and long integer and double sizes respectively. We want to create a report that shows their multiplication as currency to show order subtotals. We can accomplish this task by using the ccur() conversion function. Notice the dollar sign in front of the OrderSubtotal values.

Code:

```
SELECT OrderID, CCur(UnitPrice*Quantity) as OrderSubtotal
FROM ProductsOrders
```

Result:

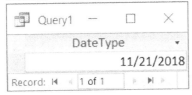

293.   The CDate() function

Convert text to dates

Discussion:

We might have inherited or imported date data in text format like "November 21 2018" or even "21 November 2018". If we want to convert these text values to a date format and store them in a date field, we can use the cdate() function.

Code:

```
SELECT cdate("November 21 2018") as DateType
```

You will achieve the same result if you use:

```
SELECT cdate("21 November 2018") as DateType
```

Result:

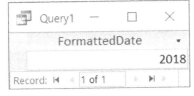

Of course, we can combine the cdate() conversion function with a date function like year() to concurrently extract the year out of our text data. (Check chapter 28 in this book for many tips on dates).

Code:

```
SELECT year(cdate("November 21 2018")) as FormattedDate
```

Result:

<table>
<tr><td>Query1   —   □   ×</td></tr>
<tr><td>FormattedDate   ▾</td></tr>
<tr><td>2018</td></tr>
<tr><td>Record: ◄   1 of 1   ► ►◄ ►</td></tr>
</table>

294.   The CStr() function
Convert numeric data to text
Discussion:
Let us assume that the previous DBA used the number data type to store zip codes. Zip codes as numbers might behave oddly in situations where we need to concatenate them for example with address numbers. The best way is to convert them to text before proceeding with any concatenation. In any case, we only use the number data type for a field if we expect to make calculations with this field. Consequently, zip codes or phone numbers should be text fields. The cstr() function will convert anything to a string (text) value.

Code:
SELECT cstr(12456) As ZipCode

Result:

295.　CHAPTER 25 DISCUSSION QUESTIONS

1. Why is it a good idea to use type conversion functions?
2. Why is it better to change the data type of a field on the fly rather than forcing a change in the design of the table?
3. How many digits can we have in a single number and how many in a double number?
4. Can we use type conversion functions to change text data to numeric data and vice versa?
5. What will happen if we try to convert a number bigger than 255 using the Cbyte() function?
6. What is the range of numbers an integer data type can hold?
7. What type conversion function do we use to return a true or false value?
8. What is the type conversion function we use to designate data as currency?
9. What is the usefulness of the Cstr() type conversion function?
10. If we have imported date data from a flat file and we want to convert it to a date format what function do we use?

296.　CHAPTER 25 HANDS-ON EXERCISES

Chapter 25 Case 1:

Create a new Access database and name it Chapter25_1.accdb. Copy the table tble_Orders_Conversion from the PracticeDatabase.accdb and paste it to Chapter25_1.accdb.

1. The inventory people want to make calculations and they need the UnitPrice field values to appear without decimals. They do not want any changes in the original data in the tble_Orders_Conversion table. Create a new query that contains the SalesRepName, OrderDate, UnitPrice, and Quantity fields from the tble_Orders_Conversion table as well as a new field named NewUnitPrice that should be an integer. Save the query as Qry1_UnitPrice_Integer.

Your result should look like:

SalesRepName ▾	OrderDate ▾	UnitPrice ▾	NewUnitPrice ▾	Quantity ▾
Anderson	May 21 2016	15.015	15	6
Anderson	May 21 2016	15.09	15	4
Anderson	May 21 2016	8.02	8	6
Anderson	May 21 2016	15.02	15	1

Record: I◀ ◀ 1 of 20 ▶ ▶I ▶⃰ No Filter Search

2. The marketing people need to send out letters to customers and they need to time those letters based on the values in the order date field. However, when they try to use the dates in the order date field they have trouble because the values are in plain text. Create a new query that contains the SalesRepName, OrderDate, UnitPrice, and Quantity fields from the tble_Orders_Conversion table as well as a new field named NewOrderDate that should be a date value in the format mm/dd/yyyy. Save the query as Qry2_OrderDate.

Your result should look like:

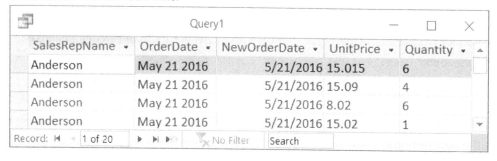

3. The marketing people need to retrieve the year value out of the order date field because they want to perform calculations based on year totals. Create a new query that contains the same fields as in question 2 and modify the NewOrderDate field to show only the year. Save the query as Qry3_Year.

Your result should look like:

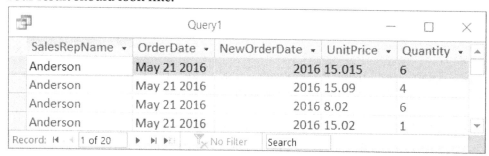

4. The inventory people need a list of customers that shows who pays above $40 for shipping cost and who below 40. Create a new query that contains the firstname, lastname, state, and another field named "SC40" that shows the category in which the customer belongs. Save the query as Qry4_Categories.

Your result should look like:

5. The sales people need to calculate order totals for customers. However, when they try to multiply the unitprice field with the quantity field they get errors. Convert the unit price and quantity fields in appropriate formats so that the sales people can perform their calculations. Create a new query that contains the FirstName, LastName, UnitPrice, and Quantity fields from the

tble_Orders_Conversion table as well as two fields named NewUnitPrice and NewQuantity on which the appropriate conversion functions are used. Name the query Qry5_Calculations.

Your result should look like:

Chapter 25 Case 2:

Create a new Access database and name it Chapter25_2.accdb. Copy the tables Customers, SalesReps, Suppliers, Products_Local, and Products_Regional from the PracticeDatabase.accdb and paste them to Chapter25_2.accdb.

1. The sales people need to change the ProductUnitPrice field to extend new prices to customers but they have trouble doing those changes because the ProductUnitPrice field is of the text data type. They also need to make the decimal points disappear from this field. Create a new query that contains the ProductName, QuantityPerUnit, CatalogLastUpdated , and a new field called NewPrice of the integer data type from the tble_Products_Conversion table that satisfies the sales people request. Save the query as Qry1_ProductUnitPrice_Integer.

Your result should look like:

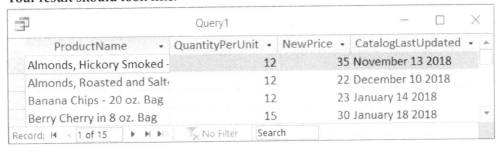

2. The sales people need to create a report using the CatalogLastUpdated date field but they have difficulty since the field data type is text. Create a new query that contains the ProductName, QuantityPerUnit, and a new field called NewCatalogLastUpdated from the tble_Products_Conversion table that satisfies the sales people request. The CatalogLastUpdated field should have the format mm/dd/yyyy. Save the query as Qry2_CatalogLastUpdated.

Your result should look like:

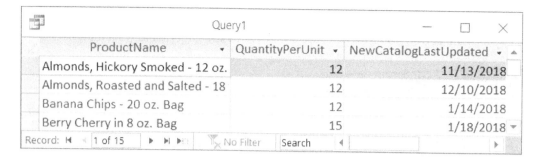

3. Continuing with the request in question 2 the sales people need to extract the year out of the CatalogLastUpdated field. Create a new query with the same fields as in question 2 from the tble_Products_Conversion table. Convert the CatalogLastUpdated field to a date field as you did in question 2 and then extract the year out of this field. Save the query as Qry3_Year.

Your result should look like:

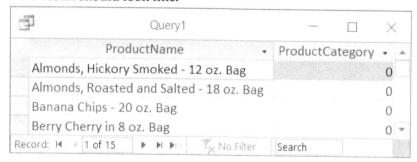

4. The inventory people need a report that shows which products require replenishment and which ones do not. Specifically, they need to know for which products the sum of the quantity per unit and the units on order is less than the reorder level and for which products is greater. Create a new query that contains the ProductName and another field, named ProductCategory, that shows the category in which the product belongs according to the criteria above. Save the query as Qry4_ProductCategories.

Your result should look like:

ProductName	ProductCategory
Almonds, Hickory Smoked - 12 oz. Bag	0
Almonds, Roasted and Salted - 18 oz. Bag	0
Banana Chips - 20 oz. Bag	0
Berry Cherry in 8 oz. Bag	0

Record: 1 of 15   No Filter   Search

5. The sales people need to make some calculations using data from the tble_Products_Conversion table. In this respect, they need the ProductUnitPrice to be of the currency data type, and the UnitsInStock and UnitsOnOrder of the integer data type. Create a new query that contains the ProductName field and three new fields one for the price named NewPrice, one for the units in

stock named NewUnitsInStock, and one for the units on order named NewUnitsOnOrder from the tble_Products_Conversion table. Save the query as Qry5_MultipleConversions.

Your result should look like:

ProductName	NewPrice	NewUnitsInStock	NewUnitsOnOrder
Almonds, Hickory Smoked - 12 oz. Bag	$35.01	30	5
Almonds, Roasted and Salted - 18 oz. B	$22.02	15	0
Banana Chips - 20 oz. Bag	$23.02	25	0
Berry Cherry in 8 oz. Bag	$30.01	35	0

Record: 1 of 15   No Filter   Search

CHAPTER 26
WORKING WITH STRINGS

We now enter the amazing world of text functions and string manipulation. Text functions produce output that it is impossible to generate otherwise. For example, we can extract part of a field value from the beginning, end, or the middle of a field based on the position of a special character. We can uppercase or lowercase a string of characters or we can add or remove spaces or characters at will. They should be in the toolbox of every database user since they have direct effects on database and table design. Knowing how to manipulate text to retrieve what we need leads to more efficient table design without uneccesary fields. The following are the text functions of Access. In this chapter, we will explore a multitude of examples of how to use them in a business.

	Function Name	Syntax
1.	Format()	Format(expression [, format] [, firstdayofweek] [, firstweekofyear])
2.	InStr()	InStr([start,] string1, string2 [, compare])
3.	InStrRev()	InstrRev(stringcheck, stringmatch [, start] [, compare])
4.	LCase()	LCase(string)
5.	Left()	Left(string, length)
6.	Len()	Len(string | varname)
7.	LTrim()	LTrim(string)
8.	Mid()	Mid(string, start [, length])
9.	RTrim()	RTrim(string)
10.	Replace()	Replace(expression, find, replace [, start] [, count] [, compare])
11.	Right()	Right(string, length)
12.	Space()	Space(number)
13.	StrComp()	StrComp(string1, string2 [, compare])
14.	StrConv()	StrConv(string, conversion [, LCID])
15.	String()	String(number, character)
16.	StrReverse()	StrReverse(expression)
17.	Trim()	Trim(string)
18.	UCase()	UCase(string)

297. Use the Ucase() function to capitalize field values
Capitalize the first and last names of customers using ucase()
Discussion:

The general syntax of the ucase() function is shown below. It takes just one argument, and it will capitalize the contents of the field on which it is applied.

ucase(field name)

Code:

SELECT UCase(lastname) AS Last, UCase(firstname) AS First, city, state, zip
FROM customers

Result:

Last	First	city	state	zip
DEMARCO	JOHN	New York	NY	12189
DEMANIA	MARY	New York	NY	12189
DEMERS	GEORGE	New York	NY	12189
DEMETRIOU	PHILLIP	New York	NY	12189

Record: 1 of 201   No Filter   Search

298. Use the strConv() function to capitalize the first character of the field only

Capitalize the first letters of the first and last names of our customers

Discussion:

We can also use the strConv() function to capitalize field values. The strConv() takes two arguments from which the second is a constant. Its general syntax appears below:

strConv (field, constant)

The constant takes three values and depending on the choice the strConv() function will produce different outputs. The table below shows the three possibilities for the constant:

strConv (field, constant)

Constant Value	Output Result
1	Converts field value to uppercase characters.
2	Converts field value to lowercase characters.
3	Converts the first letter of every word in the field to uppercase.

In this example, we will use the value 3 for the constant because we want to capitalize only the first character of each word in the last and first name fields.

Code:

SELECT strconv(lastname, 3) AS Last, strConv(firstname, 3) AS First, city, state, zip
FROM customers

Result:

Last	First	city	state	zip
Demarco	John	New York	NY	12189
Demania	Mary	New York	NY	12189
Demers	George	New York	NY	12189
Demetriou	Phillip	New York	NY	12189

Record: 1 of 201   No Filter   Search

299.   Use the format() function to capitalize fields

Capitalize the first and last names of customers using format()

Discussion:

The format() function is the third function we can use to manipulate the case of characters in a field. The general syntax of the format() function with respect to text manipulation appears below. We will use the format() function again and again in date and number fields. For the purposes of string manipulation, however, we will concentrate on this syntax:

Format(field, constant)

Constant Value	Output
<	Force all characters to lowercase.
>	Force all characters to uppercase.

Code:

SELECT format(lastname, '>') AS Last, format(firstname, '>') AS First, city, state, zip
FROM customers

Result:

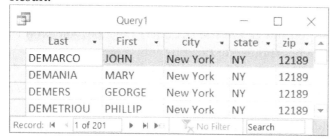

300.   Use the Lcase() function to convert field values to lowercase

Convert the first and last names of our customers to lowercase

Discussion:

The lcase() function takes only one argument—the field name—and results in converting all characters of a field value to lowercase. Its general syntax is:

Lcase(field name)

In this particular example, we use it to convert both the first and last names of our customers to lowercase:

Code:

SELECT Lcase(lastname) AS Last, Lcase(firstname) AS First, city, state, zip
FROM customers

Result:

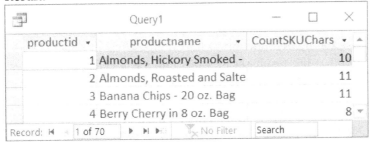

301.   Use the len() function to count the number of characters in a field

Count the number of characters in the SKU field

Discussion:

There are occasions in which we like to count the number of characters for a field in every record in the database. This is especially useful when we want to change the data type of a field or when we want to decrease its length. If we work with extraction, transformation, and loading (ETL) tools, this function is particularly useful to know exactly what is happening instead of making guesses and ending up with truncated values. The len() function is especially easy to use, it takes just one argument, and its general syntax appears below:

Len(field name)

In this particular example, we count the number of characters in the SKU field of the products table. Notice from the output that the result of the function for each record is different. We can then sort ascending or descending to display the shortest or lengthiest entries first in the output.

Code:

```
SELECT productid, productname, len(sku) AS CountSKUChars
FROM Products
```

Result:

productid	productname	CountSKUChars
1	Almonds, Hickory Smoked -	10
2	Almonds, Roasted and Salte	11
3	Banana Chips - 20 oz. Bag	11
4	Berry Cherry in 8 oz. Bag	8

Record: 1 of 70

302.   Use the instr() function to find the position of a character in a string evaluating from the beginning of a string

Find the number of characters occurring before the "-" character in the SKUs field

Discussion:

In business, we use stock keeping unit codes (SKU) to assign a unique code to products. In our products table, we do have an SKU field. This code consists of some letters and a hyphen followed by some numbers like PDKLS-3483. The letter part of the code before the hyphen signifies some larger category, and we might need to create reports and aggregations grouping only by the letter part of the

SKU code. Our problem is that the number of letters in the SKU code might not be the same all the time. At least this is what happened in my own experience. So, how can we get the string part of the SKU regardless of the number of characters it consists of? To complete this task effectively, we use the instr() function to determine the position of the hyphen in the string (PDKLS-3483). Its general syntax appears below:

$$instr(starting\ character,\ field,\ character\ to\ find)$$

In this example, we use inStr(1,sku,"-") to look for the "-" character in the SKU field starting from the first character.

Code:
SELECT productid, productname, sku, InStr(1,sku,'-') AS PartSKU
FROM Products

Result:

productid	productname	sku	PartSKU
5	California Original Pistachio	PDK-2347	4
6	Choice Apricots - 16 oz. Bag	PDKLS-2347	6
7	Cran Raisin Mix in 17 oz. Bag	PDKLS-2347	6
8	Dried Blueberries - 1 lb. Bag	PDKLS-2347	6

Record: 1 of 70   No Filter   Search

303. Use the instr() function to find the position of a blank space evaluating from the beginning of a string

Find the number of characters occurring before a blank space in the SKU field

Discussion:

For this example, I have purposely created an additional problem for us: Some of the hyphens separating the letter code of the SKU from the number code are missing because they were not typed correctly during data entry. We can still use the instr() function to find the position of those blanks. Notice the WHERE clause, which is there so that the result set includes only SKU codes with spaces between letter and number codes and not those with hyphens. Pay close attention to the result set. You will see that for the first three records the position of the blank is indicated to be at the first character. This is correct since for the first three records there is a blank to the left of the "A" letter. This is one additional problem that we might have with data and which we can solve using the ltrim() function.

Code:
SELECT productid, productname, sku, InStr(1,sku,' ') AS PartSKU
FROM Products
WHERE InStr(1,sku,' ') <> 0

Results:

productid	productname	sku	PartSKU
40	Biscuits with cream	ASDT-3456	1
41	Banana Bisquits	ADSE 2345	1
42	Chocolate Bisquits	ADST 2345	1
43	Cocoa and Hazelnut Biscuits	ADSD 2345	5

Record: ◄ ‹ 1 of 8 ► ►I ►⁕ ⫧ₓ No Filter   Search

304. Use the instr() and left() functions to extract a substring from the beginning of a string

Extract the letter part of the SKU field

Discussion:

In this example, we want to dynamically extract a substring from within a string. To do this, we use the left() and instr() functions together. First, we use the instr() function on the SKU field to obtain the numeric value of the exact position of the "hyphen" in the SKU field. Then, we use the left() function, which takes two arguments. The first is the field, and the second is the number of characters to be returned. If we apply the left() function on the string "Hello there" as Left("Hi There", 5), it will return "Hi th".

$$left(sku, InStr(1,sku,'-')-1)$$

What is the -1 doing in the instr() function? The instr() function will return the numeric position of the hyphen including the hyphen. Thus, we apply the instr() function minus one character so that we obtain the characters till the hyphen but not the hyphen itself. We do not care about the number of letters in the first part of the SKU code till the hyphen. They can be any number, and we will be able to retrieve the string we need.

Code:
```
SELECT productname, sku, left(sku, InStr(1,sku,'-')-1) AS PartSKU
FROM Products
```

Result:

productname	sku	PartSKU
Almonds, Hickory Smoked - 12 oz. Bag	PDKLS-2332	PDKLS
Almonds, Roasted and Salted - 18 oz. Bag	PDKLSD-2344	PDKLSD
Banana Chips - 20 oz. Bag	PDKLSD-2347	PDKLSD
Berry Cherry in 8 oz. Bag	PDK-2589	PDK

Record: ◄ ‹ 2 of 70 ► ►I ►⁕ ⫧ₓ No Filter   Search ‹ ›

305. Extract a substring before a space in the string evaluating from the beginning of a string

Extract the letter part of the SKU field just before a blank space

Discussion:

This example is the same as the previous one, but this time, we extract the letter code of the SKU before a space. Pay attention to the result set. The first three records contain no PartSKU values since there is a blank space in the very beginning of the field value. In the next example, we see how we remove blank spaces from the beginning of a field.

Code:

SELECT productname, sku, left(sku, InStr(1,sku,' ')-1) AS PartSKU
FROM Products
WHERE InStr(1,sku,' ') <> 0

Result:

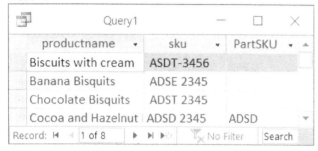

306. Use the Ltrim() function to remove spaces from the beginning of a field

Remove blank spaces from the beginning of the product name field

Discussion:

The ltrim() function takes only one argument and it will eliminate any blank spaces from the beginning of the values of a field. In this example, we are not certain if there are blank spaces at the start of the field for some product names. We can simply use the ltrim() function to make certain there are not. The ltrim() function will eliminate any blank spaces if they exist. If there are no blank spaces for this field in some records, it will leave those values unchanged. Besides, blank spaces affect how other functions such as instr() work. We can use the ltrim() function to make sure we count correctly from the beginning of the field.

Code:

SELECT Ltrim(productname) AS LeftTrimmedName, sku
FROM Products

Result:

307. Use the Rtrim() function to remove spaces from the end of a field

Remove blank spaces from the end of the product name field

Discussion:

The Rtrim() function takes one argument, and its main job is to eliminate blank spaces from the end of a field. We can use the Rtrim() function to make certain there are no blank spaces at the end of the field. If there are no blank spaces, it will leave those field values unchanged. In addition, blank spaces affect how other functions work, for example the right() function. Using the Rtrim() function, we make sure we count correctly from the end of the field.

Code:

SELECT Rtrim(productname) AS RightTrimmedName, sku
FROM Products

Result:

308. Trim blank spaces both at the end and beginning of a string

Remove blank spaces from the beginning and end of the product name field

Discussion:

The role of the trim() function is to eliminate blank spaces from the beginning and end of a field simultaneously. The trim() function takes only one argument as we can see in the example below and it is a good idea to use it when we work with strings:

Code:

SELECT trim(productname) AS TrimmedName, sku
FROM Products

Result:

309.   Insert one space dynamically before or after a field

Insert one blank space in the beginning and end of the product name field

Discussion:

This time, we have the opposite task. Instead of using the ltrim(), rtrim(), or trim() functions to remove blank spaces from the beginning, end, or both ends of a field respectively, we want to add spaces. To achieve this task, we use the concatenation character '+' to add a space in the beginning and end of the productname field. You can read a whole chapter in this book on concatenation (chapter 16).

Code:

```
SELECT (' ' +productname + ' ') AS SpacedName, sku
FROM Products
```

Result:

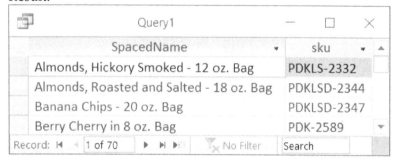

310.   Use the space() function to insert any number of spaces dynamically before or after a field

Insert ten blank spaces in the beginning and end of the product name field

Discussion:

In some cases, we might want to add any number of blank spaces in the beginning or at the end of the same field. Using concatenation characters to achieve this task will be a very messy affair. Instead, we can use the space() function to achieve the same outcome. In the example below we add ten spaces before and after the productname field:

Code:

```
SELECT (space(10)+ productname + space(10))  AS SpacedName, sku
FROM Products
```

Result:

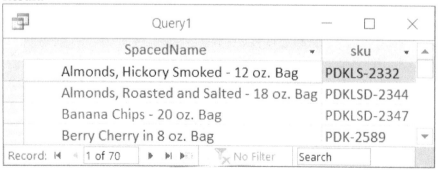

311. Use the left() function to retrieve any number of characters from the beginning of a field
Retrieve the first four characters of the SKU code
Discussion:
In some situations, the data in our database is well formatted, and we do not have to resort to combinations of functions such as left() and instr() to retrieve a substring from a string in a field. For example, if the letter part of the SKU code in our products table is always of length 4 (PDKS-2345), we can use the left function to retrieve the first four characters from this field. The left() function takes two arguments—the field name and the number of characters we want to retrieve.

left(fieldname, number of characters to retrieve)

Code:
```
SELECT productname, left(sku,4) AS 4SKU
FROM Products
```

Result:

312. Use the right() function to retrieve any number of characters from the end of a field
Retrieve the last four characters of the SKU code
Discussion:
In this example, we retrieve the last four characters from the SKU field, which, by the way, represent the number part of our SKUs (PDKS-2345). If the SKU field is well formatted, we can use the right() function to achieve this task very easily. By well formatted, we mean the number part of the SKU will always have four digits. Otherwise, we will run into trouble with the right() function. The right() function takes two arguments—the field name and the number of characters we would like to retrieve.

right(fieldname, number of characters to retrieve)

Code:
```
SELECT productname, right(sku,4) AS SKU4
FROM Products
```

Result:

productname	SKU4
Almonds, Hickory Smoked - 12 oz. Bag	2332
Almonds, Roasted and Salted - 18 oz. Bag	2344
Banana Chips - 20 oz. Bag	2347
Berry Cherry in 8 oz. Bag	2589

Record: I◄ ◄ 1 of 70 ► ►I ►⁕ No Filter   Search

313. Use the mid() function to retrieve any number of characters from any part of a field

Retrieve the first five characters of the product name field starting at character 3

Discussion:

The mid() function is practically an improved left() function, and we can use it instead of left for greater flexibility. The mid() function takes three arguments as they appear below:

Mid(field name, character to start, number of characters to get)

In this example, we use the mid() function to retrieve five characters from the productname field starting at character three.

Code:

```
SELECT mid(productname, 3, 5) As TrimmedName, sku
FROM Products
```

Result:

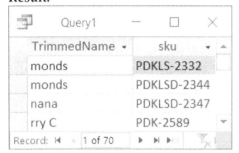

TrimmedName	sku
monds	PDKLS-2332
monds	PDKLSD-2344
nana	PDKLSD-2347
rry C	PDK-2589

Record: I◄ ◄ 1 of 70 ► ►I ►⁕

314. Use the string() function to repeat any number of characters from the beginning of a field

Retrieve the first character of the product name field repeated five times

Discussion:

The string() function will return the first character of a field value any number of times we want. It takes two arguments.

String(number of times character repeats, field name)

The string function might look simplistic, and you might wonder about its purpose. Alone, it might not be very useful, but we can use it in combination with other functions to repeat characters in the middle or at the end of a field. In addition, we can use the string() function in concatenated fields to create categories like AAA, BBB, CCC, etc. In this particular example, we repeat the first letter of the productname field five times.

Code:
SELECT string(5, productname) As Name, sku
FROM Products

Result:

315. Use the replace() function to update field values
Replace part of supplier's SKU codes dynamically
Discussion:
The replace() function provides us with great flexibility for our work. Let us suppose that one of our suppliers has recently updated the SKU codes they use, and we need to do the same for their products in our own database. From now on, products with the SKU letter codes "PDK" need to be updated to "PDS". Keep in mind that PDKSs and PDKRs need to remain as they are untouched. In addition, the number part of the SKU code needs to remain untouched. So, "PDK-2389" needs to become "PDS-2389". Consequently, we need to isolate the exact letter code "PDK", replace it with PDS, and leave the trailing numbers untouched. This is a job for the replace function. Is basic syntax appears below:

replace(field name, string to search for, string to replace with, at what character to start)

For example the expression

replace(sku, 'pdk-', pds-')

will replace "pdk-" with "pds-". Notice that the fourth argument (at what character to start) is optional, and if we leave it out, the replace function will start the evaluation at the first character of the field. We could start at any character, however.

The way we work when it comes to updates is to select the records to be updated first to make sure we will update the correct ones. Then, we write the update statement against those records. This way, just in case something goes sideways, we know which records are affected. This logic is demonstrated below with two consecutive SQL statements:

Code:

```
SELECT productname, sku
FROM Products
WHERE left(sku, 4) = 'PDK-'
```

Result:

Code:

```
SELECT productname, replace(sku, 'pdk-', 'pds-') As skuUpdated
FROM Products
WHERE left(sku, 4) = 'PDK-'
```

Result:

316. Use the strComp() function to compare the length of two fields

Compare the length of the first and lastname fields for all customers

Discussion:

In this example, we compare the length of two fields to determine if they have the same number of characters. One way to do it is to use the Len() function on both fields and then, compare the results. However, there is another quick way to achieve the same task by using the strComp() function. The general syntax of the strComp() function appears below:

$$strComp(field1, field2)$$

The strComp() function will return (-1, 0, 1, or Null) according to the table below:

Comparison Result	Output
field1 is less than field2	-1
field1 is equal to field2	0
field1 is greater than field2	1
field1 or field2 is Null	Null

In this example, we compare the length of the first name and last name fields of the customers table.

Code:

SELECT lastname, firstname, strcomp(firstname, lastname) As CompResult
FROM Customers

Result:

317. Use the strReverse() function to reverse the order of characters in a field

Reverse the order of characters in the SKU field in the products table

Discussion:

The strReverse() function is easy to use, and it takes only one argument as its syntax shows below. It will return a string in which the character order is reversed.

$$strReverse(field)$$

In this example, we apply it on the SKU field in the products table, and we see from the output that the number part of the SKU now appears first. Of course, this happens dynamically, and the actual data in the table will not be affected.

Code:

SELECT productid, strReverse(sku) As ReverseSKU
FROM Products

Result:

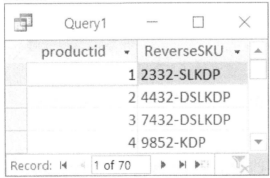

1. How many functions can we use to capitalize field values?
2. Which is the most flexible function for field capitalization?
3. How many constant values are accepted in the format() function? How many in the strConv() function?
4. What is the purpose of the len() function in Access?
5. What function can we use to find the position of a character or a blank space in a string?
6. What is the purpose of the left() function in Access?
7. Why does it make lot of sense to use the instr() and left() functions in combination? What results can we achieve?
8. What functions do we use to remove spaces from the beginning or the end of strings?
9. What function can we use to enter any number of spaces before or after a field value?
10. What function can we use to compare the length of characters of two fields?

319. CHAPTER 26 HANDS-ON EXERCISES

Chapter 26 Case 1:

Create a new Access database and name it Chapter26_1.accdb. Copy the table Customers from the PracticeDatabase.accdb and paste it to Chapter26_1.accdb.

1. The sales people need mailing labels to send out letters to customers. They want the first name of the customer capitalized for emphasis. Create a new query that contains the FirstName, LastName, City, State, and Zip fields from the customer table. Use any function you want to capitalize the FirstName field. Save the query as Qry1_FirstName.

   Your result should look like:

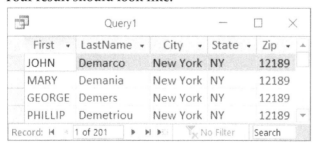

2. The sales people are thankful of your report from the previous step but they think it does not look right and they changed their mind. What they actually want is to capitalize only the first letter of the customer's FirstName and LastName fields. Create a new query that contains the FirstName, LastName, City, State, and Zip fields from the customer table and satisfies the sales people request. Save the query as Qry2_FirstCharacter.

   Your result should look like:

3. The marketing people need to send out letters to customers but they fear that some of the addresses are too long and they might exceed the space limit they have on a special pamphlet they are preparing. They are asking you to provide a report which shows the customers whose address exceeds twenty (20) characters. Create a new query that contains all fields from the customers table and satisfies the sales people request. Save the query as Qry3_NumberOfCharacters.

Your result should look like:

4. The marketing people are back asking for a list of customers for whom it is certain there are no blank spaces in front of the FirstName or the LastName fields because any blank spaces interfere with the alignment of the various paragraphs in the personalized brochures they are preparing. Create a new query that contains the FirstName, LastName, City, State, and Zip fields from the customers table and satisfies the marketing people request. Save the query as Qry4_NoBlanks.

Your result should look like:

5. The marketing people are very happy with the list you provided in question 4. They have a final request that will help the graphic designers who are working on the pamphlet. Specifically they need five blank spaces for all customers at the end of the Zip field. Create a new query that contains the FirstName, LastName, City, State, and Zip fields from the customers table and satisfies

the marketing people request. Save the query as Qry5_TrailingBlanks.

Your result should look like:

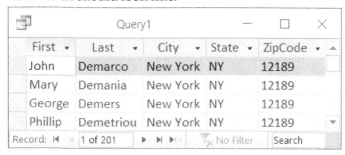

Chapter 26 Case 2:

Create a new Access database and name it Chapter26_2.accdb. Copy the table tble_Products_Strings from the PracticeDatabase.accdb and paste it to Chapter26_2.accdb.

1. The sales people need to create a new product catalog. Specifically, they need a catalog that contains the ProductName and ProductUnitPrice fields. For the Product name field they want only the portion of the name up until the dash to appear excluding any weight information. Create a new query that satisfies the sales people request and save it as Qry1_ProductName.

Your result should look like:

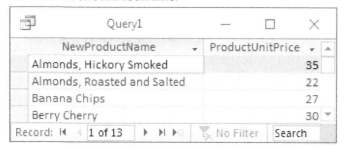

2. The sales people are back asking for another product catalog. They again need the product catalog to contain the ProductName and ProductUnitPrice fields but this time they want the "oz." notation to be replaced by "grams." Create a new query that satisfies the sales people request and save it as Qry2_Grams.

Your result should look like:

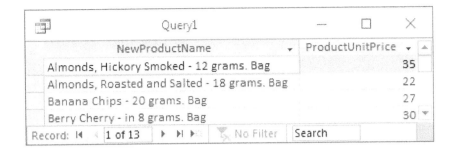

3. The supplierID field has the format XXX-XXX or XXXX-XXX with the first three or four numbers indicating the region of the supplier while the last three digits representing the product family the supplier is manufacturing for us. The production people need a list that includes the ProductName and SupplierID fields. For the supplierID field they only need the region indicator to appear. Create a new query that satisfies the production people request and save it as Qry3_Region.

Your result should look like:

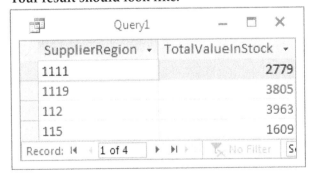

4. The inventory people liked very much the report you created for the production people and they want a similar report which will include some totals as well. Specifically, they need a report that will total the value of the inventory on hand by supplier region. Create a new query that satisfies the inventory people request and save it as Qry4_RegionTotals.

Your result should look like:

SupplierRegion	TotalValueInStock
1111	2779
1119	3805
112	3963
115	1609

Record: 1 of 4 No Filter

5. The inventory people are really amazed by the information you were able to give them. They now have one additional request. They need a report that will total the value of the inventory on hand by product family. Create a new query that satisfies the inventory people request and save it as Qry5_ProductFamilyTotals.

Your result should look like:

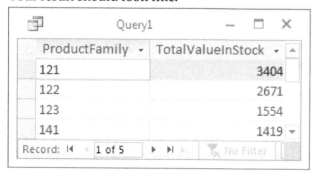

CHAPTER 27
WORKING WITH DATES

Date functions enable us to perform a superior level of work in multiple database tasks. For instance, we can create advanced reports by extracting the year or month out of a date field, and then, we can summarize data based on those years or months. Second, we can extract the quarters out of a date range and create a crosstab query showing our data by quarter. Third, we can create projected order fulfillment cycle times by adding, say, two business days to the order date field and comparing our projections with the actual shipped dates for quality control. Fourth, we can use date functions as default field values to record the exact date and time a record was inserted. Fifth, with date functions, we can convert numerical date values such as 9/20/2018 to actual named values such as September 20, 2018. Sixth, we can combine date functions with aggregate functions for exceptional data calculations and summaries. Seventh, our level of knowledge on date functions will have a direct effect on the quality of our database design since we can avoid date fields that we can create automatically from other date fields. These examples are just a small part of what we can do with date functions. The main point is that date functions do not just represent additional knowledge; they are required for truly professional work. The table below includes the date functions available in Access.

Name	Syntax	Comments
Date()	Date()	Returns a Variant (Date) containing the current system date.
DateAdd()	DateAdd(interval, number, date)	Adds or subtracts a specified time interval from a date
DateDiff()	DateDiff(interval, date1, date2 [, firstdayofweek] [, firstweekofyear])	Returns a Variant (Long) specifying the number of time intervals between two specified dates.
DatePart()	DatePart(interval, date [, firstdayofweek] [, firstweekofyear])	Returns a Variant (Integer) containing the specified part of a given date.
DateSerial()	DateSerial(year, month, day)	Returns a Variant (Date) for a specified year, month, and day.
DateValue()	DateValue(date)	Returns a Variant (Date).
Day()	Day(date)	Returns a Variant (Integer) specifying a whole number between 1 and 31, inclusive, representing the day of the month.
Hour()	Hour(time)	Returns a Variant (Integer) specifying a whole number between 0 and 23, inclusive, representing the hour of the day.
Minute()	Minute(time)	Returns a Variant (Integer) specifying a whole number between 0 and 59, inclusive, representing the minute of the hour.
Month()	Month(date)	Returns a Variant (Integer) specifying a whole number between 1 and 12, inclusive, representing the month of the year.
MonthName()	MonthName(month [, abbreviate])	Returns a string indicating the specified month.

Now()	Now()	Returns a Variant (Date) specifying the current date and time according your computer's system date and time.
Second()	Second(Time)	Returns a Variant (Integer) specifying a whole number between 0 and 59, inclusive, representing the second of the minute.
Time()	Time()	Returns a Variant (Date) indicating the current system time.
Timer()	Timer()	Returns a Single representing the number of seconds elapsed since midnight.
TimeSerial()	TimeSerial(hour, minute, second)	Returns a Variant (Date) containing the time for a specific hour, minute, and second.
TimeValue()	TimeValue(time)	Returns a Variant (Date) containing the time.
Weekday()	Weekday(date [, firstdayofweek])	Returns a Variant (Integer) containing a whole number representing the day of the week.
WeekdayName ()	WeekdayName(weekday [, abbreviate] [, firstdayofweek])	Returns a String indicating the specified day of the week.
Year()	Year(date)	Returns a Variant (Integer) containing a whole number representing the year.

Source: http://msdn.microsoft.com/en-us/library/office/ff836861(v=office.15).aspx

DateAdd(), DateDiff(), DatePart() interval argument settings.	
Setting	Description
yyyy	Year
q	Quarter
m	Month
y	Day of year
d	Day
w	Weekday
ww	Week
h	Hour
n	Minute
s	Second

Source: http://msdn.microsoft.com/en-us/library/office/gg251759(v=office.15).aspx

320.   Retrieve orders within two dates

Discussion:

In this example we want to produce a list of orders between the dates of 1/1/2019 and 6/30/2019. To achieve this task we can use the inequality and equality predicates or the BETWEEN AND operator. Of course you remember that the BETWEEEN AND operator is inclusive which means the boundary dates will be included in the result set.

Code (using BETWEEN AND):
SELECT *
FROM Orders
WHERE OrderDate BETWEEN #1/1/2019# AND #6/30/2019#
ORDER BY OrderDate ASC

Code (using inequality and equality predicates):
```
SELECT *
FROM Orders
WHERE OrderDate>=#1/1/2019# AND OrderDate<=#6/30/2019#
ORDER BY OrderDate
```

Result:

OrderID	CustomerID	SalesRepID	ShipperID	OrderDate
581	143	6	2	1/2/2019
431	29	5	1	1/3/2019
473	160	5	2	1/4/2019
146	144	1	3	1/4/2019

Record: 1 of 165 — No Filter — Search

321. Retrieve orders outside two dates

Discussion:

To retrieve orders outside two dates we need to use equality and inequality predicates as in the code below. Notice how we use the OR operator with outside date ranges.

Code:
```
SELECT *
FROM Orders
WHERE OrderDate<=#1/1/2019# OR OrderDate >=#6/30/2019#
ORDER BY OrderDate
```

Result:

OrderID	CustomerID	SalesRepID	ShipperID	OrderDate
351	56	4	1	1/14/2017
380	193	4	3	1/15/2017
854	80	9	2	1/15/2017
76	113	1	2	1/15/2017

Record: 1 of 834 — No Filter — Search

322. Use the Now() function for default field values

Discussion:

The now() function takes only one argument, and its general syntax appears below:

now()

It will output the system date and time, and it is frequently used as the default value for a date field. For example, if we open the SalesReps table, we will notice that there is a field called DateInserted with a default value of now(). This means that every time a record is inserted in this table, the system date and time will be recorded in this field. We can also use now() in a SQL statement to capture the date and time as in the statement below:

Code:

SELECT now() as CurrentDateAndTime

Result:

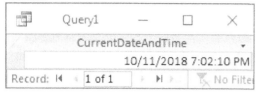

323. Find the latest order by customer

Discussion:

The sales people are asking for a report that shows the latest order for each customer. Specifically, they want to see a list that contains the last name, first name, and latest order date for each customer. There is a plethora of solutions here but we will go for the simplest one.

Solution 1:

We can quickly identify the latest order by using the max() function and the group by clause but the problem is we will not see the customer first and last names.

Code 1:

SELECT customerID, max(orderDate) As LatestOrder
FROM Orders
GROUP BY customerID

Result 1:

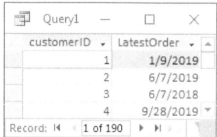

Solution 2 (wrong in most cases):

If we need the name of the customer to show we can go with a solution like the one below with the max() function, an INNER JOIN (chapter 30), and the GROUP BY clause. This solution is conceptually correct but practically wrong because in most cases we will have multiple customers with the same last name. Even if you concatenate the customers' first and last names and use the group by clause on the concatenated name, you might still get wrong results because some customers will have the same first and last names.

Code 2 (wrong in most cases):

SELECT lastname, Max(Orders.OrderDate) AS MaxOfOrderDate
FROM Customers INNER JOIN Orders ON Customers.CustomerID = Orders.CustomerID
GROUP BY lastname

Result 2:

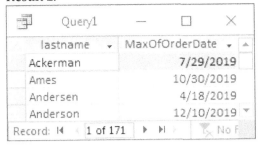

Solution 3 (correct solution)

In this example we use the group by clause on the first name, last name, and customerid fields combined. There is no way to mess up results since the CustomerID field is the primary key (PK) in the customer table and thus unique for each customer. Notice the difference in records between result 2 and result 3. Result 2 is giving us only 171 customers because we have many of them with the same last name! Result 3 is giving us the correct number of records.

Code 3

SELECT Customers.CustomerID, Customers.LastName, Customers.FirstName,
Max(Orders.OrderDate) AS LatestOrderDate
FROM Customers INNER JOIN Orders ON Customers.CustomerID = Orders.CustomerID
GROUP BY Customers.CustomerID, Customers.LastName, Customers.FirstName

Result 3

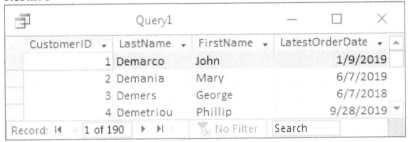

324.   Calculate the number of days, months, quarters, or years between two dates.

Discussion:

We can calculate the number of days between two dates using the datediff(interval, date1, date2) function. As you can see from the code below, date2 is greater than date1 but Access will not complain even if it is the other way around; that is to calculate the number of days to a future date. Make sure you enclose the interval argument in quotes.

Code for years:

SELECT DateDiff('d', #5/15/2017#, #6/3/2018#) As NumberOfDays

Result:

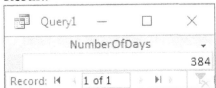

The code below will calculate time elapsed in months, quarters, and years.
Code for months:
SELECT DateDiff('m', #5/15/2017#, #6/3/2018#) As NumberOfMonths

Code for quarters:
SELECT DateDiff('q', #5/15/2017#, #6/3/2018#) As NumberOfQuarters

Code for years:
DateDiff('yyyy', #5/15/2017#, #6/3/2018#) As NumberOfYears

325.   Count the number of orders by business day of the week and within a specific quarter.
Discussion:

In this example, we calculate the number of orders by business day of the week within a specific quarter. Check how we use the datepart(interval, datefield) function in conjunction with the IN operator in the WHERE clause to isolate the business days only. By default the week in Access starts on Sunday and consequently Monday will be the second (2) day, Tuesday the third (3), and Friday the sixth (6). Also, check how we use the weekday "w" interval argument in the datepart() function in the SELECT statement.

Code:
```
SELECT datepart('w', orderdate) As BusinessDay, Count(OrderID) AS NumberOfOrders
FROM Orders
WHERE year(orderdate) = 2019 AND datepart('q', orderdate) = 2 AND datepart('w', orderdate) IN
(2,3,4,5,6)
GROUP BY datepart('w', orderdate)
```

Result:

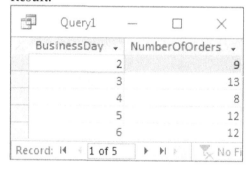

BusinessDay	NumberOfOrders
2	9
3	13
4	8
5	12
6	12

Record: 1 of 5

326.   Count the number of orders by non-business days of the week and by quarter within a specific year
Discussion:

In this example, we are looking for the number of orders in non-business days of the week, that is, Saturdays and Sundays. However, we also want to present results grouped by quarter within a specific year. Notice in the code below how we use the datepart(interval, datefield) function in the WHERE clause to isolate the non-business days of the week (Saturday and Sunday). Sunday in Access is the first (1) day of the week and thus Saturday is the seventh (7). Notice how we use the datepart() function to group twice by quarter "q" and by weekday "w".

Code:
SELECT datepart('q', orderdate) As Quarter, datepart('w', orderdate) As NonBusinessDay,
Count(OrderID) AS NumberOfOrders
FROM Orders
WHERE year(orderdate) = 2019 AND datepart('w', orderdate) IN (1,7)
GROUP BY datepart('q', orderdate), datepart('w', orderdate)

Result:

Quarter ▾	NonBusinessDay ▾	NumberOfOrders ▾
1	1	12
1	7	12
2	1	12
2	7	11
3	1	10
3	7	13
4	1	10
4	7	16

Record: ◄ ◄ 1 of 8 ► ►► ▾ No Filter | Search

327. Use the datepart() function to list orders within a month

Discussion (month):
This time the request is to create a simple list of all orders in June 2017. We can respond to this request by using the datepart(interval, datefield) function to extract the month from the OrderDate field and the year(datefield) function to extract the year. Notice the usage of "m" for the interval argument in the datepart() function.

Code:
SELECT *
FROM Orders
WHERE DatePart('m', [OrderDate]) =6 AND year(Orderdate) = 2017
ORDER BY OrderDate

Of course we could obtain the same result by leaving out the functions and just use absolute date intervals which are fine since what matters is to get the job done.

Code:
SELECT *
FROM Orders
WHERE OrderDate BETWEEN #6/1/2017# AND #6/30/2017#
ORDER BY OrderDate

Result:

OrderID	CustomerID	SalesRepID	ShipperID	OrderDate
117	182	1	2	6/3/2017
218	21	2	1	6/3/2017
396	56	4	1	6/4/2017
352	78	4	2	6/4/2017

Record: 1 of 32   No Filter   Search

328. Use the datepart() function to count the number of orders by each day of the month

Discussion:

Our manager is asking us to count the number of orders by day within June 2017. We will need to use the DatePart(interval, datefield) function to respond as in the example below:

Code:

```
SELECT DatePart('d',OrderDate) AS Day, Count(OrderID) AS NumberOfOrders
FROM Orders
WHERE Year([OrderDate])=2017 AND DatePart('m',[OrderDate]) = 6
GROUP BY DatePart('d',[OrderDate])
ORDER BY DatePart('d',[OrderDate])
```

Result:

As you can see from the result set, we obtain the total number of orders for each of the 21 days within June 2014 for which we had orders. Some days are missing because we did not have any orders in those days.

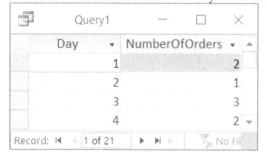

Day	NumberOfOrders
1	2
2	1
3	3
4	2

Record: 1 of 21   No Fil

329. Use the Date() function for default field values

Discussion:

The date() function is often used as the default value of a date field in case you do not want to capture the time. Its general syntax appears below:

date()

You can also use it in a SQL statement in a query or in a report to capture the current date:

Code:
```
SELECT date() as CurrentDate
```

Result:

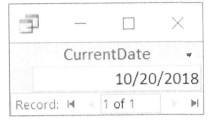

330. Use the datepart() function to count the number of orders by week

Discussion:

In this example we calculate the number of orders within each one of the 52 weeks of the calendar year 2019. Notice from the SQL code that we only have two output fields (Week and NumberofOrders) and we use the year([OrderDate]) field in the WHERE clause to limit the results within the year 2019. This is a quick way to identify order numbers and look for seasonality effects in our sales patterns.

Code:

```
SELECT DatePart('ww',[OrderDate]) AS Week, Count(OrderID) AS NumberOfOrders
FROM Orders
WHERE (((Year([OrderDate]))=2019))
GROUP BY DatePart('ww',[OrderDate])
```

Result:

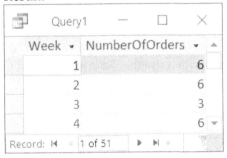

331. Use the datepart() function to count the number of orders every Monday for the last three months.

Discussion:

What if we have a request from marketing to count the number of orders for a specific day of the week and for a period of three months? It can be absolutely done and it is much less complicated than it sounds. First we use the DatePart(interval, datefield) function twice to extract the month and the week day from the Orderdate field. Then we use the Year() and Datepart() functions in the WHERE clause to isolate the year to 2019, the quarter to the first quarter of the year, and the weekday to Monday since by default in Access the week starts on Sunday which is day 1. Then, we group the results by month and day to arrive at the desired outcome. This way we can calculate all the orders for any specific day of the week and any period we would like.

Code:

```
SELECT DatePart('m',[OrderDate]) As month, DatePart('w',[OrderDate]) AS Day,  Count(OrderID)
AS NumberOfOrders
FROM Orders
WHERE year(OrderDate) = 2019  AND  datepart('q', ([OrderDate])) = 1  AND datepart('w',
([OrderDate])) = 2
GROUP BY DatePart('m',[OrderDate]), DatePart('w',[OrderDate])
ORDER BY DatePart('m',[OrderDate])
```

Result:

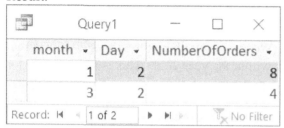

month ▾	Day ▾	NumberOfOrders ▾
1	2	8
3	2	4

Record: ◄ ◄ 1 of 2 ► ►► ▷   ▼ₓ No Filter

332.   Use the year() and datepart() functions to calculate order totals for the same week in different years

Discussion:

Management is asking for a report of order totals for the week before Christmas for all the years for which we have data in the database. Practically, we are talking about week 50 for all years in the database. For this request we need to group order totals first by year and secondly by week since we need to show the difference in sales between weeks 50 in all years. Notice in this example that we use the Year(datefield) function to extract the year out of the OrderDate field. Notice as well that we use the Datepart(interval, datefield) function to extract the week since there is no week() function in Access. Finally, notice how we use the DatePart() function in the WHERE clause to make sure we have results only for weeks that equal 50.

Code:

```
SELECT Year(OrderDate) AS [Year], DatePart('ww',OrderDate) AS Week, Sum(unitprice*quantity)
AS OrderTotal
FROM Qry_Invoices
WHERE DatePart('ww',OrderDate)=50
GROUP BY Year(OrderDate), DatePart('ww',OrderDate)
```

Result:

Year ▾	Week ▾	OrderTotal ▾
2017	50	1278
2018	50	1074
2019	50	733

Record: ◄ ◄ 1 of 3 ► ►► ▷   ▼ₓ No Filter   Search

333.   Use the year(), datepart(), or format() functions to calculate order totals by year

Discussion (year function):

On many occasions, we want to extract the year out of a date field to create aggregate summaries of our data. As we have seen, one way to achieve this task is to use the year() function, which takes only one argument. Its general syntax is:

Year(date)

In this example, we want to calculate order totals by year. We use the year() function to extract the year out of the OrderDate field in combination with the sum() aggregate function to calculate order totals. By the way, what is the meaning of the first line with a blank year and a 202 amount? This is because we have orders with a blank OrderDate. Indeed, if we open the Qry_Invoices and we sort ascending by OrderDate, we will see that we have two orders without an OrderDate value.

Code:

```
SELECT year(OrderDate) AS Year, sum(unitprice*quantity) AS OrderTotal
FROM Qry_Invoices
GROUP BY Year(OrderDate)
```

Result:

Year	OrderTotal
	202
2017	44028
2018	51164
2019	45002

Record: 1 of 4

Discussion (datepart function):

We could also extract the year from a date field using the datepart() function. The datepart() function has four arguments, but for practical situations, we only use two of them. Its simplified syntax appears below:

datepart(interval, datefield)

The interval argument is just a string indicating the date part we want to extract from the date field. For example, we would use 'yyyy' to extract the year or 'q' to extract the quarter. Do not forget the quotes in the code since without them, it will not work. Check table 1 at the end of this chapter for a list of all possible values for the interval arguments for the datepart() function for amazing flexibility in extracting date parts from years all the way down to seconds.

Code:

```
SELECT datepart('yyyy', OrderDate) AS Year, SUM(unitprice*quantity) AS OrderTotal
FROM Qry_Invoices
GROUP BY datepart('yyyy', OrderDate)
```

Result:

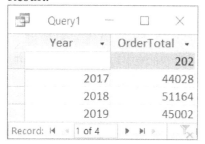

Discussion (format function):

The format function is the most flexible, and it offers more choices than the year() and datepart() functions. Officially, it takes four arguments, but again, for practical purposes, we need only two. Its simplified version appears below:

format(datefield, interval)

The interval argument is a string expression like 'yyyy' for years or 'mmmm' for months. Unlike the datepart() function, however, it will give us a lot more choices for displaying years or months. Using format, we can display the full month name, the month number with or without leading zeros, or the abbreviated month name if we want. Please check table 2 at the end of this chapter for a full list of the available choices with the format() function.

Code:
```
SELECT format(OrderDate, 'yyyy') AS Year, sum(unitprice*quantity) AS OrderTotal
FROM Qry_Invoices
GROUP BY format(OrderDate, 'yyyy')
```

Result:

Year	OrderTotal
	202
2017	44028
2018	51164
2019	45002

Record: 1 of 4

Discussion (format function):

We can use the format function to extract only the last two digits of the year by using the 'yy' argument to achieve this task.

Code:
```
SELECT format(OrderDate, 'yy') AS Year, sum(unitprice*quantity) AS OrderTotal
FROM Qry_Invoices
GROUP BY format(OrderDate, 'yy')
```

Result:

Year	OrderTotal
	202
17	44028
18	51164
19	45002

Record: 1 of 4

334.   Use the datepart() and format() functions to calculate order totals by quarter for a specific year

Discussion (with datepart):

The business goal here is to create a quarterly sales report for the year 2018. To achieve this task, we need to use two date functions. First, we will use the year() function to extract the year from the orderdate field and use this expression in the WHERE clause to limit results to 2018. Then, we use the datepart() function to group by our order totals by quarter. Of course, we could use the format function to extract quarters, which is demonstrated in the second part of this example and the result is the same.

Code:

```
SELECT datePart('q', OrderDate)  AS Quarter, sum(unitprice*quantity) AS OrderTotal
FROM Qry_Invoices
WHERE Year(OrderDate) = 2018
GROUP BY DatePart('q', OrderDate)
```

Code:

```
SELECT format(OrderDate, 'q') AS Quarter, sum(unitprice*quantity) AS OrderTotal
FROM Qry_Invoices
WHERE Year(orderdate) = 2019
GROUP BY format(OrderDate, 'q')
```

Result:

Quarter	OrderTotal
1	10172
2	9898
3	16911
4	14183

Record: 1 of 4

335.   Use the month(), monthname() datepart(), or format() functions to calculate monthly order and discount totals for a specific year

Discussion (with month):

The business goal in this example is to calculate order and discount totals by month for the year 2019. Management wants to have a look at the numbers to check the discount percentages forwarded by the sales reps. There are four different ways to achieve this result depending on the date function we use. Notice that in all four examples, the rationale is the same. We will use the year() function to isolate the year from the orderdate field and use this expression in the WHERE clause to limit results to 2019. Then, we need to use a function to isolate the month from the orderdate field so that we can group by month within the year 2019. Finally, notice that we will use two calculated fields (OrderTotal and TotalDiscount) to calculate the order and discount totals for each month.

In this first alternative, we will use the month function to extract the month from the orderdate field. The month() function has only one argument, and its syntax is below:

month(datefield)

Code:
```
SELECT month(OrderDate) AS [Month], Sum(unitprice*quantity) AS OrderTotal,
Sum((([unitprice]*[quantity])*[Discount]) AS TotalDiscount
FROM Qry_Invoices
WHERE year(orderdate) = 2019
GROUP BY month(OrderDate)
```

Result:

Month	OrderTotal	TotalDiscount
1	4012	669.7
2	3607	554.15
3	5090	805.55
4	5376	780.75

Record: 1 of 12   No Filter

Discussion (with monthname):
Suppose the management was not very happy with our first report because the month numbers confused them, and they could not quickly discern the corresponding month name. They now ask us to provide them with another report showing actual month names. We can do this immediately using the monthname() function in conjunction with the month() function. Notice that we cannot use the monthname() function by itself. We have to use it with the month() function to work as it is in the code below. Finally, see how we use the month(orderdate) function in the ORDER BY clause to have the months appear in the correct order.

Code:
```
SELECT monthname(month(OrderDate)) AS [Month], sum(unitprice*quantity) AS OrderTotal,
sum((([unitprice]*[quantity])*[Discount]) AS TotalDiscount
FROM Qry_Invoices
WHERE year(orderdate) = 2019
GROUP BY monthname(Month(OrderDate)), month(OrderDate)
ORDER BY month(OrderDate)
```

Result:

Month ▾	OrderTotal ▾	TotalDiscount ▾
January	4012	669.7
February	3607	554.15
March	5090	805.55
April	5376	780.75

Record: ◄ ◄ 1 of 12 ► ►► No Filter S

Discussion (with datepart):

We can also use the datepart() function to achieve the same result except that we will get numerals instead of month names. In other words, the result will be identical with that of the month() function.

Code:

```
SELECT datepart('m', OrderDate) AS [Month], sum(unitprice*quantity) AS OrderTotal,
Sum(([unitprice]*[quantity])*[Discount]) AS TotalDiscount
FROM Qry_Invoices
WHERE year(orderdate) = 2019
GROUP BY datepart('m', OrderDate), month(OrderDate)
ORDER BY datepart('m', OrderDate)
```

Result:

Month ▾	OrderTotal ▾	TotalDiscount ▾
1	4012	669.7
2	3607	554.15
3	5090	805.55
4	5376	780.75

Record: ◄ ◄ 1 of 12 ► ►► No Filter S

Discussion (with format):

Finally, we can use the format() function with the 'mm' argument to put a leading zero in front of the month for sorting purposes.

Code:

```
SELECT format(OrderDate, 'mm')  AS [Month], sum(unitprice*quantity) AS OrderTotal,
sum(([unitprice]*[quantity])*[Discount]) AS TotalDiscount
FROM Qry_Invoices
WHERE year(orderdate) = 2019
GROUP BY format(OrderDate, 'mm')
ORDER BY format(OrderDate, 'mm')
```

Result:

Month ▾	OrderTotal ▾	TotalDiscount ▾	▲
01	4012	669.7	
02	3607	554.15	
03	5090	805.55	
04	5376	780.75	▾

Record: ◄ ◄ 1 of 12 ► ►► ▾ No Filter S

336.   Use the datepart() function to count the number of orders by day for the whole year.

Discussion:

The goal here is to count the number of orders by week day for the whole year. That is, how many orders we had in total on Mondays, how many on Tuesdays, how many on Wednesdays etc. Notice how we use the day of the week argument ('w') in the DatePart(interval, datefield) function to isolate the days of the week and then group by them. Remember that by default Access starts the week on Sunday = 1. As you can see from the result set, we obtain some very useful information indeed. For example, we have the most orders on Saturday (day 7), followed by Sunday (day 1), that is, during the weekend!

Code:

```
SELECT DatePart('w',OrderDate) AS Day, Count(OrderID) AS NumberOfOrders
FROM Orders
WHERE Year(OrderDate)=2019
GROUP BY DatePart('w', OrderDate)
```

Result:

Day ▾	NumberOfOrders ▾
1	44
2	45
3	62
4	47
5	46
6	44
7	52

Record: ◄ ◄ 1 of 7 ► ►► ▾

337.   Use the datepart() function to count the number of orders by day of the year

Discussion:

In this example, we calculate the number of orders by day of the year. We have 365 days per year and by using the 'y' interval argument we can isolate the number of orders by the day of the year. Very useful data for some time series analysis throughout the year. From the result set, we see that from the 365 days of the year we had orders only on 213 days. In addition, we can see that from the beginning of the year we had our first orders on day 14. If we have a detailed look at the whole recordset, I bet we can make additional conclusions about the timing and volume of our orders.

Code:

```
SELECT DatePart('y',OrderDate) AS Day, Count(OrderID) AS NumberOfOrders
FROM Orders
WHERE Year([OrderDate])=2017
GROUP BY DatePart('y',OrderDate)
ORDER BY DatePart('y',OrderDate)
```

Result:

Day	NumberOfOrders
14	1
15	3
16	1
17	1
18	1
20	1

Record: 1 of 213

338. Use the datepart() or format() functions to create a crosstab report showing product sales by week for a six-month period

Discussion (with datepart):

This time, management wants a report listing total sales by week within a six-month period and within a specific year. To create this crosstab query, we need to use three date functions in combination. First, we will use the month() function to extract the month number from the orderdate field and use this as a criterion in the WHERE clause. Notice how the IN operator is used within the WHERE clause to get the first six months of the year. Since, however, we have multiple years of sales in the database, we need to include a criterion in the WHERE clause to isolate the year we want. We use the year function on the orderdate field to limit results to 2017. Finally, in the PIVOT part of the crosstab query, we use the datepart() function with the 'ww' argument to produce a column for each week. (For a detailed overview of crosstab queries, check chapter 19). As you can see from the result set, we can now examine detailed total product sales by week for a period of 27 weeks within the six-month period that we defined in our WHERE clause.

Code:

```
TRANSFORM Sum([unitprice]*[quantity]) AS Ordertotal
SELECT ProductName
FROM Qry_Invoices
WHERE month(orderdate) IN (1,2,3,4,5,6) AND year(orderdate) = 2017
GROUP BY ProductName
PIVOT datePart('ww',[OrderDate])
```

Result:

ProductName	2	3	4	5	6	7	8	9	10	11	12
All-Purpose Marinade I						56					
All-Purpose Marinade II				135			165			90	
Almonds, Hickory Smoked	75									15	
Almonds, Roasted and Salt											
Apple Cinnamon Raisin Co	60										
Artichokes in white sauce					60						

Record: 1 of 67   No Filter   Search

Discussion (with format):

We could use the format function to achieve the same task, but notice in the result set that the weeks are not in order this time.

Code:

```
TRANSFORM Sum([unitprice]*[quantity]) AS Ordertotal
SELECT ProductName
FROM Qry_Invoices
WHERE month(orderdate) IN (1,2,3,4,5,6) AND year(orderdate) = 2017
GROUP BY ProductName
PIVOT format([OrderDate],  'ww')
```

Result:

ProductName	10	11	12	13	14	15	16	17	18	19	2
All-Purpose Marinade I											84
All-Purpose Marinade II		90							105		
Almonds, Hickory Smoked		15			75				120	60	
Almonds, Roasted and Salt								75		90	
Apple Cinnamon Raisin Co				48							
Artichokes in white sauce											

Record: 1 of 67   No Filter   Search

339.   Use the day(), datepart(), and month() functions to create a crosstab report showing product sales by day of the month.

Discussion (day function):

Management is impressed by your detailed reports, and they now ask for a report of daily product sales for the month of May in the year 2019. Again, we need to use three date functions—two for criteria and one to pivot our results. In this example, we will use the month() and year() functions to isolate the year and the month in the WHERE clause and the day() function to pivot or display product sales by day. Notice that only days with product sales appear as columns in the result set.

Code:

```
TRANSFORM Sum([unitprice]*[quantity]) AS Ordertotal
SELECT ProductName
FROM Qry_Invoices
WHERE month(OrderDate) = 5 AND year(orderdate) = 2019
GROUP BY ProductName
PIVOT day(OrderDate)
```

Discussion (datepart function):

We can achieve the same result using the datepart() function with the 'd' (day) argument. For a full list of possible arguments for the datepart() function, see table 1 at the end of this chapter.

Code:

```
TRANSFORM Sum([unitprice]*[quantity]) AS Ordertotal
SELECT ProductName
FROM Qry_Invoices
WHERE month(OrderDate) = 5 AND year(orderdate) = 2019
GROUP BY ProductName
PIVOT datepart('d',OrderDate)
```

Result:

ProductName	1	4	5	9	13	14	18	22
Almonds, Roasted and Salted - 1					75			
Apple Cinnamon Raisin Cookies							60	
Chocolate Almonds in 8 oz. Bag								60
Chocolate Blueberries in 10 oz. I					20			
Chocolate Fudge		30		30				
Choice Apricots - 16 oz. Bag			45		15			

Record: 1 of 24 No Filter Search

340.   Use the weekday() and weekdayname() functions to create a crosstab report showing product sales by day of the week.

Discussion (weekday function):

In this example, we will create a report of daily product sales within a week. Specifically, management asks for a report of product sales, by day, within the 25th week of the year 2017. We will use the datepart() and year() functions in the WHERE clause to limit results to the particular year and week first. Then, we will use the weekday() function to display product sales by day within the week. The general syntax of the weekday() function appears below. It takes two arguments, datefield and firstdayofweek, and the second is optional. With the firstdayofweek argument, we can define which day we want to be the first day of the week. We can choose any day between Sunday and Saturday as the table indicates below. In this example, we left the second argument blank, which defaults the first day of the week to Sunday. From the result set, you can see the order totals by product and day of the week.

weekday (datefield, [firstdayofweek])

Argument value	First day of week
1	Sunday (default)
2	Monday
3	Tuesday
4	Wednesday
5	Thursday
6	Friday
7	Saturday

Code:

```
TRANSFORM Sum([unitprice]*[quantity]) AS Ordertotal
SELECT ProductName
FROM Qry_Invoices
WHERE datePart('ww',[OrderDate]) = 25 AND year(orderdate) = 2017
GROUP BY ProductName
PIVOT weekday([OrderDate])
```

Result:

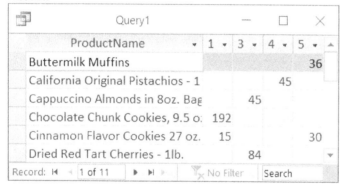

Discussion (weekdayname function)

The previous example is fine, but it will confuse management and anybody else who tries to understand what day of the week corresponds to numbers 6 or 7. To solve this problem, we can use the weekdayname() function to provide the actual day name. As you can see in the result set, the names of the days appear now as column headings.

Code:

```
TRANSFORM Sum([unitprice]*[quantity]) AS Ordertotal
SELECT ProductName
FROM Qry_Invoices
WHERE datePart('ww',[OrderDate]) = 25 AND year(orderdate) = 2017
GROUP BY ProductName
PIVOT weekdayname(weekday([OrderDate]))
```

Result:

ProductName	Sunday	Thursday	Tuesday	Wednesday
Buttermilk Muffins		36		
California Original Pistachios - 1				
Cappuccino Almonds in 8oz. Bag			45	
Chocolate Chunk Cookies, 9.5 o.	192			
Cinnamon Flavor Cookies 27 oz.	15	30		
Dried Red Tart Cherries - 1lb.			84	
Mushroom Rolls				

Record: 1 of 11   No Filter   Search

341.   Use the DateDiff() function to calculate order processing cycle times

Discussion:

Customer service has reported that customers complain about shipping. Specifically, they complain that it takes a lot of time to receive their orders after they complete the ordering process. Management is trying to determine the cause, and they need our help. They want to know if the problem is internal as a result of packaging and payment processing or if the problem is external as a result of the shipping company. They suspect the problem is internal, and they tell us to produce a report that lists how many days it takes for an order to ship from the time it has been received.

We can reply by using the datediff() function. The datediff() function takes five arguments, but for most practical scenarios, we only need to use the first three. The general syntax of the function appears below. The interval argument is a string that will determine in what interval we want to find the difference between date1 and date2. For instance, we might want to calculate the difference in days, weeks, months, or years. (Please refer to table 3 at the end of this chapter for a full list of values for the interval argument). In addition, date2 should be a later date than date1. Otherwise, the result will be negative. As you can see from the code below, we calculate the difference between orderdate and shippeddate in days. In other words, how many days elapsed between receiving and shipping an order? The results are not good at all. It takes a full five days to get the order out from our factory for the month of September 2017, which is a very long order processing cycle time.

DateDiff(interval, date1, date2[, firstdayofweek[, firstweekofyear]])

Code:
```
SELECT OrderID, datediff('d', orderdate, shippeddate) AS CycleTime
FROM Orders
WHERE year(orderdate) = 2017 AND month(orderdate) = 10
```

Result:

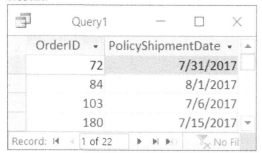

342.   Use the DateAdd() function to establish policies on expected shipping dates

Discussion:

Management is not very happy to see that it takes five days to ship an order. This means that customers will receive their orders in about ten to fifteen days total. This is unacceptable because we are in the food industry, and our products need to arrive fresh. So, management asks for our help again to produce a timetable that will list the expected shipping dates for orders. Management has determined that it should take two days at most for any order to ship, and they have established a corporate policy to be strictly enforced. We can produce target shipping dates using the dateadd() function. It takes three arguments, and its general syntax appears below:

dateadd(interval, number, datefield)

The interval argument is a string like 'd', 'm', or 'y' determining the time interval we want to add. For instance, if we want to add days to a date, we use the 'd' value. If we want to add years, we use the 'y' value for the interval argument. (For a full list of the values for the interval argument, please refer to table 3 at the end of this chapter). The number argument is the actual number of time intervals we want to add. If we want to add 15 days, for example, we use the number 15. Finally, the date argument is the date field to which we want to add a number of days, months, or years. In the code below, we add 2 days to the orderdate field:

Code:

```
SELECT OrderID, dateadd('d', 2, orderdate) AS  PolicyShipmentDate
FROM Orders
WHERE year(orderdate) = 2017 AND month(orderdate) = 7
```

Result:

OrderID	PolicyShipmentDate
72	7/31/2017
84	8/1/2017
103	7/6/2017
180	7/15/2017

Record: 1 of 22

343.   Anniversaries: Use the LIKE operator to find past anniversaries.

Discussion:

Let us assume we need a list of orders for today's date which is 10/26/2018. Practically, we need to find all orders which occurred on 10/22 of each year in our order history. A very easy and very flexible way to achieve this is by using the LIKE operator as in the code below. As you can see from the result set, we had four past orders the 22nd of October. Notice that we put the asterisk in the year part of the date. Moving the asterisk to the month or day part of the date we can achieve some additional interesting results.

Code:
```
SELECT OrderID, OrderDate, ShippingCost
FROM Orders
WHERE OrderDate Like '10/22/*'
```

Result:

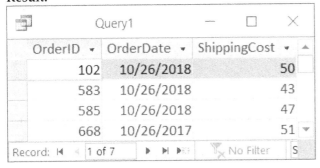

344. Anniversaries: use the DateAdd() function to find future anniversaries.

Discussion:

In this case we need to find the future date at which our sales representatives complete 20 years of service. We can do this by using the DateAdd(interval, number, date) function. Check how we enclose the 'yyyy' interval in quotes. If you do not enclose the interval argument in quotes the function will not work.

Code:
```
SELECT firstname, lastname, DateAdd('yyyy', 20 , dateofHire) AS 20yrAnniversary
FROM SalesReps
```

Result:

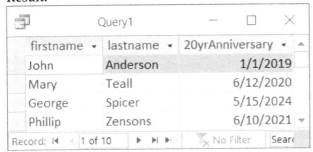

345. Anniversaries: Finding upcoming anniversaries within a specific period.

Discussion:

Now, we would like to create a list of employees with a birthday within a specific month of the year. We can do this by using the datepart (interval, datefield) function twice; first to show the day of the employee's birthday as you can see in the SELECT statement and second to isolate the month of the year as you can see in the WHERE clause. In this specific example, we are looking for employee birthdays in the month of April. Notice how we use quotes for the interval arguments in both functions ('d' and 'm') since without those quotes the datepart() function will not work.

Code:

SELECT firstname, lastname, title, datepart('d', dateofbirth) As DayOfBirth
FROM SalesReps
WHERE datepart('m', dateofbirth) = 4

Result:

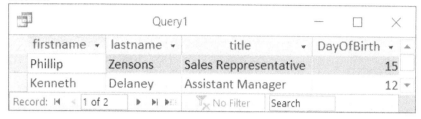

346.   Anniversaries: Calculate time elapsed such as employment length.

Discussion:

In this example, we calculate the number of employment years for each of our employees. We use the DateDiff(interval, date1,date2) function with the year ('yyyy') argument to calculate the elapsed time between the employee's date of hire and today's date.

Code:

SELECT firstname, lastname, DateDiff('yyyy', DateOfHire, Date()) AS YearsEmployed
FROM SalesReps

Result:

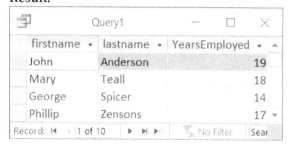

347.   Anniversaries: Calculating Employee Age

Discussion:

This time we will create a query that lists the ages of our employees. We can do this by using the DateDiff(interval, date1, date2) function which subtracts date1 from date2 and provides the difference in years, months, quarters or in any other period we need. In this particular example, we would like to see the age in years and that is why we use the 'yyyy' setting. Do not forget to include the interval setting in quotes since otherwise the function will not work.

Code:

SELECT firstname, lastname, title, DateDiff('yyyy', DateOfBirth, Date()) As Age FROM SalesReps

Result:

firstname	lastname	title	Age
John	Anderson	Sales Reppresentative	49
Mary	Teall	Sales Director	38
George	Spicer	Assitant Director of Sales	37
Phillip	Zensons	Sales Reppresentative	58

Query1

Record: 1 of 10 No Filter Search

Table 1: Datepart() function settings	
Character	**Description**
'yyyy	Year
'q'	Quarter
'm'	Month
'y'	Day of year
'd'	Day
'w'	Weekday
'ww'	Week
'h'	Hour
'n'	Minute
's'	Second

Table 2: Format function settings	
Character	**Description**
's''	Returns the second as a number without leading zeros
'ss'	Returns the second as a number with leading zeros
'h'	Returns the hour as a number
'hh'	Returns the hour as a number with leading zeros
'd'	Returns the day without a leading zero
'dd'	Returns the day with a leading zero
'ddd'	Returns the day as an abbreviation
'dddd'	Returns the full name of the day
'w'	Returns the day of the week as a number
'ww'	Returns the week of the year as a number
'm'	Returns the month without a leading zero
'mm'	Returns the month with a leading zero
'mmm'	Returns the abbreviation of the month
'mmmm'	Returns the full name of the month
'q'	Returns the quarter as a number
'y'	Returns the number of the day of the year from 1 to 366
'yy'	Returns the year as number (0-9) with leading zeros
'yyyy'	Returns the year in four-digit numeric format

Source: https://support.office.com/en-us/article/format-property-date-time-data-type-3251a423-3dd7-446e-be65-c7293eddbb43

Table 3: DateDiff and DateAdd interval argument values	
Value	Description
'yyyy'	Year
'q'	Quarter
'm'	Month
'y'	Day of year
'd'	Day
'w'	Weekday
'ww'	Week
'h'	Hour
'n'	Minute
's'	Second

348.   CHAPTER 27 DISCUSSION QUESTIONS

1. What is the usefulness of the date functions in database tasks? Can you give a couple of examples?
2. Can we extract the month out of a date field? How many date functions can we use to achieve this result?
3. What function we use to retrieve the name of the month, such as January, instead of its number, such as 1?
4. Why deep knowledge of date functions leads to better table design?
5. Why do we want to use date functions as default values in table fields?
6. What are the two functions we can use to extract quarters out of date fields?
7. How many functions can we use to extract the day out of a date field?
8. What is the purpose of the DateDiff() function? How many arguments does it take? Which ones are the most useful in practice?
9. What function can we use to add date intervals to a date field? Why is a function like this one so useful?
10. What is the difference between 'mmm' and 'mmmm' for the format function settings? Hint: Refer to the table at the end of the chapter.

349.   CHAPTER 27 HANDS-ON EXERCISES

Chapter 27 Case 1:

Create a new Access database and name it Chapter27_1.accdb. Copy the table tble_Dates from the PracticeDatabase.accdb and paste it to Chapter27_1.accdb.

1. The accounts receivable director is asking for report that will list the total value of orders by year for all years for which we have data in the database. Create a new query that satisfies the director's request and save it as Qry1_TotalOrdersPerYear.

    Your result should look like:

    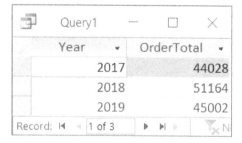

2. The accounts receivable director wants to concentrate on the year 2017. He wants a report that lists the total value of orders by month for the year 2017. Create a new query that satisfies the director's request and save it as Qry2_TotalOrdersPerMonth. Hint: make sure the director sees month names

and not month numbers.

Your result should look like:

3. The director is very happy with the reports you have provided him. Now he needs a report that will list the total orders by customer <u>and</u> year for all the years that we have data. Create a new query that satisfies the director's request and save it as Qry3_CustomerAndYear.

Your result should look like:

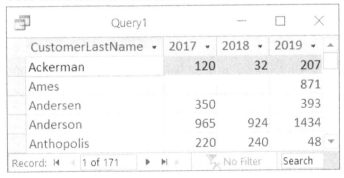

4. The accounts receivable director is back asking for a report that will list the total value of orders by quarter in the year 2017. Use the DatePart() function to achieve your task. Create a new query that satisfies the director's request and save it as Qry4_SalesByQuarter.

Your result should look like:

CHAPTER 27

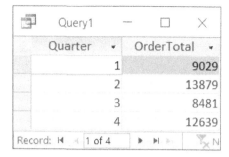

Quarter	OrderTotal
1	9029
2	13879
3	8481
4	12639

Record: 1 of 4

5. The accounts receivable director is really amazed by the information you are able to provide him. He now needs a report that will list the total value of orders by sales representative and quarter in the year 2017. Create a new query that satisfies the director's request and save it as Qry5_SalesByRepAndQuarter.

Your result should look like:

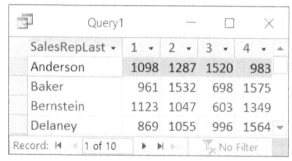

SalesRepLast	1	2	3	4
Anderson	1098	1287	1520	983
Baker	961	1532	698	1575
Bernstein	1123	1047	603	1349
Delaney	869	1055	996	1564

Record: 1 of 10   No Filter

Chapter 27 Case 2:

Create a new Access database and name it Chapter27_2.accdb. Copy the table tble_Dates from the PracticeDatabase.accdb and paste it to Chapter27_2.accdb.

1. The sales department is asking for a report that lists the total number of orders by customer state and by week for the month of May 2018. Create a new query that satisfies the sales people request and save it as Qry1_MayNumberOfOrders.

Your result should look like:

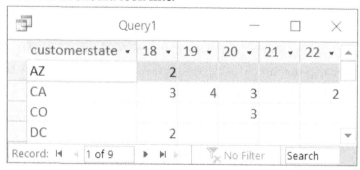

customerstate	18	19	20	21	22
AZ	2				
CA		3	4	3	2
CO				3	
DC		2			

Record: 1 of 9   No Filter   Search

368

2. HR is asking for the total value of orders by sales rep and by week of the year in the month of May 2018. Totals should be given in currency format. Create a new query that satisfies the HR request and save it as Qry2_MayOrderTotalsByEmployee.

Your result should look like:

3. The sales people are asking for a report that will list the total order amount by city only for the months of January, May, and September in the year 2018. Create a new query that satisfies the sales people request and save it as Qry3_TotalsByCity. The total amount field should be in currency format. HINT: we are looking for totals for the three months and not for totals by month.

Your result should look like:

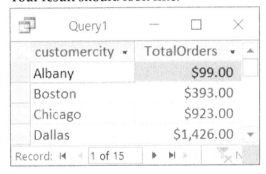

4. The shipping director set a new rule that all orders should arrive to the customer within ten days of the order date. She needs a report that includes the OrderID, customerlastname, orderdate, and the RequiredArrivalDate fields where the RequiredArrivalDate field is ten days after the order field. She will compare these results with what actually happened. Create a new query that satisfies the director's request and save it as Qry4_RequiredArrivalDate.

Your result should look like:

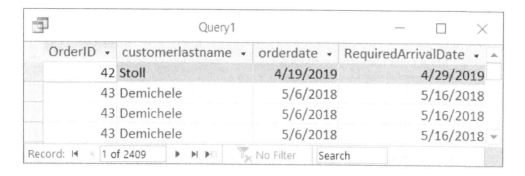

5. The HR director is asking for a report that will list the name of the sales representative and the number of years he or she is with the company. Create a new query that satisfies the director's request and save it as Qry5_EmployeeSeniority.

Your result should look like:

Your own result might be slightly different since your own current system date will be different from the current system date at the writing of this book.

CHAPTER 28
UPDATE SQL STATEMENTS

Update statements are powerful tools for the advanced user, administrator, and developer. They provide astonishing flexibility and control to complete a task in minutes for which you would otherwise need hours. For example, suppose we have a database of 100 suppliers and a few thousand products associated with each supplier. Every week, due to promotional campaigns, pricing strategies, or replenishment costs, our suppliers might change their prices and since their products constitute our own raw materials we need to update our prices. After all, the only constant in business is change. Change will affect your operations, and, in the end, your data. Since this is true, you must be ready for lightning speed changes to your operational data.

Your suppliers will never update their product prices at the same time and at the same percentage rates. This scenario is valid only for theoretical books. What actually happens is that suppliers will send you a price update when their business operations dictate, and this update will most probably be different from everyone else's. So, how do you account for situations like this? Of course, you use flexible update statements that you can reuse effectively. This chapter starts with simple examples and ends up with powerful conditional updates for manipulating your data.

Keep in mind that you cannot undo the results of update statements or update queries. Consequently, my advice and my own policy is to first use a SELECT statement to check the records to be updated and then, run the update itself. This is actually common industry practice. We never run an update statement in the blind.

The general syntax of an update statement is shown below:

UPDATE table
SET fieldvalue1 = value1, fieldvalue2 = value2, fieldvalue3 = value3…
[WHERE condition]

We can also run updates on queries (updateable ones). We might construct a dataset having data from multiple tables and run the update against the query. (I have examples of this in the chapter). In addition, we can update a table based on the values of another table or query. We can easily achieve this by using subqueries. Before we delve into examples, let's make sure we understand what cascade updates are and how they work in Access.

350.   What are cascade updates, how to use them, and what they mean
There are cases in which we have to update the values of primary keys in our tables. Usually, these changes are mandated by entities external to the organization, such as the government. For example, up until now, we might have used the social security number of an employee as the primary key for the employees table. As a result, SSN functioned as the foreign key to record all related activities for that

employee (sales, HR records etc.) Now, the government steps in and says that we cannot do that anymore. This means that we have to change the SSN value for the employee in the employees table, and, most importantly, we need to change all of its occurrences in related tables. So, if this employee worked for us for 10 years, he might have 260 paystub records in the database. We might actually have thousands of references that we need to update for this employee.

Doing so manually is an impossible task, especially if we have several thousand employees. This is where cascade updates come in. Cascade updates will allow us to change the value of the primary key in the primary table, and the database engine will change all the foreign key values in related tables. Let's go through a practical example to see how cascade updates work.

Customers	
CustomerID	Name
1	John
2	Mary
3	George
4	Stacy

Orders		
OrderID	CustomerID	OrderDate
1	2	9/10/2019
2	2	10/10/2019
3	1	11/10/2019
4	3	11/11/2019

Products	
ProductID	ProductName
1	A
2	B
3	C
4	D

ProductsOrders		
OrderID	ProductID	Quantity
1	2	2
2	2	5
3	1	3
4	2	4

In the figure above, let's assume that we need to change Mary's primary key value from 2 to 222. To achieve this we first need to turn cascade updates on for the relationship between customers and orders. Then, we can simply change the primary key value from 2 to 222. The database will ask us to confirm the action, and once the updates are completed, this is how the same tables will look:

Customers	
CustomerID	Name
1	John
222	Mary
3	George
4	Stacy

Orders		
OrderID	CustomerID	OrderDate
1	222	9/10/2019
2	222	10/10/2019
3	1	11/10/2019
4	3	11/11/2019

Products	
ProductID	ProductName
1	A
2	B
3	C
4	D

ProductsOrders		
OrderID	ProductID	Quantity
1	2	2
2	2	5
3	1	3
4	2	4

The database will automatically change all of the references of CustomerID=2 to 222 in the Orders table. I strongly recommend having cascade updates turned off except when you actually want to make changes to primary key values. This is a precaution in case an end user changes the value of a primary key by accident. So, how do we use cascade updates in Access?

1. Click on the "Database Tools" tab. Then, in the group "Relationships", click on "Relationships".

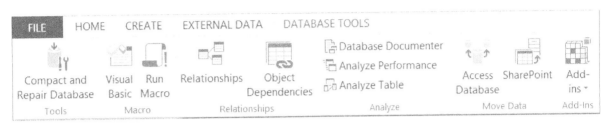

This will open up the relationships window as shown below:

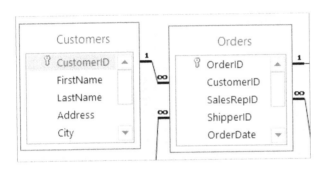

2. Double click on the relationship line between customers and orders. The following screen will appear. Click on "Cascade Update Related Fields", and click "OK".

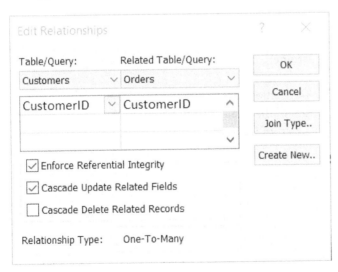

Now, we are ready to open the customer table and change the value of the primary key for any customer. Our change will be propagated throughout the database where the database finds a foreign key value, in this case a CustomerID value, which is equal to the primary key we changed. Remember to edit the relationship again and turn off "Cascade Updates" once the records are updated.

351.   Update a single field value in a single record

Update address information for a single customer

Discussion:

In this example, our goal is to update the address information for one of our customers. Notice the criteria in the query. They need to uniquely identify the customer we want to update. We will use a SELECT statement beforehand just to make sure we do not have another customer with the same first and last names.

```
SELECT *
FROM tbls_Customers_Upd
WHERE lastname = 'Demizio' AND firstname = 'Michael'
```

Code:

```
UPDATE tbls_Customers_Upd
SET Address = '12 Lark Street'
WHERE lastname = 'Demizio' AND firstname = 'Michael'
```

Result:

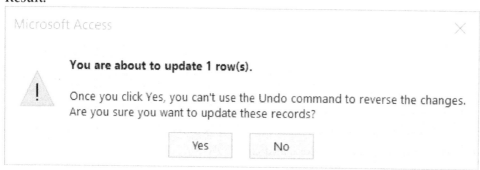

352.   Update multiple field values in a single record

Update address and city information for a single customer

Discussion:

Our job now is to update both the address and city information for a customer. In other words, we will update two fields of the same record. The criteria remain the same, but notice how the two fields that we are updating are separated by a comma in the SET part of the code.

```
SELECT *
FROM tbls_Customers_Upd
WHERE lastname = 'Demizio' AND firstname = 'Michael'
```

Code:

```
UPDATE tbls_Customers_Upd
SET Address = '12 Lark Street', city = 'Albany'
WHERE lastname = 'Demizio' AND firstname = 'Michael'
```

Result:

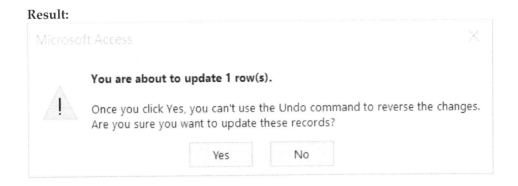

353. Update a field value in multiple records

Update zip codes for all customers in a certain city

Discussion:

Our job request is to update zip code values for all of our customers in Denver, Colorado. It might look simple, but we need to pay attention and make sure the city of Denver does not exist in any other state. If it does, we need to add one more criterion in the WHERE clause to identify the state as well. Always run a SQL statement in advance to make sure your operation will affect the correct records.

```
SELECT *
FROM tbls_Customers_Upd
WHERE city = 'Denver'
```

Code:

```
UPDATE tbls_Customers_Upd
SET zip = '22215'
WHERE city = 'Denver'
```

Result:

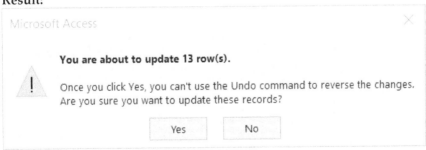

354. Update multiple field values in multiple records

Update city, zip, and address information for all customers in Dallas, Texas

Discussion:

Because of erroneous data entry, customers that show up from Denver, Colorado are actually from Tucson, Arizona. Consequently, we have to update their zip, city, and state information. We need to update multiple field values in multiple records in the database. This is possible by using multiple update values in the SET clause of the update statement. We must always check our criteria in the WHERE clause to make sure they identify the records we want to update.

```
SELECT *
FROM tbls_Customers_Upd
WHERE city = 'Denver'
```

Code:
```
UPDATE tbls_Customers_Upd
SET zip = '22730', city = 'Tucson', state = 'AZ'
WHERE city = 'Denver'
```

Result:

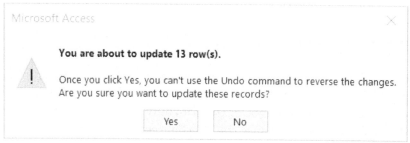

355. Update using calculated values

Update product prices increasing them by a certain percentage

Discussion:

One of our suppliers has sent us updated prices, and we need to increase our own prices for the products from this supplier by 5%. To achieve this, we use a calculated field in the SET clause as you can see in the code below. In the WHERE clause, notice that instead of the supplier name, we use the supplier ID to make sure we identify the correct product records for this supplier. This is common practice for criteria in the WHERE clause because primary key values are unique. Therefore, we do not need to worry if we have two suppliers with the same name in the database. Finally, notice in this example that we work with the query "Qry_SupplierPrices" which combines the information of suppliers and their products. Running update statements against queries is fine and sometimes desirable because they provide us with just the information we need rather than looking at huge tables. In this particular example, our supplier, "Home of Snacks", has increased prices by 5%, and we will increase our own prices by the same amount.

```
SELECT *
FROM Qry_SupplierPrices
WHERE supplierID = 1
```

Code:
```
UPDATE Qry_SupplierPrices
SET ProductUnitPrice = ProductUnitPrice * (1+0.05)
WHERE supplierID = 1
```

Result:

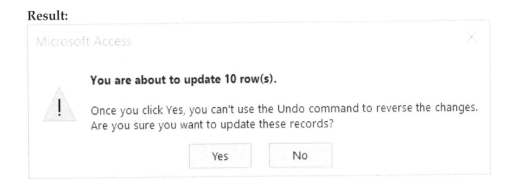

356.   Update conditionally using the switch() function

Update product prices using different update conditions for every supplier

Discussion:

As you might expect, in everyday work scenarios, our suppliers, customers, students, or partners do not set up meetings to send us uniform and standardized information just so that we can have a nice time with our operations. Instead, they send us their own percentage increases and not at the same time. So, what can we do to take care of this business fact in minutes instead of making it an operational and administrative nightmare? We can combine the powers of the update statement and the switch() function. As you can see below, our suppliers sent us percentage updates ranging from 2% all the way up to 15%. Using one update statement with the switch() function, we obtain the following: First, we can take care of all the updates in minutes. Second, the statement is so clean that it is reusable the next time we need to do the same job. Third, suppose that some of our suppliers have not sent us any updates. We can leave the statement below as is and update the ProductUnitPrice with itself as is the case with supplierID=5 where nothing is updated.

Code:

```
UPDATE Qry_SupplierPrices
SET ProductUnitPrice =
SWITCH (
supplierid=1,     ProductUnitPrice*(1.1) ,
supplierid=2,     ProductUnitPrice*(1.05),
supplierid=3,     ProductUnitPrice*(1.1) ,
supplierid=4,     ProductUnitPrice*(1.05) ,
supplierid=5,     ProductUnitPrice ,
supplierid=6,     ProductUnitPrice*(1.02) ,
supplierid=7,     ProductUnitPrice *(1.03),
supplierid=8,     ProductUnitPrice*(1.05) ,
supplierid=9,     ProductUnitPrice*(1.15) ,
supplierid=10,    ProductUnitPrice*(1.1) ,
)
```

Result:

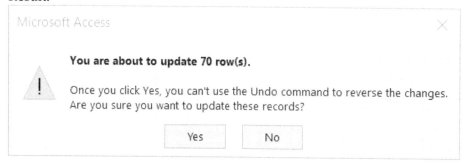

357. Update records in a table using criteria from another table
Update the products table using criteria from the suppliers table
Discussion:

In this example, our goal is to update prices in the tbls_Products_Upd table using criteria from the Suppliers table. We can achieve this using a subquery. The subquery will retrieve supplier ids from the Suppliers table and will update the corresponding product prices in the tbls_Products_Upd table. Specifically, the subquery will retrieve supplier ids for suppliers in Boston or Dallas and feed those ids in the WHERE clause of the main update statement. The business request is to update product prices from suppliers in Boston and Dallas by 20% for all their products. The problem we solve through the subquery is that the tbls_Products_Upd table does not contain any city information which we need to obtain from the Suppliers table.

Code:

```
UPDATE tbls_Products_Upd
SET ProductUnitPrice = ProductUnitPrice * (1+0.20)
WHERE SupplierID IN
(SELECT SupplierID FROM Suppliers
WHERE city= 'Boston' or city = 'Denver')
```

Result:

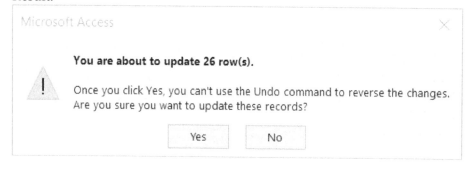

1. What is the primary goal of update statements?
2. Can we undo the result of an update statement if we change our mind?
3. What is a good safety strategy to follow before we use an update statement?
4. What is the role of cascade updates in relational databases?
5. Why it is a good idea to keep cascade updates off and use them only when needed?
6. Can you provide an example situation in which it makes sense to use cascade updates?
7. Can we update multiple values in a single record with a single SQL statement?
8. Can we update multiple values in multiple records by using a single SQL statement?
9. What function can we use to update records based on multiple conditions?
10. What technique can we use to update records in one table using criteria from another table?

359.   CHAPTER 28 HANDS-ON EXERCISES

Chapter 28 Case 1:

Create a new Access database and name it Chapter28_1.accdb. Copy the table Products from the PracticeDatabase.accdb and paste it to Chapter28_1.accdb.

1. The inventory people want to change the UnitsOnOrder quantity from 0 to 5 for the Almonds, Roasted and Salted - 18 oz. Bag product with ProductID=2. Create a new query that satisfies the inventory people request and save it as Qry1_UnitsOnOrder.

Your result should look like:

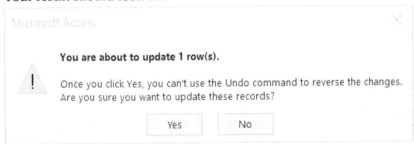

2. The inventory people now want to change the ProductUnitPrice and UnitsInStock to 32 and 30 respectively for the product Banana Chips - 20 oz. Bag with ProductID = 3. Create a new query that satisfies the inventory people request and save it as Qry2_UpdateTwoFields.

Your result should look like:

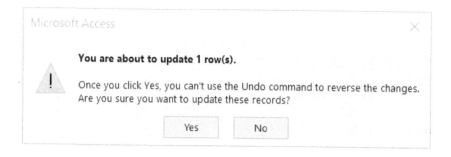

3. The replenishing department just called in and notified us that we need to add five dollars to the price of all products from the supplier with SupplierID = 5. Create a new query that satisfies this request and save it as Qry3_UpdateMultiplePrices.

Your result should look like:

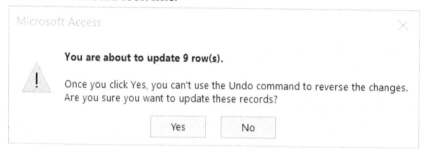

4. The purchasing department just called and informed us that we need to make the following changes for the supplier with SupplierID = 3. Create a new query that satisfies this request and save it as Qry4_UpdateMultipleFieldsAndRecords.

    a. Change the QuantityPerUnit to 35.
    b. Add 12 dollars to the price of each of the products.
    c. Change the ReorderLevel to 15.

Your result should look like:

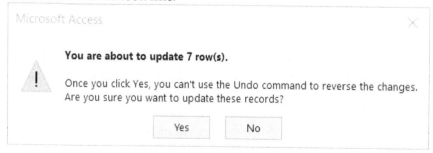

5. The purchasing department called in again and informed us that the supplier with SupplierID = 5 increased their prices by 7.5%. Now we need to increase our own prices by the same amount. Create a new query that satisfies this request and save it as Qry5_PercentageIncrease.

Your result should look like:

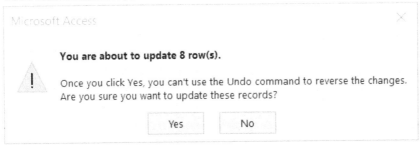

Chapter 28 Case 2:

Create a new Access database and name it Chapter28_2.accdb. Copy the tables ProductsOrders and SalesReps from the PracticeDatabase.accdb and paste them to Chapter28_2.accdb.

1. HR called in and said that the city for the employee Anderson John is wrong and it needs to be changed to "Los Angeles". Create a new query that satisfies the HR request and save it as Qry1_EmployeeCity.

   Your result should look like:

   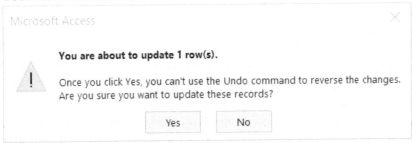

2. HR called in again and said that for the employee John Thomas the zip code needs to be updated to 83044 and the date of hire to 5/10/2009. Create a new query that satisfies the HR request and save it as Qry2_EmployeeZipHireDate. HINT: Do not forget to enclose your date with number signs (#).

   Your result should look like:

   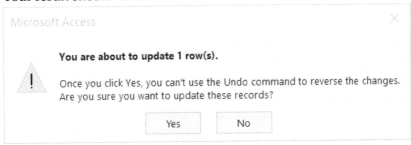

3. One of the sales reps called and she said that in the ProductsOrders table, for the OrderID= 692 and ProductID = 10, the unit price is wrong and needs to be updated to 20. Create a new query that

satisfies the sales rep request and save it as Qry3_UnitPrice.

Your result should look like:

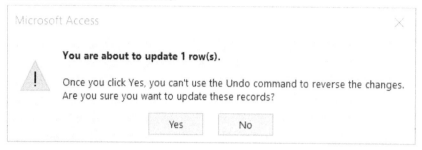

4. Another salesrep called in and said that in the ProductsOrders table, for OrderID = 783 and ProductID = 70, the unitprice needs to be decreased by 5 dollars and the discount needs to be increased by 3%. Create a new query that satisfies the sales rep request and save it as Qry4_Calculated.

Your result should look like:

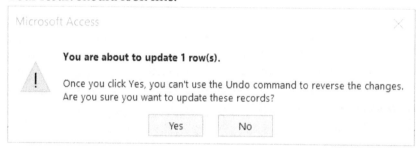

5. We have a request from accounts receivable to increase the prices of all products in the order with OrderID = 784 by 15%. Create a new query that satisfies the accounts receivable request and save it as Qry5_MultipleRecords.

Your result should look like:

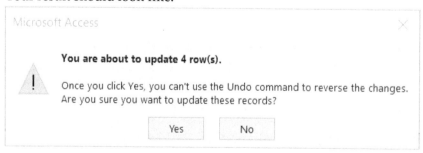

CHAPTER 29
DELETE STATEMENTS

The principal role of delete statements is to remove multiple records in one operation. Instead of deleting table rows manually, we use delete statements to delete many of them with one SQL statement. The general syntax of a delete statement appears below, and while it looks simple, it can become an amazing tool when coupled with criteria and subqueries.

> DELETE
> FROM table
> WHERE criteria

As with update statements, we cannot undo the results of delete statements. Thus, once we delete a set of records, there is no way to get them back. Consequently, we should always backup our data or keep the deleted records in a temporary or historical table just in case we made a mistake. In this chapter, we will see how easy it is to move records to other tables before deleting them. Furthermore, it is professional practice to run a SELECT statement before a delete statement to determine if the result set contains the records we want to delete. Before we run any code in this chapter, we should learn about the role of cascade deletes. For all of the examples in this chapter, cascade deletes are off, and we should keep them off in our databases unless we specifically want to take advantage of their functionality in specific situations. We want cascade deletes off so that we do not accidentally delete a record in a table and then the database deletes all related records in related tables.

360. What are cascade deletes, how to use them, and what they mean

In order to understand cascade deletes in full, let's work with the record of a customer from five years ago who is no longer in business. We want to delete this customer from the database so that it does not come up in queries and does not take up space.

We could simply go to the customers table and try to delete this record. However, if there are associated orders with this customer, the database will not allow us to delete it since we would then end up with orphaned records in the orders table. Referential integrity rules do not allow this to happen, and we would not be able to delete the customer. For a full explanation of referential integrity, check chapter 4. To delete this customer manually, we should first go to the orders table and delete all of the orders associated with this customer. However, since we also have a many-to-many relationship between Orders and Products, we first need to go to the ProductsOrders table and delete the associations (records) of Orders and Products for that customer. If we need to delete the customer Mary from the database, we need to do the following in the order provided:

Customers	
CustomerID	Name
1	John
2	Mary
3	George
4	Stacy

Orders		
OrderID	CustomerID	OrderDate
1	2	9/10/2019
2	2	10/10/2019
3	1	11/10/2019
4	3	11/11/2019

Products	
ProductID	ProductName
1	A
2	B
3	C
4	D

ProductsOrders		
OrderID	ProductID	Quantity
1	2	2
2	2	5
3	1	3
4	2	4

- Delete from the ProductsOrders table the two records with OrderIDs 1 and 2. For example, the order with orderID 1 contains the product with ProductID 2.
- Delete from the Orders table the orders with orderid = 1 and 2 since they belong to Mary.
- Finally, delete Mary's record with CustomerID = 2 from the Customers table.

Even in this simple scenario, deleting a customer is an involved process. Imagine the scenario where you have hundreds of customers with thousands of associated orders. It would be humanly impossible to remove customers manually.

This is where cascade deletes come in. By using cascade deletes, we can delete a customer in the primary table, and the database itself will delete all references to that customer in all related tables. In this example, if cascade deletes are on, when we delete Mary from the customers table, the database will automatically delete all of Mary's references in the Orders and ProductOrders tables reliably and at once. To turn cascade deletes on, follow these steps:

1. Click on the "Database Tools" tab. Then, in the group "Relationships", click on "Relationships".

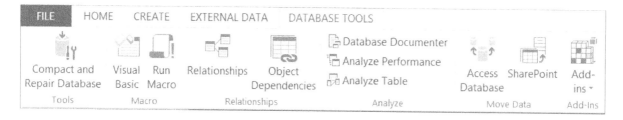

2. This will open up the Relationships window. Double click on the relationship line between Customers and Orders.

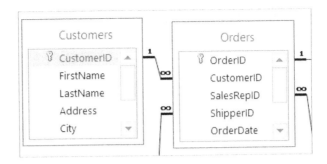

3. The following screen will appear. Click on "Cascade Delete Related Fields", and click "OK".

4. Repeat step two for the relationship between the tables Orders and ProductsOrders, and enable cascade deletes as well.

5. At this point, if we open the customers table and delete Mary's record, all of Mary's orders will be deleted from the Orders table, and all respective associations between Orders and products will be deleted from the ProductsOrders table.

For the purposes of this chapter, cascade deletes are off. In addition, we will be working on the tbls_Orders_DEL table, which is just a copy of the Orders table in which we can delete records at will.

361.　Delete a single record in a table
Delete a specific customer's order
Discussion:
The goal in this example is to delete a customer's order. Notice how we use the OrderID as the criterion in the WHERE clause. The OrderID is the primary key of the Orders table, and it will uniquely identify the record for deletion. Try to use primary key values for criteria instead of fields such as customer names, which might have duplicates in the table with the result of deleting records you do not want to delete. In addition, always run a SELECT beforehand or a SELECT INTO so that you can identify or backup your data respectively. I will show you how you can use the SELECT INTO to make a temporary table for deleted data. For this example, you need to follow four steps:

Step 1: Run a SELECT statement to uniquely identify and verify records for deletion. Never run a delete statement directly.

SELECT *

FROM tbls_Orders_Del

WHERE orderid = 20

Step 2: Turn on cascade deletes for the relationship between the tables Orders and ProductsOrders.

Step 3: Run the DELETE statement

DELETE

FROM tbls_Orders_Del

WHERE orderid = 20

Result:

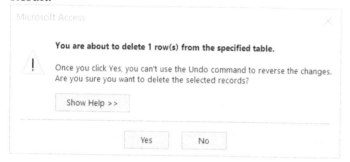

Step 4: Turn off cascade deletes for the relationship between the tables Orders and ProductsOrders so that nobody can delete any orders by mistake. If they are off, the database will give a referential integrity warning. We can open the Orders table and try to delete any record to have a look at the referential integrity message. Check chapter 4 for a full explanation of referential integrity consequences.

362. Delete multiple records in a table

Delete all orders for a specific customer

Discussion:

In this example, we want to delete all orders for customerid= 2, i.e. Mary. To achieve this task, we will use the CustomerID field in the WHERE clause, which is the primary key for the customers table and the foreign key in the orders table. Our task involves four steps as they appear below:

Step 1: Run a SELECT statement to uniquely identify and verify records for deletion.

SELECT *

FROM tbls_Orders_Del

WHERE customerid = 2

Step 2: Turn on cascade deletes for the relationship between the tables Orders and ProductsOrders. We do not need to turn cascade deletes on for the relationship between the tables Customers and Orders since we are not deleting the customer herself in this case—just her orders.

Step 3: Run the DELETE statement

DELETE
FROM tbls_Orders_Del
WHERE customerid = 2

Result:

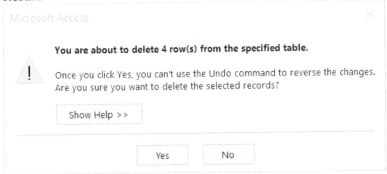

Step 4: Turn off cascade deletes for the relationship between the tables Orders and ProductsOrders so that nobody can delete any orders by mistake.

363.   Delete records in a certain date range
Delete multiple orders from multiple customers within a date range
Discussion:
This is an example of how we can use date criteria to delete orders within a specified date range. In this date range, we might have multiple orders from multiple customers.

Our four steps to delete all orders for a specific date range appear below:

Step 1: Run a SELECT statement to uniquely identify and verify records for deletion.
SELECT *
FROM tbls_Orders_Del
WHERE orderdate BETWEEN #10/15/2017# AND #10/17/2017#

Step 2: Turn on cascade deletes for the relationship between tables Orders and ProductsOrders.

Step 3: Run the DELETE statement
DELETE
FROM tbls_Orders_Del
WHERE orderdate BETWEEN #10/15/2019# AND #10/17/2019#

Result:

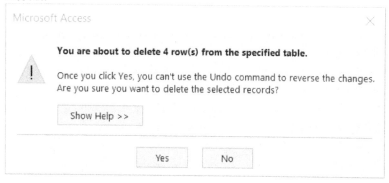

Step 4: Turn off cascade deletes for the relationship between tables Orders and ProductsOrders so that no one can delete any orders by mistake.

364.   Delete duplicate records while controlling if you want to delete the earliest or the latest ones

Delete earliest or latest duplicate customer orders

Discussion:

Let's discuss the setup of this example so that you can understand it in detail. First, in the table tbls_Orders_DEL, records with orderid 1001, 1002, and 1003 are duplicates. Specifically, the record with orderid = 1 is identical to 1001, the record with orderid = 988 is identical to 1002, and the record with orderid = 990 is identical to 1003. Keep in mind that these records have identical field values but different primary keys values.

The burning question is which records we should delete; the earliest ones or the latest ones? We know that a record with a lesser orderid value was entered before a record with a higher orderid value since the primary key is an autonumber. In the following example, we discuss both alternatives in detail. In any case, the four steps to follow appear below:

Step 1: Run a SELECT statement to uniquely identify and verify records for deletion.
The SQL statement below will SELECT the records with smaller orderid values. Notice we use a subquery to obtain what we need. In the main SELECT statement, we select all orders from the tbls_Orders_Del table that do not belong in the subquery. Consequently, we need to check what the subquery will fetch. The subquery itself will fetch the duplicate records with the maximum orderid values in the tbls_Orders_Del table. From the six duplicated records, it will select the three with the maximum orderID values (1001, 1002, and 1003). The main SELECT statement will fetch what is left from the six duplicated records, i.e. 1, 988, and 990. We can also use the NOT IN operator instead of the "<>" inequality predicate to obtain the same results. I know it is counter intuitive to use max() to get the earliest records, but max() is used in the subquery to identify duplicates with maximum primary key values. Then, the main SELECT statement will fetch all duplicates not in the subquery. The logic is the same the other way around for the next example:

SELECT OrderID, CustomerID, OrderDate, ShippingCost
FROM tbls_Orders_Del AS T2
WHERE OrderID <>
(SELECT Max(OrderID)
FROM tbls_Orders_Del AS T1
WHERE T2.CustomerID = T1.CustomerID AND T2.SalesRepID = T1.SalesRepID AND
T2.ShipperID = T1.ShipperID AND T2.OrderDate = T1.OrderDate)

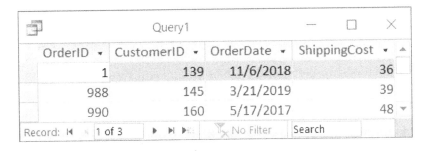

This SQL statement will select the latest duplicate records:
SELECT OrderID, CustomerID, OrderDate, ShippingCost
FROM tbls_Orders_Del AS T2
WHERE OrderID <>
(SELECT Min(OrderID)
FROM tbls_Orders_Del AS T1
WHERE T2.CustomerID = T1.CustomerID AND T2.SalesRepID = T1.SalesRepID AND
T2.ShipperID = T1.ShipperID AND T2.OrderDate = T1.OrderDate)

OrderID	CustomerID	OrderDate	ShippingCost
1001	139	11/6/2018	36
1002	145	3/21/2019	39
1003	160	5/17/2017	48

Record: 1 of 3   No Filter   Search

Step 2: Turn on cascade deletes for the relationship between the tables Orders and ProductsOrders.

Step 3: Run the DELETE statement
DELETE
FROM tbls_Orders_Del AS T2
WHERE OrderID <>
(SELECT Min(OrderID)
FROM tbls_Orders_Del AS T1
WHERE T2.CustomerID = T1.CustomerID AND T2.SalesRepID = T1.SalesRepID AND
T2.ShipperID = T1.ShipperID AND T2.OrderDate = T1.OrderDate)

Result:

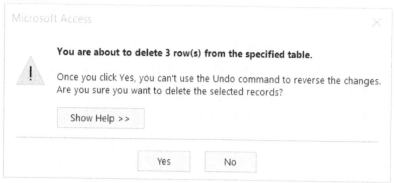

> **Microsoft Access** ✕
>
> ⚠️ **You are about to delete 3 row(s) from the specified table.**
>
> Once you click Yes, you can't use the Undo command to reverse the changes. Are you sure you want to delete the selected records?
>
> [Show Help >>]
>
> [Yes]   [No]

Step 4: Turn off cascade deletes for the relationship between the tables Orders and ProductsOrders so that nobody can delete any orders by mistake.

365. Delete ALL duplicate records (originals plus duplicates) that have the same field values and same primary key values

Delete all duplicate customer orders including original and duplicate orders

Discussion:

In this example, our goal is to delete all duplicate orders, including the original orders. We are working on a scenario where six records are identical such as records with orderids 1, 3, and 5. The records with orderid = 2 and 4 are unique and should not be touched. Notice that for this example, I have created a new table named tbls_Orders_Del2.

OrderID	CustomerID	SalesRepID	ShipperID	OrderDate	RequiredDate	ShippedDate	ShippingCost
5	123	2	2	11/14/2017	11/29/2017	11/19/2017	40
5	123	2	2	11/14/2017	11/29/2017	11/19/2017	40
3	137	2	2	6/29/2018	7/14/2018	7/4/2018	34
3	137	2	2	6/29/2018	7/14/2018	7/4/2018	34
2	184	2	1	7/25/2018	8/9/2018	7/30/2018	39
1	139	2	2	11/6/2018	11/21/2018	11/11/2018	36
1	139	2	2	11/6/2018	11/21/2018	11/11/2018	36
4	165	2	1	12/14/2019	12/29/2019	12/19/2019	48

Record: ◄ ‹ 1 of 8 › ► ►◄   No Filter   Search

tbls_Orders_DEL2

The four steps to run in a real situation are the following:

Step 1: Run a SELECT statement to uniquely identify and verify records for deletion from the table tbls_Orders_DEL2.

SELECT OrderID, CustomerID, SalesRepID, ShipperID, OrderDate
FROM tbls_Orders_DEL2
WHERE orderid IN(
SELECT OrderID
FROM tbls_Orders_DEL2
GROUP BY OrderID, CustomerID, ShipperID, OrderDate
HAVING count(*)>1)

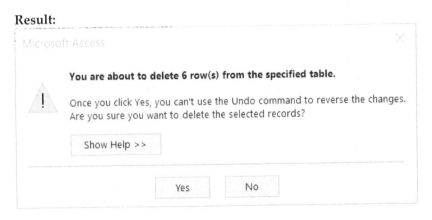

Step 2: Turn on cascade deletes for the relationship between the tables Orders and ProductsOrders.

Step 3: Run the DELETE statement
DELETE
FROM tbls_Orders_DEL2
WHERE OrderID IN(
SELECT OrderID
FROM tbls_Orders_DEL2
GROUP BY OrderID, CustomerID, ShipperID, OrderDate
HAVING count(*)>1)

Result:

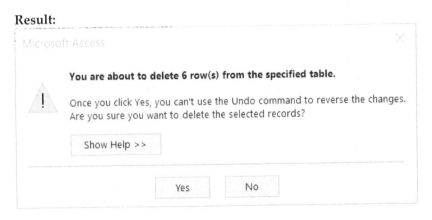

Step 4: Turn off cascade deletes for the relationship between the tables Orders and ProductsOrders.

366.   Use SELECT INTO to back up records before deleting them
Create a temp table to back up customers' orders before deleting them
Discussion:
In this example, we delete records from the tbls_Orders_DEL table but just in case we need these records later on, we back them up on the fly in a new table using a SELECT INTO statement. In addition, if we want to append the deleted records in a historical table, we can easily do so by using the INSERT INTO statement, which has the functionality of an append query. The bottom line is that the code of both SQL statements for SELECT INTO or INSERT INTO will be exactly the same with the code of the DELETE statement changing only its first line.

Code:

```
SELECT * INTO TempTable
FROM tbls_Orders_Del
WHERE orderdate
BETWEEN #10/15/2019# AND #11/15/2019#
```

Result:

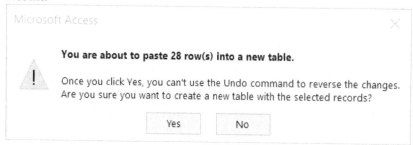

DELETE
```
FROM tbls_Orders_Del
WHERE orderdate
BETWEEN #10/15/2019# AND #11/15/2019#
```

Result:

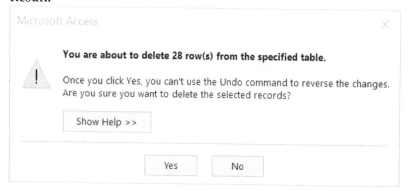

367.   Delete records in a table based on values in a different table using a subquery

Delete records from the orders table using criteria from the customers table

Discussion:

This time, we have a request from management to delete all orders from Los Angeles for a customer with the last name of Orlando. The problem is we do not have a state field and a last name field in the orders table. This is ok since we can use a subquery to easily delete records in one table based on criteria from a different table. In a production environment, follow the steps below:

Step 1: Run a SELECT statement to uniquely identify and verify records for deletion.

SELECT *
FROM tbls_Orders_DEL
WHERE CustomerID IN
(SELECT CustomerID FROM Customers
WHERE city= 'Los Angeles' AND lastname = 'Orlando')

Step 2: Turn on cascade deletes for the relationship between the tables Orders and ProductsOrders.

Step 3: Run the DELETE statement
DELETE
FROM tbls_Orders_DEL
WHERE CustomerID IN
(SELECT CustomerID FROM Customers
WHERE city= 'Los Angeles' AND lastname = 'Orlando')

Result:

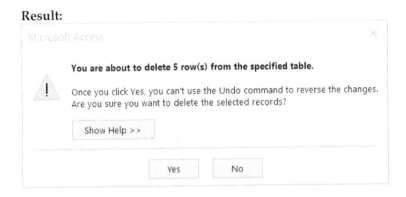

Step 4: Turn off cascade deletes for the relationship between the tables Orders and ProductsOrders.

368.   Delete records in a table based on calculations in a different table
Update address information for a single customer
Discussion:
This time, the request from management is to delete all orders with a grand total of more than $500. We need to resort to the ProductsOrders table for criteria, make calculations on this table, and use the calculated fields as criteria. It sounds like a big deal, but it is not.

A sample dataset from the ProductsOrders table appears below. Notice the pairs of OrderIDs and ProductIDs so that you know what product is included in what order. For example, order 2 contains products 23, 24, 32, and 70.

To be able to comply with the request of management, we first need to calculate order subtotals or, in other words, total amounts for each product. To put it yet another way, we multiply unitprice*quantity. Once we have the order subtotals, we need to calculate order totals. To do this, we use the SUM() function and the GROUP BY clause. Finally, since we only want order totals which exceed $500, we insert the criterion ">500" in the HAVING clause. Please note that we use HAVING instead of WHERE since HAVING is applied after the records are grouped while WHERE is applied before they are grouped.

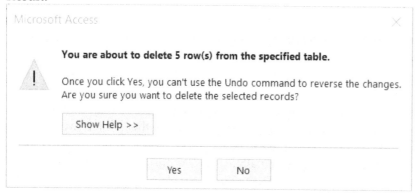

OrderID ▼	ProductID ▼	UnitPrice ▼	Quantity ▼	Discount ▼
34	1	15	4	0.15
36	1	15	2	0.2
66	1	15	6	0.15
85	1	15	4	0
91	1	15	3	0.15
148	1	15	1	0.2
165	1	15	4	0.15
225	1	15	5	0.2

Record: ◄ ◄ 1 of 2411 ► ►I ►⃰ 🏷No Filter Search ◄ ►

Step 1: Run a SELECT statement to uniquely identify and verify records for deletion.
SELECT *
FROM tbls_Orders_DEL
WHERE OrderID IN(
SELECT Sum([unitprice]*[quantity]) AS totalOrder
FROM ProductsOrders
GROUP BY OrderID
HAVING Sum([unitprice]*[quantity])>500)

Step 2: Turn on cascade deletes for the relationship between the tables Orders and ProductsOrders.

Step 3: Run the DELETE statement
DELETE
FROM tbls_Orders_DEL
WHERE OrderID IN(
SELECT Sum([unitprice]*[quantity]) AS totalOrder
FROM ProductsOrders
GROUP BY OrderID
HAVING Sum([unitprice]*[quantity])>500)

Result:

Microsoft Access

You are about to delete 5 row(s) from the specified table.

Once you click Yes, you can't use the Undo command to reverse the changes.
Are you sure you want to delete the selected records?

Show Help >>

Yes   No

Step 4: Turn off cascade deletes for the relationship between the tables Orders and ProductsOrders.

CHAPTER 29 DISCUSSION QUESTIONS

1. What is the basic goal of delete statements in relational databases?
2. Can we undo the results of delete statements just in case we deleted records by mistake?
3. What is a good strategy to follow before we use a delete statement?
4. What is the role of cascade deletes in relational databases?
5. Why it is a good idea to keep cascade deletes off and use them only when needed?
6. Can you provide an example of a business occasion in which it makes sense to use cascade deletes?
7. If we have duplicate records in a table what kind of function can we use to select the latest ones for deletion?
8. How can we delete all duplicate records in a table using a single SQL statement?
9. What SQL command can we use to backup records in a different table before we delete them from the current one?
10. What technique can we use to delete records in one table while using criteria from a different table?

370. **CHAPTER 29 HANDS-ON EXERCISES**

Chapter 29 Case 1:

Create a new Access database and name it Chapter29_1.accdb. Copy the tables Products and Suppliers from the PracticeDatabase.accdb and paste them to Chapter29_1.accdb.

1. The inventory people want you to delete from the database the product "Dried Blueberries - 1 lb. Bag". Create a new query that satisfies the department's request and save it as Qry1_DeleteProduct.

   Your result should look like:

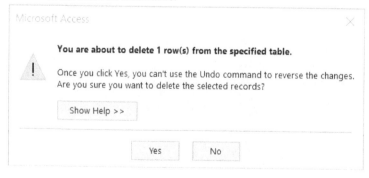

2. The inventory people are back and they want you to delete from the database all the products with prices between $15 and $19. Create a new query that satisfies the department's request and save it as Qry2_DeleteManyProducts.

   Your result should look like:

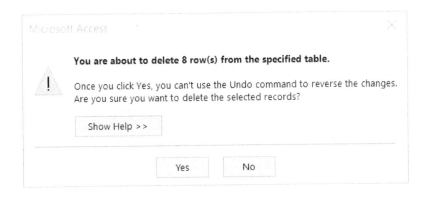

3. The inventory people are very happy with your work because you saved them a lot of time. Now, they want to delete additional records from the Products table but they need a backup copy of it before they proceed. Create a new query that creates a backup copy of the products table and save it as Qry3_Backup.

Your result should look like:

4. The management of the company decided to suspend operations with the suppliers from Dallas after a government directive for potential pollutants in their products. They want you to delete all the products in the products table from suppliers in the city of Dallas. Create a new query that satisfies the management's request and save it as Qry4_Dallas. HINT: You need to use a subquery to achieve this result.

Your result should look like:

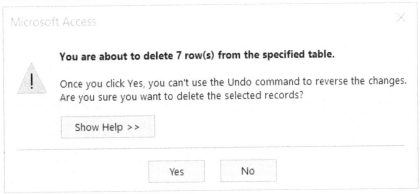

5. Prices in the Northeast went way out of control and the management decided to replace the suppliers there with others from the Southeast of the country. Create a new query that deletes all products from suppliers in the states of NY and MA and save it as Qry5_NY_MA.

Your result should look like:

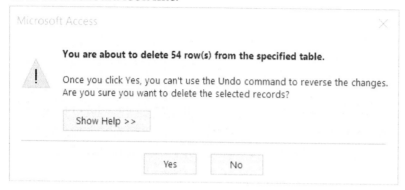

Chapter 29 Case 2:

Create a new Access database and name it Chapter29_2.accdb. Copy the tables Customers, Orders, SalesReps, and ShippingCompanies from the PracticeDatabase.accdb and paste them to Chapter29_2.accdb.

1. The shipping department called in and said that the customer Zartons Lisa from Los Angeles does not exist and they ask you to remove this record from the database. Create a new query that satisfies this request and save it as Qry1_DeleteCustomer.

Your result should look like:

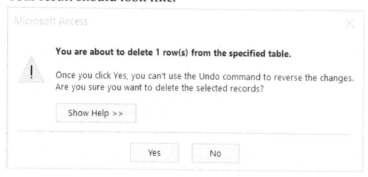

2. The sales department sent us a message saying that since we are not doing business with customers in the city of Albany, New York we can delete the customers from that city. Create a new query that satisfies the sales people request and save it as Qry2_DeleteCity. HINT: Make sure that you delete customers from Albany, NY only since there are twenty eight (28) Albanys in the USA!

Your result should look like:

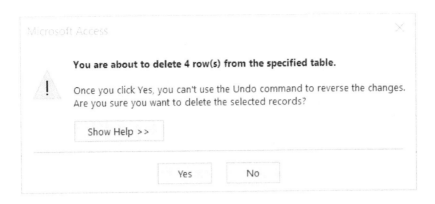

3. HR wants us to delete some records of employees who are not working for us any longer. Specifically, they want us to delete any employee who was hired before 12/31/2000. Create a new query that satisfies the HR request and save it as Qry3_DeleteEmployee.

    Your result should look like:

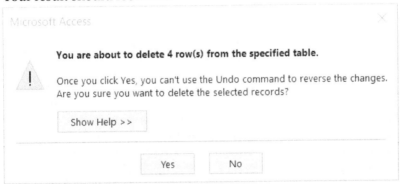

4. The sales manager called in and she is asking us to delete all orders put in by any sales rep from the city of Dallas. Create a new query that satisfies the request of the manager and save it as Qry4_DeleteSalesRepOrders. HINT: You need to use a subquery to achieve this result.

    Your result should look like:

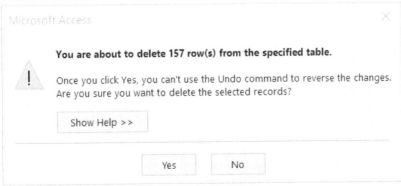

5. The shipping people called in and are asking us to delete all orders placed between #1/1/2017# and #1/31/2017# through any shipping company in the city of Boston. Create a new query that satisfies this request and save it as Qry5_DeleteBostonOrders.

Your result should look like:

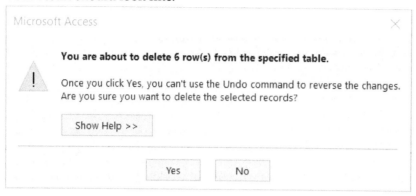

CHAPTER 30
WORKING WITH JOINS

The power of joins is a bit of a hidden jewel in the world of databases and data analysis. Developers and power users alike stay away from a good understanding of joins, mostly because they perceive them as complicated and impractical concepts. Both beliefs are false. You must understand joins to understand databases, and they are actually easy to use. They just look complicated. Devoting some time to understand the remarkable muscle of joins will transform the way you work and give you amazing flexibility in your everyday work tasks. In this chapter, we will look at practical applications of joins through realistic scenarios. In fact, this is the only way someone could convince me to use joins: Show me what they can actually do in practice.

In relational databases, we keep data in separate tables. We keep supplier information in the suppliers table, customers in the customers table, and orders in the orders table. This is what we call the physical structure or design of the database. This is done so that normalization rules apply in the database where we keep our business transactions (orders, quotations, invoices). What we are interested in, however, are the conceptual invocations from a relational database. We would like to generate and send out information, such as invoices, in a way that makes sense to our customers and us. In this respect, joins are links that we establish between tables with the goal of retrieving related information.

In this chapter, we will explore the use of inner, left, and right joins. Among these three, inner joins are the most commonly used in practical applications. Left joins are useful in certain business scenarios, while right joins can be used to check the integrity of the database and identify any orphaned records.

371.   Inner Joins
Find customers who actually have some orders
Discussion:
Let us assume our supervisor has a very simple request: She wants a report of customers who actually ordered something from us. The customers table might include people who asked for quotations, leads, or it might include customers who have not ordered anything for some time. How can we answer this request? We can go back to the chapter about duplicate, orphaned, and related records and use a subquery such as:

Code:
SELECT FirstName, LastName, Address, City
FROM Customers
WHERE CustomerID
IN (SELECT CustomerID from Orders)

Result:
Notice the number of customers returned is only 190. However, in the customers table, there are 201 customers. So, 11 customers have not had any orders at all for the historical data we have.

401

We can achieve the same result using a join. Let's create a new query in design view and add the customers and orders tables. There is a one-to-many relationship between customers and orders. For one customer, there might be multiple orders, but each order definitely belongs to one customer. Add the fields LastName, FirstName, City, and Address from the Customers table to the query.

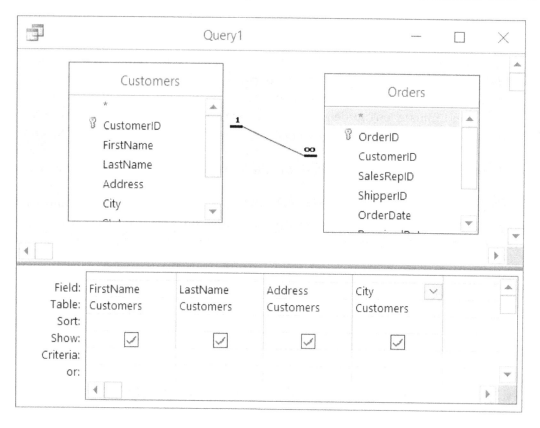

Double-click on the relationship line between customers and orders. The following dialog box comes up. By default, MS Access will join two tables through an inner join or, in other words, include records from each table where there is a common CustomerID value. By the way, CustomerID is the primary key (PK) in the customers table and the foreign key (FK) in the orders table.

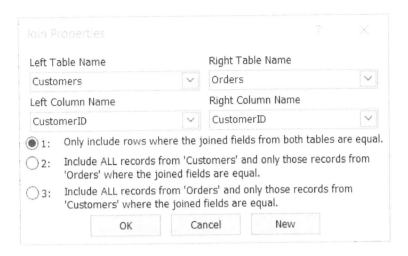

This is the case of an inner join. Notice that an inner join will give us the customers who have orders. If there are any customers without orders, they will not appear in the result set. In addition, if there are any orders without associated customers, they will not appear either. Only where the two tables match on the CustomerID will records be returned. The SQL code for the inner join appears below. Notice that the database returned 1000 records. This is because there are 1000 cases in which the CustomerID in the customers table has an associated CustomerID in the orders table. The eleven customers without a CustomerID in the orders table will not appear in the result set of this inner join.

Code:
SELECT FirstName, LastName, Address, City
FROM Customers
INNER JOIN Orders ON Customers.CustomerID = Orders.CustomerID

Result:

Discussion:
The initial request, however, was to present a list of unique customers who have orders. We do not need any repeated customer names in the result set. To achieve this, we need an inner join and a GROUP BY clause by last name, first name, and address fields. Notice how the number of customers returned is the same as that returned by the subquery we used in the beginning of this example.

Code:

SELECT FirstName, LastName, Address, City

FROM Customers

INNER JOIN Orders ON Customers.CustomerID = Orders.CustomerID

GROUP BY FirstName, LastName, Address, City

Result:

Oops! What happened here? The result is exactly the same like the subquery's in the beginning of this example. Simply, Access sorts by the first field in the GROUP BY clause, in this case, FirstName.

To solve this problem, we add the CustomerID field in the SQL statement and the result now is identical with that in the subquery. We do not even need to sort by CustomerID.

Code:

SELECT Customers.CustomerID, FirstName, LastName, Address, City

FROM Customers

INNER JOIN Orders ON Customers.CustomerID = Orders.CustomerID

GROUP BY Customers.customerID, FirstName, LastName, Address, City

Result:

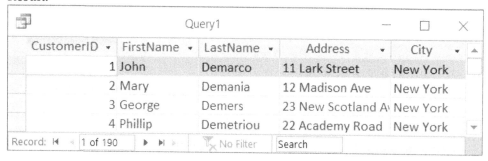

372. Left Joins

List all customers whether they have orders or not

Discussion:

There are cases in which we do not want to retrieve only the matching records from two related tables. For instance, we might want to list all customers from the customers table and their associated orders where they exist. In this case, the output of our query will list all records from the customers table and their associated orders in the orders table. For customers without orders, it will return blank values for fields from the orders table such as the OrderDate and ShippingCost fields.

The figure below shows the query design for an inner join, which is the default join type when we create a query in Access.

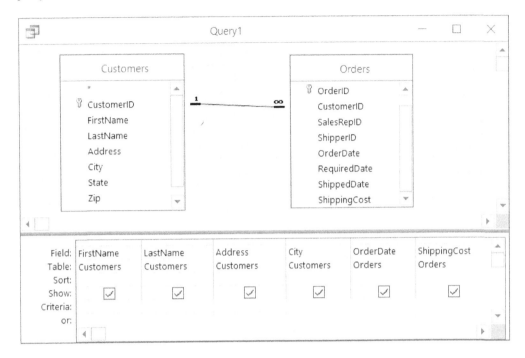

Double-click on the relationship line between customers and orders. The Joins dialog box comes up. Change the join type to number 2: "Include ALL records from Customers and only those records from Orders where the joined fields are equal".

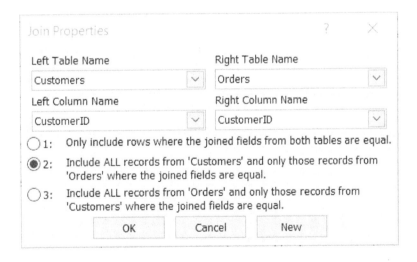

The query design now changes to the one below. Notice the relationship arrow that now has a point toward the Orders table. This is the visual sign that there is a left join relationship between these two tables.

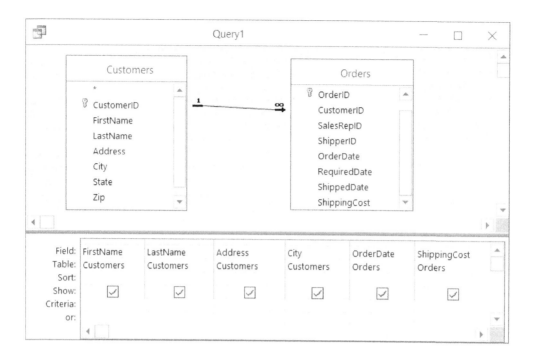

A left join will output all customers from the Customers table and any related fields from the Orders table based on matches on the CustomerID field. If there are any customers without orders, they will still appear in the result set. If there are any orders without associated customers, they will not appear in the result set.

Code:

SELECT FirstName, Lastname, Address, City, OrderDate, ShippingCost
FROM Customers LEFT JOIN Orders ON Customers.CustomerID = Orders.CustomerID

Result:

Note that the database returned 1011 records. This is because there are 1000 records in which the CustomerID in the customers table has an associated CustomerID in the orders table. In addition, we have 11 customers without a CustomerID in the orders table, but they will appear in the result set because this is a left join. There will be blank values for the OrderDate and ShippingCost for the customers without any orders.

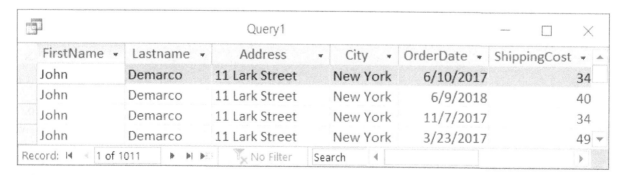

373. Right Joins
List all orders including those without customers
Discussion:
In this scenario, we want to produce a list of all orders from the orders table whether or not they have any matching records in the customers table. If a record from the orders table has a matching record in the customers table, this is fine and should actually be the case for all orders. If our query returns any records in which the fields from the customers table are blank, these are orphaned records. This means that we have orders without customers, and the integrity of our database is compromised. Let's start with a normal query and see how we can change it to a right join query.

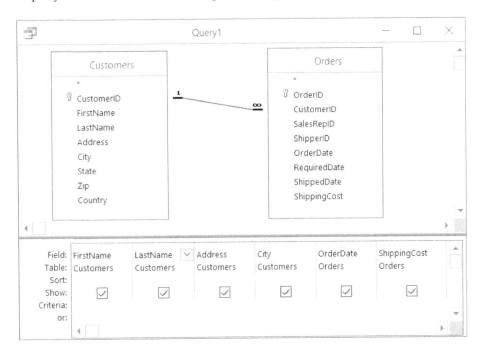

Double-click on the relationship line between customers and orders. The Joins dialog box comes up. Change the join type to number 3: "Include ALL records from Orders and only those records from Customers where the joined fields are equal".

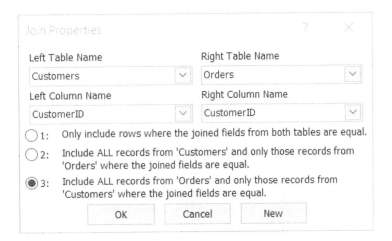

A right join will output all of the orders from the orders table and any related customers from the customers table based on matches on the CustomerID field. If there are any orders without customers, they will still appear in the result set. If this is the case, these orders are considered orphaned records, and they need to be investigated very closely and eliminated from the database. In addition, we need to have a look at the database design to see how it is possible that these orders are there in the first place. This can happen only if referential integrity is off. If it is off, turn it on.

Then, we need to deal with the orphaned records. We cannot have orders without customers because first, it does not make sense and second, because our database integrity is compromised. Maybe these were orders belonging to existing customers and entered with the wrong CustomerID as the foreign key while referential integrity was not on. If this is the case, change the value of the CustomerID field in the orders table to associate them with existing customers in the customers table. If we cannot find any customers to associate the orphaned orders, we must delete them from the database. Notice the relationship arrow that now has a point toward the customers table. This is the visual sign that there is a relationship with a right join between these two tables.

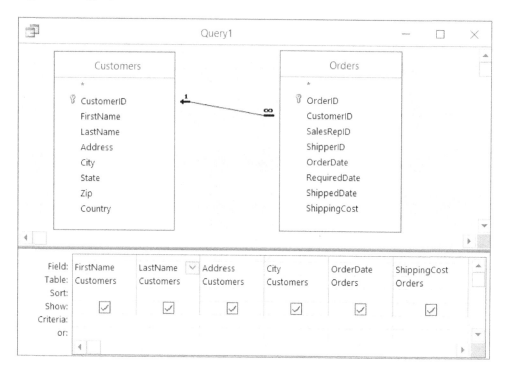

Code:
SELECT FirstName, LastName, City, Address, OrderDate, ShippingCost
FROM Customers
RIGHT JOIN Orders ON Customers.CustomerID = Orders.CustomerID

Result:
Notice that the database returned 1000 records. This is because there are 1000 records in which the CustomerID in the orders table has an associated CustomerID in the customers table. As you know, there are 11 customers without a CustomerID in the orders table, but they will not appear in the result set because this is a right join listing ALL records in the orders table and only associated customers in the customers table. Notice that we do not have any blank values for the lastname, firstname, and address fields from the customers table, which means we have no orphaned records in the orders table.

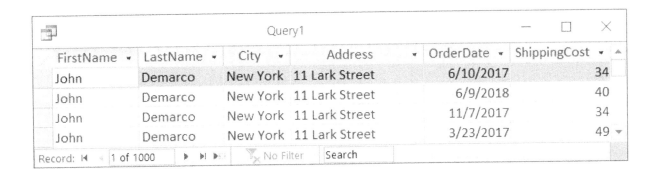

374.   Cross Joins

Derive the Cartesian product of two tables

Discussion:

A cross join, also called a Cartesian product, will join every record in one table with every record in the other table. Let us work through an example. In the sample database the suppliers table contains ten records and the products table contains seventy records. A cross join between the two will result in seven hundred records. Each supplier will be joined to every single product row which means there will be seventy rows per supplier.

The general syntax for a cross join in Access is   SELECT * from TABLE1, TABLE2

Code:

SELECT * FROM Suppliers, Products

Result:

Suppliers.SupplierID ▾	CompanyName ▾	ContactName ▾	ContactTitle ▾	Address ▾
1	Home of Snacks	Pedro Adkins	Sales Manager	22 Taft Street
2	American Foods, LLC.	John Marrey	Purchasing Manager	30 Maplewood Ave
3	American Imports Inc.	Maria Hopkins	Sales Manager	10 Silver Street
4	America's Greatest Snacks, Inc.	Andrew Daves	Sales Manager	12 Avon Ln

Record: ◄ ◄ 1 of 700 ► ►► No Filter   Search

The cross join does not have a graphical representation in the relationship between the two tables. That is, there is no line between the two tables that will indicate a cross join as you can see in the image below.

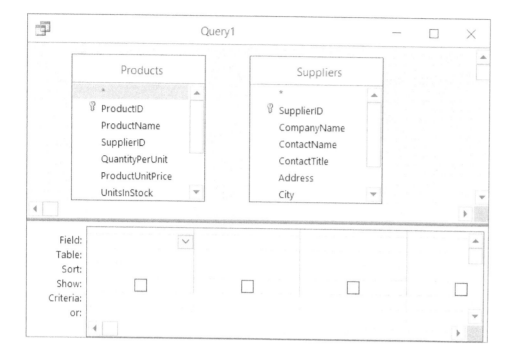

375.   Cross Joins with the WHERE clause

Create the Cartesian product of specific fields

Discussion:

The goal in this example is to obtain a list of sales representatives and suppliers who reside in the same city. Such a list is very useful because it will give us the "load" of sales reps in each city. That is, it will enable us to see how many suppliers are serviced by each sales rep in each city. Depending on the results, we might want to reallocate the work load of the sales reps to optimize their performance. In the code below notice how we define the table name for each city field since it exists in both tables.

Code:

SELECT salesreps.lastname, salesreps.city, Companyname, suppliers.city
FROM
Suppliers cross join salesreps
where suppliers.city = salesreps.city

Result:

As you can see from the result set, for each sales rep we can see the corresponding suppliers who operate in the same city, along the name of the city.

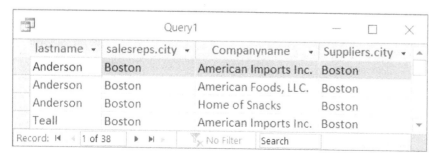

376.   Natural Joins

List suppliers and sales reps from the same city

Discussion:

A natural join will connect two tables on a common field which is different than the standard (PK, FK) combination. For instance, the standard way of joining the tables Customers and Orders is to use the CustomerID field which is the primary key in the Customers table and the foreign key in the Orders table.

In our example below, we are using the city field to join the Suppliers and SalesReps tables. The result set will include records from both tables where the value of the city field is identical. That is, it will give us suppliers and sales reps who are located in the same city.

Code:

```
SELECT salesreps.lastname, salesreps.city, Companyname, suppliers.city
FROM Suppliers inner join salesreps
ON Suppliers.City = SalesReps.City
```

Result:

Notice how the result set of this "natural join" is the same with the result in the previous cross join example with the where clause.

377.   Self Joins

What is a self join and when do we use it

Discussion:

All the examples to this point have joined two separate tables. For example, we have joined the customers and orders tables to list customers who have orders, to show customers without orders, or even to identify orders without customers (orphaned records). In a self join, we still join two tables but we join a table to itself. Let us work on an example to fully understand the concept. The figure below includes the tbls_Products_Joins table twice.

The business rationale behind this example is that each product consists of multiple component products but it can also be a component to other products. Notice how some products consist of two components, some of them have only one component, and some others have no components at all. Notice the hierarchical relationship between products here. A product might have multiple components and one of its components might have sub components. For example, product D consists of products E and C. Product C in turn consists of products D and H. Product H consists of product E. At the same time, we see that products A and I do not have any subcomponents at all. To capture and work on these intricate relationships among rows in the same table we use self joins.

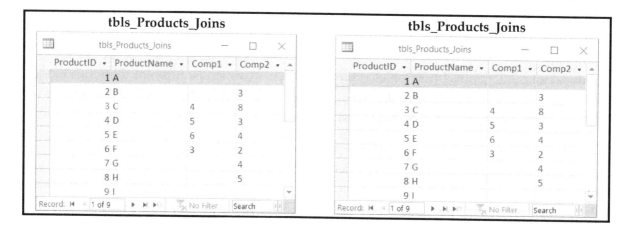

378.   Self Joins with Inner Joins

Show products which have components

Discussion:

Even in self joins, it is important to select the correct join type, such as an inner join, left join, or right join, between the two identical tables to list the records we need. In this example, we use an inner join to connect the ProductID and Comp1 fields to see how many products have a first component. For this example, we present the design of the view to visualize the inner join between the two tbls_Products_Joins table. Since we cannot use the same table name twice we provide two alternative and shorter names, p1 and p2, for the tbls_Products_Joins table. As you can see from the result set, only products which do have a first component show up in the list. Any products without a first component will not show up in the list due to the inner join we have used.

Code:

```
SELECT p1.productID, p1.productname, p2.productname as Component1
FROM  tbls_Products_Joins AS p1 inner JOIN
tbls_Products_Joins AS p2 ON p2.Comp1 = p1.ProductID
```

Design:

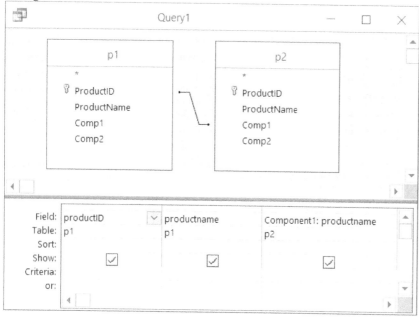

Result:

productID	productname	Component1
4	D	C
5	E	D
6	F	E
3	C	F

Record: ⏮ ◄ 1 of 4 ► ⏭ ▶* No Filter   Search

379.   Self Joins with Left Joins

Show all products whether they have components or not

Discussion:

In this example, we use a left join to connect the ProductID and Comp1 fields to list all products whether they have a first component or not. We present the design of the view to visualize the left join between the two tbls_Products_Joins table. Also, we still use the p1 and p2 short names for the tbls_Products_Joins table. As you can see from the result set, all products will appear in the result set whether or not they have a first component.

Code:

```
SELECT p1.productID, p1.productname, p2.productname as Component1
FROM  tbls_Products_Joins AS p1 left JOIN
tbls_Products_Joins AS p2 ON p2.Comp1 = p1.ProductID
```

Design:

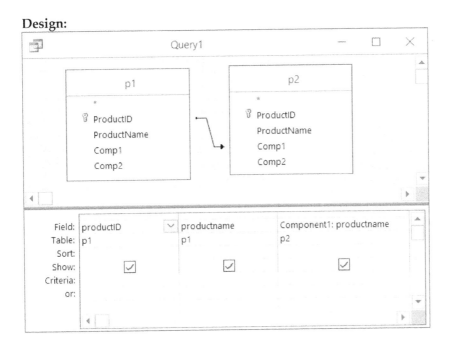

Result:

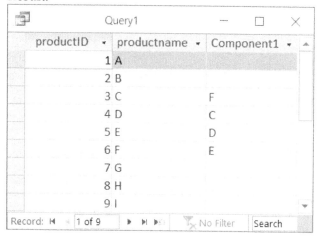

CHAPTER 30 DISCUSSION QUESTIONS

1. What is the main purpose of joins in relational databases?
2. Why are the concepts of joins and normalization related?
3. Why do we relinquish flexibility if we do not have knowledge of joins?
4. What do we mean by the physical design of the database?
5. What is the usefulness of an inner join?
6. What is the purpose of a left join?
7. What is the rationale behind a right join?
8. How can we find orphaned records using joins?
9. How the concept of right joins is related to referential integrity?
10. What kind of a join do we need to use to find suppliers without products in our database?

381. **CHAPTER 30 HANDS-ON EXERCISES**

Chapter 30 Case 1:
Create a new Access database and name it Chapter30_1.accdb. Copy the tables Orders and SalesReps from the PracticeDatabase.accdb and paste them to Chapter30_1.accdb.

1. The sales director needs a list of sales representatives who actually have some orders in the orders table. Create a new query that contains the firstname, lastname, and address fields from the SalesReps table and satisfies the director's request. Use a subquery to achieve this task. Save the query as Qry1_SalesRepsOrders_subquery.

   Your result should look like:

2. You need to achieve the same task as in number 1 but using a join this time. Create a new query and save it as Qry2_InnerJoin_SalesRepsWithOrders.

   Your result should look like:
   The order of records is different from the previous example but the result is the same.

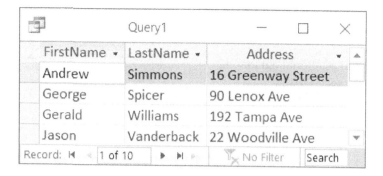

3. The sales director needs a report that lists sales reps and their respective order information. He wants the report to include all sales reps whether they have orders or not. Specifically, from the SalesReps table he needs to see the lastname, firstname, and address fields, while from the Orders table he would like to see the orderdate and required date field. Create a new query that satisfies the director's request and name it Qry3_LeftJoin_AllSalesReps.

Your result should look like:

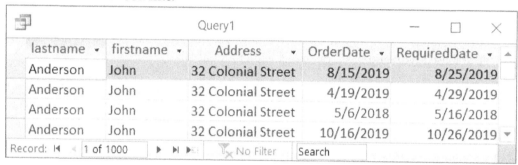

4. This time the sales director needs a report that will list all orders and their related salesreps information. Specifically, from the SalesReps table he needs to see the lastname, firstname, and address fields, while from the Orders table he would like to see the orderdate and RequiredDate field. Create a new query that satisfies the director's request and name it Qry4_RightJoin_AllOrders.

Your result should look like:

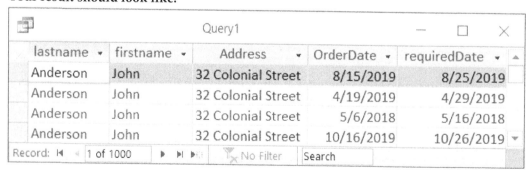

5. Along with the report in question 4, you suggest to the sales director a report that will include any potential orphaned records from the orders table. That is, a report of orders without corresponding

sales reps. Create a report to list orphaned records from the Orders table if any. Use a join to achieve this task. Create a new query that satisfies the director's request and name it Qry5_Orders_OrphanedRecords. HINT: See chapter 23 for help on this task. As you can see from the image below, there are no orphaned records in the Orders table.

Your result should look like:

Chapter 30 Case 2:

Create a new Access database and name it Chapter30_2.accdb. Copy the tables tble_ProductsNS and Suppliers from the PracticeDatabase.accdb and paste them to Chapter30_2.accdb.

1. The inventory director needs a list of the suppliers from which we currently have products in our database. Create a new query that includes the CompanyName, ContactName, and ContactTitle fields from the Suppliers table and satisfies the director's request. You need to use a join to achieve your goal and the supplier names must appear only once in the result set. Save it as Qry1_InnerJoin.

Your result should look like:

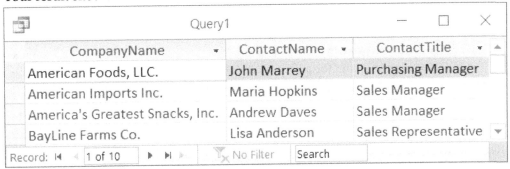

2. The inventory director now needs a list of suppliers and their respective product information. She needs the list to include all suppliers whether or not they currently have products in the inventory. Create a new query that includes the CompanyName, ContactName, and ContactTitle fields from the Suppliers table and the ProductName, ProductUnitPrice, and UnitsInStock fields from the Products table and satisfies the director's request. You need to use a join to achieve your goal and the result set should be sorted by CompanyName ascending. Save the query as Qry2_LeftJoin.

Your result should look like:

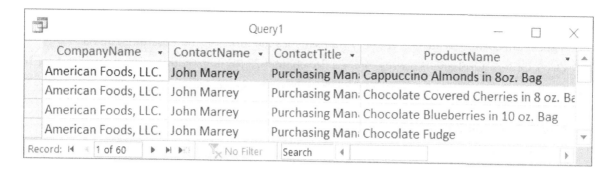

3. The inventory director got word that there is a discrepancy in the products table. Specifically, she was told that some products do not have associated supplier information making replenishing impossible. Consequently, the director is asking for a report that will list the CompanyName field from the Suppliers table and the ProductName, ProductUnitPrice, and UnitsInStock fields from the Products table. She needs to see all product information whether or not they have an associated supplier. You need to use a join to achieve your goal and the result set should be sorted by ProductName ascending. Save the query as Qry3_RightJoin.

Your result should look like:

CompanyName	ProductName	ProductUnitPrice	UnitsInStock
Old York Foods, Inc.	All-Purpose Marinade I	29	27
Cape Cod Snacks Co.	All-Purpose Marinade II	39	26
Home of Snacks	Almonds, Hickory Smoke	35	40
Home of Snacks	Almonds, Roasted and Sa	22	32

Record: 1 of 70   No Filter   Search

4. The inventory director is now asking for a list that includes products without suppliers in the database. This list needs to include the ProductName, ProductUnitPrice, UnitsInStock, and ReorderLevel fields from the Products table. You need to use a subquery to achieve this task. Create a new query that satisfies the director's request and save it as Qry4_OrphanedSubquery. HINT: Refer to chapter 23.

Your result should look like:

ProductName	ProductUnitPrice	UnitsInStock	ReorderLevel
Dried Cranberries - 34 oz.	35	15	20
Raw Sunflower Seeds in 19 oz.	25	12	20
Chocolate Almonds in 8 oz. Ba	25	21	25
Dark Chocolate Apricots in 20	46	38	25

Record: 1 of 10   No Filter   Search

5. You need to achieve the same result as in number 4 but using a join this time. Create a new query and save it as Qry5_OrphanedJoin.

Your result should look like:

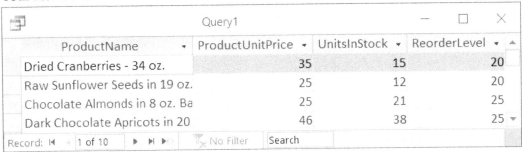

ProductName	ProductUnitPrice	UnitsInStock	ReorderLevel
Dried Cranberries - 34 oz.	35	15	20
Raw Sunflower Seeds in 19 oz.	25	12	20
Chocolate Almonds in 8 oz. Ba	25	21	25
Dark Chocolate Apricots in 20	46	38	25

Record: 1 of 10   No Filter   Search

CHAPTER 31
WORKING WITH SUB-QUERIES

A subquery is a query nested within another query. Subqueries are primarily used to achieve results in a single step instead of using multiple queries. Specifically, subqueries are used in the following scenarios:

1. Create dynamic search lists with IN or NOT IN
2. Create dynamic search lists with EXISTS or NOT EXISTS
3. Find records in a table using criteria from another table using IN
4. Find records in a table using criteria from another table using EXISTS
5. Find orphaned records
6. Find duplicate records
7. Find unrelated records
8. Return a single value
9. Perform dynamic aggregations with aggregate functions
10. To create temporary tables that combine data from multiple tables using UNION
11. Update records in one table using criteria from another table
12. Delete records in one table using criteria from another table
13. Relate two tables on fields other than the primary keys
14. Create crosstab reports

Let us explore the scenarios above through practical examples.

382. Create dynamic search lists with IN or NOT IN
Find orders for which you extended no discounts for at least one of the products included in the order

Discussion:
Our goal in this example is to retrieve orders for which we provided no discount for at least one of the products contained in the order. That is, for at least one of the products contained in these orders, the discount rate was 0. Keep in mind that there might be multiple products in each order. In addition, notice that the ProductsOrders table is the table in between that establishes the many-to-many relationship between the Orders and Products tables. Consequently, the logic should be to first look in the ProductsOrders table for all of the products with zero discounts. Using the OrderID from this result (the subquery) you will be able to find the corresponding order records in the Orders table. From the result, we can see that out of the 1000 orders in the Orders table, we provided at least one non-discounted product for 136 orders.

Code:
```
SELECT *
FROM orders
WHERE orderid
IN (SELECT orderid FROM ProductsOrders WHERE (Discount) =0)
```

Main Query Result:

OrderID	CustomerID	SalesRepID	ShipperID	OrderDate	RequiredDate
2	184	2	1	7/30/2018	8/9/2018
5	123	2	2	11/19/2017	11/29/2017
7	165	2	2	12/1/2018	12/11/2018
24	127	4	1	3/12/2017	3/22/2017

Record: 1 of 136   No Filter   Search

Subquery Result:

orderid
2
5
7
24

Record: 1 of 140

Notice that we have a discrepancy: The subquery returned a list of 140 orders, while the main query returned a list of only 136 orders. What happened? As you can see in the picture below, there are some orders like OrderID=390 which contain two products, and we provided no discounts for either of them Order 390 appears twice in the subquery but only once in the main query, which means that the final count of 136 is correct.

	390	68	4	2	2/5/2018

ProductID	UnitPrice	Quantity	Discount	Click to Add
13	15	4	0	
45	5	5	0	

383.   Create dynamic search lists with EXISTS or NOT EXISTS

Find orders for which we extended no discounts for at least one of the products included

Discussion:

A more effective and faster solution than using the IN predicate is to use EXISTS. In this example, we are again looking for non-discounted products in orders, and we will obtain the exact same result as in the previous example. O and P are simply abbreviated names for the Orders and ProductsOrders tables respectively.

Code:
SELECT *
FROM Orders O
WHERE EXISTS (SELECT OrderID FROM ProductsOrders P WHERE O.OrderID = P.OrderID AND discount = 0)

Result:

OrderID	CustomerID	SalesRepID	ShipperID	OrderDate	RequiredDate
2	184	2	1	7/30/2018	8/9/2018
5	123	2	2	11/19/2017	11/29/2017
7	165	2	2	12/1/2018	12/11/2018
24	127	4	1	3/12/2017	3/22/2017

Record: 1 of 136   No Filter   Search

384.   Find records in a table with criteria from another table using IN
Find customers with orders in the fourth quarter of the year 2019
Discussion:

In this example, we will use the IN predicate with two date functions to retrieve customers with orders in the fourth quarter of 2019. Keep in mind we are looking for customer names and not orders placed in that period.

Code:
SELECT FirstName, LastName, Address, City, State, Zip
FROM Customers
WHERE CustomerID IN
(Select CustomerID FROM Orders WHERE
DatePart('q',[OrderDate])=4 AND Year([orderdate])=2019)

Result:

FirstName	LastName	Address	City	State	Zip
Robert	Demaggio	34 Princeton Dr	New York	NY	12110
Paul	Demarist	89 Mercer Street	New York	NY	12110
Jim	Devito	102 Lexington Ave	New York	NY	89890
David	Vanderback	91 Fifth Ave	New York	NY	89890

Record: 1 of 60   No Filter   Search

385.   Find records in a table with criteria from another table using EXISTS
Find customers with orders in the fourth quarter of the year 2019
Discussion:
We can obtain the same output with the previous example by using EXISTS.

Code:

```
SELECT *
FROM Customers C
WHERE EXISTS
(Select CustomerID FROM Orders O WHERE C.CustomerID = O.CustomerID AND
DatePart('q',[OrderDate])=4 AND Year([orderdate])=2019)
```

Result:

FirstName	LastName	Address	City	State	Zip
Robert	Demaggio	34 Princeton Dr	New York	NY	12110
Paul	Demarist	89 Mercer Street	New York	NY	12110
Jim	Devito	102 Lexington Ave	New York	NY	89890
David	Vanderback	91 Fifth Ave	New York	NY	89890

Record: 1 of 60 — No Filter — Search

386. Find orphaned records

Find orders without customers

Discussion:

In this example, we are looking for orders without customers which is an oxymoron. If we indeed find any orders without customers, we need to delete them from the database and check the referential integrity settings for the one-to-many relationship between the tables Customers and Orders. In this example, we use the table tbls_orders where I put some orphaned records for demonstration purposes. As we can see from the result set, three orphaned records are found.

Code:

```
SELECT *
FROM tbls_orders
WHERE CustomerID
NOT IN (SELECT CustomerID FROM Customers)
```

Result:

OrderID	CustomerID	SalesRepID	ShipperID	OrderDate	RequiredDate
1500	250	11	2	1/20/2017	2/4/2017
1501	251	12	2	11/18/2017	12/3/2017
1502	252	14	3	2/5/2018	2/20/2018

Record: 1 of 3 — No Filter — Search

387.   Find duplicate records using a subquery

Find all duplicate records in a table

Discussion:

Our goal in this example is to use a subquery to find all duplicate records in the tbls_Orders table. Keep in mind that these records have identical field values and identical primary keys values. So, they are exact duplicates. If you need to find duplicate records based on the values of one, two, or multiple fields, consult chapter 23 where we list various scenarios for duplicate records. As you can see from the result set in this example, there are 11 duplicate records in this table.

Code:

```
SELECT *
FROM tbls_Orders WHERE OrderID IN(
SELECT OrderID
FROM tbls_Orders
GROUP BY OrderID
HAVING count(*)>1)
ORDER BY OrderID
```

Result:

OrderID	CustomerID	SalesRepID	ShipperID	OrderDate	RequiredDate	ShippedDate	ShippingCost
8	71	3	1	4/1/2019	4/16/2019	4/6/2019	36
8	71	3	1	4/1/2019	4/16/2019	4/6/2019	36
45	93	1	3	10/23/2017	11/7/2017	10/28/2017	46
45	93	1	3	10/23/2017	11/7/2017	10/28/2017	46
254	198	3	2	7/15/2017	7/30/2017	7/20/2017	36
254	198	3	2	7/15/2017	7/30/2017	7/20/2017	36
820	46	8	1	9/4/2019	9/19/2019	9/9/2019	39
820	46	8	1	9/4/2019	9/19/2019	9/9/2019	39
993	99	10	2	10/14/2017	10/29/2017	10/19/2017	49
993	99	10	2	10/14/2017	10/29/2017	10/19/2017	49
993	99	10	2	10/14/2017	10/29/2017	10/19/2017	49

Record: 1 of 11   No Filter   Search

388.   Find unrelated records

Find customers without any orders

Discussion:

This time, we will use NOT EXISTS to find customers who have not submitted any orders at all. Practically, we are looking for customers in the customers table without any related orders in the orders table. This is not a problem when it comes to database integrity. It is just a business fact. We might want to initiate a promotional campaign for these customers, for example. The "C" and "O" designations are just abbreviations for the Customers and Orders tables respectively. You can write the SQL statement without using these abbreviations.

Code:

SELECT FirstName, LastName, Address, City, State, Zip

FROM Customers C

WHERE NOT EXISTS (SELECT CustomerID FROM Orders O WHERE C.CustomerID = O.CustomerID)

Result:

FirstName	LastName	Address	City	State	Zip
Erin	Erin	28 Karrie Terrace	Los Angeles	CA	94851
Allan	Cimo	24 Crestwood CT	New York	NY	45357
Kelly	Costa	45 Sixth Ave	Philadelphia	PA	56789
Arnold	Webster	53 Southern Blvd	Miami	FL	88987

Record: 1 of 11 — No Filter — Search

389. Return a single value using the max() function

Find the latest shipped order from the orders table

Discussion:

Let's assume we need to present the details of the latest order we shipped. We can achieve this result with a single query where in the subquery we find the maximum (latest) shipped date in the orders table and use this date as a criterion in the main query to list the details of our latest order.

Code:

SELECT OrderID, CustomerID, SalesRepID, ShipperID, OrderDate

FROM Orders

WHERE shippeddate = (SELECT max(ShippedDate) FROM Orders)

Result:

OrderID	CustomerID	SalesRepID	ShipperID	OrderDate
4	165	2	1	12/19/2019

Record: 1 of 1 — No Filter — Search

390. Create dynamic aggregations (working on one table)

Find products with prices above the average product price

Discussion:

In this example, we are looking for products with above average prices. We want the database to calculate the average price per product, compare every product price to the average price, and display only those products which exceed the average price. It looks like a lot for a single SQL statement, but it is possible. The essence of this SQL statement is in the WHERE clause where we ask the ProductUnitPrice to be bigger than the average ProductUnitPrice using the inequality predicate ">" and the aggregate function avg().

425

Code:

```
SELECT productname, ProductUnitPrice
FROM Products
WHERE (ProductUnitPrice) > (SELECT avg(ProductUnitPrice) FROM Products)
ORDER BY ProductUnitPrice DESC
```

Result:

productname	ProductUnitPrice
Coffee biscuits	50
Pepper Cheese Box 3.75 oz.	50
Pizza croutons	49
Chocolate Chip Cookies	49

Record: 1 of 30 — No Filter — Search

391. Create dynamic aggregations with EXISTS (working with two tables)

List order information with shipped invoices above $500

Discussion:

This time, we need to retrieve orders with a total of over $500. Our problem however is that we need to list order information from the Orders table while making calculations on the ProductsOrders table where we keep product prices and quantities. We can achieve this task using a subquery with EXISTS and GROUP BY, which will run very fast as well.

The crucial part of this piece of code is in the GROUP BY clause. We need to group by OrderID in the subquery since in the ProductsOrders table, the same OrderID appears multiple times because there might be multiple products in the same order. However, we want our subquery to produce only one OrderID per order. In addition, we use the HAVING clause because we do not know beforehand what orders have a total of $500 or more. By using the HAVING clause, we are telling the database to first calculate the order totals through the sum() function, group the results by order, and then, apply the filter HAVING (Sum([unitprice]*[quantity]))>500).

Code:

```
SELECT OrderID, OrderDate, RequiredDate, ShippedDate, ShippingCost
FROM orders O
WHERE EXISTS
(SELECT orderid, Sum([unitprice]*[quantity])
FROM ProductsOrders P
WHERE O.OrderID = P.OrderID
GROUP BY orderid
HAVING Sum([unitprice]*[quantity])>500)
```

Result:

OrderID ▾	OrderDate ▾	RequiredDate ▾	ShippedDate ▾	ShippingCost ▾
308	10/20/2018	10/30/2018	10/25/2018	41
354	4/28/2017	5/8/2017	5/3/2017	44
404	11/23/2018	12/3/2018	11/28/2018	36
609	5/9/2019	5/19/2019	5/14/2019	33

Record: ◄ 1 of 5 ► ►I ►: No Filter Search

392. Create temporary tables using a subquery and UNION

Retrieve person information from the customers and suppliers tables and create a temp table with the combined results

Discussion:

Let's assume that a fellow employee has asked us for a combined list of names and addresses of our customers and suppliers because she wants to send out a common greeting card to all of them. We can create a temporary table with the combination of names using the SELECT INTO and UNION statements in combination. Notice how single quotes (") are used in the SQL statement for suppliers since in that table, there are no first and last name fields.

Code:

```
SELECT lastname, firstname, address, city, state, zip INTO tempPeopleTable
FROM
(SELECT lastname, firstname, address, city, state, zip
FROM customers
UNION
SELECT ContactName, " , address, city, state, zip
FROM suppliers)
```

Result:

Microsoft Access ×

⚠ **You are about to paste 211 row(s) into a new table.**

Once you click Yes, you can't use the Undo command to reverse the changes. Are you sure you want to create a new table with the selected records?

[Yes] [No]

393. Update records in one table using criteria from another table

Update product prices in the products table using criteria from the suppliers table

Discussion:

Management has decided to increase the prices of products from suppliers in Boston and Dallas. This is because transportation costs from those cities have increased considerably lately. We need to update prices in the products table using criteria from the suppliers table. This time, we also need to use filtering criteria within the subquery statement. The subquery in this example needs to retrieve the SupplierIDs of suppliers in Boston and Dallas which will be used by the main query to update product prices in the products table. Notice that in the products table, every record contains a SupplierID value.

Code:

```
UPDATE tbls_Products_Upd
SET ProductUnitPrice = ProductUnitPrice * (1+0.20)
WHERE SupplierID IN
(SELECT SupplierID FROM Suppliers
WHERE city= 'Boston' or city = 'Dallas')
```

Result:

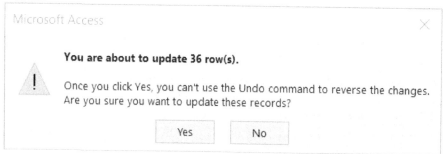

394. Delete records in one table using criteria from another table

Delete order information in the orders table using criteria from the customers table

Discussion:

This time, our task is to delete orders from customers in Los Angeles and Orlando. These orders will be processed by another distribution center, and we do not want them to clutter our database and affect our reports. In essence, the subquery will retrieve the CustomerIDs of these customers from the Customers table. Then, the main query will use these CustomerIDs to delete the orders that contain them in the tbls_Orders_DEL table. Always remember to run a SELECT statement first before deleting records. (Check chapter 29 for a full overview of DELETE statements).

Code:

```
DELETE
FROM tbls_Orders_DEL
WHERE CustomerID IN
(SELECT CustomerID FROM Customers
WHERE lastname = 'Orlando')
```

Result:

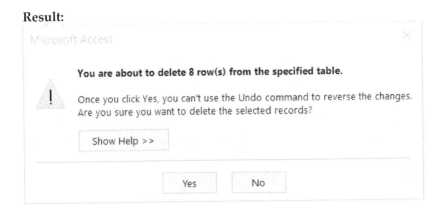

395.   Relate two tables on fields other than the primary keys using EXISTS

Find customers who reside in the same city as that of sales representatives

Discussion:

Our supervisor asks for a list of customers who live in the same city as our sales representatives. So, if we have a sales representative in Orlando, Florida, our supervisor wants us to identify all of the customers living in that city. We need to create a relationship between the Customers and SalesReps tables based on the city field. We can accomplish this task using the subquery below. As you can see from the result set, we have 54 customers living in the same cities as our salespeople.

Code:

```
SELECT FirstName, LastName, Address, City, State, Zip
FROM customers
WHERE exists
(SELECT *
FROM salesreps
WHERE customers.city = salesreps.city)
```

Result:

396.   Create a crosstab report with a subquery

Create a crosstab report that shows the number of orders by customer

Discussion:

In this example, we have a request from management to present a report that will list the number of orders by customer and by year. This is a crosstab query, but we can actually use subqueries to create this report. As you can see from the code below, we can use a subquery to calculate the number of orders from the Orders table as they relate to each customer in the Customer table.

Code:

```
SELECT lastname, firstname,
(SELECT Count(*) FROM Orders O WHERE O.CustomerID = C.CustomerID AND (year(orderdate) = 2017) ) AS [2017],
(SELECT Count(*) FROM Orders O WHERE O.CustomerID = C.CustomerID AND (year(orderdate) = 2018) ) AS [2018],
(SELECT Count(*) FROM Orders O WHERE O.CustomerID = C.CustomerID AND (year(orderdate) = 2019) ) AS [2019]
FROM Customers AS C
ORDER BY lastname
```

Result:

lastname	firstname	2017	2018	2019
Ackerman	Nicholas	2	2	1
Allen	Alfred	0	0	0
Ames	Pindar	0	0	5
Andersen	Thomas	2	0	2
Anderson	Joseph	1	3	1
Anderson	Peter	3	3	3
Anderson	Paul	2	2	2
Anthopolis	Ricky	1	2	1
Aversa	Scott	2	0	0
Baker	Matthew	2	3	3

Record: 1 of 201   No Filter   Search

The above SQL example will work in any relational database, and it represents a way to create crosstab reports. However, in Access, we have the option to create the exact same report by taking advantage of the TRANSFORM and PIVOT statements for crosstab queries to obtain the same results in a faster and easier way without the need to write multiple subqueries. In addition, if we needed our report to present ten years of sales history, we would have to write ten subqueries. Instead, by using crosstab queries, we can achieve the same result with simpler code below.

Code:

```
TRANSFORM Count(Orders.OrderID) AS CountOfOrderID
SELECT Customers.LastName, Customers.FirstName
FROM Orders INNER JOIN Customers ON Orders.CustomerID = Customers.CustomerID
GROUP BY Customers.LastName, Customers.FirstName
PIVOT Year([Orderdate])
```

Result:

LastName ▾	FirstName ▾	<> ▾	2017 ▾	2018 ▾	2019 ▾
Ackerman	Nicholas		2	2	1
Ames	Pindar				5
Andersen	Thomas		2		2
Anderson	Joseph		1	3	1
Anderson	Paul		2	2	2
Anderson	Peter		3	3	3
Anthopolis	Ricky		1	2	1
Aversa	Scott		2		
Baker	Matthew		2	3	3
Balfur	Carolyn		1	2	1

Record: ◄ ‹ 1 of 190 ► ►► ▸ No Filter   Search

Notice that 201 customer records returned using subqueries, while only 190 using TRANSFORM. This is because TRANSFORM left out customers without any orders, while the subqueries code returned all customer records—even those without any orders displaying 0s for all three years for those customers. Look for example at the customer Allen Alfred, record number two in the previous image, in the result of the subqueries code. This customer will not be included using the TRANSFORM statement. This is not a problem of the crosstab or subqueries code. It is simply a fact that there are some customers in the database that have no orders yet. This fact makes things a bit more complicated, but it happens. We just need to know how crosstab queries and subqueries fare under these circumstances.

397. CHAPTER 31 DISCUSSION QUESTIONS

1. What exactly is a subquery?
2. Why is it useful to use subqueries?
3. When we use the IN or NOT IN operators with subqueries what are we trying to build?
4. How can we perform dynamic aggregations with subqueries?
5. How can we perform existence tests using subqueries?
6. Can we use subqueries to find orphaned records?
7. How can we create customized categories using subqueries?
8. What kinds of questions are answered by subqueries which return single values?
9. What extra functionality do subqueries provide to UPDATE statements?
10. Can we create crosstab reports with subqueries? How do they compare with crosstab queries that use the pivot and transform statements?

398. CHAPTER 31 HANDS-ON EXERCISES

Chapter 31 Case 1:

Create a new Access database and name it Chapter31_1.accdb. Copy the tables tble_OrdersNS, Products, ProductsOrders, and SalesReps from the PracticeDatabase.accdb and paste them to Chapter31_1.accdb.

1. The sales reps got word that there are orders in the system without associated sales people. This fact results in lost commissions for them. They ask you to identify these orders so that they can get the appropriate commissions. Create a new query that includes all fields from the tble_OrdersNS table and satisfies the sales reps request. Save the query as Qry1_OrphanedRecords.

Your result should look like:

OrderID	OrderDate	RequiredDate	ShippedDate	ShippingCost
957	9/4/2017	9/14/2017	9/9/2017	46
964	3/20/2019	3/30/2019	3/25/2019	47
965	7/29/2018	8/8/2018	8/3/2018	51
966	2/15/2019	2/25/2019	2/20/2019	40

Record: 1 of 9   No Filter   Search

2. The sales director is asking for a list of salespeople who have no associated orders in the tble_OrdersNS table. Create a new query that includes the FirstName, LastName, Address, City, State, and Zip fields from the salesreps table and satisfies the sales director's request. Save the query as Qry2_UnrelatedRecords.

Your result should look like:

432

3. The sales director is back asking for a list of orders whose shipping cost is greater than the average shipping cost of the orders in the tble_OrdersNS table. Create a new query that includes the OrderID, CustomerID, OrderDate, and ShippedDate fields from the tble_OrdersNS table and satisfies the sales director's request. Save the query as Qry3_AboveAverageShippingCost.

Your result should look like:

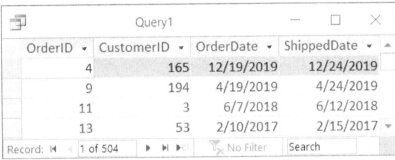

4. The sales director needs a similar report as in number 3 but one that only shows the number of orders whose shipping cost is greater than the average shipping cost of all the orders in the tble_OrdersNS table. Create a new query that satisfies the sales director's request. Save the query as Qry4_Count AboveAverageShippingCost.

Your result should look like:

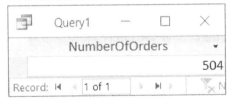

5. The sales director is asking for a list of products with sales above $3,000 without taking into consideration any applied discounts. Create a query that includes the fields ProductName, ProductUnitPrice, UnitsInStock, and UnitsOnOrder from the products table and satisfies the sales director's request. Save the query as Qry5_HiVolumeProducts.

Your result should look like:

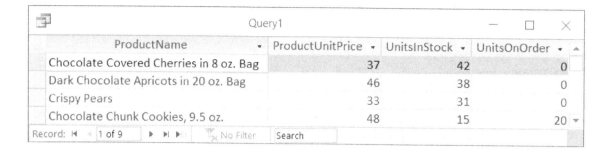

Chapter 31 Case 2:

Create a new Access database and name it Chapter31_2.accdb. Copy the tables tble_Orders and SalesReps from the PracticeDatabase.accdb and paste them to Chapter31_2.accdb.

1. The sales manager needs a list of sales people with orders in the months of January, February, March, April, May, and June of the year 2019. Create a new query that includes the firstname, lastname, and title fields from the SalesReps table and satisfies the sales manager request. Save the query as Qry1_RepsWithOrders.

    Your result should look like:

    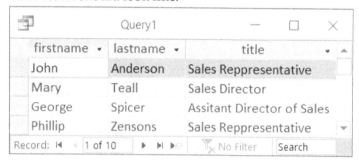

2. The sales manager is back and this time she is asking for a list of sales people without any orders in the month of June 2019. Create a new query that includes the firstname, lastname, and title fields from the SalesReps table and satisfies the sales manager request. Save the query as Qry2_RepsWithoutOrders.

    Your result should look like:

3. The accounts receivable people need to know the details of the latest order that was input in the system based on the OrderDate field. Create a new query that includes the OrderID, CustomerID, OrderDate, and ShippedDate fields from the Orders table and satisfies the accounting people request. Save the query as Qry3_MostRecentOrder.

Your result should look like:

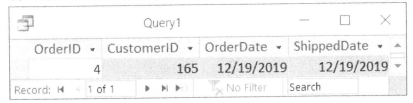

4. The inventory people need a list of orders for which the shipping cost is greater than the average shipping cost of all orders. Create a new query that includes the OrderID and OrderDate fields from the Orders table and satisfies the inventory people request. Save the query as Qry4_HighShippingCost.

Your result should look like:

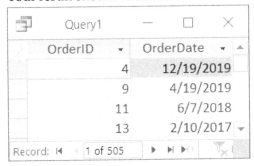

5. The sales manager needs an additional report. She needs a crosstab report that lists the number of orders by sales person and by year for the years in the database which are 2017, 2018, and 2019. Create two new queries that satisfy the sales manager request. The first query should be a pure SQL query and the second one should use the TRANSFORM AND PIVOT statements. Save the queries as Qry5_NumberOfOrdersA and Qry5_NumberOfOrdersB.

Your result should look like:

lastname	firstname	2017	2018	2019
Anderson	John	0	37	40
Baker	Jim	34	34	33
Bernstein	Michael	2	34	37
Delaney	Kenneth	10	28	27
Simmons	Andrew	53	44	47
Spicer	George	0	35	32
Teall	Mary	62	34	30
Vanderback	Jason	60	50	38
Williams	Gerald	17	18	22
Zensons	Phillip	64	31	32

Record: I◄ ◄ 1 of 10 ► ►I ► No Filter Search

Your result should look like:

LastName	FirstName	<>	2017	2018	2019
Anderson	John			37	40
Baker	Jim		34	34	33
Bernstein	Michael		2	34	37
Delaney	Kenneth		10	28	27
Simmons	Andrew		53	44	47
Spicer	George			35	32
Teall	Mary	1	62	34	30
Vanderback	Jason		60	50	38
Williams	Gerald		17	18	22
Zensons	Phillip		64	31	32

Record: 1 of 10   No Filter   Search

Why do we have an extra column in the second solution? Consult chapter 19 if you need help with this question.

APPENDIX I
THE SAMPLE DATABASE

The Entity Relationship Diagram (ERD) of the database is shown below:

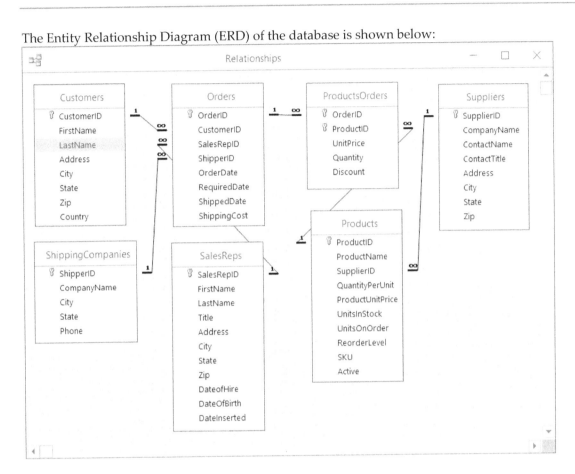

1. There is a one-to-many relationship between Customers and Orders.
2. There is a many-to-many relationship between Orders and Products with the table ProductsOrders functioning as the join table. The table ProductsOrders holds all of the details about each particular order and what products it contains. Its primary key is the combination of the primary keys of the Orders and Products tables.
3. As you can see from the ERD, there are also one-to-many relationships between the ShippingCompanies and Orders tables, Suppliers and Products, and SalesReps and Orders. The SalesReps table is our employees table, i.e. our salespeople.

The tables you see in the ERD diagram are the main tables in the database. However, we have created copies of the main tables so that you can work on examples without affecting the main tables. All of the secondary tables have the prefix "tbls", and you can work on them at will, deleting or updating data without affecting the main tables of the database. Just in case something goes wrong, however, you can download the database again as you please.

INDEX OF TERMS

Made in the USA
Middletown, DE
10 September 2023

38289506R00256